Performance and politics in popular drama

Performance and politics in popular drama

*Aspects of popular entertainment
in theatre, film and television
1800–1976*

Edited by
DAVID BRADBY
Lecturer in French and Drama, University of Kent at Canterbury

LOUIS JAMES
*Reader in English and American Literature
University of Kent at Canterbury*

BERNARD SHARRATT
*Lecturer in English and American Literature
University of Kent at Canterbury*

CAMBRIDGE UNIVERSITY PRESS
CAMBRIDGE
LONDON · NEW YORK · NEW ROCHELLE
MELBOURNE · SYDNEY

Published by the Press Syndicate of the University of Cambridge
The Pitt Building, Trumpington Street, Cambridge CB2 1RP
32 East 57th Street, New York, NY 10022, USA
296 Beaconsfield Parade, Middle Park, Melbourne 3206, Australia

First published 1980

Printed in Great Britain at the
University Press, Cambridge

Library of Congress Cataloguing in Publication Data
Main entry under title:
Performance and politics in popular drama
Bibliography:
Includes index.
1. Drama — History and criticism — Addresses,
essays, lectures. 2. Theatre — Political aspects —
Addresses, essays, lectures. 3. Popular culture
— Addresses, essays, lectures. I. Bradby,
David. II. James, Louis. III. Sharratt, Bernard.
PN1643.P4   809.2'9   79-12036
ISBN 0 521 22755 0

Contents

Contents

Contributors

DAVID BRADBY, lecturer in French and Drama, University of Kent; has previously taught in Glasgow and Nigeria. Publications include *Adamov: Research Bibliography and Checklist*, edited (London, 1975) and on Adamov in *La Nouvelle Critique*, 66 (1973), Jean-Paul Sartre, *Kean*, edited (Oxford, 1973); and *People's Theatre*, with John McCormick (London, 1978).

J. S. BRATTON, lecturer in English, Bedford College, London, since 1968; educated at Oxford. She has published *The Victorian Popular Ballad* (London, 1975) and slide sets about Wilton's Music Hall and Astley's Amphitheatre, 1976 and 1979.

STUART COSGROVE is from Perth, Scotland and graduated in English and Drama at the University of Hull. He has written a number of articles on workers' theatre, contributes to various black music magazines, and is currently writing a book on the United States Federal Theatre. In 1977 he was awarded a scholarship to study theatre in New York.

DEREK FORBES, Head of the Department of Drama, Middlesex Polytechnic, specialising in the teaching of theatre history; BA and MLitt Bristol University. Following periods as a schoolmaster and county drama organiser, he taught drama in Colleges of Education. He has directed over thirty shows, from a civic pageant to Shakespeare at the Minack theatre, and he is a committee member of the Society for Theatre Research. Publications include articles in *New Theatre Magazine*, *Educational Drama*, *Speech and Drama*, etc.

A. E. GREEN, lecturer in Folk Life Studies, University of Leeds; has previously held appointments in English Literature and Folklore at University College, London and the Memorial University of Newfoundland, Canada. He has written on various aspects of popular performing arts, notably folk-song and verse-recitation.

ANTONY D. HIPPISLEY COXE, author of *A Seat at the Circus*, has contributed articles on various aspects of the circus to many publications including the *Encyclopaedia Britannica*, *Theatre Notebook* and *The Times*, as well as taking part in radio and television programmes on the same subject. He has lectured at the Royal Society of Arts and other institutions, and his collection of circus books, historical documents, prints etc. is now with the Theatre Museum, London, to which he acts as consultant.

W. D. HOWARTH, Professor of Classical French Literature, University of Bristol, since 1966; Fellow and Tutor in Modern Languages, Jesus College, Oxford, 1948–66. His books include editions of plays by Anouilh and Molière; *Life and Letters in France: the Seventeenth Century* (London, 1965); *Explications: the Technique of French Literary Criticism*, with C. L. Walton (Oxford, 1971); *Molière: Stage and Study. Essays in Honour of W. G. Moore*, edited with Merlin Thomas (Oxford, 1973); *Sublime and Grotesque. A Study of French Romantic Drama* (London, 1975); *Comic Drama: The European Heritage*, editor (London, 1978), and he is currently working on a book on Molière for the CUP Major European Authors series.

LOUIS JAMES, Reader in English and American Literature, University of Kent; has taught in various universities, in Africa, the Caribbean and the United States. Publications include *Fiction for the Working Man 1830–50* (London, 1963); *The Islands In Between*, editor (London, 1968); and *Print and the People 1819–51* (London, 1976), as well as numerous articles on African and Caribbean literature and on Victorian popular literature.

MARTIN KANE, lecturer in German, University of Kent, since 1968. He has published articles on George Grosz, Thomas Mann, Walter Kempowski, and Christa Wolf, and numerous reviews of contemporary German fiction and lyric poetry for the *International PEN Bulletin*.

JOHN McCORMICK, lecturer in French and Drama, Trinity College, Dublin, since 1970; has also taught at the University of Glasgow and in Finland. He is chairman of the Irish Institute of Drama and the Allied Arts. Publications include *Le Théâtre Britannique contemporain* (Brussels, 1972); E. Ionesco, *Tueur sans Gages*, critical edition with notes (London, 1972); *People's Theatre*, with David Bradby (London, 1978).

DAVID MAYER, Senior Lecturer in Drama, University of Manchester; author of *Harlequin in His Element; English Pantomime, 1806–1836*

(Cambridge, Mass., 1969), and co-editor with Kenneth Richards of *Western Popular Theatre* (London, 1977). Other publications include 'The Sexuality of Pantomime' and a study of Billy Purvis in *Theatre Quarterly*; many articles on nineteenth-century theatre music and on pantomime in *Theatre Notebook* and other theatre research publications; frequent contributions of theatre criticism to *Plays and Players*.

DOUGLAS A. REID, lecturer, Department of Economic and Social History, University of Hull; has lectured at Nene College, Northampton, and Bristol University. He is completing a PhD thesis on 'Popular Leisure and Popular Culture: Birmingham 1750–1875'.

NICK RODDICK, lecturer, Department of Drama, Manchester University; studied at Oxford and Bristol Universities and taught for four years in the French Department, Trinity College, Dublin. Film and twentieth-century French theatre are his main specialisations; PhD on the relationship between eighteenth-century French theatre and contemporary moral philosophy; publications include articles on eighteenth-century subjects, including a strike at the Comédie-Française in 1765. He is currently researching a study of Warner Brothers' 'social conscience' pictures in the thirties.

RAPHAEL SAMUEL, tutor, Ruskin College, Oxford, since 1964; lives in Spitalfields. He has been closely associated with the History Workshop conferences, edited the series of History Workshop pamphlets and is editor of *History Workshop Journal*.

BERNARD SHARRATT, lecturer in English and American Literature, University of Kent; has also taught at the University of the West Indies. He read English at Cambridge and did research on nineteenth-century working-class autobiographies. Publications include articles on Beckett, Coleridge, Foucault, Seamus Heaney, William Morris, and the sociology of Roman Catholicism. He has also written a book on Marxist theory and the reading of literature.

NICK WORRALL, Senior Lecturer, Humanities Department, Middlesex Polytechnic; Soviet correspondent of the British Associate Centre of the International Theatre Institute and contributor to their publication *International Theatrelog*. His publications include articles on the work of Meyerhold in the Soviet theatre for *Theatre Quarterly* and *Drama Review*; 'Vladimir Mayakovsky', *Theatrefacts*, 13 (1977); contributions on Soviet theatre to the forthcoming revised edition of the *Oxford Companion to the Theatre*.

Preface

This book arises from a conference held at the University of Kent at Canterbury in September 1977. Subtitled 'a festival and an inquiry', the conference placed a central emphasis on performance: the Joint Stock Theatre Company and the Strathclyde Theatre Group both gave performances, and there were showings of three films: *1789*, *The Poseidon Adventure*, and *Soulcaking at Antrobus*. In discussion, it was possible to confront the issues raised by popular and political theatre and film from the point of view of both creators and critics. In this way the conference organisers hoped to prevent the separation of the issues into tidy specialisations, whether academic or practical, and to provoke a new awareness of the continuities and disjunctions in forms of popular drama since the beginning of the nineteenth century.

The papers selected for publication have been rewritten in the light of what was said and experienced at the conference and the editorial introductions to the three parts emphasise the links and connections that can be made between one form or century and another. But the papers have also been selected with a view to their range and heterogeneity, so that the book as a whole deliberately juxtaposes diverse areas of interest, leaving the reader to make his or her own connections.

D.B.
W.L.G.J.
B.S.

Acknowledgements

We should like to thank all those who participated in the 1977 conference in whatever capacity and especially the members of the Strathclyde Theatre Group and the Joint Stock Theatre Company.

The conference was made possible by a generous grant from Southern Television, to whom we are extremely grateful, and the performance by Joint Stock was assisted by a grant from the South East Arts Association.

PART ONE

SPECTACLE, PERFORMANCE AND AUDIENCE IN NINETEENTH-CENTURY THEATRE

Introduction

Louis James

Contemporary interest in popular drama is not an adventitious one. It is part of a much wider shift in the basis of cultural concern; indeed, it is part of the revaluation of modern society itself. This gives the present study both its impetus and its difficulty. We not only approach areas of theatre that have previously been neglected, but we have to find appropriate critical terms which take into account the contemporary cultural debate. We have to be exploratory; yet we have to find some sense of direction or we will be lost.

In the past, popular drama has been studied under at least four categories, which have often been deployed within, or have relied for their specification upon, a quasi-chronological account. The first, which we may call *folk drama*, is related to a pre-literate, rural society. It is traditional, close to ritual and the everyday life of the common people. Industrialism and the growth of cities in the nineteenth century broke up the older genre. Large theatres were built to entertain the masses, exploiting possibilities of spectacle and sensation, and the star actor. This was the era of *commercial* working-class theatre, music hall and melodrama. But the division of theatre along lines of the class of the audience was always uncertain, and with the development of film and then television we arrive at the period of *mass media*. In reaction to this, the radical elite created *agit-prop* theatre, attempting to restore drama to the people as part of the class struggle.

These categories and accounts are useful as far as they go, but they hide some dangerous assumptions. Each category of popular drama tends to have been taken over by particular critical approaches, each with its own interests, emphases, questions and implied answers. Folklorists, with some notable exceptions, have generally been concerned with the traditional elements in folk theatre and have a tendency to posit a golden age of communal creativity. Scholars of mass entertainment in the capitalist era have tended to focus on popular theatre in terms of the exploitation of the working classes. Such emphases often have good reasons behind them, but they can also make it difficult to explore popular theatre with the open mind the subject demands. One must return repeatedly to the experience, the theatrical reality. Here one finds that the issues are as complex as they are in 'academic' drama, though in different ways. Popular drama can be at once clichéed and professionally expert, escapist and relating to deep levels of audience experience, ephemeral yet able to capture our attention with moments of complete conviction.

The following papers do not solve all the critical problems raised by popular drama, but they are aware of them. The early essays in this part of the book consider questions of content and context. Those on water drama, circus and the theatre of war move away from the traditional critical concerns with plot and character, to consider plays relying on different kinds of skill and presentation. They are 'entertainments', yet they also inhabit the border country between theatre and journalism.

These papers both take us away from what we think of as 'major' plays, and also bring us back to them. Considering a drama such as J. H. Amherst's *Battle of Waterloo*, it is difficult not to make some comparisons with Brecht's Epic Theatre — there is even, in the camp-follower Molly Maloney, a distant relative of Mother Courage. Melodrama in its prime looks backwards to Shakespeare and forward to expressionism. Nor is this kind of claim the conditioned nervous twitch of the academic mind. Popular drama demands our attention because of its vitality, and the awareness it brings of the heritage of working-class culture. But, as such 'popular' dramatists as Aeschylus, Shakespeare and Brecht have well known, it is an essential part of any live theatrical tradition.

Was Jerrold's Black Ey'd Susan
more popular than Wordsworth's Lucy?

Louis James

Melodrama, that once ragged waif, has been brought in from the cold. A decade ago, 'melodramatic' was a term of critical abuse: now 'Melodrama' has its volume in Methuen's 'Critical Idiom' series,[1] along with 'Romanticism' and 'The Epic'. She has been washed, given clean clothes, and warmed by academic fires. There are murmurs about aristocratic parentage. Shakespeare? Bernard Shaw wrote that if melodrama was good enough, 'why, then one has *Lear* or *Macbeth*'.[2] Sophocles? Eric Bentley pointed out that the key emotions of melodrama, 'Pity' and 'Fear', were also those Aristotle prescribed for tragedy.[3] Robert W. Heilman, in *Tragedy and Melodrama* (Seattle, 1969), argued against melodrama's status as tragedy, but gave it the dignity of academic investigation; in 1976 Peter Brooks in the most penetrating study of the genre to date, *The Melodramatic Imagination*, applied the concept to Balzac and Henry James. Will Melodrama prove to be *the* contemporary heroine and Muse? Eisenstein traced the film concept of montage back, through Dickens, to melodrama,[4] and today melodrama dominates cinema and television screens for reasons other than those of Russian cinematic technique.

Or has there been a melodramatic twist to our story? Look again at the now clean and bespectacled young lady with all those new books. Has there been a switch somewhere in the plot? How remote are considerations of 'the melodramatic imagination' from the drawled, heavily mannered speech, the acrobatically stylised gestures, the crudely emotional audience reaction at the Surrey or the Britannia melodrama of the 1840s? Is the real Melodrama still out there somewhere in the snow? There is nothing wrong in the intellectualisation of 'popular' cultural traditions: it would, I think, be possible to prove that there has been an element of this in every major turn of English literary history, not only in Wordsworth's use of the ballad tradition which has given me my title,[5] although, as I will suggest, the parallel between the impact of melodrama and the significance of Wordsworth's

3

Lyrical Ballads (1798) is particularly interesting. The status of this paper makes it yet another attempt to 'academicise' a popular genre. But we should be aware of what we are doing. I also wish to suggest ways of approaching melodrama which may come nearer to the original form than do some other current views.

Theories about melodrama

To start with Bernard Shaw. One would have expected Shaw, with his hate of the 'theatrical and hysterical'[6] tendency of English audiences, to have attacked melodrama. But he separated melodrama from late-nineteenth-century theatre in general, and noted that when he introduced all the conventions of melodrama into *The Devil's Disciple* in 1897, the play was praised for its *originality*.[7] Shaw liked melodrama for the same reasons that made him admire Bunyan: he considered it philosophical, democratic and well crafted. It is 'a simple and sincere drama of action and feeling', in its range of experience accessible both to philosopher and labourer. 'One has to go straight to the core of humanity to get it.' In its form it reflects the variety of life, depending upon contrasts between 'types of youth and age, sympathy and selfishness, the masculine and the feminine, the serious and the ridiculous and so on'. It is philosophical because it must 'represent conduct as producing swiftly and creating in the individual the results which in actual life it only produces in the race in the course of many centuries'.[8] While *The Devil's Disciple* turned melodramatic principles on their head, he directed that it should be acted for the effects of serious melodrama;[9] a burlesque production, such as the Royal Shakespeare Company's 1976 presentation, changes the play's meaning and impact.

In 1948, Wylie Sypher described melodrama as the key modality of the nineteenth century.[10] Each era, he argued, has its mental framework through which it explains and orders its experience. In the eighteenth century the dominant concern with order and balance gave us Newtonian physics, the rhyming couplet, and the landscape gardening of Capability Brown. In the modern age we think in terms of relativity, the organising principle of Einstein's theory, the novel sequences of Faulkner, or a progression of paintings by Picasso. In the nineteenth century the modality was that of melodrama, the dialectic of two absolute forces in conflict towards a resolution — the 'good' heroine against the 'bad' villain, Malthus's struggle of population against the laws of subsistence, the class conflict of

Worker against Capitalist of Marx and Engels, or Darwin's natural selection of species.

To whatever extent this theory is valid, most academic critics have agreed that melodrama itself is an inadequate artistic form, crude in its emotions and simplistic in its morals. It may arouse sensations of terror, wonder or pathos in the audience, but these feelings are aroused for their own sake, rather than emerging from a significant situation. Unlike tragedy, it does not move through sensation to awe at the human condition. Tragedy, Heilman has argued, is more profound because it explores the crisis of inner personality; melodrama presents only 'types'.[11]

But is this not making a comparative value judgement about different dimensions of dramatic experience? For Eric Bentley, the 'unreality' is functional. 'Melodrama sometimes uses the "irrational" type of fear in a more direct form such as that of Frankenstein's monster or Dracula. More often it lets irrational fear masquerade as the rational: we are given reasons to fear the villain, but the fear actually aroused goes beyond the reason given.'[12] In this it is expressing an aspect of our psychological experience. Similarly, the improbabilities of melodramatic plot may from one angle appear absurd, while from another they image the experience of living in an absurd universe. For, writes Bentley, the power of melodrama comes from its ability to affect the irrational but profound levels of the human psyche: 'melodramatic vision is paranoid'. Even the acting style of melodrama contributes to this. 'That we are all ham actors in our dreams means that melodramatic acting, with its large gestures and grimaces and its declamatory style of speech, is not an exaggeration of our dreams but a duplication of them. In that respect, melodrama is the Naturalism of the dream life.'[13] While Bentley does not note this as an example, it is illuminating to compare basic melodrama with German expressionist theatre and film, and even with a surrealist film such as Cocteau's *Orphée*.

By another argument, melodrama is essentially dramatic because it takes to its extreme the element of play within drama itself. The spectator expects, say, the hero to marry the heroine at the end, not because we are experiencing reality, but because we go to the theatre to enter voluntarily into a game where certain expectations are set up and fulfilled. In the clichés of melodrama, then, this element of 'game' is completely realised: there is no pretence that we are *not* enjoying plot and character played by rules. Such an approach brings us to the central and perhaps ultimately unpassable gap at the centre

5

of our appreciation of melodrama. Melodrama is hard to rediscover because it is, to modify R. A. Foakes's definition of Romantic poetry, the drama of *assertion*,[14] not one of questioning, and the significance of this assertion is an experiential one that can only be measured in terms of a communal theatrical interaction of actors and audience. As J. L. Styan has pointed out, the key to the popularity of melodrama is in the audience response:[15] the early-nineteenth-century theatre-goer was able to enter into the experience both believing and not believing in a way that we, in a different age, cannot recover. All we can do is to attempt to assess the intellectual and emotional perspectives the original audience might have brought to a melodrama performance. While this will be essentially inadequate, some aspects are available, and may appear surprising.

Psychological theories of the passions and the acting tradition

One door opens onto another. Consideration of the physical expression of moral and emotional states goes back to medieval theories of the Humours and even Theophrastus's *Characters*, which remained surprisingly popular throughout Europe right into the nineteenth century, when an English illustrated version was published in 1836. But a convenient and central starting point is Charles le Brun's *Conférence . . . sur l'expression générale et particulière* (1698) which was constantly translated, expanded and adapted: one popular early English translation by J. Smith was published in 1701. This influential little work analysed the passions from the basic extremes, such as 'Extreme Anger', to the subtler expressions such as 'Admiration', 'Esteem' and 'Veneration'. Of particular importance was the accompanying series of striking illustrations, showing how the face appeared under each emotion. Le Brun also considered bodily gesture, but in little detail. Smith's translation included a brief supplement on Le Brun's theory of physiognomy. Johann Caspar Lavater, in his *Essays on Physiognomy* (1798), again vividly illustrated, followed Le Brun's theories through with much greater detail and complexity. He became influential not only through translations and adaptations — the British Museum notes three English translations, which were apparently published within four years of their publication in France — but through the popular Victorian science of phrenology, which his work initiated. The line of investigation continues to Darwin's *Expression of Emotions* (1872) which was illustrated with photographs; it was considered

by William James in his *Principles of Psychology* (1890),[16] and,
if it seemed to be exploded by Jung's and Freud's concern with the
unconscious, is experiencing a new revival with interest in 'body
language'.

The way in which this interest in the physical expression of
emotion has developed hand in hand with the history of art lies outside the scope of this short paper. Le Brun was himself an artist,
and when William Hogarth was commissioned to paint Garrick as
Richard III (1746) he turned in part for his inspiration to Le Brun's
Family of Darius before Alexander the Great, and Le Brun's illustration of 'Fear'.[17] Hogarth's work shows an expert interest in the
expression of the passions, and this enabled him in his picture
series to bring together psychological and socio-moral concerns.
They are also dramatic tableaux: 'my picture was my Stage', he wrote,
'and men and women my actors who were, by means of certain
Actions and expressions, to Exhibit a dumb show'.[18] Continuously
popular into the nineteenth century, they made the natural bases
for theatre: *Industry and Idleness* (1747), for instance, was made
into at least two melodramas a hundred years after its first appearance.
Further, Hogarth helped to establish the line of Victorian genre and
narrative painting which likewise told a story, and told it in dramatic
terms. Melodrama is related to the 'picture' in many ways. One of
them was in its direct links with Victorian narrative art. A series like
Cruikshank's *The Bottle* (1847) or Wilkie's *The Rent Day* and
Distraining for Rent were immediately and naturally made into
plays.[19]

The science of the expression of the passions also directly affected
dramatic theory. Michael Booth quotes the theatrical periodical
The Prompter of as early as 1735: 'every passion has its peculiar and
appropriate look, and every look its adopted and particular gesture'.[20]
In 1785—6 J. J. Engel published his *Ideen zu einer Mimic*, a popular
work adapted into English by Henry Siddons as *Practical Illustrations
of Rhetorical Gestures* (1822). Strongly influenced by Le Brun,
but also drawing on a wide range of examples from literature, art,
and philosophy, Engel explored the social and psychological bases
for theatrical action, and illustrated them with illustrative prints
enlarged and made more sensationally vivid by Siddons. Engel stresses
that theatrical gestures must be simultaneously *expressive* and
picturesque, but significantly sees no conflict between the two
concerns. *Practical Illustrations* was an expensive and theoretical
work, but Le Brun's influence extends to actors' handbooks, primarily

7

concerned with the practical side of the profession, like Leman
Thomas Rede's compact *The Road to the Stage* (1827). Rede appended a 'celebrated analytic review of the effect of various emotions
on the human frame' which, if not made a substitute for the actual
passion, 'will not be regarded with indifference by those really
studying the stage'.[21] The review is roughly based on Le Brun.

Theories of the physical expression of emotion help us to see why
melodramatic acting was not, as is conceived today, a set of unreal
clichés, but to some extent an attempt at psychological realism. As
William James indicated,[22] psychological theories were remarkably
close to melodramatic acting styles. In Rede's 'analytic review',
for instance, as in Le Brun, '*Grief*, sudden and violent, expresses
itself by beating the head or forehead, tearing the hair, and catching
the breath, as if choking; also by screaming, weeping, stamping with
the feet, lifting the eyes from time to time to heaven, and hurrying
backwards and forwards.'[23]

This helped to confirm theatre in its concern with the portrayal

Gestures of melodrama, from Skelt's *Characters in Othello*.

8

of passion. But, paradoxically, it also shaped melodrama's concern with types. Lavater in particular was interested in the way physical genres were linked to moral classifications, and it is not too far a step from the typology of 'Affection' or 'Hatred' to the types of the hero, the heroine, or the comic man. Again, the conventions of melodramatic characters must be seen against an age in which phrenology was a popular science, and in which the interest in classifying 'types' ranged from such popular series as Kenny Meadow's *Heads of the People* (1848) to Mayhew's *London Labour and the London Poor* (1851–64) and the beginnings of sociology.

Romanticism sets the scene

Humble and rustic life was generally chosen, because, in that condition the essential passions of the heart find a better soil in which they can attain their maturity, are less under restraint, and speak a plainer and more emphatic language; because in that condition of life our elementary feelings co-exist in a greater simplicity, and, consequently, may be accurately contemplated, and more forcibly communicated.

The dialogue is 'natural and characteristic . . . There is no extravagance of idea — no elaborate research after simile and metaphor, no display of pomp and inflated expression: the thought seems to arise from the moment, and the words appear to be suggested by the circumstances which pass under the eye of the spectator.' The first quotation is from Wordsworth's 'Preface' to the second edition of *Lyrical Ballads* (1800), the second from the *Times* review of the first English play to be called a 'melodrama', Holcroft's *A Tale of Mystery* (1802).[24]

    The emergence of the Romantic movement and melodrama in England were contemporary and connected in many ways. To find the appropriate expression for direct and powerful emotions, Wordsworth turned to rustic and to simple folk, including children, simple heroines, silent outcasts such as the Leech Gatherer and the Cumberland Beggar; even, to the delight of hostile critics, an idiot boy. Melodramas relied on similar foci for the emotions, innocent heroines, children, dumb figures — *A Tale of Mystery* concerns Francisco, a dumb man.[25] They went further and used animals — the dog of Pixérécourt's *The Hound of Montargis*, the extraordinarily trained horses of Astley and Ducrow. Yet even here, as Arthur Saxon has pointed out, there was a crudely Romantic attitude. 'Darwinism and the theory of the indifferent universe was still some fifty years in the future; nature was viewed, with childlike simplicity, as being sympathetic to man.'[26]

The same is true for the setting. Wordsworth's fascination with

Black drizzling crags that spake by the way-side,
As if a voice were in them, the sick sight
And giddy prospect of the raving stream,
The unfettered clouds and region of the Heavens,
Tumult and peace, the darkness and the light

(Prelude, Bk VI, lines 631–5)

was given stage expression in a melodrama such as *A Tale of Mystery*, with its evocation of 'the wild mountainous country called the Nant of Arpennaz; with pines and massy rocks . . . The increasing storm of lightning, thunder, hail, and rain becomes terrible.'[27] The attraction to the strange and the wonderful that inspired Coleridge's *The Rime of the Ancient Mariner* (1798) was felt by audiences at spectacle and gothic melodramas. Most important, the wild and strange setting in some Romantic poems and certain types of melodrama was used both to give a sense of the wonderful, and to highlight the passions of the characters — whether Holcroft's Romaldi, who emerges in the storm 'pursued, as it were, by heaven and earth',[28] or Coleridge's exiled, tormented Mariner.

Of specific importance to melodrama was the Romantic attitude to music. The first work designated by the author as a '*mélodrame*' was Jean-Jacques Rousseau's *Pygmalion* (1774), a monologue with action scored against violin music, and written with Rousseau's concept of the connection between music and human emotion in mind. Engel and Siddons wrote specifically about the relation of different kinds of music to dramatic gesture, and theorised about how music directly reflected emotional states in a way which pre-figured the stage directions in *A Tale of Mystery* — 'music to express chattering contention', 'threatening music', 'joyful music' and the like. Romantic theory of music and of the 'simple' character is illustrated in a pantomimic section Milner added to Mary Shelley's story in the melodrama *Frankenstein*, where the Monster is interestingly made more sympathetic than in the original. Trapped among mountainous rocks, Emmeline saves the Child from the Monster by pulling from her dress a small flageolet, and playing, the Monster becoming 'powerfully affected'.

As the air proceeds his feelings become more powerfully excited — he is moved to tears: afterwards, on the music assuming a lively character, he is worked up

10

*to a paroxism of delight — and on its again becoming mournful, is quite subdued,
till he lays down exhausted at the foot of the rock to which* Emmeline *is
attached.* [29]

Enter the acrobats

Such a scene is essentially both Romantic and melodramatic, but
theatrically one need not look to these specific sources of inspiration.
The action is one from popular dumb-show and 'serious pantomime',
rooted in popular entertainment going back much earlier. Pixérécourt
and the English translations or rough adaptations of his melodramas
appearing from the turn of the century were popular and influential,
but both English and French melodrama drew on common popular
traditions of mime to music which enabled Holcroft, while writing
the first named English melodrama, to demand elaborate miming,
and to expect both actors and audience to be able to interpret it.
As Rede noted, *distinguishing* this from 'melo-drame', 'Kean and
Young have both considered music essential — the latter gentleman
is an excellent *pianiste*; and the late John Kemble, whenever he had
music at his exits, was as particular in his observance of it as any
serio-pantomimic performer.'[30] When he does write about 'melo-
drame', which he takes as a separate genre, Rede couples it with
'serious pantomime', 'where a certain number of things are to be
done upon the stage during the execution of so many bars of music;
the cues too for entrances and exits are frequently only the changes
of the air, and unless the ear is cultivated (if naturally bad) the
performer will be led into error'.[31]

In understanding this we are hindered by a lack of the detailed
information about travelling fairground and other barnstorming
entertainments in the eighteenth century that is now becoming
available for the nineteenth century. For as Marian Hannah Winter
points out for France,[32] the catalyst that transformed the theory of
writers like Engel into what we know as melodrama was the theatre's
contact with the popular tradition of entertainment, dumb-show,
magic and illusion, and in particular, acrobatics. Melodramas were
usually done in a mixed programme, including such arts as comic
dancing and acrobatics, and, equally important, the same actors
'doubled up' in both. For melodramatic acting is essentially a physical,
indeed a violently physical, style, dominated by athletic figures
such as the ex-sailor T. P. Cooke, and O. Smith. Part of the related
revolution in 'legitimate' acting styles was led by Edmund Kean,
acrobatically trained in Richardson's travelling theatre and other

11

troupes. Even death on the stage was, for the melodramatic actor,
energetic; 'exhibited by violent distortion, groaning, gasping for
breath, stretching the body, raising, and then letting it fall';[33]
or in the perilous rigid 'prat fall'. There is at least one account of a
death so powerful that the actor was asked for — and gave — an
encore.[34]

For the acrobatic tradition of extreme controlled movement
allowed melodrama to bring together two disparate dimensions:
the concern with passion and movement, and the demand for the
romantic and the picturesque. The style is essentially balletic and
operatic — writers on the acting profession such as Rede indicate
the importance of dancing and singing for training the actor. The
actor must study even the ways of moving gracefully on and off
the stage. The gestures themselves are large and precise: Boucicault
demanded that they be 'distinct and deliberate. When you look at
a person you do not turn your eye, but you turn your whole head.
If you want to point, do *that (with the arm straight out from the
shoulder)* — the action must go from the shoulder.'[35] The action
creates a picture and moves into tableau. 'Another thing is, do not
let your gesture be too short . . . You do not know how long you can
rest upon a good one. It tires you, but it will not tire the spectator.'[36]

Yet the nature of the gestures gives the acting a constant sense of
energy. This is related constantly to the emotive inner structure of
each scene, and to the other characters. The actors in melodrama
react to each other with the direct intensity of a magnetic field.
Engel illustrates this with a picture of a character reacting backwards
and forwards from a snake, and in Siddons's translation declares,
'the rule which subsists with respect to the desire which carries us
towards an agreeable object agrees equally well with that which
removes us from an unpleasant one'.[37] Equally important, the
tendency of melodrama to flow into the significant static tableau
is energised by the basic effect of violent destruction of this tableau,
of alternation of mood and scene. Eisenstein rightly identified
this as a key effect of melodrama, and, as 'montage', took it over as
the basis of his cinematic technique. It is the 'dynamic' effect of
'parallel action' that can 'mill the extraordinary, the unusual, the
fantastic, from boring, prosaic and everyday existence'.[38]

This 'montage' of mood and gesture, which can be found built into
any good melodrama writing, was achieved by rapid scene changing,
using sliding 'flats'. But it exists even within a single character in a
scene or speech. As Boucicault also wrote, the personality exists on

three planes — the 'inner man, as when he is alone'; the 'domestic man, as he is to his family', and the 'man as he stands before the world . . . they are all in the one man, and the dramatist does not know his business unless he puts them into the one character'.[39]

An example of this can be seen in J. B. Buckstone's *Luke the Labourer: or the Lost Son* (1826), usually taken as the first fully anglicised melodrama, and a good early example of the way in which the 'heroic' style of Pixérécourt becomes transferred into a domestic situation. Luke, when an unemployed labourer, had been refused help from Farmer Wakefield, and had to watch his wife die of starvation. In Act I, Scene 2, Luke in revenge has contrived to have Wakefield arrested for debts, and he enters the cottage to confront the farmer's family, unaware that Wakefield has been released and is sitting, in a domestic tableau, reunited with his wife and daughter. As he strides through the door he is a confident individual, his 'private' self. He reaches the front-of-stage before Wakefield calls out, 'Well, sir, your business here?' and Luke crumples. He is again the labourer in front of his master, his 'public' self. 'I ha noa business in particular, I ha noa — only a — how came you out o' gaol?' As the dialogue develops between Luke and Wakefield, memories of his past injuries overwhelm Luke. He talks to Wakefield, but also to himself — he becomes his 'middle self': 'I were out o' work week after week, until I had not a penny in the world, nor a bit o' bread to put into mine nor my wife's mouth. I then had a wife, but she sickened and died — yes, died — all — all along o' you.' Finally he passes into reverie, his 'private' self, ignoring the listeners as he relives his agony of distress. 'I sat thinking, wi' my wife in my arms — she were ill, very ill.' He is only woken back to his 'middle self' by the impact of Wakefield's daughter throwing herself at his feet, begging him to save her father from more confrontation. Luke cries, '[my eyes] are dry as dust again', and he grapples with Wakefield. The actor must be able to convey these shifts in self-awareness within the total emotional flow of the scene, which has an almost balletic structuring. In performance, however, the characters have the essential help of the music, which underlines the phases of the action and works alongside the strong rhythmic patterns of the prose. Without music, the scene has only a vestige of its potential impact.

Such stylisation relates melodrama, I would argue, more closely to popular traditions than Wordsworth was able to come in the *Lyrical Ballads*. Wordsworth took the lyric simplicity of the ballad, but did not have the critical vocabulary to explain its dramatic formulation of experience into basic and universal themes of love and death, fear and joy. Aware that ballads were not naturalistic, he fell back on his inadequate definition of his own poetry as '*selecting* from the real language of men'[40] (my italics). But melodrama, while for many of its early critics it achieved Wordsworth's aims of expressing the elementary passions of mankind, was also in the direct tradition of thematic ritualisation that gave those passions an appropriate form. As John Cawelti has written of popular literature, melodrama, in addition to narrative, possesses the structure of 'collective ritual, game and dream'.[41] Melodrama contains within itself the basic ballad pattern. It also includes to a significant degree popular dance and song: *Black Ey'd Susan* was not only inspired by Gay's song, it used throughout nautical airs and embodied both sea and rural dances.

Melodrama and the two traditions

There are two common misconceptions about melodrama. The first is that it is synonymous with Victorian nineteenth-century theatre. This was of course a complex pattern of genres, including different varieties of tragedy and comedy, farce, 'serious' and 'comic' pantomime, burletta, ballet, and burlesque. The second is that it was a simple and 'popular' form. The reality is more complicated. For the first four decades of the century, melodrama was watched and enjoyed by a wide range of social classes.[42] By the mid century, partly because of changing patterns of theatre-going, but also because of wider changes in attitudes to emotion and intellect, melodrama began to split into two streams. Even with a production such as that by Charles Kean of Dion Boucicault's *The Corsican Brothers* (Princess Theatre, 1852), we find a refinement of theme and treatment addressed to a 'respectable' audience.

The universal themes of joy and terror implicit in early melodrama become consciously examined — even the telepathy of the Corsican brothers is at one remove from the simple guilt and innocence of *A Tale of Mystery*. By the time Irving produced Leopold Lewis's *The Bells* to a dress-suited Lyceum audience in 1871, guilt has become subtly internalised: Mathias is sentenced and strangled by nothing but his own conscience. The genre of melodrama had become available for the complexities of fiction — Robert Louis Stevenson's *Dr Jekyll and Mr Hyde* (1886); Oscar Wilde's *Picture of Dorian Gray* (1891) or Henry James's *Turn of the Screw* (1898).

14

On the other hand, the 'popular' melodramatic tradition continued, increasingly a subject for intellectual condescension and amusement, in working-class theatres such as the Britannia, Hoxton, and in touring groups and provincial performances: a production of *Maria Marten* in a Lincolnshire barn seen in 1961 was played and received 'straight' by its audience of labourers. The 'popular' tradition was carried over, as critics like J. L. Fell[43] have shown, directly into early film: the silent film in particular returned melodrama to its source as mime to music. In 1976 at the end of a lecture on melodrama David Mayer showed an episode which illustrated many points he had been making. The episode was the current instalment of the BBC's *Dr Who*.

NOTES

1 James L. Smith, *Melodrama* (London, 1973).
2 Bernard Shaw to Ellen Terry (26 March 1896), in *Ellen Terry and Bernard Shaw: A Correspondence*, ed. Christopher St John (New York, 1931), p. 21; cited by M. Meisel, *Shaw and the Nineteenth-Century Theatre* (Princeton, 1963), p. 184.
3 Eric Bentley, *The Life of the Drama* (London, 1965), p. 200.
4 Sergei Eisenstein, 'Dickens, Griffith, and the Film Today', reproduced in G. Mast and M. Cohen, *Film Theory and Criticism* (New York, 1974), pp. 302–7.
5 See, e.g. G. Malcolm Laws, *The British Literary Ballad* (Carbondale, 1971) for a discussion of the popular and elitist tradition in song.
6 G. B. Shaw, 'Preface' to *Three Plays for Puritans* (Harmondsworth, 1946), p. xxi.
7 *Ibid.*, p. xxiv.
8 G. B. Shaw, *Our Theatre in the Nineties*, 3 vols. (London, 1932) vol. 1, p. 93.
9 See Meisel, *Shaw*, pp. 194–206.
10 Wylie Sypher, 'Aesthetic of Revolution: the Marxist Melodrama', *Kenyon Review*, 10 (Summer, 1948), pp. 431–44.
11 R. B. Heilman, *Tragedy and Melodrama* (Seattle, 1968), p. 79.
12 Bentley, *Life of the Drama*, p. 201.
13 *Ibid.*, p. 205.
14 R. A. Foakes, *The Romantic Assertion* (London, 1958).
15 J. L. Styan, *Drama, Stage and Audience* (Cambridge, 1975), pp. 130–6; 71–2.
16 William James, *The Principles of Psychology*, 2 vols. (1890), vol. 2, ch. 25. James quotes a wide range of views on the expression of the emotions in ways clearly relevant to melodramatic stylisation.
17 See S. Shesgreen, *Engravings by Hogarth* (New York, 1973), plate 57.
18 Hogarth, *Autobiographical Notes*, cited by Shesgreen, *Engravings*, p. xxii.
19 *The Bottle* was credited with some eight dramatic versions; Wilkie's pictures became the popular melodrama, Douglas Jerrold's *The Rent Day* (1832).

20 M. R. Booth, *English Melodrama* (London, 1965), p. 205.
21 L. T. Rede, *The Road to the Stage* (1827), p. 77.
22 See James, *Psychology*, Bentley, *Life of the Drama*, pp. 205—6.
23 Rede, *Road to the Stage*, p. 78.
24 Cited by J. O. Bailey, *British Plays of the Nineteenth Century* (New York, 1966), p. 224.
25 For an important discussion of the place of the inarticulate in melodrama, see Peter Brooks, *The Melodramatic Imagination* (London, 1976), ch. 3.
26 A. Saxon, *Enter Foot and Horse* (New Haven, 1968), p. 8.
27 T. Holcroft, *A Tale of Mystery* (1802), Act II, Scene 3.
28 *Ibid.*
29 H. M. Milner, *Frankenstein: or, the Man and the Monster!* (1826), Act II, Scene 4.
30 Rede, *Road to the Stage*, p. 63.
31 *Ibid.* p. 62.
32 M. H. Winter, *The Theatre of Marvels* (New York, 1964) *passim.*
33 Rede, *Road to the Stage*, p. 93.
34 [Thomas Wright], A Journeyman Engineer, *Some Habits and Customs of the Working Class* (1867), p. 165.
35 D. Boucicault, 'The Art of Acting', Dramatic Museum of Columbia University *Papers on Acting*, 5th series (1926), cited by R. W. Corrigan, ed., *Nineteenth Century British Drama* (New York, 1967), p. 30.
36 *Ibid.*, pp. 32—3.
37 H. Siddons, *Practical Gestures of Rhetorical Gesture and Action* (1822), p. 103; see also pp. 85—93.
38 Eisenstein, 'Film Today', p. 303.
39 Boucicault, 'The Art of Acting', pp. 39—40.
40 Preface to the second edition of *Lyrical Ballads* (1800).
41 J. G. Cawelti, 'The Concept of Formula in the Study of Popular Literature', *Journal of Popular Culture*, (1969), pp. 381—90.
42 See, e.g. Douglas Reid's account of Birmingham audiences in this volume.
43 J. L. Fell, *Film and the Narrative Tradition* (Norman, Oklahoma, 1974).

Word and image in Pixérécourt's melodramas: the dramaturgy of the strip-cartoon

W. D. Howarth

What importance should we give to Pixérécourt's well-known statement, 'I am writing for those who cannot read'? How literally should it be taken, and what are its implications for anyone inquiring into the nature of popular drama in early-nineteenth-century France? It could reasonably be argued that the degree of literacy of a theatre audience is irrelevant to the production of a spectacle designed to be seen and heard; and no doubt those who approve of the gradual emancipation of European drama from what they regard as excessively literary influences would applaud Pixérécourt's statement as heralding a move away from text towards spectacle. On the other hand, it is possible to interpret the 'popular' character of his melodramas in a different light, and to see this genre, for all its visual spectacle and despite its apparent anti-literary tendency, as one still dependent on literary traditions, one in which the spoken word is still used in a recognisably 'literary' manner, even if this manner is generally simplified and often debased. I propose in this paper to examine the relationship between spoken word and visual image in a number of representative plays; and I shall attempt to justify the phrase 'the dramaturgy of the strip-cartoon'.

The emergence of melodrama in the years around 1800 is best explained by the fusion of two developments, one popular and one literary, in the drama of the preceding generation. The importance of the *pantomime*, or musical mime-play, to which enterprising directors of independent theatres resorted in order to circumvent the monopoly of spoken and sung drama held by the official houses, has been stressed by Pitou and others.[1] However, the formula of *pantomime* did not remain stable for very long, and the fact that it soon evolved into a bizarre hybrid with the contradictory label of 'pantomime dialoguée' seems to indicate the inadequacy of pure mime to express the range of thoughts and emotions that melodrama was later to attempt. It would in any case be wrong to give too much prominence

17

to these affinities with popular antecedents; and Geoffroy, the contemporary critic, for one had no doubt that the new melodrama
represented a degenerate form of the literary drama of the previous
century: 'a kind of tragedy fit for the lower classes'.[2] Others since
Geoffroy have taken a similar view, seeing the principal sources of
melodrama either in Voltaire's tragedy or in Diderot's domestic
drama; and however important the links, through *pantomime*, with
the popular traditions of the fairground theatres, it is clear that such
links do not of themselves fully account for the peculiar characteristics
of Pixérécourt's melodrama.

The literary drama of the previous generation was by no means a
static recitative lacking all visual appeal. On the one hand, in tragedy,
'melodramatic' features of plot, as well as a tendency towards
spectacle on a grand scale, were already well established; on the other
hand, in sentimental domestic drama, the use of *pantomime* and
tableaux compensated to some extent for the acknowledged inadequacy
of the spoken word. However, both of these genres obviously remained
forms of drama in which speech was paramount; and the prose of
drame bourgeois, no less than the verse of tragedy, was a highly
stylised medium, with its own specialised form of literary rhetoric.

But whereas verse tragedy catered for the traditionalist spectators
of the Comédie-Française, and Diderot's *drame* appealed to less
conservative members of the same culture-group — and whereas such
novelties as the *pantomime* also attracted cultured patrons looking
for lighter entertainment — melodramas of the 1800s were written
for a quite different kind of spectator. The new genre came into
being at the end of a decade in which the old monopoly had been
broken, the prestige of the Comédie-Française had seemingly been
irrevocably shattered by the repeated closure of the theatre and the
imprisonment of half the company, and Parisian theatres generally,
now more numerous, had become much more responsive to political
and social changes.[3] The theatre-going public was no longer confined
to those with a certain level of education and culture: Grimod de la
Reynière, writing in 1797, speaks of a new mania for the theatre
that had spread through all ranks of society. There was now a new
kind of audience, who had lived through the revolution and had a
well-developed taste for violent sensations: 'soldiers; adolescents who
would be better suited to the classroom than to the theatre; the
lowest grades of the working class; finally, a few clerks, a class which
used to have some education, but is now semi-illiterate'. Such audiences,

says La Reynière, 'are so ignorant of the most basic elements of
grammar and versification that they don't know verse from prose;
they can't tell comedy from farce, bombast from sublimity, pathos
from cheap sentimentality . . . And these are the judges in whose
hands the future of the French theatre rests!'[4]

This is a graphic portrait of Pixérécourt's audience, the 'illiterate'
for whom he claimed to be writing. And at first sight, when we look
at the spectacular effects of his finales, the crude sentimentality of
his dramatic climaxes, and the lack of sophistication of his comic
scenes, we might be forgiven for assuming that the purpose of such
plays was simply to exploit the naivety of these uncultured audiences
by offering them a totally undemanding form of entertainment.
Pixérécourt was no mere entertainer, however; still less was he a
cynic, prepared to exploit for his own benefit the naivety or gulli-
bility of others. 'Unlike the Roman crowd who called for bread and
circuses', says La Reynière, 'the people of Paris want only circuses'
— but Pixérécourt, who had an unshakeable conviction in the didactic
force of the theatre, was determined to give them moral sustenance
as well, and his melodramas were all conceived with that end in
view.

Charles Nodier, in his flattering introduction to the four-volume
Théâtre choisi of Pixérécourt (1841—3), explicitly links the playwright's moral purpose and his prose style. Drawing attention to the
sudden interruption of the church's moral role in the revolutionary
decade, he suggests that melodrama 'took the place of the silent
pulpit'; Pixérécourt, he says, was conscious of his lofty mission, as
of a veritable apostolate, 'and the most important condition of any
apostolate is a knowledge of the language proper to the country in
which one is going to exercise one's mission'. Contemporary French
usage, Nodier maintains, was marked by a taste for extravagant,
bombastic rhetoric, a debased form of revolutionary oratory, per-
petuated in the political clubs, the law courts and the press; and it
was only by adopting the same hollow verbiage that a popular dramatist could capture the imagination of his audiences.

It is impossible to say how far Pixérécourt's turgid manner in fact
derives from a conscious attempt to speak the language of his spectators, and how far it reflects earlier literary influences — for after
all, the characters of Diderot and Mercier had often spoken in a
similar declamatory style. But whatever its source, there is no difficulty
in recognising the diction of Pixérécourt's characters as speech inflated

well above the level of normal colloquial usage. The following highly literary examples of hyperbole, apostrophe, balance and repetition are typical of the 'Corneille of the boulevards':

— Ah! Monsieur, il faudrait être entièrement dépourvue de sentiments et de délicatesse, pour ne pas chérir le plus estimable, le plus généreux des hommes!

— Modeste asile où, pendant vingt ans, je n'ai connu que l'innocence et la paix, plût au ciel que je ne t'eusse jamais quitté!

— La triste Eliza, vouée de nouveau à l'opprobre, en butte à la calomnie, va se voir haïe, méprisée, abandonnée de tout le monde.

— Ah! je suis trahie, déshonorée, perdue! Victime des adroites séductions d'un imposteur, il ne me reste rien, plus rien! O mon père! la voilà donc accomplie votre terrible prédiction! la misère, la honte, l'opprobre sont désormais l'unique partage de la malheureuse Valentine.[5]

Pixérécourt's characters are ever ready to resort to the moral maxim, a prose equivalent of the *sententiae* familiar from the tragedy and the *haute comédie* of a century and a half:

— Un père offensé qui pardonne est la plus parfaite image de la divinité.

— L'homme vertueux punit, mais il n'assassine pas.

— Si l'on savait ce qu'il en coûte pour cesser d'être vertueux, on verrait bien peu de méchants sur la terre.

— Quand on sait se faire aimer, on est rarement dans le cas de punir.

— Qu'il est affreux, le sort d'un criminel, éternellement placé entre le remords et la crainte du châtiment.[6]

Finally, nothing betrays the literary ancestry of this new genre so much as the soliloquies in which sinners acknowledge the voice of conscience. Here are the closing lines from a long soliloquy by Macaire, the villain of *Le Chien de Montargis*:

En horreur à moi-même, dévoré de remords, tout couvert du sang de mon semblable, je marche à pas précipités vers l'échafaud qui me réclame, et qui peut seul mettre un terme aux effroyables tourments que j'éprouve; et voilà où les passions déréglées conduisent un homme assez faible, assez lâche pour s'abandonner sans résistance à leur fatal empire.[7]

Mutatis mutandis, these are the self-incriminating accents of a whole series of tragic characters stretching back to Racine's Phèdre.

The passages of extremely economical writing, on the other hand —

those sequences, for instance, in which characters converse in a crude approximation to the stichomythia of classical verse drama:

— Votre nom?
— Polina. (*A part*) Quel espoir . . . ! (*Haut*) Le vôtre?
— Polaski.
— Vous êtes . . . ?
— Polonais.
— Les Cosaques . . . ?
— Vaincus.
— Edwinski . . . ?
— Sauvé.
— Zamoski . . . ?
— Mort.
— O Providence!
— On vient . . . ![8]

may well suggest a more obvious analogy with the cartoonist's reductive techniques. There are also, of course, episodes in which essential dramatic action is accompanied by no verbal commentary at all. To take just one example, in *Le Pèlerin blanc*, when the Count, disguised as an elderly retainer in his own castle, saves his young sons who are in the power of Roland, the evil *intendant*, by switching bottles so that the latter drinks the poison he has prepared for the boys, this vital sequence, on which the dénouement will depend, takes place without a word being uttered — not even one of the asides by which Pixérécourt's good, as well as his evil, characters habitually keep the less perceptive spectators informed of what is going on. But very few sustained dramatic sequences in Pixérécourt depend entirely on visual rather than on spoken communication; and in many cases where this might be expected, the visual is pointedly translated into the medium of speech. For instance, the sign-language of the dumb characters, Francisque in *Coelina* and Eloi in *Le Chien de Montargis*, is accompanied at the most crucial points by an explicit commentary spoken by their interpreters; while in the latter work in the case of the dog itself, that representative of divine justice whose action in 'accusing' his master's murderer provided the anecdotal source of the play, Pixérécourt seems deliberately to have avoided the challenge to let visual action speak for itself: Dragon's inspired intervention takes place offstage and has to be reported, and his only appearance on stage also needs to be interpreted by a spoken commentary.

However, if the visual spectacle is seldom allowed any genuinely autonomous standing — if generally speaking not only the moral values, but also most of the actions are generated by dialogue of very conventional style — it can also be shown that Pixérécourt's dialogue too lacks the self-sufficient, autonomous quality of the classical text. The speech of Pixérécourt's characters depends on visual reinforcement to a degree that is difficult to imagine when one has nothing but the text to rely on. There can be no doubt about the literary ancestry of the rhetoric of melodrama, but to read the dialogue on the printed page certainly tends to give a disproportionate emphasis to its conventional literary qualities. It is abundantly clear that in the theatre it was not an intellectual appeal to the minds of his spectators that the dramatist was seeking, but an affective appeal to their sensibility; and in that affective appeal the interrelationship between the spoken word and the accompanying image was absolutely vital.

In this regard, Pixérécourt's grandiose operatic finales may seem to be examples of spectacle for the sake of spectacle, pure visual entertainment for simple-minded spectators. Yet if we look at what is surely the most sensational of these spectacular scenes, the eruption of Vesuvius at the end of *La Tête de mort*, it can be seen that the physical setting of the play — the ruins of Pompeii, with the volcano brooding ominously in the background — is by no means an arbitrary adjunct to the human action. There is an evident affinity between the forces of nature and the divine justice that Réginald and his accomplices have offended; human notions of right and wrong are powerfully reinforced by the intervention of the natural order, and this primitive form of the pathetic fallacy is certainly implicit in the final stage direction as the volcano erupts, covering the body of Réginald (who has just died of remorse) and killing the other evildoers:

Tous les personnages se tournent avec effroi vers la gauche et sont frappés de terreur; ils veulent fuir en poussant de grands cris; mais un torrent de lave se précipite des hauteurs à gauche dans les excavations du fond. Tout le monde recule à cette vue. Quand l'excavation est remplie, la lave déborde et s'avance dans la grande rue qu'elle inonde . . . Les soldats menacent les bandits, qui sont renversés et détruits par la lave. Le corps de Réginald en est couvert, et disparaît sous les scories brûlantes. Un torrent venant de la gauche traverse le théâtre dans sa largeur et va tomber à droite dans une cavité où s'étaient réfugiés quelques bandits. On entend leurs cris de détresse. Le théâtre est entièrement inondé par cette mer de bitume et de lave; une pluie de pierres embrasées et transparentes et de cendres rouges tombe de tous côtés . . . La couleur rouge dont tous les objets sont frappés, le bruit épouvantable du volcan, les cris, l'agitation et le désespoir des personnages, chacun dans leur sens, tout concourt à former de cette effrayante convulsion de la nature un tableau horrible et tout à fait digne d'être comparé aux Enfers.[9]

Here, the natural setting is no mere picturesque backcloth: the volcano becomes an active participant in a cosmic drama. We may compare the stage direction at the beginning of Act III of *Coelina*, where the disruption of the moral order, with the temporary triumph of Truguelin and the banishment of the heroine and her father, is symbolised by the violent storm that accompanies the action: 'au lever du rideau toute la nature paraît en désordre; les éclairs brillent de toutes parts, le torrent roule avec fureur, les vents mugissent, la pluie tombe avec fracas, et des coups de tonnerre multipliés qui se répètent cent fois, par l'écho des montagnes, portent l'épouvante et la terreur dans l'âme'.[10] No wonder that Truguelin comments: 'Il me semble que tout dans la nature se réunit pour m'accuser.'[11] Similarly, in *Le Monastère abandonné*, the 'fearful storm' that has served as a background to the self-incriminating soliloquy of the real criminal, Bastien, is interpreted by Piétro as harmonising with his own uneasy conscience: 'Quelle nuit! à peine ai-je pu sommeiller quelques instants! le bouleversement de la nature, le désordre de mes pensées, m'ont tenu dans une agitation continuelle.'[12]

It would be no exaggeration to regard Pixérécourt's whole *oeuvre* as a vast metaphysical drama portraying a Manichaean conflict on a cosmic scale. Nevertheless, the individual episodes of this struggle are normally acted out in a less spectacular setting, and the visual illustrations of the ways of Providence are seldom as striking as in *La Tête de mort*, or even as in certain parts of *Coelina* or *Le Monastère abandonné*; so that as regards the relationship between the spoken and the visual in his plays taken as a whole, the domesticated dumb-show deriving from the *drame bourgeois* tradition is much more significant than the occasional spectacular *tour de force*. In the more mundane settings of the domestic melodramas, Providence may not show its hand quite so openly — but its workings can nevertheless be seen as well as heard. As in the gothic novel, occult correspondences are taken for granted; the place where a crime has been committed, the weapon with which it was committed, as well as the hour at which the deed was done: all of these are capable of operating powerfully on the mind of the wrongdoer. Thus, in the same way that Truguelin is affected when he revisits the scene of his crime — 'Ciel! . . . que vois-je? . . . ce pont . . . ces rochers . . . ce torrent . . . c'est là . . . là . . . que ma main criminelle versa le sang d'un infortuné . . . O terre! entr'ouvre-toi! . . . abîme dans ton sein un monstre indigne de la vie . . . '[13] — Piétro in *Le Monastère abandonné* also suffers at the tangible reminder of the crime he thinks he has committed: '*Neuf*

*heures sonnent à la grosse horloge du Monastère. Ces sons prolongés
et retentissants inspirent la terreur. Piétro s'arrête et compte à
voix basse; après la huitième heure, il s'écrie comme s'il pouvait
arrêter la marche du temps*: Arrête! . . . c'est assez . . . Voilà l'heure
où je fus maudit.'[14]

In these and similar ways, the playwright underlines his somewhat
simplistic message: the eventual punishment of the evildoer is forecast
by a system of signs and portents, by which Providence uses the
material world to work on an uneasy conscience. Moreover, the
uneasy conscience constantly betrays itself by physical signs. The
comforting message — that the unscrupulous characters who exploit
their fellow-men never enjoy the real happiness that only virtue can
bring — is expressed, as we have seen, in the form of soliloquies or
conventional asides to the audience; it is also frequently reinforced
by reference to visual indicators. Carlo, the righter of wrongs in
La Tête de mort, speaks of Réginald as follows: 'Tout doit légitimer
le soupçon qui m'a conduit ici. Toujours solitaire et sombre, jamais
je ne l'ai vu sourire. Son extérieur grave et composé, sa froide réserve,
cette habitude mélancolique et douloureuse annoncent un coeur
chagrin, une conscience bourrelée. Il craint d'être deviné.'[15] More
specifically, characters blush, or go livid, as a sign of guilt:

— Savez-vous, Monsieur, qu'avant d'accuser un homme d'un délit aussi grave,
il faut avoir des preuves?
— J'en ai une irrécusable.
— Quelle est-elle?
— Ta pâleur.[16]

They start apprehensively, recoil in fear, and continually betray their
guilty conscience: at the appearance of the mute Francisque, his
victim of eight years earlier, Truguelin 'recule de quelques pas, et
paraît frappé de terreur'; Macaire, returning after the murder of
Aubry, enters 'avec l'air égaré d'un homme qui vient de commettre
un crime'; and the same Macaire, perhaps the most obviously conscience-
stricken of all Pixérécourt's criminals, has constantly to be reproved
by his accomplice, Landry, because the visible signs of his remorse
threaten to give the guilty pair away.

The aside to the audience is, of all the features of the dialogue of
melodrama, the one with the most obvious counterpart in the
cartoonist's art. The comments at first hand by participants in the
action — 'Fâcheux contretemps!', 'Quel supplice!', 'D'où vient que
le coeur me bat avec tant de force!'[17] and countless similar inter-
jections — are the nearest equivalent of the 'balloons' representing

unspoken thoughts; and it would surely be right to imagine these
asides being delivered with the accompaniment of appropriately
theatrical gestures providing a stylised show of annoyance, anguish,
or apprehension. There are sequences in which a dialogue is punctuated throughout by this kind of comment; for instance, every encounter between Raymond and Isouf, in *Les Ruines de Babylone*,
where each is trying to deceive the other, is built up on this basis:

— Tu as raison. (*A part*) Je crois qu'il me trompe.
— (*A part*) Sachons s'il est instruit. (*Haut*) Et, cependant, quel progrès avez-
vous fait? qu'avez-vous appris?[18]

These scenes have a likely source in the verbal duel between Figaro
and Count Almaviva in Act III of *Le Mariage de Figaro* — though it
may well be felt that contrived, patterned dialogue of this sort
remains more appropriate to comedy than to would-be serious drama.
    Another use of the aside is to provide a comment at second hand,
as it were, by a bystander. At its simplest, this is illustrated by the
scene in which Coelina overhears Truguelin and his accomplice
plotting the death of Francisque:

Truguelin: A minuit. S'il résiste . . .
Germain: Il est mort.
Truguelin: Retirons-nous.
Coelina (*à part*): Les monstres!
Truguelin: J'entends du bruit.
Germain: On vient . . . C'est lui.
Truguelin: Lui! pourquoi différer?
Germain: Il n'est pas temps encore.
Truguelin: Tu veilleras.
Germain: Vous agirez.
Coelina (*à part*): Les scélérats![19]

The device is constantly exploited in this way, for the author habitually
makes use of the good characters in order to draw attention to the
motives of the evildoers. Bataille, for instance, the honest ex-soldier
of *La Femme à deux maris*, remarks as he hides behind a statue to
overhear his generous master offering to save the life of the unworthy
Isidore Fritz: 'Quoi qu'en dise Monsieur, je veux veiller sur lui: il
n'y a jamais rien de bon à attendre des méchants.'[20] Although in the
passages just quoted there are no stage directions to indicate any
visual accompaniment to the verbal expression of emotion or sentiment, Pixérécourt's plays do contain a wealth of stage directions
which show how speech was intended to be reinforced by such
means. The following examples, all taken from *Coelina*, suggest a

repertory of conventional facial and gestural expressions that would
be readily understood by the audience:

D'un air contraint et avec un faux intérêt.

S'efforçant de se remettre de son trouble.

Avec un grand sang-froid.

D'un ton brusque, après avoir jeté un regard de mépris sur Truguelin.[21]

More obviously, at moments of emotional crisis characters raise
their hands towards heaven, throw themselves at each other's knees,
embrace one another and swoon; while in addition to such cases in
which dialogue is supplemented by the conventional language of
gestures, there is of course abundant gestural by-play involving
disguise, letters, weapons, and all the other material objects which
are given so prominent a place in the dramaturgy of melodrama[22]
(the passage referred to above from *Le Pèlerin blanc* is a good example
of this). Such a technique once again suggests that of the cartoonist,
in its reliance on a stereotyped language of signs designed to produce
the desired affective appeal to an unsophisticated audience.

Not that there are no parallels to be found in more sophisticated
art-forms. The text of Racine's tragedies, for instance, contains many
significant references to tears, sighs and gestures, and to the ways
in which a character's facial expression betrays his emotions (not to
mention the ancillary role of gesture as established by a century or
more of acting tradition); and it is well known that a painter like
Poussin had recourse to an accepted code of gestures, clearly identifiable with a range of corresponding emotions (see for instance his
Judgement of Solomon). But from Racine and Poussin to Diderot
and Greuze, and thence to Pixérécourt, such correspondences become
steadily more banal — largely because they are so much more explicit,
and leave so much less to the imagination of the spectator. By the
same token, the *tableaux* of which Pixérécourt and his contemporaries
were so fond (and cf. the stage direction 'Picture' in English melodramas) — '*[Truguelin] tire un poignard de son sein, et se précipite
sur Francisque qui fait feu de la main gauche. Germain vient vivement
le saisir par le bras droit et lui arrache son arme. Tableau*' (*Coelina*,
Act I, Scene 16)[23] — can be shown to be a cruder development of the
feature which Diderot had incorporated into his domestic drama in
imitation of painters like Greuze: 'Une disposition [des] personnages
sur la scène, si naturelle et si vraie que, rendue fidèlement par un

peintre, elle me plairait sur la toile, est un tableau.'[24] Cruder, because while in even the more dramatic of Greuze's 'narrative' paintings (e.g. 'Le Mauvais Fils puni') he has chosen to portray a sentimental climax by means of an essentially static emotional display, and while Diderot explicitly recommends the *tableau* as a static alternative to the *coup de théâtre*, it can be seen from examples like the one quoted from *Coelina* that Pixérécourt tends to use the *tableau* in order to 'freeze' a violent climax, so that it becomes in his hands a fundamentally unstable device.

When Artaud called for 'a new physical language, based no longer on *words* but on *signs*'; when he specified that 'it is not a question of doing away with conventional speech, but of endowing language with the sort of meaning that it possesses in our dreams'; and when he then went on to say that the only form of Western theatre to have succeeded in breaking down the 'descriptive' theatre of the neo-classical age had been the Romantic melodrama of the early nineteenth century, one cannot help thinking that this was an example of wishful thinking.[25] For surely the mixture of the spoken and the visual in Pixérécourt's melodrama is not significantly different from the mixture in Voltaire's tragedy or in Diderot's *drame bourgeois*: what is different is the level on which the whole operates. Pixérécourt's is essentially still a *descriptive* form of drama, to use Artaud's term: the language of signs and gestures is a closed one, with clear-cut correspondences between the visual and the spoken, not the sort of open system whose interpretation depends on the free exercise of the spectator's imagination.

Similarly, when the author of an excellent recent study of melodrama, Peter Brooks, writes: 'The gestures that we see on stage, the visible movements, can perhaps best be considered . . . the vehicle of a metaphor whose tenor is a vaguely defined yet grandiose emotional or spiritual force that gesture seeks to make present without directly naming it, by pointing toward it',[26] this would appear to be valid only insofar as the role of gesture in melodrama can be considered to be independent of the spoken word. It is true that the gestures of Pixérécourt's characters are almost always hyperbolic — but so is their language; and as I have attempted to show, the nature of this hyperbole is essentially reductive: the polarisation of motives into extremes of good and evil, expressed in the most explicit terms, the use of gesture as a schematised representation of equally explicit responses, renders the emotional effects crude and unsubtle. The art-form in which melodrama really comes into its own, as what Brooks

27

calls 'an intensified, primary, and exemplary version of what the most ambitious art, since the beginnings of Romanticism, has been about',[27] is surely nineteenth-century opera; while the same critic also argues convincingly that the melodramatic mode, as a means of 'uncovering, demonstrating, and making operative the essential moral universe in a post-sacred era',[28] is successfully exploited by a novelist like Balzac. Even if we grant that the theatrical melodramas of the 1800s were written with a similar aim, it must regretfully be acknowledged that the achievements of this form fall far short of those of later (and more sophisticated) manifestations of the melo-dramatic mode. The close interrelationship of the systems of speech and visual image, and above all the explicitness of both, mean that the 'gestural semiotics' of melodrama, far from lifting the genre on to a higher imaginative plane, for the most part plays down to the understanding of a simple-minded audience.

It may seem unduly dismissive to talk of the 'dramaturgy of the strip-cartoon'. Pixérécourt's dialogue does not descend to the 'Aaargh!' and 'Ouch!' of the present-day practitioners, and the contemporary parody reproduced by Brooks: 'Oui!! . . . non!!! mais . . . non, non!!!!! Se peut-il? Quoi! . . . Oh grands dieux!!!!!! . . . Malheureux, qu'ai-je fait????? . . . Barbare!!!!!! . . . Hélas!! . . . O jour affreux! . . . ô nuit épouvantable!! . . . Ah! que je souffre!! . . . Mourons!!!! . . . Je me meurs . . . je suis mort!!!!!!! . . . aie, ay! aie!!!!!!!'[29] was no doubt directed not so much at the master himself as at his less am-bitious imitators. Nevertheless, in the mutual dependence of word and image; in the polarisation of characters into elementary stereo-types of good and evil; in the abuse of the aside to guide the audience's reactions; in the over-simplified function of the soliloquy; in the undemanding explicitness of both speech and gesture; in the fondness for static tableaux representing emotional states in a highly stylised manner: in all of these ways, Pixérécourt's practice involves an impoverishment of dramatic art for the benefit of naive and uncultured spectators; and the analogy with the cartoonist presenting a simple story in palatable form for the relatively unlettered is perhaps not too wide of the mark.[30]

Postscript

Having read the other conference papers, and listened to the other speakers, I am sure that an excellent case can be made out for con-sidering Pixérécourt and his contemporaries as the first creators of a distinctively popular drama in modern times. French melodrama of the 1800s may not have been 'popular' in the sense in which some of the later contributors to the conference chose to use the term, that is 'dedicated to the overthrow of a political system in which power does not rest in the hands of the people' — but it is certainly 'popular' in the primary sense in which the term is applied to both dramatic and non-dramatic literary forms: that is, to indicate those works which are addressed to an unsophisticated public, lacking the education and the culture which are necessary to appreciate more traditional forms. In the case of popular drama, as I have shown, this involves an increasing reliance on the non-literary, and to some extent the non-verbal, elements of theatre; but a similar reductive process operates in other popular art-forms, and the analogy with the cartoonist's technique is only one of the parallels that could be suggested. Some time after writing this paper, I happened to hear a radio talk in which the managing director of the *Daily Mirror* — a paper which, though it could not be described as popular in the sense of 'revolutionary', is incontestably popular in the primary meaning of the word — spoke of the difficulty of 'expressing serious ideas in words of one syllable'. I suppose it could be said (though the speaker did not put it in precisely this way) that the aim of the *Daily Mirror* is to serve as the political conscience of a certain class of reader, more easily reached by its blend of banner headlines, unambitious vocabulary and simplified sentence structure, its sensationalism and its homely familiarity ('Come Off It, Harold!') than by the formal, intellectualised argument of a *Times* leader. The shock tactics can easily mislead one as to the *Mirror*'s purpose, but there can be no doubt that this is essentially serious and responsible. By the same token, Pixérécourt was a dramatist with a wholly serious purpose; and using remarkably similar means,[31] he set out to serve as the moral conscience of the post-revolutionary age.

NOTES

1 Cf. A. Pitou, 'Les Origines du mélodrame français à la fin du XVIIIe siècle', *Revue d'histoire littéraire de la France*, 18 (1911), pp. 256–96.
2 Quoted by C.-M. Des Granges, *Geoffroy et la critique dramatique* (Paris, 1897), p. 404.
3 Cf. M. Carlson, *The Theatre of the French Revolution* (Ithaca, New York, 1966).
4 Quoted by W. G. Hartog, *Guilbert de Pixérécourt, sa vie, son mélodrame, sa technique et son influence* (Paris, 1913), p. 71.

5 — Ah! Sir, one would need to be totally lacking in delicacy of feeling not to cherish the most worthy, the most generous of men!

— Humble dwelling where for twenty years I knew naught but innocence and peace, would to heaven I had never left you!

— The wretched Eliza, once more destined to shame, again the object of calumny, will see herself hated, despised, abandoned by everyone.

— Ah! I am betrayed, dishonoured, lost! A victim of the clever seductions of an impostor, I have nothing, nothing left! Alas, dear Father, your terrible prophecy has now come true! Nothing but shame, disgrace and destitution shall henceforth be the lot of the unhappy Valentine.

6 — A wronged father who forgives his child is the most perfect representation of the deity.

— The virtuous man punishes, but he does not kill.

— If only men knew what it costs to stop being virtuous, there would be hardly any villains left on earth.

— Whosoever is able to make himself loved, seldom needs to punish.

— How terrible is the lot of the criminal, forever placed between remorse and the fear of punishment.

7 A source of horror to myself, consumed by remorse, bathed in the blood of my fellow-man, I hasten towards the scaffold that awaits me, and which can alone put an end to the frightful torments that I undergo; for that is where unbridled passions drive whoever is weak and cowardly enough to give himself up without a struggle to their fatal dominion.

8 — Your name?
— Polina. (*Aside*) What hope . . . ! (*Aloud*) Your own?
— Polaski.
— You are . . . ?
— Polish.
— The Cossacks . . . ?
— Beaten.
— Edwinski . . . ?
— Safe.
— Zamoski . . . ?
— Dead.
— O Providence!
— Someone is coming . . . !

9 All the characters turn to their left in fear, and are struck with terror. They cry out, and try to flee; but a torrent of lava rushes down from the heights to the left, into the excavations backstage. Everyone retreats at the sight of it. When the excavation is filled up, the lava overflows and sweeps down the main street, smothering it completely . . . The soldiers

threaten the bandits, who are overwhelmed and wiped out by the torrent of lava. Réginald's body is covered by it, and disappears beneath the burning slag. A stream of lava coming down from the left crosses the whole width of the stage and pours into a pit in which some bandits had taken refuge. Their cries of terror can be heard. The stage is completely inundated by a sea of bitumen and lava; a shower of glowing, transparent rocks and red-hot ashes falls everywhere . . . The red glow in which all these objects are bathed, the terrifying noise of the volcano, the cries, the commotion and the universal despair, all combine to make this dreadful upheaval of nature a picture of utter horror, worthy to be compared with the Nether Regions.

10 'When the curtain rises, the whole of nature seems to be in disarray; lightning flashes everywhere, the mountain stream rages furiously, the wind howls, the rain beats down noisily, and repeated peals of thunder, multiplied a hundredfold by the mountains' echo, strike terror and dismay into every heart.'

11 'The whole of nature seems to conspire to accuse me.'

12 'What a night! I have hardly slept more than a moment! the wild disorder of nature, the confusion of my thoughts, kept me in a continual turmoil.'

13 'Heavens! . . . what do I see? . . . the bridge . . . the rocks . . . the stream . . . 'twas there . . . there . . . that this criminal hand of mine shed the blood of a poor unfortunate . . . Open up, O earth! . . . engulf for ever a monster who does not deserve to live . . .'

14 *The big monastery clock strikes nine. Its prolonged, reverberating strokes are truly terrifying. Piétro stops and counts under his breath; at eight, he cries out, as if to bring time to a halt*: Stop! 'tis enough . . . That is the hour at which I was accursed.'

15 'Everything helps to justify the suspicion which led me to this place. Always sombre and solitary, I have never known him to smile. His stern, composed expression, his cold reserve, his melancholy, sorrowful manner: all this denotes a tormented heart, a conscience ill at ease. He is afraid of being found out.'

16 — Are you aware, Sir, that before accusing a man of so serious a crime, you need to have proof?
— I have an irrefutable proof.
— And that is . . . ?
— Your pallor.

17 'Cursed mishap!', 'What torture!', 'How is it that my heart beats so wildly!'

18 — You are right. (*Aside*) I think he is deceiving me.
— (*Aside*) Let's find out if he knows the truth. (*Aloud*) What progress have you made in the meantime? What have you learned?

19 — At midnight, then, if he resists . . .
— He's a dead man.
— Let us withdraw.
— (*aside*) The monsters!
— I hear a sound.
— Someone is coming . . . It is he.
— He! why delay?

> — It is not yet time.
> — You'll keep a look-out.
> — You'll do the deed.
> — (*aside*) The villains!

20 'Whatever my master may say, I intend to look after him: there's never any good to be expected from wicked men.'

21 *In a forced manner, and showing an assumed interest.*

    Endeavouring to recover his composure.

    With complete composure.

    In a brusque manner, after glancing scornfully at Truguelin.

22 Cf. V. Hugo, *Ruy Blas*, ed. A. Ubersfeld (Besançon and Paris, 1971), vol. 1, pp. 69–70, 'Une Dramaturgie de l'objet'.

23 '*Truguelin draws a dagger from his bosom, and rushes at Francisque, who fires with his left hand. Germain darts forward, seizes him by his right arm, and disarms him. Tableau.*'

24 'An arrangement of the characters on stage, so natural and true to life that if it were rendered faithfully by an artist, the painting would give me pleasure: that is a tableau.' Diderot, *Writings on the Theatre*, ed. F. C. Green (Cambridge, 1936), p. 29.

25 *Le Théâtre et son double* (Paris, 1964), pp. 81, 116, 142.

26 *The Melodramatic Imagination: Balzac, Henry James, Melodrama and the Mode of Excess* (New Haven, 1976), p. 72.

27 *Ibid.*, pp. 21–2.

28 *Ibid.*, p. 15

29 'Yes!! ... no!!! but ... no, no!!!!! Could it be? What! ... Ye gods !!!!!! ... Unhappy wretch, what have I done????? ... Cruel one!!!!!! ... Alas!! ... O dreadful day! ... O horrible night!! ... Ah! how I suffer!! ... Let us end it all!!!! ... I am dying ... I am dead!!!!!!! ... aaaaah!!!!!!!!' *Ibid.*, p. 210.

30 The special issue of the *Revue des sciences humaines* devoted to 'Le Mélo-drame', 162 (1976), contains some useful articles both on the dramaturgy and on the language of Pixérécourt and other French dramatists of the period.

31 Due allowance must of course be made for the characteristic differences between the French and English languages. Pixérécourt's dialogue retains, for an English reader, a certain rational, abstract quality that is largely absent, for instance, from Holcroft's *Tale of Mystery*; but French will always, at any level, be more abstract, less vivid and colourful, than its English counterpart: one has only to look at advertisements and public notices in the London Underground and the Paris Métro, or to compare *Paris-Presse* with the *Daily Mirror*.

Joseph Bouchardy: a melodramatist and his public

John McCormick

Je suis heureux de terminer l'histoire de l'Ambigu en signalant le succès le plus productif qu'ait obtenu ce théâtre. M. Joseph Bouchardy est la providence des directeurs; il les enrichit tous, il fait maintenant avec *Lazare le pâtre* des recettes inouïes, miraculeuses, des recettes aussi extraordinaires que celles du *Sonneur de Saint-Paul* qui a procuré à la Gaîté plus de 200,000 francs de bénéfices.[1]

I

Joseph Bouchardy, 1810–70, 'le grand impresario des terreurs du boulevard', was the author of a score of *drames*[2] and a successor to Pixérécourt, whose plays he read avidly in his youth.

Bouchardy's plays cannot be examined without a look at the audiences for which they were designed. All but a handful were staged at either the Ambigu or the Gaîté. These two theatres, classified by Napoleon as places where melodramas might be performed, had originally been situated next to one another on the Boulevard du Temple. After a fire in 1827 the new Ambigu was reconstructed on the Boulevard Saint Martin, almost next door to the Théâtre de la Porte Saint Martin. The Gaîté was burnt down in 1835, and the new theatre which rose again on the same site, had, like the Ambigu, an enlarged seating capacity. These new buildings were being erected at a time when the boulevards were becoming more fashionable places of resort and losing much of their earlier fairground appearance.[3] The bourgeois take-over of the theatre of the boulevards is best symbolised by the persistent popularity and the ideological values of the plays of Eugène Scribe at the Gymnase. The modern concept of boulevard theatre derives more from the tradition of Scribe and the Gymnase than from that of Pixérécourt or Bouchardy at the Gaîté. Strongly affected by the general *embourgeoisement* of the theatre, the Gaîté and the Ambigu managed to remain predominantly popular. In the early twentieth century the Ambigu could still refer to itself as 'le théâtre du mélodrame populaire', and a 1905 cartoon

shows the audience of the gods extremely involved in the performance and shouting advice to the characters as it might have done in
the 1830s. The Gaîté survived its demolition by Baron Haussmann and
the transplantation from the Boulevard du Temple to the Square
des Arts et Métiers (now Papin) in 1862. According to Buguet,[4]
the popular public hesitated before following the theatre. However,
a review of the Dumas/Meurice adaptation of *Hamlet* in 1867 gives
an indirect indication of the situation when it mentions that the
fashionable audience was the exception, not the rule, 'dans ces
parages chers aux habitués du mélodrame'.

As Maurice Descotes has pointed out,[5] when Théophile Gautier
went to one of the melodrama theatres he found the audience
picturesque — it was a public to which he did not belong. Likewise,
the Boillys, Daumiers and other illustrators of the period have left
a very colourful impression of the *paradis* of these theatres, tightly
packed, predominantly youthful and unruly, with a sprinkling of
soldiers and grisettes and the occasional woman feeding a baby.
Equally, the unrestrained emotions of the audience are frequently
depicted and contrast strongly with the satirical cartoonist's expressions of wooden boredom and large stomachs to be seen at the
Comédie-Française.

Dans les théâtres de mélodrames, il n'est pas besoin de chercher à distinguer
ce qui se passe dans les coeurs: les spectateurs, pendant la représentation, ne
vous laissent pas le moindre doute à cet égard; et quand la toile se baisse, les
exclamations, les commentaires prouvent quel intérêt cette masse prend à ce
qu'elle écoute et à ce qu'elle voit.[6]

By comparison with plays performed at the Comédie-Française
or the Gymnase, Bouchardy's plays were written for a popular
audience. Some indication of the composition of this audience may
be gleaned from an examination of the price structures at the Gaîté
and the Ambigu during his major period of activity and popularity
(1837—52). For this to have any meaning, we need to look at the
earnings and real incomes of the working class at the time. According
to L. Chevalier,[7] the period 1815—50 was one of static or diminishing
salaries, with an upturn coming early in the second Empire. Between
1820 and 1849 there was a tendency towards lower prices, but this
was followed by a sharp increase between 1849 and 1857. Because
of the greater use of female labour and machinery, Parisian workers
were often less well-off than workers in other towns. The decline
of the apprenticeship system coupled with immigration to the
capital tended to swell the ranks of the unskilled proletariat. In the

1830s and 1840s an unskilled worker earned, on average, about
two francs a day, but these were years of depressions and periods
of unemployment (notably 1836–7 and 1847).[8] A working day
could be thirteen to fifteen hours, but a number of days would be
lost as a result of holidays, overproduction or even civil disturbances.
In 1845, Villeneuve-Bargemont estimated that a bachelor would
need at least 502 francs a year to subsist in Paris, and a family
750.[9] A high proportion of the working-class population, even with
comparatively full employment, was thus below subsistence level
and can hardly be thought of as forming part of the theatre public.
One can probably assume that a worker earning two francs a day
might go to the theatre occasionally if he was celibate, but that
once he had a family he would no longer be in a position to spend
fifty centimes on the cheapest place at the Gaîté or Ambigu. His
theatre visits would be limited to the over-crowded free performances
of 14 July or 15 August. The area around the Boulevard du Temple,
stretching eastwards from the rue Saint Denis, was one which contained
many small industries, and the workers here tended to be better off
than those in the larger textile factories. A more skilled artisan, such
as a stone-mason or a cooper, or one engaged in the luxury trades,
might expect to earn four to five francs a day. Another important
social grouping was the *petite bourgeoisie*, for which Mlle Daumard
uses the term *bourgeoisie populaire*.[10] This group, much in evidence
in the area, consisted largely of small shopkeepers and traders who in
most cases were former workers or still had very close links with the
working and artisan classes. Usually they had little capital beyond
their stock and furniture, and their shops or premises were rented.
With them one might include various *déclassés* such as bankrupts
or soldiers on half-pay, and also poorer members of the liberal
professions and a number of *petits rentiers*, often retired servants,
living on a small annuity.

One has the impression that during the 1830s and 1840s frequentation of the Gaîté and Ambigu was predominantly local and that
like Montparnasse or Montmartre in 1900 they were *théâtres de
quartier*. *Le Réveil de l'Ambigu*, a one-act prologue by Dutertre
to celebrate the re-opening of the Ambigu after a closure of some
months in 1841 because of bankruptcy, presents local shopkeepers
discussing the closure in couplets:

On ferm' l'Ambigu Comique
C'est affreux

A ces lieux
Il faut faire nos adieux.

C't'établiss'ment au quartier donn' la vie,
Là l'peuple se plaît, il aime à v'nir s'asseoir,
Et si l'théâtre encourag' l'industrie,
C'est en même temps, le délass'ment du soir.[11]

It then goes on to introduce a *petit rentier*, Pluchoiteau, who has
come all the way from Pontoise to see *Lazare le pâtre*, unaware that
the theatre has closed in the middle of its successful run. A description
of the Ambigu at the time of this closure mentions its generally
dilapidated condition and the dirtiness of the seats, which hardly
suggests an attempt to attract a very elegant public. However, the
better-off classes did make up a certain section of the public and
were undoubtedly drawn by the more resounding successes. In the
late 1840s both theatres were extensively renovated and seats became
bookable in advance. By 1852 a five-franc seat cost seven francs if
booked in advance, and a further segregation of the audience was
encouraged by having a separate box office for the cheapest seats.
A description of the refurbished Ambigu of 1847 seems to imply an
increased attempt on the part of the director, Antony Béraud, to
attract a smarter public:

Oh! vieux mélodrame des temps antiques, que tu serais mal à l'aise, avec tes
sabres de bois, tes cordes à puits, tes tasses de poison égueulées, devant ce
public d'aujourd'hui, en habits noirs et en robes de soie, en cravates blanches et
en cachemires, en gants jaunes et les bras adorablement entourés d'adorables
bracelets.[12]

The exact social composition of an audience is difficult to determine,
varying both according to the day of the week and the play performed.
Eugène Sue makes his grisette, Rigolette, who earns about thirty
sous (1 fr. 50) a day, spend this amount on the occasional Sunday
evening visit to the theatre. Sunday night was the popular night. It
had been in the eighteenth century, and Napoleon's police had even
felt it necessary to introduce a regulation governing the theatres of the
boulevards du nord which stipulated that performances on Sunday
should start at 5 p.m. instead of 6.30, so that the working population
would not be too tired on Monday. In 1837, which was a particularly
brilliant year for the Porte Saint Martin, the Gaîté and the Ambigu
(*Gaspardo le pêcheur* drawing crowds almost non-stop at the latter),
the *Courrier des spectacles* observed that 'le lundi est un autre
dimanche pour l'Ambigu Comique et pour la Gaîté qui regorgeait
hier de spectateurs'.[13]

36

Through the 1830s and 1840s performances at these three theatres ordinarily began between 5 p.m. and 6 p.m. Programmes were long. The Porte Saint Martin would sometimes offer no less than three full-length *drames* as an evening's fare. One satirical cartoon shows a jaded audience leaving the theatre at 2 a.m. having been treated to a lengthy bill including a Dumas play and, possibly (the first part of the title is not visible), *Lazare le pâtre*. Programmes at the Opéra or the Comédie-Française at this period generally started at about 7 p.m. and were rather shorter. A more fashionable boulevard theatre, such as the Variétés, tended to begin at about 6.45 p.m. In the 1850s the melodrama theatres generally started at 7 p.m. which suggests that their managements were now more concerned with the convenience of the better-off section of the audience.

Considering the economic facts mentioned above, it is not surprising to find very little modification in overall prices in the theatres of the 1830s and 1840s. The table indicates the range of prices (the dearest and the cheapest seats) at the Comédie-Française, the Variétés and the three main melodrama theatres. Between 1828 and 1835 one

	1828	1835	1852
Comédie Française	6 fr. 60—1 fr. 80	6 fr. 60—1 fr. 0	8 fr. 0—2 fr. 0
Variétés	5 fr. 0—1 fr. 25	5 fr. 0—1 fr. 25	6 fr. 0—0 fr. 75
Porte Saint Martin	5 fr. 0—0 fr. 75	5 fr. 0—0 fr. 60	5 fr. 0—0 fr. 50
Ambigu	3 fr. 60—0 fr. 60*	5 fr. 0—0 fr. 50	5 fr. 0—0 fr. 50
Gaîté	3 fr. 60—0 fr. 60	4 fr. 50—0 fr. 50	5 fr. 0—0 fr. 50

*These are the figures for 1827, before the Ambigu was burnt down, but they would almost certainly have been those for 1828, which are not given in the *Almanach des spectacles*.

notices the increase in the prices of the better seats at the Ambigu and the Gaîté, and the drop in those of the cheaper seats, corresponding no doubt to the fall in prices and earnings, at all theatres except the Variétés, which was clearly becoming less interested in the popular public. By 1852 the range between dearest and cheapest has become wider at the Comédie-Française and the Variétés, and the Gaîté has brought its top prices into line with the other two melodrama theatres, whilst the Porte Saint Martin has done likewise with its cheapest places, dropping their price by ten centimes. In fact the

melodrama theatres all had a concealed price increase in the charge
for advance booking, which effectively raised their top prices to seven
francs at this period. Without entering into further figures, it is worth
observing that the difference between the highest and lowest prices
at the melodrama theatres is proportionately far greater than at the
other two, and this also suggests increasing stratification of the
public according to economic categories.

Audience composition is easier to estimate from the 1850s, when
numbered seating became general. Even in 1852, seats in the third
and fourth galleries and the parterre of the Ambigu were not numbered,
and the same applied to the cheap seats at the Gaîté. In 1835 the
Ambigu could take nearly 2,000 spectators (the old theatre fitted only
1,230); the newly constructed Gaîté had increased its capacity from
1,254 to 1,818; and the Porte Saint Martin seated 1,803 (by 1852
this figure had been increased to 2,069). The larger seating capacity
was the result of the top galleries opening out into big amphitheatres.
According to Donnet and Kaufmann,[14] the Ambigu had an amphitheatre that held 600. If we add to this the second and third galleries
and the parterre (all the seats costing 1 fr. 50 or less), it is clear that
over half the seats were within reach of a very large section of the
classes populaires. The same is still true in 1852, when only about a
third of the seats at the Gaîté or the Ambigu cost more than 1 fr. 50.
For 2 fr. 50, admission was gained to all but the front rows of the
orchestra, the first gallery, the open boxes around the parterre, or the
less good seats of the balcony. (The same price at the Comédie-
Française would give access only to the parterre or the galerie des
deuxièmes loges.) The more elegant public, paying five francs for a
seat in the first two tiers of stage-boxes or the loges grillées[15] around
the balcony, would have amounted to only three or four per cent of
the audience, although, on the occasion of a particularly successful
play, it might well overflow into the better orchestra and balcony
seats, which were normally occupied by the better-off, but not
fashionable, bourgeoisie.

Theatre-going from the 1830s on was associated with social prestige.
Audiences went to be seen as much as to see. The huge chandelier
in the middle of the auditorium remained lit throughout the performance until late in the century. At the Ambigu, however, the chandelier
could be drawn up during the performance, thus allowing for greater
scenic effect and giving a clearer view of the stage from the top
galleries, but making it less easy to see the toilettes of the ladies in
the boxes. Ample evidence shows that the Gaîté and Ambigu remained

predominantly theatres where audiences went to enjoy themselves
and not out of any sense of social obligation. Consequently, despite
an increasing amount of middle-class frequentation, the encroachment
of a bourgeois ethos in the repertoire, and a tendency to greater
class stratification (indicated by price and comfort), these theatres
to a large extent resisted the *embourgeoisement* that had overwhelmed other theatres by the time of the second Empire and had
made the very word *boulevard* almost synonymous with *bourgeois*.

II

Unlike most of the regular purveyors of melodramas for the boulevard
theatres, Bouchardy seldom worked in collaboration.[16] He took his
craft very seriously and each play was the result of nearly a year's
work. He did not participate in the vogue for adapting novels and his
plots, even if they sometimes contained themes explored by other
authors, were all original. The essence of a Bouchardy plot is the
creation of the greatest possible number of situations. If the basic
model is Pixérécourt, it is Pixérécourt highly condensed (Jules Janin
suggested that the last act alone of *Le Secret des cavaliers* contained
enough material for twenty *drames*). By purely literary standards this
may be viewed as decadent,[17] but as popular theatre there is no question about its appeal to audiences of the latter half of the reign of
Louis Phillippe, an appeal deriving largely from this very complication.

The elements that make up a Bouchardy plot — lost children (or
parents), separated husbands and wives, wills and inheritances
falling into the wrong hands, thrones usurped, unjust imprisonment,
the avenging of crime — all belong to a remarkably small and apparently
hackneyed stock. All the elements are immediately recognisable to
an audience familiar with the basic patterns and codes of melodrama,
but Bouchardy's gift is to produce the expected at an unexpected
moment, or to hold off for an incredibly long time a dénouement
that seems to be just around the corner. The complexities of plot
were a constant problem for reviewers obliged to describe the action
as lucidly as possible.[18] Yet in the theatre this mattered far less and
the non-verbal elements coupled with the instantaneous value of the
situation in performance meant that audiences did not altogether
share this concern of the reviewers. However, in the later plays
complexity sometimes gained the upper hand at the expense of
the dramatic and interest in the characters became too slight for
them to be able to sustain the intrigue. This was probably one cause

for the failure of *L'Armurier de Santiago*, which expected the audience to retain an absurd amount of expository material before a not very clear action could get under way.

The basic melodrama formula, which presents a reassuring world where virtue will ultimately triumph, is still there, but the emphasis has shifted slightly. The moral imperatives of Pixérécourt have become more of a pretext than a guiding force. The last act, often perfunctorily brief (two scenes, representing a bare two pages of text in *Lazare le pâtre*), is little more than a situation, a confrontation between protagonists, giving great satisfaction to the audience (and producing an effective final tableau). By this stage the worst of the dramatic tension is generally past. The forces of good have rallied at the end of the penultimate act, little peril is left and most of the recognition scenes have occurred. All attention can now be given to the unmasking and punishment of the villain. In the final confrontation of *Lazare*, the wicked Judael admits his guilt to Lazare, but tells him he has no proof, whereupon a curtain at the back of the stage is opened to reveal the duke and his court (including the executioner) who have heard everything.

Bouchardy retains the clear-cut figures of melodrama, uncomplicated by the psychological shading or internal conflicts of so many later nineteenth-century plays. The characters are cast according to *emplois* and the audience is never in any doubt about their moral value. The *traître* has not a single redeeming feature; he is in a position of power or wealth, but this position is generally the result of crime; he is often a nobleman who has betrayed his lord during a period of civil strife (*Le Sonneur de Saint-Paul*, *La Soeur du muletier*), a close relative who usurps or wishes to usurp the throne (*Lazare le pâtre*, *Pâris le bohémien*), or a mere adventurer who already has a criminal past (*Christophe le Suédois*, *Les Orphelines d'Anvers*). Only one of the *drames*, *Les Enfants trouvés*, is without a villain. With a very small cast (if we exclude a chorus of foundlings) it revolves around the idea of a father, the Maréchal d'Ancre, becoming the rival of a son he had unjustly abandoned, on suspicion of illegitimacy, twenty years earlier. There is little peril, no deaths are involved, and the ending is exceptionally happy and sentimental.

The *traître* has assistants who are generally utilities. Some of them are developed into complete roles, in which case they are often comic parts, more in need of money than actually committed to evil. They lack the driving force of the villain, usually take to their heels at the end of the play, or else change sides, and sometimes (as Arvide in

Christophe le Suédois) upset evil plans completely through incompetence or a particularly grotesque stroke of irony.

Amongst the sympathetic characters are the *jeune premier* and *première amoureuse* (sometimes two of each) who have either lost their parents or are ignorant of their identity, and are under threat of the greatest peril. We either learn of their birth in the exposition or see them as infants in a prologue, and from this point onwards a two-generation structure is established that is central to Bouchardy's dramaturgy. The young men are well intentioned but easily duped and do not carry the main burden of the intrigue. A few of the younger female roles offer possibilities to an actress. Marie in *Les Orphelines d'Anvers* and Ketty in *Le Secret des cavaliers* have important scenes where they feign blindness and madness respectively to deceive the *traître*. However, Marie of *Le Sonneur de Saint-Paul*, after an affecting scene with her supposed father in the first act, is kidnapped and, although we know that she is in danger, we do not see her again until the last lines of the play. If we consider the large number of plays of the period in which chastity is a central issue, it is interesting to note that Bouchardy's young women are always victims of the lust for money or power, and not of sexual lust. Basically, however, all these plays are reducible to a two-man struggle and all the other characters are little more than utilities or pawns.

The key part is not a *jeune premier*, but a *premier rôle*, a mature man aged between thirty-five and fifty (who may have to appear fifteen or twenty years younger in a prologue). Gifted with extraordinary tenacity and ready for all disguises, he will, if necessary, wait years for justice, and is even prepared to renounce the joys of parenthood in order to preserve a child over whom he will watch and whom he will protect as a sort of extension of Providence.

These heroes (frequently eponymous) have a remarkable singleness of purpose, but never less than two identities. If Jean the coachman conceals Jean the mountaineer (*Jean le cocher*), Bertram the sailor (*Bertram le matelot*) supposes himself to be Georges, son of the executioner of Mary Queen of Scots, but is in fact the rightful Lord Hamilton, and the bellringer of Saint Paul's (*Le Sonneur de Saint-Paul*) is, of course, John the Scottish hunter, formerly John the London innkeeper. In the latter case the disguise is not merely one of profession or habitat; it is also heightened by a different series of points of reference: he is John the blindman (shot in the prologue by William Smith, alias Bedfort, the *traître*, he remains blind for sixteen

years). Bouchardy exploits the use of gesture that accompanies and
portrays blindness, thus emphasising the helplessness of John, just
as Pixérécourt had used the muteness of Humbert in *Coelina*. At
the same time, he employs blindness strictly as a plot device, allowing
John to recover his sight and rediscover the mother of his child in
Act III and identify the villain in Act IV. Lazare the shepherd
(*Lazare le pâtre*), alias Rafael Salviati, passes fifteen years as an
obscure dumb prisoner, and then, at the end of Act II, electrifies
the audience by opening his mouth and articulating a signal that will
save his son's life.

Looked at from a twentieth-century point of view, Bouchardy
would seem to have been fascinated with the question of identity.
If none of his major characters can be called detailed psychological
studies, all of them present a fragmented view of personality, where
personality itself is defined by appearance, action and situation, not
essence. The two most self-consciously theatrical pieces are *Pâris
le bohémien* and a late *comédie-drame*, *Philodor*. The first was written
to provide a flamboyant role for Frédérick Lemaître at the Porte
Saint Martin and allows the main character, a former gypsy, loyal
servant and intimate friend of the late duke Visconti (not in fact
dead), to appear as a swaggering strolling player, complete with
mandoline, as an irascible elderly general, whose identity he had
borrowed on a previous occasion, and as a Jewish money lender.
During most of the play he is presumed dead and is thus able to
act in the interests of his own son, generally assumed to be the son of
the duke. *Philodor* goes a step further by having as its central figure
an actor who is described as possessing 'le rare talent de savoir prendre
toujours le masque du personnage qu'il veut représenter'.[19] An act
set in his dressing-room allows the audience to see him in a variety of
costumes for a melodrama taking place offstage.

Every possible effect that can be derived from disguise or unknown
identity is exploited. Most of the plots depend on the slow unveiling
of the identity of various characters to other characters individually.
The timing of the different revelations is all-important. The *traître*'s
power depends on his knowing slightly more than everybody else or
being the sole possessor of a vital piece of information that allows
all the loose ends to be tied up. The reversal of his fortunes in the
penultimate act is directly related to the rapidly diminishing number
of possible revelations or recognitions.

Contemporary critics commented on the lack of motivation of
events and of a sense of causality. A character had only to be mentioned

and this was generally a signal that he or she would appear almost
immediately. The audience promptly picked up this signal, accepted
it and even applauded this type of entrance because of its wish to see
that character on the stage at that moment.

Quant à nous, de telles pièces nous font l'effet de ces rêves fourmillants, où
vont et viennent mille figures bizarres, et où les événements les plus incroyables
se succèdent, sans égard aux temps et aux lieux, et sont admis par le dormeur
comme les choses du monde les plus ordinaires et les plus simples.[20]

At a time when theatre was becoming increasingly interested in
social issues (poverty, prisons, the situation of women, illegitimacy)
and obviously contemporary themes, Bouchardy kept open the
doors of an unreal and semi-fantasy world in which it is the rule,
not the exception, for those of noble status to marry virtuous persons
of humble extraction (we might contrast this with the more bourgeois
theatre of Scribe, where the misalliance is presented as undesirable for
the family and the social order).[21] Many of the reasons that brought
a popular public to see Bouchardy's plays were similar to those that,
today, bring workers to the Châtelet rather than to the more self-
conscious *théâtres populaires*.[22] Despite a similarity in underlying
structures and situations, he was not interested in the exaggerated
realism in presenting the poorer classes or the social purpose which
is so much in evidence, and largely intended for the middle-class
reader, in Eugène Sue's *Mystères de Paris* or dramas based on this
type of material. Frankly escapist in tone, Bouchardy's *drames* are
all costume pieces set in specific historical periods and employing
in secondary roles characters who actually existed. In only two of
them do we so much as enter the nineteenth century. The actions
are set in a collection of palaces (places of power, corruption and
often danger), prisons (symbols of oppression, helplessness and peril)
and poor dwellings (generally the abode of virtue and often set in
the countryside). This is the standard visual vocabulary of the older
melodrama, with the scenery providing a silent comment on the
situations in a language immediately familiar to the public. There is
no doubt about the importance of setting for Bouchardy. It is not a
mere picturesque background (though this may be a part of its value),
but is fully used in both a suggestive and practicable manner. For
example, every door and window carries a charge and is used for the
significant entrance, overhearing, watching for a sign, concealing a
vital offstage action or making possible (often by opening a large
double door or curtain) an expressive tableau, especially as part of
the dénouement.

Despite the potential resources of the Gaîté and the Ambigu for elaborate productions (the latter had staged Maillan and Merville's adaptation of *Le juif errant* in 1834 with a cast of over thirty, numerous extras in costumes of various periods, a ballet and spectacular scenic effects), Bouchardy made very little use of the spectacular for its own sake. He did not venture into the *féerie* or the dream or vision play. One set per act, with a very occasional change during the act, was sufficient.[23] Despite the immense use of coincidence and the very significant role of Providence, his plays are down to earth and distinctly lacking in the metaphysical. Even a subject such as hypnotism (*La Croix de Saint Jacques*) loses all its mystery at his hands and becomes yet another device, like a disguise, which permits the villain to obtain information he could not otherwise possess.

III

Bouchardy's plays symbolise an era in the theatre. Lazare, John the bellringer and Gaspardo, helped by their creators, Mélingue, Francisque *aîné* and Guyon, became types with whom audiences identified and who, in the 1860s and 1870s, are referred to with nostalgia as representing an epoch. For about fifteen years Bouchardy satisfied the popular imagination and his works were also translated and played fairly widely outside France, especially in Spain. Continuing popularity for reading and, presumably, performance in the provinces is indicated by the fact that *Lazare le pâtre* was reprinted seven times between 1850 and 1859, *Le Sonneur de Saint-Paul* seven times between 1851 and 1869, and *Jean le cocher* as late as 1872.

At a period when censorship prevented much direct political statement in the theatre, and when most authors operated a sort of auto-censorship, Bouchardy expresses a fundamentally populist ethos. If there was nothing in his plays to which the liberally minded bourgeoisie in the audience could take exception, a large part of the appeal was to those who might feel oppressed by poverty or the system. His villains are authoritarian, class-conscious abusers of power, his ideal monarchs always just, virtuous and democratic in the extreme. Again and again he gives an idealised working out to the pent up political frustrations of the popular classes under the July monarchy. *Gaspardo le pêcheur* was described by a reviewer as 'l'histoire de trois hommes du peuple outragés au même degré par le duc de Milan, Marie Visconti, et qui, s'étant unis pour une même vengeance, arrivent, au bout de vingt-cinq ans, à renverser leur ennemi commun'.[24] The Ambigu marked the proclamation of the Republic in 1848 by staging a revival of this play the next day.

Between 1837 and the early 1850s Bouchardy's popularity was as great as that of his contemporary, Eugène Scribe, but by the late fifties his plays no longer drew the crowds. *Le Secret des cavaliers* (1856), 'un Joseph Bouchardy au grand complet', to which Jules Janin devoted eight columns[25] and commented on the enthusiastic response of the first-night audience, ran for a bare month, and *Micael l'esclave*, whose dénouement 'a fait couler bien des larmes et qui en fera couler longtemps encore dans la salle de la Gaîté',[26] was scarcely more successful in 1859. The author's reputation was still sufficient for his last play, *L'Armurier de Santiago*, to be staged at the recently built Théâtre Impérial du Châtelet in 1868, but this time the critics treated the play as outmoded and it closed after a fortnight.

It is difficult to offer any single reason for Bouchardy's decline in popularity. One is undoubtedly the ephemeral nature of the theatre and its dependence on tastes — Scribe, after a long and successful career, went out of fashion very quickly in the 1860s. Bouchardy chose to work on a very limited area, and having chosen this area he worked it in as much detail as he had the metal plates during his earlier career as an engraver, extracting countless variations from a relatively small number of situations. As the years went by it became apparent that ingenuity and a splendid sense of the theatrical were in themselves insufficient compensation for the comparative lack of content. Without going over into the more psychological drama of Sardou, he had stretched the historical melodrama as far as it would reach.

Not in the least concerned with theatre as literature, Bouchardy escaped the great danger of the bourgeois theatre of the nineteenth century, the substitution of literary values for dramatic ones. Language for him was a support to action and situation, not a substitute for it. It is as a craftsman and not as an *homme de lettres* that he should be evaluated. As a craftsman he possessed what is today recognised as one of the quintessential qualities of popular theatre: the ability to tell a story in terms to which the popular imagination could relate.

NOTES

1   I am happy to conclude the history of the Ambigu by drawing attention to the greatest financial success ever achieved by this theatre. Monsieur

Joseph Bouchardy is a gift from providence for theatre directors — he makes their fortunes for them. At the moment *Lazare the Shepherd* is an unheard-of box office success, whose takings are every bit as astounding as those of *The Bellringer of Saint Paul's*, which netted more than 200,000 francs for the Gaîté.

E. Deligny, *Histoire de l'Ambigu-Comique depuis sa création jusqu'à ce jour* (Paris, 1841), p. 117. Bouchardy's earliest plays, *Le Fils du bravo* (1836), *Un Petit Coup de vin blanc* (1837), both *vaudevilles* in one act, and the one-act *Hermann l'ivrogne* (1836), were written in collaboration with Deligny.

2 Other than the two *vaudevilles* mentioned in note 1, *Un Vendredi*, a *vaudeville* written for the Variétés in 1849, and his one *comédie-drame*, *Philodor* (1863), all his plays are serious *drames* with a historical background. He describes his plays as *drames*, not *mélodrames*, which they were in fact. All had music to accompany them. The composers, Artus, Chautagne, Béancourt and Mangeant, were the conductors of the theatres where they were performed. Chautagne's *barcarolle* from *Gaspardo le pêcheur* was extremely popular and a selection of tunes from the play was used for the balls given at the Ambigu in 1837. In the published texts of the plays there are ample, if not regular or consistent, indications of music to accompany pantomime, cover scene changes, create atmosphere and serve as leit-motifs for different characters.

3 For a description of the Boulevard du Temple in the 1830s see Robert Baldick, *The Life and Times of Frédérick Lemaître* (London, 1959), p. 98.

4 Henry Buguet, *Foyers et coulisses: Histoire anecdotique des théâtres de Paris* (19 vols., Paris, 1873—85) 'Théâtre de la Gaîté' (1875).

5 Maurice Descotes, *Le Public de théâtre et son histoire* (Paris, 1964), p. 243.

6 'In the melodrama houses there is no need to try and make out how people are reacting. During the performance the audience leave one in no doubt about this and, when the curtain falls, the exclamations and comments show the interest taken by this mass of people in what it sees and hears.' H. Auger, *Physiologie du théâtre* (Paris, 1839), vol. 3, p. 278.

7 L. Chevalier, *La formation de la population parisienne au XIXe siècle* (Paris, 1950).

8 H. See, *Histoire économique de la France* (Paris, 1951).

9 Cited by See, *Histoire économique*. He also gives an example (vol. 1, p. 182), taken from Blanqui, of the budget of a worker's family near Lille in 1848. The husband earns two francs a day, his wife ten to fifteen centimes from making lace, and they have four children. The week's expenditure amounted to 12 fr. 75:

24kg of bread at 22 centimes per ½kg	5 fr. 40
scraps of meat three times a week	0 fr. 75
butter, treacle or fruit	1 fr. 30
potatoes and haricot beans	1 fr. 0
½pinte (nearly a pint) of milk a day	0 fr. 35
rent of cellar	1 fr. 50
coal	1 fr. 35
soap and light	1 fr. 10

The family received a distribution of 3 kg of bread and some clothes once a fortnight.

10 A. Daumard, *La Bourgeoisie parisienne de 1815 à 1848* (Paris, 1963).
11 They're closing the Ambigu Comique
    Its frightful
    To this spot
    We must say farewell.

    This establishment gives life to the neighbourhood,
    The (ordinary) people enjoy themselves there, and love to come and sit there,
    And, if the theatre encourages hard work,
    It is also people's relaxation in the evening.

12 'Oh, melodrama of the days of yore, with your wooden swords, your well-ropes
    and your chipped cups of poison, how out of place you would feel today
    faced with an audience in black tail-coats and silk dresses, white ties and
    cashmir shawls, with yellow gloves and delicious arms wearing delicious
    bracelets.' *Notice sur l'Ambigu Comique, nouvelle salle* (Paris, 1847).
13 'Monday is another Sunday for the Ambigu Comique and the Gaîté which
    had a packed house yesterday.'
14 A. Donnet and J. A. Kaufmann, *Architectonographie des théâtres*, (Paris,
    1837–40), vol. 1. Figures for numbers of seats in Donnet and Kaufmann do
    not always correspond with those given in the *Almanach des spectacles*. They
    allow the old Gaîté 1,545 seats and the Comédie-Française 2,100 (as opposed
    to the *Almanach*'s 1,522). The figure of 2,000 may be slightly inflated for
    the Ambigu, although in 1875 this theatre did have 1,900 seats.
15 In 1835, Jacques le Souffleur had described boxes in the following terms in
    his *Dictionnaire des coulisses*: 'Il y a deux sortes de loges, celles où les femmes
    se mettent pour être vues et ne pas voir, et celles où elles veulent voir et
    ne pas être vues.' The persistence of the *loge grillée* at the melodrama theatres
    is, if needed, a further indication of their lack of social status.
16 See note 1. The only major play for which Bouchardy had a collaborator was
    Léa ou la soeur du soldat (1847), written with Paul Foucher. It is interesting
    to note that this is one of the few plays in which women have major roles,
    and the only one in which the *traître* is a woman.
17 See in particular some of the extremely perceptive comments made by
    Peter Brooks in *The Melodramatic Imagination* (New Haven, 1976), pp. 88–9.
18 The Bibliothèque Nationale has *analyses-programmes* for performances of
    Lazare le pâtre at the Théâtre des Célestins, Lyon, in 1841, and of *Jean le
    cocher* in Toulouse in 1861. In both cases the synopsis of the plot requires
    about four pages.
19 Act I, Scene 4.
20 'Such plays remind me of those complicated dreams swarming with thousands
    of strange figures and with the strangest events following one another without
    any regard to time or place, and which the sleeper himself accepts as the
    most ordinary and simple things in the world.' Théophile Gautier in his
    review of *Lazare le pâtre*, quoted by Maurice Tourneux in his article on
    Bouchardy in *Le Grand Dictionnaire universel du XIXe siècle* (Paris 1866).
21 See Descotes, *Le Public de théâtre*, ch. 9.
22 See Richard Demarcy, *Eléments d'une sociologie du spectacle* (Paris, 1975).
23 *La Croix de Saint Jacques* is slightly exceptional in that it demands three
    changements à vue.

24 'The story of three men of the people, all victims of the violence of Marie
Visconti, duke of Milan, who unite to satisfy their common revenge and
who, twenty-five years later, succeed in overthrowing their common enemy.'
A. Luch, review in *L'Artiste*, série 1, vol. 12 (1837), p. 237.

25 'A full-scale Joseph Bouchardy.' *Journal des débats*, 29 December 1856.

26 '. . . has caused many tears to flow and will keep them flowing for a long
time yet in the auditorium of the Gaîté.' Albéric Second in *L'Entr'acte*,
20 April 1859.

Theatres and dates of first performances of Bouchardy's plays

Play	Theatre	Date
Le Fils du bravo	Ambigu	1836
Hermann l'ivrogne	Ambigu	11 June 1836
Un Petit Coup de vin blanc	Ambigu	1837
Gaspardo le pêcheur	Ambigu	14 January 1837
Longue Epée le Normand	Ambigu	1 December 1837
Le Sonneur de Saint-Paul	Gaîté	2 October 1838
Christophe le Suédois	Ambigu	29 October 1839
Lazare le pâtre	Ambigu	7 November 1840
Pâris le bohémien	Porte Saint Martin	18 April 1842
Les Enfants trouvés	Ambigu	2 April 1843
Les Orphelines d'Anvers	Ambigu	3 October 1844
La Soeur du muletier	Gaîté	11 October 1845
Bertram le matelot	Gaîté	3 March 1847
Léa ou la soeur du soldat	Gaîté	6 August 1847
Un Vendredi	Variétés	7 April 1849
La Croix de Saint Jacques	Gaîté	15 December 1849
Jean le cocher	Ambigu	11 November 1852
Le Secret des cavaliers	Ambigu	24 December 1856
Micael l'esclave	Gaîté	18 April 1859
Philodor	Gaîté	3 January 1863
L'Armurier de Santiago	Châtelet	30 September 1868

The music of melodrama

David Mayer

The purpose of this paper is to demonstrate and reinforce observations
I have made on earlier occasions:[1] that nineteenth-century popular
entertainment continues and elaborates the eighteenth-century practice of combining in various forms drama and music, and further, that
when, on the continent and thereafter in England, Ibsen, Henry
Arthur Jones, Pinero, Wilde, Granville-Barker, to name but a few
pioneering playwrights, introduced the so-called New Drama, one of
the sharpest breaks they made with established theatrical custom was
to end the practice of accompanying dramatic action with music.
Serious drama, call it melodrama or tragedy,[2] was suddenly music-
free. Hedda Gabler's short bursts of piano-playing and subsequent
suicide, Paula Tanqueray's death, the Reverend Michael Feversham's
admissions of sin and hypocrisy happen against offstage silence, not
above and in addition to the woodwinds, strings, and brasses of a
thirty-piece pit-orchestra. We in the twentieth century have inherited
a comparatively new practice, not a long-established tradition, and,
mistakenly, we have taken the older tradition to be some peculiar
manifestation of the Victorian stage. I am increasingly convinced
that our failure to take into account the extent to which drama was
staged, and staged by choice, with full orchestral accompaniment
derives from a misreading of testimony given before committees of
Parliament and statements in the press by partisans of minor theatres
who, before the Licensing Act of 1843, were attempting to curtail
the monopoly of the patent houses and who fastened on the obligation under the 'burletta' licence to provide music as a point to
press their attack. Contrary to these partisan statements, the minors
as well as the patent theatres employed and enjoyed accompaniment
from full pit-orchestras rather than infrequent and unwished for
chords struck from untuned pianos.

Nowhere is the use of musical accompaniment more pervasive and
continuous, from ten years before the start of the nineteenth century

until well after the First World War, than in the melodrama. As the term informs us, melody is a part of melodrama's appeal. And, as elsewhere in this volume we are encouraged to consult the plays and the theatrical techniques of Pixérécourt, we must not fail to acknowledge this Frenchman's overt appeal to the emotive powers of music. Moreover, if we are prepared to step further back in time by a mere eight or nine years to the Paris and London of 1791–2, we will find in the 'rescue' or 'escape' operas of Cherubini, Kelly, Storace, as well as the theatrically more familiar name of Kemble, the ingredients of Pixérécourt's 'melo-drames' and more than a foretaste of Nick Roddick's disaster films. There, in Paris and London alike, performed before audiences who did not make firm distinctions between drama and opera, were avowedly musical dramas that specialised in spectacular escapes from natural and man-made disasters, virtue and honest love rewarded, evil paying its overdue debts and perishing in earthquakes or conflagrations or beneath collapsing battlements.[3]

But my purpose is to argue neither the antiquity nor the paternity of melodrama, but to implant the facts that, whenever possible, whenever theatrical managements could afford the services of a composer-conductor and a theatre orchestra for him to conduct, melodrama was scored and elaborately orchestrated, and the score was carefully integrated with the text and with dramatic action during performance. Writing in 1881 Percy Fitzgerald paid tribute to this use of music in West End melodrama:

The music that illustrates the progress of a drama, though perhaps little recognised, is often of much merit and interest. Full of grace and colour, it lingers on the ear and reflects the dramatic passion of the situation. It is surprising to find some obscure leader devising a truly dramatic 'leit motive', which is thereafter associated with the play. In Paris this mode of illustration is far more in favour than with us, and the great melodramas of the Chatelet, Porte St Martin, and Ambigu, which last from seven till midnight, are regularly accompanied from beginning to end by a current of music, now agitato, now patetico, now passionato. A few years ago, even here, it was a custom that some long speech of particular interest should be regularly accompanied by suitable music, the actor measuring his phrases so as to finish when the music finished, all the stringed instruments having this mute end. In a good dramatic melodrama the entrance of a hero is attended by some particular melody, and always with good effect. In 'Charles I' an old French air of a plaintive cast heralded this unhappy monarch, and will be recalled with pleasure. Mathias in 'The Bells' was attended by another of more mysterious cast, and in the 'Lyons Mail' there was a particularly significant melody. Mr Stoepel is responsible for these.[4] The well-known ghost melody in the 'Corsican Brothers' became dear to the memory and attained the greatest reputation. But this is really owing to a law of association, as the original character of the scene would have invested any air that was at all appropriate with a similar mystery. In truth, the melody has been traced as a colourable variation of a young lady's piano-piece, not well known, as a 'reverie' by one Rosellen. Whatever credit, however, there is attached to it, it is now established, belongs to Varney ... [5]

Fitzgerald here recognises that music is an affecting and effecting device to underline and emphasise the emotional content of a play's action, to further concentration, very probably masking the improbabilities that we so often recognise in melodrama, and maintaining momentum of the play's headlong rush from sensation to sensation, from crisis to emotional crisis. He mentions the composers' tendency to accord musical treatment to certain fixed moments in a melodrama and to devise memorable themes for characters and incidents, but he makes no mention that in the melodramatic score these themes are stated, repeated, quoted on these occasions for reasons of sentiment, subliminal association with other actions or characters, or for deliberate irony or mockery, transposed in major and minor keys, varied in tempi and volume, and above all, performed in various combinations by strings, woodwinds, brasses and percussions to give to the play colour and variety and bold or subtle shifts in mood.

If the music of melodrama as well as melodrama itself has had a bad press, it may be because melodramatic music, just as melodramatic incidents, characters, and dialogue, could be readily assembled from ready-made parts, even as mosaics are fashioned from ready-cut chips of coloured tile. Jimmy Glover, who was Master of Music at Drury Lane under Augustus Harris and Arthur Collins, described an occasion when he composed music on the mosaic-making principle for Andrew Melville (who was known as 'Realise the Poster Melville' from his practice of buying up stocks of illustrated posters, then insisting that his designers and performers imitate the illustration):

One Christmas Eve morning, 1888, he wired me to come to Birmingham and write the music for his first pantomime 'St George and the Dragon', to be produced on Boxing Morning ... I arrived at Birmingham at three, and took down a list of forty numbers to be written or scored, nearly a month's work, and at six o'clock offered to go home and try to get some idea of how it was to be done. 'Nonsense,' said Melville, 'we produce a new drama tonight called 'Bitter Cold', or 'Two Christmas Eves', and I want about sixty 'melos' numbers for that. Take them down.' At this time musical directors travelled with a book of 'agits', i.e. *agitatos*, 'slows', — that is, slow music for serious situations — 'pathetics', 'struggles', 'hornpipes', *'andantes'* — to which all adapted numbers called 'melos' any dramatic situation was possible. Armed with my chart I got through the middle of the evening when I saw a man writhing in agony on the stage. 'My God! — I'm dying — curse her! She has poisoned me — but if there is justice in heaven may the rest of her life be a hell on earth-gug-gug-gug', writhed the actor and down he fell prostrate. Just then the tube whistle blew hard. 'Who's there?' said I. 'Melville,' was the reply. 'Well, what of it?' I answered. 'Play up, old man.' 'I've no cue.' 'Cue be d—d! Don't you see a man dying on stage? Give us four bars of "agit".'[6]

Understandably, such music invited a derisive response. Percy Fitzgerald, who commended the music of West End melodrama, was distinctly ironic on the subject of melodramatic music at the Transpontine playhouses:

Still flourishes that mysterious music which always strikes in when melodramatic emotion is waxing strong. What more natural, when the lion-hearted sailor (who is so droll all through, so ready at the cry of female distress), when he engages in that truly terrific combat, at unprecedented odds — seven to one — what more natural than that his feelings should be translated by hurried and agitated music, by fiddle and gallopade of bows? Again, what so natural as that when smugglers, or robbers, or captives trying to make their escape should, when moving lightly on tiptoe past the unnatural tyrant's chamber, be kept in time by certain disjointed and jerking music, with a grasshopper or robin-red-breast rhythm? Again, what more desirable that when the grayhaired Count in the braided frock, whose early life will not bear much looking into, turns to the villagers, and, in tones that seem to come from the region of his boots, says that 'Adela is indeed his chee-ild!' — what so becoming as what is called 'A chord!' of startling character, making listeners jump from their seats? Still more in keeping is that slow, agonising strain which steals in when all the guests are crowding into the drawing-room, with horror and consternation in their countenances, and gather slowly about the lady in white, whose father, husband, lover, or brother has just disappeared, or been shot in a duel, or absconded. Sad uplifting of hands — characteristic grouping, and effective tableau, as drop-scene comes down slowly to the agonising music, closing in all decently![7]

Perhaps one reason why authors and critics may adopt such a patronising tone to the music of melodrama is that the composers of its scores are generally but one notch above the anonymous, so obscure and insignificant that biographical data is hard to come by. Few such composers appear in musical directories and then only briefly. We know that most were dignified with the title of 'chef d'orchestre' or 'master of music' at one theatre or another, but it is significant that the British Library has been unable to decide questions relating to copyright of the works of several important chefs d'orchestre because so few details about their lives, including approximate date of death, are known. This is not to say that their names were omitted from playbills and programmes or that their services went unrecognised. George R. Sims, who wrote or co-authored some twenty-five melodramas

52

between 1881 and 1914, devoted two chapters of his autobiography[8] to enumerating and praising his musical collaborators.

In Sims's realm of late-nineteenth-century melodrama, two names stand out, Michael Connolly and Henry Sprake. Connolly worked but twice with Sims, composing the score for *The Lights o' London* (1881) and *The Romany Rye* (1883). He was also associated with Wilson Barrett and Henry Arthur Jones, providing among other scores the music for *The Silver King* (1882). Henry Sprake, who composed the incidental music for fourteen of Sims's melodramas, identifies himself on the title page of each manuscript score as 'Conductor, Royal Adelphi Theatre, the Strand.' His job as conductor involved the multifold tasks of auditioning and engaging musicians, conducting musical rehearsals, composing and orchestrating incidental music for any Adelphi piece lacking music, engaging and supervising the music copyists who produced duplicate band-parts, and conducting one or two performances nightly. Sprake, despite Sims's claim that he was a former army bandsman, may also have been an accomplished violinist, for in each surviving set of scores the conductor's part is also identified as the band-part for the first violin. Then, as now, it was quite an ordinary occurrence to conduct a chamber orchestra or pit-band from the orchestra leader's chair.

Melodrama's dependence upon musical accompaniment and the degree of collaboration between playwright Sims and composer Sprake are both illustrated through the prompt-script and score to Sims's and Henry Pettitt's Adelphi success *London Day By Day* (1889). One prompt-script and one score do not convincingly demonstrate a century-long union of melodramatic dialogue, action, and music, but it is not stretching fact to insist that this set is in many respects typical of numerous surviving scripts and scores. My particular choice of Sims–Pettitt script and Sprake score lies in Sims's notation of the music cues in his prompt-script and Sprake's written instructions in the score, joint practices which render the aural instantly visible.

The score to *London Day By Day*, depending upon whether or not one counts repeats, is comprised of some thirty-five to forty-five musical pieces. Some are of no more than a few brief moments' duration. Others, the cues and segue pieces, intended to connect scene-ends, scene changes, and beginnings of new scenes with emotionally evocative melodies, are several minutes in length. Each of these pieces is numbered in sequence, although some numbers in the sequence have no music by them, merely the injunction to repeat a numbered theme introduced earlier in the score. Each number in the score (see extract) corresponds to a circled number in the margin of the prompt-script (see extract), and we may understand that each of these numbers, in the original script circled in violet ink, refers to some line of dialogue that is to cue the appropriate music from the pit. From this circled number, a wavy violet line descends along the script's margin, graphically indicating the duration of each music cue and the point at which the music is to cease. In the accompanying example, containing three numbered cues and a segue piece, the wavy lines are almost continual, and this scene is in no way atypical of other scenes in this play or of other melodramas.

In nearly all such scripts and scores there is a variable that complicates the conductor's work. These are the bracketed passages in the text, cuts which Sims and Pettitt insisted be made when the play is performed twice nightly. On such two-house nights the conductor must somehow abridge his music, but as no corresponding cuts are indicated in the score, we must assume that the cuts were made according to the custom of pit-orchestras by simply fading out the music, first dropping in volume before stopping altogether, the audience being too absorbed in the drama to notice.

Sprake's directions in the score, expressed in musicians' polyglot, indicate dynamics and specific instructions to enhance performers' onstage efforts: 'allegretto', 'andante', 'andantino', 'tempo di marcia', 'temp di valse', 'sordine' (sic), 'mutes', 'mutes off', 'till [a character's name] on'. And the practice that Fitzgerald in 1881 had described as a bygone custom, the synchronising of speech to accompanying muted music, was still in use eight years later according to the injunction to cue twenty-eight: 'Tremolo—Marks [an alcoholic solicitor suborned and blackmailed into chicanery by the play's two villains] speaks through this — moderato agitato.'

The illustrated passages of text and music are drawn from the second scene of the fourth act, set in the chamber of Maude Willoughby, the wife wronged and deserted by the villain DeBelleville. DeBelleville would now court the heroine Violet Chester, hoping to marry her before she can discover that she is heiress to a fortune. To Maude's rooms come first Violet's lover, the play's hero Frank Granville, and, immediately thereafter, DeBelleville. Frank Granville comes to ask Maude's assistance against DeBelleville, prompting Maude to reveal the secret of her early unhappy marriage to this villain. Moments later DeBelleville enters, attempts to keep Maude silent, and, when it is apparent that neither bribes nor threats will succeed, murders her before rushing from the chamber into the street. Cue 31, played

at the moment Maude reveals to Frank her secret, repeats the previous
cue, a tender and sentimental *andante* played at the rise of curtain
to establish Maude's loneliness. A further piece of music, cue 32,
restates Maude's isolation, beginning after Frank's departure and
continuing as she examines her marriage certificate and soliloquises,
'I wonder how many lonely hearts there are like mine to-night in
this great City!' With DeBelleville's entrance the music ceases, to be
resumed, *allegro agitato* in cue 33, as husband and wife quarrel.
This music is hurried, rising and falling, until, toward its end, co-
inciding with Maude's final death struggles, the same notes or groups
of notes are repeated with heavy emphasis. Cue 33 segues into an
andante, a musical comment on Maude's lonely death, and this
piece itself segues into the hurried music which opens the next scene,
the street into which DeBelleville runs.

As we note the almost continual presence of music in this particular episode of revelation, domestic quarrelling, attempted black-
mail, murder and flight, it will be well to recall that Sims's dramas
were repeatedly commended and as often attacked by London
critics for their almost excessive stage realism. Sims could be described
by Augustin Filon as the author of 'a kind of popular humour together with a touch of Zolaism',[9] and by H. G. Hibbert as 'Zola
diluted at Aldgate Pump'.[10] Although musical accompaniment is
conspicuously unrealistic and not in the least Zolaesque, both the
above critics and all others, whether praising or attacking Sims's
work, exempt music from their observations. My inference is that
the presence of music was an almost unassailably strong convention,
to be taken for granted, even when, as in *London Day By Day*, it
was scored for first and second violins, flute, clarinet, cornet, trom-
bone, bassoon, oboe, horns, and drums. On tour such luxurious
instrumentation might dwindle; when funds ran low it was certain
to. But music was, nonetheless, an essential ingredient of the play.
In an autobiographical novel Jerome K. Jerome recalls of his tour
with a fit-up company an orchestra reduced to a cornet and violin
and how in small towns 'a piano, hired in the town, represented the
orchestra. We couldn't get a piano on one occasion, so the proprietor
of the hall lent us his harmonium.'[11]

The size of the Victorian theatre orchestra may have been inconsistent — strings, woodwinds, brasses, and percussion in houses
prosperous enough to afford as full an orchestra as managers considered necessary, but other houses making do with a single cornet
and fiddle or a wheezy harmonium when the luck ran out. But the

Prompt-script from Act IV Scene 2 of *London Day by Day*, showing notation of music cues.

19

FRANK. And why not?

MAUD. Because I am his wife. (Falls in chair L. of table.) ㉛

FRANK. His wife!

MAUD. His wife - his wife! For the sake of my own future - I would have kept silent. For your sake, and that of the sweet and gentle girl you love - I have spoken - Go to her and tell her that she need fear her enemy no more. If he asks her to be his wife again - she can answer that he has a wife living - who if he threatens to send her to an English prison, will send him to a French one for life.

FRANK. At last! At last! Now, M. de Belleville, Violet is no longer at your mercy, but you are at mine! (Going down R.)

MAUD. (Rise) Mr Granville, before you go promise me that you will not use this knowledge unless you are compelled. Use it only to save her, not to injure him. Remember, he is my husband. He has wrought me only shame, and sorrow, but I loved him once. That love is dead, but the memory of it comes back and pleads to me to spare him even now.

FRANK. Madam, you have lifted too great a load from my heart for me willingly to do that which would cause you one moment's pain. (Takes MAUD'S hand.) I can never forget the service you have rendered me to-night, I shall always remember with gratitude, and pray that happier years may be in store for you yet. Good-bye. God bless you.

(EXIT R.D.)

MAUD. Happier years! There are no happier years for me. (Goes to desk L.) Here are the letters and papers he left behind him in his flight - they would send him to his doom. (Takes papers out) A copy of our marriage certificate. (Closes desk - sighs, cross to window looks out R.C.) I gave this man my love, and he has spoilt my life. Poor little dream, how soon you passed away. London!..I wonder how many lonely hearts there are like mine to-night in this great City! ㉜

(Bell. Crosses to door R.)

(surprised)
Who's that? Perhaps Mr Granville returned.

56

Music score from Act IV Scene 2 of *London Day by Day*, showing written
instructions for cues.

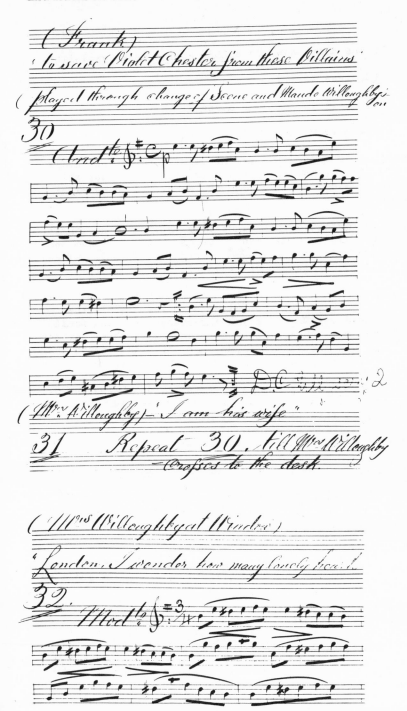

20

(Opens door, sees De BELLE. starts back, exclaims:)

MAUD.   You! (Crosses to L.)

BELLE.   Yes, madam, it is I - your husband!

MAUD.   You have no right here!

BELLE.   (Folding his arms.) [I have no right here?] C'est drole
ça! You forget, madam, that you are my wife - that all
you have is mine, and that you are mine. It is my right
to be here.

MAUD.   You have forfeited that right long ago. [I am no longer
the foolish girl you married. You gave me my freedom and
I have earned my independence] I was your dupe, [I refused
to be your accomplice, and] I will not be your victim.
Go!

BELLE.   [You wish to be free? you wish to forget the tie that
binds us, and yet] to-night you threatened me. You would
not listen to me then, there were too many to hear our conversation, but now we are alone, and you shall listen to
me. (Seizing her hand.)

MAUD.   Nothing that you can say will alter my determination.]
If to-morrow I hear that you have abandoned your merciless
plot, against this girl, I will hold my peace.

BELLE.   And if I do not obey your commands?

MAUD.   Then I will claim you as my husband. (Lets go her hand.)

BELLE.   Maud, I tell you I am desperate. This girl's fortune
alone can save me, and you alone know the secret that can
prevent it. Come, [if you will not give me your silence] I
will buy it, make your own terms.   (33.)

MAUD.   Terms! I would rather die than purchase my life by such
infamy. Man! Man! You have wrecked my life, you shall not
blast and ruins hers. (Cross R.)

BELLE.   You refuse! Eh bien, ma chère, I know what to do now.
[You will not let me wed another woman, you claim to be my
wife.] You shall be my wife. [From this moment I am the
husband of Maud Willoughby, all the world shall know it.]
This is my home. I am your husband, now, madam, I'll make

58

till De Bellville's on

(De Bellville)
'I will buy it, make your own terms'

33

your life a hell so terrible that you will pray for death
[to break the chains that I will bind about you until they
eat into your flesh and crush your heart.]

MAUD.   And if you ~~attempt to~~ do that it will cost you your life.
(Crosses L.)

BELLE. My life!

MAUD.   Yes. For I will cry aloud the secret which I have kept
buried in my heart.

BELLE. And what is that?

MAUD.   I will tell the police [that which will put them upon the
track of an assassin, the man they have searched for in
vain, the man] who robbed and murdered a wealthy Russian, at
an hotel in Nice!

BELLE. Mon Dieu - She knows!

MAUD.   Now you know why I shrink from you, why I forbid you
ever to call me wife again. [I am your wife, and being so,
I have remained silent, but] if you are merciless, so will I
be too. Move one step further in your infamous plot and
I will [rid] myself of you for ever, and [send] you to [end]
your days [in] the galleys or [on] the guillotine.

BELLE. Never, I would rather kill myself...I would rather kill
you. (Locks door, puts key in pocket.)

MAUD.   (Moving away) Ah, you will not do that!

BELLE. (Following her) It is my life against yours now. You
would betray me, you would send me to the guillotine, you
would speak the words that would ruin me to-morrow. ~~Perhaps~~
you have spoken your last words to-night.

MAUD.   You will not murder me! Ah, help! Help!

(MUSIC Business, struggle, he stabs her, she
falls with scream on sofa L.C. De BELLE. turns
down lamp, unlocks door and EXITS R.)
(Moonlight on the sofa, where MAUD is lying.)

Dwell on Picture

Gong....Change.

60

till Maude Willoughby's Killed and on Couch —
then Segue.

Segue.

And^{te}

till Scene changed and lights up
then Segue C.S.

need for music never varied, for it was music that helped to focus attention on the stage. Music vividly and explicitly described aurally the visible action of scenes, identified characters for audiences through recognisable themes, and coaxed an extra measure of emotional acquiescence from rapt spectators. Whilst there was melodrama, invariably there was music.[12]

But let Jerome K. Jerome have the final word:

At last, everybody having been supplied with his or her part, and the leader of the band having arrived, the rehearsal really commenced. The play was one of the regular old-fashioned melodramas, and the orchestra had all its work to do to keep up with it. Nearly all the performers had a bar of music to bring them on each time, and another to take them off; a bar when they sat down, and a bar when they got up again; while it took a small overture to get them across the stage. As for the leading lady, every mortal thing she did or said, from remarking that the snow was cold, in the first act, to fancying she saw her mother and then dying, in the last, was preceded by a regular concert. I firmly believe that if, while on stage, she had shown signs of wanting to sneeze, the band would at once have struck up quick music. I began to think, after a while, that it must be an opera, and to be afraid that I should have to sing my part.[13]

NOTES

1 Cf. my 'Nineteenth Century Theatre Music', *Theatre Notebook*, 30: 3 (1976), pp. 115—22.

2 The term *melodrama* was applied with diminishing frequency in the second half of the nineteenth century to plays which bear the usual characteristics of melodrama, especially to pieces offered by the more genteel theatres. At these houses, *drama* was the preferred term, although few patrons could have been misled by the substitution.

3 For thorough discussions of 'escape opera', cf. Roger Fiske, *English Theatre Music in the Eighteenth Century* (Oxford, 1973), pp. 516, 518, 526—7, and Basil Deane, *Cherubini*, Oxford Studies of Composers 3 (London, 1965), pp. 1—17.

4 Robert Stoepel composed the score for Henry Irving's 1877 revival of Charles Reade's *The Courier of Lyons*. However, the score to *The Bells* (1871) was the composition of E. Singla.

5 Percy Fitzgerald, *The World Behind the Scenes* (London, 1881), p. 285.

6 James Glover, *Jimmy Glover, His Book* (London, 1911), pp. 240—1.

7 Fitzgerald, *The World Behind the Scenes*, pp. 312—3.

8 George R. Sims, *My Life: Sixty Years' Reflection of Bohemian London* (London, 1917), pp. 212—27.

9 Augustin Filon, *The English Stage* (London, 1897), p. 301.

10 H. G. Hibbert, *A Playgoer's Memories* (London, 1920), p. 133.

11 Jerome K. Jerome, *On the Stage and Off: The Brief Career of a Would-be Actor* (London, 1891), p. 202.

12 The duration of the practice of supporting melodramas with full incidental

music extended into the twentieth century. As late as 1912 Samuel French's *Alphabetical Catalogue of the Principal Plays* contained a section advertising (pp. 42–3) 'Music on Hire'. The scores include those for melodramas. Among the melodramas listed are the following, the bracketed number indicating the number of band-parts available, not the number of instruments actually required: *Black Ey'd Susan* (8), *The Colleen Bawn* (8), *The Corsican Brothers* (6), *The Dumb Man of Manchester* (8), *Guy Mannering* (8), *Lost in London* (8), *Luke the Labourer* (8), *Mazeppa* (10), *The Miller and His Men* (5), *The Octoroon* (10), *The Shaughraun* (8), *The Streets of London* (9), *The Ticket of Leave Man* (8). The same advertisement offers the promise of 'Incidental Music Suitable for Lively Rise of Curtain, Entrance of Characters, etc., Hurry, Combat, Apparitions, Pathetic Situations, Martial, etc., etc., Price Piano 4s., Full Orchestration 5s.'

13 Jerome, *On the Stage and Off*, pp. 50–1.

Popular theatre in Victorian Birmingham

Douglas A. Reid

In St Paul's Square in Birmingham, during the 1840s, there was a
rule-making workshop, where one Dyke Wilkinson and his fellow
apprentices would often divert their master's ivory from its ordained
function to the clandestine fashioning of dice. The subsequent sale
of these dice was a useful source of pocket-money, 'generally spent',
said Wilkinson, 'on sixpenny seats in the gallery of the old Theatre
Royal'.[1]

It is from such fragments of evidence that a picture of working-
class theatre-going in mid-nineteenth-century provincial England may
be constructed. The subject forms a significant but unexplored aspect
of the history of theatre and of working-class culture, and it is a
major objective of this paper to establish systematically some of the
dimensions of this area. Who went to the theatre? When did they go?
Where did they sit? What plays were most popular? How were they
received? The inquiry will be structured around the Birmingham
Theatre Royal from the 1840s to the 1870s, a period chosen because
it has both a theatrical and social coherence; occasionally, however,
where evidence is available, the questions will be extended to other
theatres.

When entering new territory a reconnaissance photograph is always
useful, and so it will be desirable here to anticipate our conclusions
somewhat. The evidence demonstrates that the pit and gallery of
the theatre in early- to mid-Victorian Birmingham were largely
peopled from the working class — a term which is used here in an
umbrella, descriptive capacity, encompassing a significantly varied
social reality. The most popular types of play are seen to have been
melodrama — no surprise to the received assumptions about the
period — and Shakespeare — a very much unappreciated historical
fact. In fact, interpretation of audience responses is a problematical
activity, and, in contrast to the available notions about the limitations

65

of popular taste, this author is forced to conclude by registering
the complexity of the popular culture studied here.

I

The playhouse to which Dyke Wilkinson referred was the third to be
erected on its New Street site. The original theatre had been built
in 1774; it had a handsome facade bearing the sculpted heads of
Garrick and Shakespeare which survived the otherwise disastrous
fires of 1792 and 1820. James Guest (a radical printer) recorded the
latter conflagration and observed that the new theatre 'which can
scarcely be equalled out of London, either for accommodation or
elegance, like the phoenix, out of its own ashes, sprang up in the
short space of seven months . . . brilliantly lighted with gas and . . .
[able to] contain more than 2,000 persons'.[2] There were two tiers
of boxes capable of holding 720 people, but the pit had room only
for 480; above, there was bench-space for 1,050 gallery 'gods'.[3]
In situation, the theatre had developed none of the environmental
drawbacks associated with the Theatre Royal, Drury Lane; in fact
it was claimed that 'the neighbourhood of the Birmingham Theatre
is particularly respectable and is not the dwelling place of the vicious'.[4]

The New Street theatre was not the first to be built in Birmingham
— the town's theatrical history went back to the 1740s — but the
1774 venture represented an attempt by some of the leading citizens
to establish a much grander theatre, one more commensurate with
the growing economic and social importance of the town, and one
which would 'tend to improve the morals, the manners or taste of
the people'.[5] At this time — with a population of about 40,000 —
Birmingham was the third largest English provincial town; this
position it was to maintain, though on a vastly increased scale,
throughout the succeeding century: 178,000 in 1841, 344,000 in
1871. Its growth and prosperity was based upon a mass of metal-
working trades; 'in 97 trades not common to all large towns . . .
there [were] in Birmingham at least 2,100 firms'.[6] Manchester may
have been the mecca of the mechanic and the cotton spinner, but
the symbolic Birmingham industrial worker was the 'artisan' in one
of the myriad divisions of the brass, button, gun or jewellery trades.
Confusingly, 'artisan' was a label borrowed from the traditional
crafts which very much kept the reference to them, for Birmingham,
as a populous place, had a great many shoemakers, carpenters,
tailors, cabinet-makers, coach-makers and the like. It followed that

66

the most numerous employers were small workshop masters, and 'artisans . . . comprised about half the adult male population of early Victorian Birmingham'.[7] Consequently, wage rates tended to be high for the period; a skilled man could earn over £2 per week though the average man probably earned much less; in 1862 'the lowest wages of men able to do men's work, e.g. as porters, packers, jobbing, &c.' were said to be 14/- or 15/-.[8]

From this economic base there arose a social structure in which variety rather than concentration, independence rather than subordination, were the striking features. The dominant social image was of social mobility, not of class conflict.[9] Nevertheless, if Birmingham apparently had no aristocracy of great capitalists such as Manchester had, and no real aristocracy like London's, the relative absence of socio-economic gulfs should not mislead us into supposing that there was no extended status hierarchy based on wealth. Any consideration of the development of Edgbaston as a suburb makes this abundantly plain.[10] Less obviously, perhaps, a status hierarchy stretched downwards from an 'aristocracy of labour'.

As a matter of policy, then, and as a matter of economic prudence, the Birmingham theatre aimed to attract a cross-section of local society as its audience. For the first sixty years and more of its existence gallery places cost 1/-, pit places 2/- or 2/6, and box seats 3/6 or 4/-; at these prices fifty-five per cent of the optimum revenue of £260 was derived from the box patrons.[11] Up until 1808 the theatre season had been only four summer months, but that year a winter season was introduced, as if to justify the achievement of the Royal Patent in 1807 (although a permanent stock company was not built up until the 1830s). Whether in fact there was in Birmingham 'a sufficiency of play goers to render a long season productive' must have been a question which successive managers despairingly asked themselves, for the next three decades were one long melancholy tale of decreasing attendances and declining morale.[12] Of course neither the situation nor its approximate causes were peculiar to Birmingham: many theatres suffered from the alteration in middle-class estimation of the drama and from working-class penury brought about by the vicissitudes of the economy in these decades. Nevertheless, the imposition of a strong managerial hand by Mercer H. Simpson in 1838 helped to recover some stability and respectability for the Theatre Royal; and it had the additional merit of persuading the Birmingham press to begin that more detailed commentary on theatrical affairs which provides my chief source of evidence. Perhaps

one of the contributory causes of Simpson's twenty-four-year reign
as manager was his immediate decision to halve the price of a gallery
seat from one shilling to sixpence, to lower the pit price to one
shilling, and the upper and lower boxes to two and three shillings
respectively.[13] Prices in general were falling over the long term, but
he certainly must have felt it was none too soon a move when he
observed music hall competition beginning to flourish in the next
decade.

Henry Holder, landlord of the Rodney Inn, Coleshill Street,
established the first Victorian music hall in Birmingham in 1846.
It held 600 people and was said to attract 200—300 most nights of
the week, with a programme which included 'artistes' from the
'Liverpool and Manchester Theatres', from London's Vauxhall
Gardens and from the Grecian Saloon at the 'Eagle', City Road.[14]
Nevertheless, it was not until the 1860s that the full force of music
hall competition was felt by the Theatre Royal. Minor halls had
come and gone, but from 1863 onwards Day's Crystal Palace Concert
Hall, the London Museum Concert Hall in Digbeth and an extended
Holder's Concert Hall offered 4,700 seats between them to the
Brummies.[15] Of course, the fiercest competition to the Theatre
Royal would be that of other theatres, but for nearly twenty years
after the 1843 Theatres Act had theoretically taken away its monopoly
the Theatre Royal held the competition down.[16] It successfully
opposed applications for a magistrates' licence to turn a circus
amphitheatre into a theatre, and, by threatening to prosecute, sup-
pressed a defiant 'temporary theatre' and amateur and other dramatics
in public houses.[17] In 1854 a serious rival did gain a foothold when
Tonks' Colosseum was opened in the vast newly built Bingley (Exhibition) Hall, but its size was its financial undoing and it did not
begin a second season.[18] Not until the 1860s did the New Theatre,
Moor Street, and the Prince of Wales, Broad Street, manage to
establish a measure of theatrical pluralism in Birmingham. At the
New Theatre 'Melodrama was the order of the day — or night. Ghosts
glided, ruffians stalked and interesting young ladies — with their
back hair down — were benighted in the depths of gloomy forests
and carried off to the Bandit's Lair nightly to the rapture of ap-
preciative but unremunerative audiences.'[19] In fact the Moor Street
theatre only lasted from 1861 to 1864. Why? With box prices at
2/- (and 1/- at half-price time) was there insufficient wealthy patronage?
Or was the high unemployment rate of the early sixties a factor? Or
did Moor Street succumb to music hall competition? Whatever the

answer, the Theatre Royal also felt the draught in 1863 and complained of the two new theatres and of the 'three attractive Music halls which have withdrawn a large number of the Attendants at the Theatre Royal'.[20] Yet the other new theatre — the Prince of Wales — was by no means having an easy time of it, and was not firmly established until the later 1860s. Then it carved out a role for itself as the theatre of the touring companies whereas the stock company plus visiting 'stars' were the order of the day late into the 1870s at the Theatre Royal. The Prince of Wales, while not totally eschewing melodrama and Shakespeare, tended to prefer burlesques, light opera, and pantomime. Although it was a huge theatre — holding nearly 3,000 people in 1866 — it attempted to be 'fashionable' rather than 'popular' and introduced orchestra stalls and the 'dress circle' to Birmingham.[21] Consequently the atmosphere of the pit and gallery at the Prince of Wales was bound to differ from that still obtaining at the Royal. The pit was now separated from the stage by two rows of stalls, and the era of the touring companies resulted in much less of a reciprocal relationship between pit and gallery and actors. Nevertheless, the social constituency of pit and gallery appears to have been much the same — at least when melodrama and Shakespeare were played.

II

Who went to the theatre? Consider the following evocation of 'the heaped-up gallery . . . on a Monday night' in the 1840s: 'every corner crammed with juvenile life; heads reeking with perspiration, and bodies squeezed into the smallest possible compass. Bonnets and caps transformed into impromptu fans, and some few experienced celestials taking it coolly, with the upper portions of their bodies divested of all covering, excepting their calico of questionable hue.'[22] The impression here conveyed is of a largely youthful, very proletarian gallery audience, and this was almost exactly confirmed by a police report from 1840.

On Monday last, November 30, went to the gallery of the theatre . . . and ascertained from the check-taker that there were nearly 1,200 persons in the gallery; of this number there were probably 600 girls and boys under 16 years of age, and 200 more from 16 to 20 years. The greater proportion are boys.

Thus roughly half the gallery were juveniles and those under twenty formed two-thirds of the total gallery crowd; they were mainly 'apprentices' or other children employed in manufactories.[23] The range of occupations of the residue of adults is indicated by the candlestick polisher, bricklayer, gun-finisher, brassfounder, glass blower, copper-plate printer, watch finisher, gun-maker, stone-mason, and clothier who appeared in the police court after gallery incidents between 1841 and 1852.[24] They comprised a representative variety of the Birmingham working class, with artisans well to the fore.

It is interesting to note, however, that significant numbers of artisans used to frequent the pit. A theatre critic reflected on the raising of the pit price from 1/- to 1/6 for a special performance in 1843: 'On Monday night . . . the pit admission was augmented 50 per cent . . . The consequence was, the driving out of nearly all the ordinary pit frequenters — workmen, and their wives and sisters, and younger clerks and shopmen, to whose scanty incomes a shilling is a sort of *maximum* of expenditure.'[25] When prices were again temporarily raised in 1846 the critic observed: 'Broadcloth lined the pit, where fustian more often reigns.'[26] Court cases involving pittites were rather fewer than those involving the gallery, but they lend weight to an impression of a rather mixed social composition in the pit. An unidentified 'young women', a Mrs Jane Earp and a certain Isabella Brindley had the misfortune to have their pockets picked, but the only males who achieved police court prominence were a gun-maker, a 'confectioner' and a medical student.[27]

A central justification for treating the 1840s to the 1870s as one period is that the social composition of the theatre remains broadly similar. Certainly the gallery appeared to be as youthful and as mixed by sex in the 1870s as in the 1840s. Witness the complaint from 1873: 'It is really disgraceful to see young children admitted unattended, at ages varying from 8 to 12 years, making our theatres little better than penny gaffs.' And there is presumptive evidence that women, of various ages, continued to make the gallery a place of recreation; the frequent notices that 'Children in arms will not be admitted' show how well established that custom was.[28] Again, the presence of large numbers of working-class youths and young men may be indicated by the labourers, tool-maker, tube-maker, tailor's assistant, stamper, boatman, filer, and carpenter's son, all aged between thirteen and twenty-three, who caused trouble in the gallery in 1873 and 1874.[29]

Evidence is scantier as regards the pit in the 1870s, though the impression one has is that its social composition was still as mixed and could vary from play to play. Certainly it was looked down upon in more than a literal way by the occupants of the lower boxes. In

1876 the Theatre Royal manager explained: 'A great improvement of the Lower Boxes will be effected by lowering the Pit — much annoyance often occurring to the Lower Box audience by the contiguity of the Pit audience.'[30] But this disdain should not mask the social divisions *within* the pit, to which a local schoolmaster (presumably not a unique representative of the lower professions) testified:

In the pit there was the assiduous enforcement of the order, 'Close-up, please', and it was carried out by a policeman who, at times, and when he knew he dared to do it, did not hesitate to use his cane to urge a closer contact between those already seated and those who wanted to get a seat.[31]

Indeed, on a popular night, the pit and gallery audience had often to be of a certain robust constitution even to survive getting into the theatre. In 1853 a complainant told how he arrived early and got near the gallery door in order to secure a good place.

About ten minutes before admittance several fellows with heavy boots on got upon the shoulders of some persons at the outside of the crowd, walked across the heads of the people, until they got to the doors, where they wedged themselves down into the places of the first comers. Hats were kicked off, bonnets torn, and faces scratched by the boots of the fellows.

The slang for this among apprentices was 'going over'; 'In the same way the pit was terrorised' in the 1860s. As late as 1881 a 'local pit-goer', concluded that if a remedy could not be found then 'the pit, for popular performances, must be left to the roughs'.[32]

Having survived the entrance the people then had to negotiate the stairs:

Oh! the gallery . . . at the Royal! I remember the tortuous way of the stairs, the twists and turns thereof, the cruel pushes, the stoppage at the pay box and up again . . . Nor were the habitués of 'high Olympus' particular in those days. A pal in front, if he had secured a seat for a chum coming in later, would save it till the arrival of the latter, who had no objection to being tossed or rolled over the heads of the audience until he was ultimately landed in his 'reserved seat'.[33]

Unfortunately, shortly after the curtain rose on a Saturday night in 1873, Thomas Millbanks, aged 13, a shoemaker's son,

made a 'roll' from the top of the gallery over the heads of the audience to reach his companions who were seated in the front row . . . The attention of . . . Millbanks' companions having been attracted to the opening scene in the piece, they failed to catch him as he came rolling over, and so, with headlong force, he cleared the boundary rail in the gallery and fell smash into the pit.

At the inquest, the coroner inquired of a police constable:

'Have you ever seen such gambolling or tumbling done before?'
'Many times; but I have never seen them tumble into the pit.'
'Boys or men?'
'Both boys and grown up young men.'[34]

The predominant social cast of the gallery, then, and sometimes of
the pit was working-class; they were the locations of 'sportively-
inclined artisans' and others.[35] Knowing this, we may appreciate the
nuances of remarks on theatre attendances. When all parts of the
theatre were proportionally full it was a 'splendid house', but in
contradistinction to 'the popular portions were well filled' we note
'a large and fashionable audience', or 'a highly fashionable . . . [and]
so brilliant an audience'.[36] In 1842 dress box occupants were described
more specifically as 'our provincial gentry', as well as 'the upper of
our middle classes'. There are also scattered references to 'highly
respectable' tradespeople: a chandler and his wife and a shoemaker's
wife in the upper boxes.[37] In the 1850s and early 1860s, Joseph
Gillott, steel pen manufacturer, patron of J. M. W. Turner, and one
of the richest men in Birmingham, was a frequent visitor to the snug
smoking room of the 'Hen and Chickens'. He usually left early, 'and
went from there almost nightly, to the Theatre Royal, where he
occupied, invariably, a back seat of a certain box, and here, if the
performances were a little dull, he would often enjoy a comfortable
nap'.[38] When we come to 1873 we find a reviewer complaining of
the Prince of Wales: 'Of course there was a beggarly array of empty
boxes. The "upper ten" of Edgbaston were conspicuously absent.
There was no music to attract . . . no fashion to be part of.' Throughout the 1870s the corners of the upper circle of boxes 'were generally
considered, after 9 p.m. [half-price time] , the property of the
jeunesse dorée of the period'.[39] Thus the theatre was something of
a social microcosm. It had gentry and bourgeoisie in the boxes, close
to the pit but increasingly concerned to distance themselves. The
pit clearly presented a shifting scene: artisans, shopkeepers, school-
teachers, probably other impecunious professionals (occasionally
'roughs'). A youthful and predominantly working-class gallery audience
formed the largest and most separate section of the house.

What was the social calendar of the theatre? Significantly, it was
shaped in response to the general recreational calendar of the working
class, and between 1840 and 1870 this calendar visibly changed under
the impact of opposition to the traditional 'Saint Monday'.[40] In 1840
it was truly observed that Monday 'is generally kept as a holiday by a
great portion of the working classes'; the concomitant of the Monday

holiday was hard work and long hours at the end of the week: 'It was the regular thing . . . not to have done paying the hands till 9 on Saturday nights.'[41] It followed that on Saturday nights the playhouse was subsidiary to the pot-house, and there were only nine Saturday performances at the Theatre Royal in the two years 1840 and 1841 together. It also followed — insofar as disorderliness was an index of popular attendance — that Monday nights had a special reputation; as the *Journal* noted: 'We understand that the lessees of the Birmingham Theatre are about to adopt measures for preserving better order in the gallery, especially on Monday evenings, when the uproar is so continuous as to prevent the majority of the audience from hearing a greater part of the performance.' It was no accident that even though new plays were presented on the first weekday 'the dress circle . . . is never full on an "unfashionable" Monday'.[42] It is surprising therefore to read, in October 1853, of a 'House filled in almost every part, on that most dramatically dreary and commercially busiest night of the week' — a Saturday.[43] The mystery is explained by the success of a Saturday half-holiday campaign which was gathering momentum in Birmingham in the early 1850s. In the third quarter of the nineteenth century the holiday emphasis was gradually shifted from Monday to Saturday, and, although both nights continued as popular occasions, in 1873, on a Saturday, pit and gallery were filled 'of course', and the *Post* observed: 'It is needless to say that on a Saturday night the "gallery gods" muster in strong force at the theatres.'[44]

One night consistently escaped the presence of the 'gods' and that was Friday. In 1813, R. W. Elliston, then Theatre Royal manager, designated Friday as 'fashionable night': 'On this evening, without inconvenience perhaps to any individual, an expectation might be held out that the best company of Birmingham and its neighbourhood, would be collected at the Theatre. An elegant place of periodic assemblage might thus be established.' In 1868 the tradition was 'still powerful enough . . . to make the Friday's box attendance the largest and best dressed of the week'.[45] It was a good night for 'the best company' because it was the night when the working population were working their hardest and least able to afford entrance to the theatre. Saturday apart, popular attendance almost certainly tailed off towards the end of the week; it is interesting that court cases involving 'gods' and 'pittites', whether as accusers or accused, dwindled in this way.[46]

III

At this point it would be logical to turn directly to the plays, but it is not possible to assess their reception without a full consideration of the conditions in which they were performed. Before this can be done, however, two general points must be made about the quality of the evidence.

Contemporaries — particularly theatre critics and writers — tended to condemn all noisiness from the popular sections of the theatre out-of-hand. In part this reflects the way in which manners and mores reflect dominant ideological and social tendencies. In the eighteenth century (indeed, into the nineteenth) theatre boxes were often quite as noisy as the galleries, but the reformation of manners which worked through all sections of society in these years led to a new sensitivity about deviation from bourgeois manners, particularly in the popular sections of the theatre. Therefore, if we accept *prima facie* the blanket condemnations of influential contemporaries we may well misconstrue the historical situation under discussion.

A further distortion of perspective may occur because newspapers tend to define 'news' as whatever is unusual or untypical in the perceived pattern of events; it follows that the Birmingham newspapers may unintentionally have presented an impression of greater gallery disturbance than there actually was. One or two chance references in the other direction may help to restore the balance, and ought to be borne in mind in the discussion of rowdiness which follows. The ability of Joseph Gillott to 'enjoy a comfortable nap' during dull performances is hardly consonant with constant noisiness in the gallery; nor is the case of the pickpocket who, it was said, 'took advantage of the opportunity afforded him by the *fixed attention* of the company in the gallery *upon the performance*, to effect his purpose with greater security'.[47]

I would suggest that there were in fact three categories of noise and disturbance displayed in the theatres. There might be the normal noisy reflection of the theatre's role as a social centre. There might be 'ritual noise' marking the course or significance of the evening. Finally, there might be the hullabaloo of disorder and/or deliberate disturbance.

Firstly, then, 'normal noise'. The theatre was undoubtedly a major social centre for the working people of Birmingham. Apart from the drinking places, the Town Hall, and the short-lived People's Hall, it was one of the few secular public meeting places in Birmingham in

74

the early 1840s, and the venue for many assignations; it was said to be 'a very frequent case for an apprentice . . . to obtain leave to quit his work at half past 5 on Monday to go to the theatre, and to keep a place for a female companion, who comes when she leaves her work at 7'.[48] The large numbers of youths and girls meant that talking, laughing, showing off, joking would have been endemic to the gallery; and 'vulgar and sometimes obscene exclamations . . . [were] frequently witnessed'! Then there were the cries of babies-in-arms, the chattering of children, and, sometimes, 'the handing of a huge stone bottle about in the gallery'.[49] To gallery ale must be added ginger beer, and apples, oranges and nuts, dispensed from the baskets of men and women who made their way between the benches; no doubt this led to disturbance. One particular case has been recorded:

Lucia di Lammamoor was the opera, and in the middle of Edgardo's impassioned curse, interpreted by Reeves with rare dramatic power and effect — 'pop!' went a ginger beer bottle in the gallery — whereupon the great singer and actor in disgust at the ludicrous interruption stopped dead, and of course entirely spoiled the climax of the piece.[50]

On some calendar occasions the festiveness of the gallery audience made them unresponsive even to such an actor as Macready, who, one evening in 1850, wrote in his diary: 'Acted Iago, taking great pains; was most affectionately received. But the Easter Monday gallery was not an audience to appreciate the kind of performance.'[51]

Perhaps the second category of noisiness which may be distinguished was the ritualised clamour with which some of the 'gods' punctuated the course of a play or marked the significance of an evening.

Observe the conduct of many of them on the commencement of any stage of the performance — the change of a scene, or the commencement of an act. The moment the bell rings, a deafening shout of 'order' is set up, when perhaps almost the only disorder is the shout in question. On crowded nights, however, the ring of the bell is the signal for a chorus of whistles, whose piercing performances render the ears for a time insensitive to the ordinary sound of mortal voice.[52]

There was evidently a sense of participation in the shaping of the evening, and a relationship between audience and actors that is foreign to today's experience. At one level this developed into a *claque* system (of which, space unfortunately forbids analysis here), at another it was marked by banter from the gallery addressed to the actors. For instance, there was the case of a tragedian, in the 1860s, 'who was very tall and thin — over six feet in height':

One night he was playing Hamlet, and was dressed in the traditional dark suit with a very thin pair of nether garments on, which displayed his lower limbs to too great an advantage. The performance had gone on smoothly up to the second scene of the third act, where Hamlet is giving the players the following advice: 'Let those that play your clowns speak no more than is set down for them: for there be of them that will themselves laugh, to set some quantity of barren spectators to laugh too.' Just at this moment one of the 'gods' in the gallery shouted out, 'You were about when the legs were given out.' The roars of laughter all over the house quite upset the poor tragedian for the evening; and during his brief stay in the town he contented himself afterwards in appearing only in less ambitious pieces.[53]

Finally, there was the objectionable noise of disorder and deliberate disturbance. Here again — in the former case at least — a full understanding of the context ought to mitigate the offence. As one 'E.W.' complained in 1848, the first of 'the many causes that conspire to the disorderly state of our theatre . . . [was] that of admitting numbers of persons who cannot be seated into the pit and gallery'. Consequently, 'others coming in afterwards, and finding all places occupied, thrust themselves between the benches, and by brute force displace or crush between the seated parties'. Was it remarkable then that 'rarely . . . an evening passes, when the house is tolerably full, that one or two fights do not occur in the gallery'?[54] Nor was Macready's comment surprising when he 'Acted King Lear to such a house as never before was seen in Birmingham. Acted my best, but the house though very attentive, was too full to enjoy the play.'[55]

The relevant context of deliberate disturbance was historical as well as structural. Such disturbances had a long history in Birmingham (and, of course, elsewhere), and apart from the hustings the theatre was perhaps the last location where an 'eighteenth-century' commotion could still occur. The theatre is singular of course in that it constitutes a 'closed' or only semi-public arena where social disruption can occur without necessarily having implications for the whole social order; witness the remarkable riot which took place in 1838, stimulated by a public dispute between an actor and the manager of the Theatre Royal. In the intervals between these gentlemen's struggles on the stage and scuffles in the boxes the gallery audience had 'amused themselves by singing the national chaunt of *Rule Britannia* and *We Won't Go Home Till Morning*', but 'finding all hope of accommodation at an end, a call was made to clear the pit', and the gods began to tear up the gallery benches and throw them down into the pit; after about twenty minutes' work the chandeliers were smashed, the light was gone, and the audience dispersed.[56] Again, in 1841, an example was set by persons of superior rank. Two senior officers of the Birmingham garrison fomented a disturbance by paying a man to throw bags of flour from the gallery into the pit, where they landed on Henry Parker and his wife, 'and some friends of his who were in mourning'. To make matters worse, when they left the theatre it was raining![57]

However, the kind of riotous behaviour by large sections of the gallery seen in 1838 was never repeated, and one's impression is that men and boys in the gallery became more physically restrained as the mid-century decades wore on. Certainly, deliberately disorderly scenes continued to occur, but contemporary comment and historical investigation both suggest that they became less frequent and less popular. I hope to show elsewhere that they could more and more be laid specifically at the door of youth's delinquencies or be attributed to the excesses of *claqueurs*; for the present purposes it is only necessary to understand the outline of the context of the performances, especially Shakespearian performances.

IV

Melodrama, pantomime and Shakespeare were the types of drama most popular in the Birmingham theatres. Pantomime raises issues which are *sui generis*, however, and since the evidence of melodrama and Shakespeare taken together is more than adequate to our theme, pantomime will not be dealt with here.

Melodrama has been identified by contemporaries and historians alike as the quintessential popular drama. This is partly because of the circumstances of its birth (in the popular theatres of revolutionary Paris, where the characteristic music in support of the dialogue was first applied), partly because of the great development of unfashionable London theatres in the nineteenth century, and partly because of the structure of the genre. The triumph of vice over virtue — it has been assumed — offered a vicarious justification to the members of an oppressed proletariat. The violent action, surprising vicissitudes, and sensational stage effects which marked the course of most melodramas have been assumed to appeal primarily to the crude tastes of an uneducated crowd eager for sensation.[58]

This identification of melodrama with the populace was first made in the nineteenth century, of course, by theatre critics who reported or claimed to detect a special affinity between pit and gallery audiences and melodramas. In 1841 houses were good for the criminal melodrama *Jack Sheppard* at the Birmingham Theatre Royal — 'especially in the pit and gallery'. The critic commented:

Jack and *Fanny*, the thief and the ———, are a nice pair to run in harness. It is grievous to see such performers as Mrs Keeley and her good-humoured little husband, wasting their acknowledged powers on such irredeemable trash . . . The excuse for the repeated exhibition of these dramas (precious dramas) is, that they please the gods! If such be the case, the gods deserve to be whipped, for their vicious taste, rather than have their vicious taste pandered to.

In 1847, *Taming a Tartar, or Mazourkafobia* was but another of the long line of melodramas said to have 'contributed mightily to the gratification of pit and gallery'. Numerous other examples could be quoted from our period which, like *British Born* in 1873, were described as being 'a great piece for the gallery'.[59]

This common contemporary equation of pit and (especially) gallery and melodrama has been accepted *tout court* by Professor Michael Booth. Melodrama, he states, 'was essentially entertainment for the industrial working class; it grew up with them and died away when they turned to other means of amusing themselves'.[60] Incongruously — for 'it was a city virtually without a factory proletariat' — Booth develops his theme with regard to London. His main assertion is that there was a direct relationship between the taste of 'sub-literate' metropolitan audiences and their 'monotonous, drab and squalid' living and working conditions: 'Condemned to anonymity in life and work, struggling on the borderline of poverty and starvation, it is not surprising that they sought excitement, forgetfulness, and a better world in their entertainment.'[61]

But Booth is guilty of over-simplifying this issue. London is not England. Its size and the unprecedented scale of class-based residential segregation have encouraged a too easy identification of melodrama solely with his 'sub-literate' working class. In Birmingham it is much easier to see that melodrama was by no means attractive exclusively to working-class audiences. In Birmingham, in 1853, *Uncle Tom's Cabin* was said to have 'run . . . without any parallel amongst melodramatic pieces'; in 1878 — when fifty-four freed negro slaves enlivened the play with 'curious dances, impressive melodies, clever renderings upon the banjo, and remarkably grotesque performances' — 'Every part of the theatre, but more particularly the *upper boxes*, pit and gallery, was well filled.' Even at the 'sensational drama', *Haunted Houses*, in 1872 — 'a piece which had piled into it enough matter for half a dozen of those wonderful creations which . . . delight . . . transpontine and East End audiences' — even at this 'the

78

boxes were fairly filled'. Professor Booth had in fact noticed similar evidence in London but he explained it away with the observation: 'Later in the century melodrama became a fashionable source of pleasure for the upper classes, but its basic energy was proletarian.'[62] One is tempted to ask: are there no fashions among the poor?

In a later book, however, Booth has himself formulated propositions which encompass both working-class and middle-class reactions to melodrama. There, he has argued that although the artistic pleasures of the working and lower middle classes were 'crude and vulgar' those of the 'more educated classes inclined also to the simple and unsophisticated'.

What both the reading and play-going public looked for was a great deal of sentiment and strong pathos, domestic suffering and domestic bliss, a good story line, sensation and violence, a stern morality, much positive virtue and its reward in the almost inevitable happy ending, eccentric humour, and native English jollity and spirit.[63]

Although his argument is not confined to melodrama here, how well it fits much of the genre! In fact melodrama can be seen to embody many important characteristics and features of the 'Victorian' age. This interpretation receives support from the recent work of Louis James referring nineteenth-century melodrama to the contemporary science of phrenology and the psychology of opposed types; 'absolutist' melodramatic attitudes to emotion and intellect that might seem exaggerated today need to be seen in their total context.[64] To adapt Booth's metaphor, perhaps the 'mass' of melodrama was proletarian, but its energy was 'Victorian'.

The argument cannot be settled so simply and neatly, however; the weight of the stereotype of a simple-minded proletarian audience demands further shifting. Professor Booth is a representative, if sophisticated, proponent of this theme when he argues that 'subliterate' audiences found Shakespeare 'on the whole too literary', so that melodrama was 'suitable for their 'coarse and noisy ranks': 'It has a refreshing lack of pretension about it; there is no messing about with intellectuality. It always goes straight to its emotional and physical point and never deviates from there.'[65] Since melodramas were simple and non-intellectual they were therefore quintessentially proletarian, or so the reasoning appears to run.

Two main objections may be lodged against this view. Firstly, it does of course lump together all the gallery and the pit in a quite uncritical and unhistorical way, thus ignoring the careful distinctions which must be made. There is no need to rehearse the evidence of the social constituencies of pit and gallery, but there is need to introduce a further useful distinction: between regular and occasional attenders. It is suggested here that there was a hard core of regular theatre-goers, which was supplemented by occasional attenders whose numbers fluctuated according to the weather, the competition, or the fashion. At the beginning of our period it was felt that 'that part of [Birmingham's population] . . . which is playgoing does not much more than suffice to supply the theatre for a few nights'. It was an assumed consequence that 'the gods above and the men below are composed week after week of nearly the same individuals'.[66] This assumption is almost certainly valid throughout the period (other evidence is cited below) and it helps to explain the following comment on the return of *Jack Sheppard* to the Theatre Royal, in 1852:

it again draws houses full in certain parts . . . We have even heard of hundreds being turned away from the pit and gallery doors . . . One fact, however, came prominently out — the audience was not the intelligent and discriminating audience generally seen within the walls of the theatre — it was of a different character altogether.[67]

We must distinguish between the real patrons, knowledgeable and committed, who sustained the theatre through thick and thin, and those others who came and went, who followed trends and fashions, particularly, perhaps, the young; the rising population and the rising appetite for theatrical entertainment were of course constantly producing more recruits for both categories.

Secondly, the simple-minded proletarian audience stereotype understates, indeed ignores, the common sense of the common people and assumes that because melodramas were evidently popular that the 'gods' deserved to be either 'whipped or pitied'. There is a hidden assumption which vitiates so much that is spoken or written about 'popular culture', which is that because many melodramas (for instance) were *written* as though their audiences were simpletons, therefore they all *were* simpletons.

A distinction must be made between unschooled intellects and native wit; wit applied to appreciating plays by many a regular playgoer. The case can be made because there is a remarkable news-paper interview from the 1880s with one, Dick Field, the 'King of the Gallery' at the Birmingham Theatre Royal. Field had earlier achieved prominence as the leader of the gallery *claque* but by the 1880s he had gone back to being 'a decent artisan' — a dipper and gilder in the brass trade.

Field's reminiscences demonstrate a clear awareness of the structure of melodrama and show that the stereotyping which is taken so seriously by the literary critics was itself a source of enjoyment for the audience.

Robert Barton was a great favourite with the gallery boys, and at one time, when he had a succession of bad parts — mostly villains — they helped him by always applauding him and letting the hero shift for himself. 'Of course' says Dick, 'its easy enough for a lover or a hero to get plenty of applause, but its hard for a villain, and so we used to call Barton before the stage every time he did anything, whatever it was' — 'If it was a cold-blooded murder for instance?' 'Yes, anything.'[68]

This illuminating reminiscence makes ambiguous many seemingly straightforward reports of audience responses. At Charles Reade's *Joan, or Life in the Black Country*, 'the ruffian Don Lowrie could not have had a better compliment than the howls and execrations of a righteously indignant gallery', yet how far was this proof of simple conviction and how far an almost ritual response to a well-appreciated melodramatic situation? Similarly, with the 'groans and hoots of the audience' directed against the villain Lazarre in *Proof*?[69]

During the discussion of audience behaviour an analogy with the modern association football stadium may have formed in the minds of many readers, and it does seem an especially appropriate parallel when a comment on *Haunted Houses* (1872) is considered: 'Mr Mackenzie, as Daniel Blake . . . played rather too much for gallery applause, which, as he appeared on the point of death several consecutive times, he received most liberally.' Yet another comment (this time from 1879) conveys a sense of the popular audience participating in the course of the play; not as an anonymous mass of the 'coarse and noisy' but as *aficionados* of melodrama who appreciated an actor in a well-understood role: 'The part of Nat Gosling, the old jockey, was well sustained by Mr George Thorne, who elicited rounds of applause by his cool manner of checking the four black-legs, who desire to "nobble" Flying Scud. The audience bestowed cheer after cheer upon the actor, who certainly played his part to perfection.'[70]

Interpretation of melodrama has usually centred on large themes: melodrama as a source of escape from the world of care, as a source of excitement in a drab environment, as a source of vicarious fear and sadism or of vicarious vindication when the inept middle-class hero is saved by the resourceful working man.[71] Most of these themes have a certain plausibility, and could be *illustrated* by Birmingham evidence, though nothing of their impact is precisely calculable. What

81

can be said here is that these socio-psychological models are less likely to apply to regulars schooled in the traditions of the theatre, than to the occasional playgoers whose attendances reflected the ebb and flow of larger cultural tides. It is quite apparent that a close study of reactions to melodrama and the assumptions which have been made about it does lead one to a view of the complexity rather than the simplicity of this popular culture. Perhaps, above all, an awareness of the common sense of the common people has to be maintained.

V

A similar sense of proportion must be kept when popular reaction to Shakespearian plays is considered. It is first necessary to remark that Shakespearian productions drew consistently good popular audiences in the period under discussion; this is a noteworthy historical fact. In 1845, for instance, *Hamlet* was played to 'a crowded house' with a gallery 'crammed to suffocation' and a pit 'no less closely packed'. Throughout the 1840s W. C. Macready's Shakespearian representations were fully followed by pit and gallery; when he played *Henry VIII* in 1848 'the pit presented a perfect sea of heads; and thence upwards to the highest benches in the gallery, the theatre seemed to be a vast pyramid of perspiring faces'.[72] It is true that the conventional wisdom of the 1840s and 1850s was that 'fierce melodrama or gorgeous spectacle' were more performed than Shakespeare, yet by the 1870s the amount of Shakespearian performance (or that of other serious drama, such as *Medea* or Sheridan Knowles's *Virginius*) at the Theatre Royal had doubled, to comprise approximately thirty per cent of the annual programme. (At the same time, melodrama, which had taken up half the programme at the beginning of the 1840s, took only a quarter at the commencement of the later decade; the difference was made up by the expansion of pantomime, light opera, comedy and burlesque.)

In the 1870s, Shakespearian roles were most popularly played by Barry Sullivan. In 1873, for example, he was at the Royal to play in *The Lady of Lyons*, *The Stranger*, *Hamlet*, *Macbeth* and *Richard III*, 'winning enthusiastic applause in all . . . and drawing crowded audiences, more especially in his Shakespearian assumptions'. Pits and galleries were several times 'crammed to inconvenience' as Sullivan repeated these successes.[73] Other actors and other plays — *The Winter's Tale*, *Romeo and Juliet*, *A Midsummer Night's Dream*,

82

Henry V — were also popular, especially (as with *King Lear* in 1879) in the pit and gallery. 'It is somewhat singular that in the humbler parts of the house Shakspere [*sic*] should find more admirers and patrons than in the more "aristocratic" circles. Whereas the pit and gallery had pretty nearly their full complements, the boxes and stalls were scantily filled.'[74]

It is perhaps a measure of the influence of Hollywood and of television that such historical facts should have been so submerged in our consciousness. Looked at in a historical perspective, there is in fact no cause for surprise that Shakespearian plays were popular; after all, popular radicalism, which was still in flood in the 1840s, has been authoritatively described as 'an intellectual culture'. In 1819 the Birmingham 'Church and King' men had sought a battle with the reformers in the theatre; the familiarity of the radical bookseller, James Guest, with the Theatre Royal has already been noticed; in 1848 it was entirely in keeping with this tradition that Edward Newton, an unemployed artisan, should spatter a letter of protest with lengthy Shakespearian quotations.[75]

The station of such self-educated artisans would ideally have been the pit. 'As a point of vantage' it was said to be 'the best place in the house'. It was cheap enough, yet less subject to disruption than the gallery. 'The pit has had a dramatic education' wrote an experienced journalist a few years later; 'The members are regular attendants at the Temple of Thespis, and the pit knows at once what is good bad or indifferent.'

The criticism of the pit . . . if rough and ready, is formed upon a sound basis. Listen between the acts to the remarks passed around you on a new exponent of a celebrated part, and you will hear comparisons drawn between the present performance and all the great ones who have trod the boards.

Hence a contrast was drawn between the 'spontaneous acumen' of this audience and the 'kid-gloved denizens of the "circle" and "stalls"' who 'languidly wonder whether this is good and that is bad'. Not surprisingly then, it was recollected that 'the Birmingham pit knew their Shakespeare so well that they could prompt any actor who went astray'.[76]

However,

During 1865, the well-remembered Shakespearian actor, Mr William Creswick, fulfilled more than one welcome engagement at the 'Royal' . . . For those days this most creditable production [*The Tempest*] had quite a run, but I remember hearing Mr Creswick say that he was quite certain neither pit nor gallery understood the play, and he talked of issuing a little pamphlet, in explanation of it.[77]

But this opinion seems to fly in the face of common sense, for if neither pit nor gallery understood the play, what were they doing there and why did Shakespearian productions continue to draw them? Even the social attractions of the gallery must have begun to pall when the play was incomprehensible. An extra element of enigma is added by the frequent disturbances which took place during Shakespearian performances. In 1868 Barry Sullivan faced a gallery making so much noise that he 'in vain played through three acts of *Richard III*' and only after he made 'an earnest appeal for silence' did he obtain 'some sort of a hearing'. Again, in 1872, Sullivan played the hunch-backed king on a Saturday night and 'owing to the noise and confusion caused by the gallery audience, scarcely ten words could be heard'. In 1877, the 'cat calls and hootings were so incessant and deafening that the first scene and many other parts of the play were enacted in dumb show, the speakers being quite inaudible'.[78] Shakespeare and Sullivan seemed sadly unlucky to suffer excessive noise from the 'gods' quite so often. Was it that by the 1870s the regular attenders of the Theatre Royal had expanded to include large numbers who could not understand Shakespeare, and hence became disruptive out of boredom?

An examination of the pattern of disruption suggests, however, that there was by no means a *general* failure to understand Shakespeare, for three plays only garner these disruptive audiences: *Richard III*, *Hamlet* and *Macbeth* — the most exciting and thrilling in the conventional Shakespearian canon. This strongly suggests that the ghosts, murders and battles of this trio drew into the theatre a noisy lot of youths who, because they were not regulars, were less disposed to appreciate the plays quietly. Thus, galleries which for other reasons could be very noisy places anyway were supplemented by groups of raw and noisy youths. Even so, there is evidence that under the impact of powerful acting these youths responded. In 1873 Sullivan played Hamlet and 'kept the immense audience spellbound', almost every speech was greeted with applause, although 'in the absence of "the unfortunate Prince of Denmark" the gods were somewhat troublesome and noisy'. There is a parallel example, from 1845, of the impact which a leading actor could make — the man in question being none other than William Creswick, also playing Hamlet. 'He laboured under great disadvantages in having a noisy audience, but it was a high compliment to the talents of the actor, that the sea of voices which swelled and rolled on during the bye-play of the piece was hushed to a perfect calm whenever it was his cue to speak.'[79]

84

So, emphasis must be placed not on Shakespeare's plays occasioning rows from an uncomprehending gallery but on a popular audience which comprehended very well but which was sometimes joined by an excitable lot of youths who were nevertheless brought to silence by extremely effective acting.

Of course there were different levels of response within the regular audience. To judge from the only direct personal account from Birmingham, Dick Field derived the highest pleasure from following particular actors and from moments of high stress and drama. His interviewer noted that 'Dick is still an enthusiast in stage matters. Whenever an old friend, such as Barry Sullivan or T. C. King, comes down he cheerfully pays his sixpence and goes to see him.' 'King was always his favourite tragedian, and *Verginius* [*sic*] his favourite play. He liked King in that part because: "You see it was his own daughter, and he could do what he liked with her when he was murdering her. He was a beautiful murderer — beautiful!"' *Virginius*, by Sheridan Knowles, was a nineteenth-century Roman tragedy written in the Elizabethan style; Field went on to mention a domestic tragedy of the eighteenth century: 'Sullivan is very good in *The Gamester*. First he wants to die, then he don't. It's fine!'[80] Clearly, Dick Field does at least understand what is going on! And we can insist on this basic premiss with regard to most of the pit, and many of the gallery, audiences throughout our period.

When the evidence is weighed it becomes quite clear that to assume incomprehension on the part of the popular audience is far too simplistic, and it ignores much positive evidence thrown up by an attempt to place plays, players and playgoers in their full social context. Some theatre historians might be tempted to explain the popular following of Shakespeare in terms of its melodramatic qualities but this is to take too much notice of a certain popular following while ignoring a different and quieter popular audience for Shakespeare. It is to underestimate the pit and gallery, for reasons which this essay has attempted to point out. To redress the balance it is apposite to end not with Michael Booth but with the contemporary theatre chronicler T. E. Pemberton: 'Birmingham pits and galleries understand their Shakespeare very well indeed.'[81]

NOTES

This paper has been a long time in the making, but I owe particular and recent debts to the Bristol University Economic and Social History Seminar, to Louis

85

James, and to Dorothy Thompson, for help in bringing it to (what I hope is) a successful conclusion.

The following abbreviations are used in the notes:

BJo *Birmingham Journal*

BMN *Birmingham Morning News*

BRL Birmingham Reference Library

CEC *Children's Employment Commission*

Gazette *Birmingham Daily Gazette*

Mail *Birmingham Daily Mail*

Post *Birmingham Daily Post*

PP Parliamentary Papers

1 Dyke Wilkinson, *Rough Roads, Reminiscences of a Wasted Life* (London, c. 1912), p. 34.

2 William Hutton, *The History of Birmingham* (Birmingham, 1835), pp. 287–8; though cf. G. J. Kohl, *England, Wales and Scotland* (London, 1844), p. 12, for a contrary opinion on the merits of the 'accommodation'.

3 [Joseph Parkes], *The Plagiary 'warned'. A Vindication of the Drama, the Stage, and Public Morals, from the plagiarisms and compilations of the Revd. John Angell James . . . in a letter to the Author* (Birmingham, 1824), p. 74.

4 *Ibid.*, p. 75.

5 Historical Manuscripts Commission, *Fifteenth Report, Appendix, Part I. The Manuscripts of the Earl of Dartmouth*, vol. 3 (1896), pp. 234–5.

6 *Local Reports on the Sanitary Condition of the Labouring Population of England*, PP, 1842, HL, xxvii, p. 215.

7 T. R. Tholfsen, 'The Artisan and the Culture of Early Victorian England', *University of Birmingham Historical Journal*, 4 (1953), p. 144.

8 *CEC, 1862, Third Report of the Commissioners*, PP, 1864 [3414–1], xxii, p. 165.

9 Asa Briggs, *Victorian Cities* (Harmondsworth, 1968), pp. 186–7.

10 David Cannadine, 'Victorian Cities: How Different?', *Social History*, 4 (Jan. 1977), esp. pp. 468–82.

11 [J. Drake], *The Picture of Birmingham* (Birmingham, 1825), p. 36.

12 *BJo*, 28 April 1838.

13 J. A. Langford, *A Century of Birmingham Life*, 2 vols. (Birmingham, 1868), vol. 2 p. 608; *Report from the Select Committee on Public Houses*, PP, 1852–3 (855), xxxvii, QQ.8752–3.

14 *BJo*, 27 June 1846, 27 Nov. 1847.

15 *Report from the Select Committee on Theatrical Licences and Regulations*, PP, 1866 (373), xvi, QQ.5721, 7379, 7524.

16 On the 1843 Act, see Watson Nicholson, *The Struggle for a Free Stage in London* (New York, 1906).

17 Minutes of the Committee of the Theatre Royal, Birmingham, 29 Dec. 1843; 27 Dec. 1844; 31 Dec. 1845; 30 Dec. 1846; 31 Dec. 1847; 31 July, 19 Dec. 1860 (BRL 662469).

18 BRL 60831 (newspaper cuttings), p. 181.

19 *Mail*, 30 March 1872.

20 Theatre Royal, Minutes, 28 Dec. 1863 (BRL 662469).

21 [C. S. Adcock], *Fifty Years Memoirs of the Prince of Wales Theatre* (Birmingham, 1911); Prince of Wales Theatre, Programmes 1863–73 (BRL 57544).

22 *BJo*, 24 Jan. 1846.
23 *CEC (Trade and Manufactures), Appendix to the Second Report of the Commissioners, pt I, Reports and Evidence from Sub-Commissioners*, PP, 1843 [432], xv, pp. f172—3.
24 *BJo*, 11 Dec. 1841; 27 Sept., 29 Nov. 1845; 3 and 31 Jan., 7 and 21 March, 11 April, 26 Oct. 1846; 8 and 16 Oct. 1847; 18 Jan., 31 May, 7 June, 20 Sept. 1851; 28 Feb. 1852.
25 *Ibid.*, 25 March 1843.
26 *Ibid.*, 21 Nov. 1846.
27 *Ibid.*, 29 Nov., 6 Dec. 1845; 7 Feb. 1846; 6 Oct. 1849; 15 June 1850.
28 *BMN*, 12 April 1873; *Gazette*, 20 Feb. 1873; *Theatre Royal Advertiser and Evening Programme*, e.g. 18 Feb. 1864.
29 *Gazette*, 5 March 1873; *Post*, 17 and 20 Feb., 28 March, 1 and 2 April 1873; *Mail*, 21 Sept. 1874.
30 Theatre Royal, Minutes, 6 July 1876.
31 E. L. Levy, *Birmingham Theatrical Reminiscences, Jubilee Recollections (1870—1920)* (Birmingham, 1920), pp. 3—4.
32 *BJo*, 19 Nov. 1853; BRL 302179 (newspaper cuttings), pp. 163—4; *Post*, 13 Sept. 1881.
33 Levy, *Reminiscences*, pp. 3—4.
34 *Gazette*, 17 Feb. 1873; *Post*, 20 Feb. 1873.
35 *Mail*, 29 Dec. 1979.
36 e.g. *Post*, 18 Nov. 1873
37 *BJo*, 26 Nov. 1842; 27 March 1841; 22 Oct. 1842.
38 E. Edwards, *Personal Recollections of Birmingham and Birmingham Men* (Birmingham, 1877), pp. 98—9.
39 *Mail*, 24 June 1873; Levy, *Reminiscences*, p. 4.
40 Douglas A. Reid, 'The Decline of Saint Monday, 1766—1876', *Past and Present*, 71 (May 1976), pp. 76—101.
41 *BJo*, 15 Feb. 1840, and 24 Jan. 1846; *CEC, 1862, Third Report*, p. 84.
42 *BJo*, 5 and 29 Dec. 1845.
43 *Ibid.*, 29 Oct. 1853.
44 Reid, 'Decline of Saint Monday', pp. 86—9, 99—101; *Gazette*, 1 Sept. 1873; *Post*, 17 Feb. 1873.
45 Langford, *Century of Birmingham Life*, pp. 376, 378; *Mail*, 12 May 1880.
46 *BJo*, 18 Feb. 1843; 29 March, 27 Sept., 29 Nov. 1845; 7 Feb., 7 and 21 March 1846; 16 Oct. 1847; 11 Jan. 1851.
47 For Gillott see note 38 above; *BJo*, 18 Jan. 1851 (my italics).
48 *CEC, Second Report*, 1843, p. f173.
49 *BJo*, 14 Oct. 1848.
50 'Delta', History of the Stage in Birmingham, part II (BRL 60830).
51 William Toynbee (ed.), *The Diaries of W. C. Macready*, 2 vols. (London, 1912), vol. 2, p. 463.
52 *BJo*, 14 Oct., 30 Dec. 1848; 1 March 1845.
53 *Birmingham Weekly Mercury*, 24 April 1901. Since this chapter was written I have come across another vivid illustration of this relationship — this time from the 1840s and 1850s — which deserves full quotation. The

source is J. T. Bunce, 'Birmingham Life Sixty Years Ago' in the *Birmingham Weekly Post*, 10 June 1899.

> The Birmingham theatre . . . public . . . liked the stock company. Particular actors, through being long on the staff, became special favourites, even their mannerisms seeming to endear them to the audiences, and being welcomed by unfailing applause. There must be still a good many readers who will remember with interest two actors of this class — Mr. 'Bobby' Atkins, a clever low comedian, and Mr. John Barton, whose department was that of 'general utility'. Whatever parts they undertook, these actors were always Atkins and Barton — there was no disguising their voices, their little tricks of speech, their stereotyped movements; the characteristics which, in fact, made them so popular. The gallery, especially, was on more than friendly — indeed intimate — terms with them, addressing them by their Christian names, sometimes criticising them freely, and sometimes offering them encouragement by observations which would have been embarrassing if addressed to strangers.

54 *BJo*, 14 Oct. 1848.
55 Toynbee, *Diaries of Macready*, vol. 2, p. 463.
56 *BJo*, 29 Sept., 6 Oct. 1838; *Aris's Birmingham Gazette*, 8 Oct. 1838.
57 *BJo*, 20 Feb. 1841.
58 This formulation owes something to a review by F. J. W. Hemming in *The Times Higher Education Supplement*, 5 May 1978. In general, see Phyllis Hartnoll, *Oxford Companion to the Theatre* (Oxford, 1967), pp. 631—2; George Rowell, *The Victorian Theatre* (London, 1967); M. R. Booth, *English Melodrama* (London, 1965); and — especially illustrating the last point — see W. D. Howarth, 'Word and Image in Pixérécourt's Melodramas: the Dramaturgy of the Strip-Cartoon', this volume, esp. pp. 18—19.
59 *BJo*, 22 Aug. 1840, 9 Oct. 1847; *BMN*, 1 July 1873.
60 Booth, *Melodrama*, p. 52.
61 *Ibid.*, pp. 56—60, Cf. Gareth Stedman Jones, *Outcast London* (Harmondsworth, 1976), p. 337.
62 *BJo*, 25 April 1853; *Gazette*, 10 Sept. 1878 (my italics); 1 Oct. 1872; Booth, *Melodrama*, p. 52.
63 M. R. Booth (ed.), *English Plays of the Nineteenth Century*, vol. I, *Dramas 1800—1850* (Oxford, 1969), pp. 6—7. It is only fair to add that Michael Booth has recently come to a recognition of the virtues of 'history from below'; see his statement 'East End and West End: Class and Audience in Victorian London', *Theatre Research International*, New Series, 2:2 (Feb. 1977), pp. 98—103.
64 Louis James, 'Was Jerrold's Black Ey'd Susan More Popular than Wordsworth's Lucy?', this volume.
65 Booth, *Melodrama*, pp. 38, 56—61.
66 *BJo*, 18 Jan. 1840.
67 *Ibid.*, 23 Oct. 1852.
68 BRL 60831 (newspaper cutting, *c.* 1879—81); see also *BMN*, 7 June 1873 and *Post*, 9 June 1873.
69 *Mail*, 23 Sept. 1879; 6 Aug. 1878.
70 *BMN*, 1 Oct. 1872; *Mail*, 5 Aug. 1879.

71 See, for example, Booth, *Melodrama, passim*; Kathleen Barker, *Entertainment in the Nineties* (Bristol, 1973), p. 7; Bernard Sharratt, 'The Politics of the Popular? — from Melodrama to Television', this volume, esp. pp. 277—81.

72 *BJo*, 18 April 1841; 14 June, 29 Nov. 1845; 24 April 1847; 8 July 1848; 23 June, 17 Nov. 1849.

73 *Post*, 18 and 25 Nov. 1873; 2 April 1877; *BMN*, 8 Nov. 1872, 22 April 1873; *Gazette*, 2 April 1877.

74 *Gazette*, 11 March 1879.

75 E. P. Thompson, *The Making of the English Working Class* (Harmondsworth, 1968), pp. 781, 785; *Edmond's Weekly Recorder and Saturday's Advertiser*, 16 and 30 Oct. 1819. For James Guest see note 2 above; for Edward Newton, see *BJo*, 19 June 1848.

76 *The Birmingham Dramatic News*, 10 Oct. 1885; and BRL 302179 (newspaper cutting, Oct. 1919).

77 T. E. Pemberton, *The Theatre Royal, Birmingham, 1774—1901. A Record and some Recollections* (Birmingham, 1901), pp. 42—3.

78 T. E. Pemberton, *The Birmingham Theatres: a Local Retrospect* (Birmingham, 1889), p. 59; *BMN*, 25 April 1872; *Post*, 25 Oct. 1877.

79 *BMN*, 22 and 28 April 1873; *BJo*, 29 Nov. 1845.

80 As note 68.

81 Pemberton, *Royal*, pp. 42—3.

Water drama

Derek Forbes

The history of the association of water with the drama is as old as the recorded history of the drama itself. During the century leading up to 1200 *BC* the Egyptian drama known as *The Triumph of Horus* was performed on, in, and around the sacred lake within the temple precincts of Edfu.[1] Romans enjoyed the sea-battle entertainment known as the 'Naumachia', for which special flooded arenas were built.[2] In the religious plays of the late middle ages real water occasionally makes its appearance, as in the moat surrounding the playing-place of *The Castell of Perseverance*,[3] and in the Valenciennes passion play of 1547 which has its own 'sea', used for a variety of episodes.[4] Allegorical water-shows became a part of the royal and civic revels of the renaissance. In England, these included the Earl of Leicester's shows for Queen Elizabeth on the water at Kenilworth as part of the 'Princely Pleasures' of 1575,[5] and the entertainments offered to the Queen by the Earl of Hertford at Elvetham in 1591 on a specially excavated lake, as well as London Lord Mayor's Shows in which George Peele led the way in 1591 for much subsequent water-pageantry with the first Lord Mayor's Show on record that contains a speech delivered from a stage afloat on the Thames.[6]

With the restoration of the monarchy in 1660 came the development of scenery and illusion in the public theatres in England. The use of water on stage in the form of hydraulic effects became fashionable. A theatrical fountain spouts as early as 1665, if we may go by Dryden's stage directions for *The Indian Emperor*. By 1692 *The Fairy Queen* requires cascades, side-fountains, and a central fountain 'where the Water rises about twelve Foot'.[7] At about this time Henry Winstanley built a 'Water Theatre' in Piccadilly, to feature 'the greatest curiosities in waterworks, the like never performed by any'. The trick fountains, spouts, and mingled fire-and-water effects of Winstanley's Waterworks were used to create moving tableaux, a 'flying dragon', for example, and 'a prospect of the Coaches going to

Hide Park [*sic*] in cascades of water'. After Winstanley's death
in 1703 in the collapse of his greatest waterwork of all, the first
Eddystone lighthouse, the Piccadilly Water Theatre fitfully continued to operate under the direction of his widow and was open
to the public as late as 1713.[8] Its end is misted over.

Before the end of the eighteenth century a lake and cascade using
real water were seen on the stage of one of the patent theatres. This
was at the rebuilt Drury Lane Theatre in 1794. The lake was contained
in a great basin large enough for a boat to be rowed about in it; it
was fed from a water-course built to resemble a rocky stream-bed,
down which water flowed from tanks installed in the theatre's attics.[9]
The water tanks, together with an iron safety curtain, were meant as
a fire precaution. The demonstration to the public of 'real water' on
stage was not initially given as an effect integrated into a play but
formed a separate show: George Colman got up a 'Pantomime
Epilogue' as an after-piece, in which Miss Farren presented the water
to the public in the character of a superior housekeeper:

> The very ravages of fire we scout,
> For we have wherewithal to put it out . . .
> Behold, obedient to the Prompter's bell
> Our tide shall flow, and *real* waters swell.
> No *river*, of meand'ring *pasteboard* made;
> No gentle tinkling of a *tin cascade*;
> No *brook* of *broad-cloth* shall be set in motion;
> No ships be wrecked upon a *wooden ocean*;
> But the pure element its course shall hold,
> Rush on the scene, and o'er the stage be rolled.

James Boaden was not impressed. 'All this nonsense had proceeded
from engineers', he says, but was 'caught at' by managers because of
its 'strong effect upon the public mind'.[10] Hence we find at Drury
Lane Theatre in 1803 a production of *The Caravan* by Frederick
Reynolds, in which, so Charles Dibdin the younger records, 'a Dog
jumped into a small reservoir of "sea water" and preserved a child
from drowning'.[11] Dibdin may have taken this as a challenge. In the
following year he embarked upon his own series of aquatic productions
at Sadler's Wells Theatre, where he was manager and writer.

When he first promoted 'Aqua-drama' in 1804, Charles Dibdin
constantly advertised his plays as being given in a tank of 'real water'.
When defending his use of the term 'real water' he allowed himself
to be scornful of the technical effects used for feigning 'artificial'
water on stage:

The Public knew we could, in common with all Theatres, produce *artificial* water, and wrap up our rivers when not used, in tarpaulins, to keep our waters from the dry rot, and, therefore, it was requisite that they should be unequivocally informed that they would actually see *Water*, and not Wood, Canvas, and Whalebone, painted.   (*Memoirs*, pp. 98–99)

It is not my present purpose to demonstrate the detailed evidence for the development of dry water effects in the standard illusionistic theatre.[12] It must be noted, however, that when Charles Dibdin the younger became the supreme impresario of drama in a marine or nautical setting, he was building on a thematic tradition that had already been well established in the drama of the eighteenth century, though normally such plays had been staged dry, using feigned water effects. It is useful, therefore to keep in mind something of the development of the nautical drama genre and its broad social and political context.

As part of *The Critic* in 1779, Sheridan staged an ambitious theatrical sea-battle (using 'dry' effects). It seems that the type of the marine or naval scene was so familiar in the theatre of the day that he was confident he could mock its conventions. This he did brilliantly. The climactic Armada battle of Puff's play calls for fleets to engage and advance, and for the 'Spanish fleet [to be] destroyed by fire-ships, etc.'. If we try to envisage what happened in 1779, it should be in the knowledge that Drury Lane Theatre was then served by Philippe de Loutherbourg, one of the greatest contrivers of stage illusion of all time. The Armada play in *The Critic* may have been parody, but the fun did not lie in a technically maladroit presentation. As A. C. Clinton-Baddeley has observed, 'Sheridan made the joke the other way round, burlesquing not with a minimum but with an excess of patriotic splendour.'[13] Contemporary accounts refer to the battle as 'executed in the most masterly manner', and 'miraculous'. Cecil Price quotes the *London Evening Post* as saying: 'The deception of the sea was very strong, and the perspective of the ships, together with the mode of their sailing, truly picturesque.'[14]

The emergence of nautical drama in the latter half of the eighteenth century can be partly accounted for in Puff's own words: 'Ay, this is always the way at the theatre: give these fellows a good thing, and they never know when to have done with it' (*The Critic*, Act II, Scene 2). One other reason for the popularity of naval plays is that they reflected the nation's patriotism during a time of almost constant war. The bluejackets and their ships represented not merely deeds of great valour; they were equally the symbol of the 'wooden walls' whereby the island's security was assured. It was craggy 'Old Jervie', Earl St Vincent, himself a naval victor of renown, who as First Lord answered in Parliament a question about the possibility of invasion by the French: 'I do not say they cannot come; I only say they cannot come by sea.' In the Drury Lane season of 1793—4 Sheridan gave *The Glorious First of June*. This was another play with a spectacular nautical battle as its climax, staged using dry effects. Rapidly scrambled together, the piece was given less than five weeks after the actual battle. On its first night, 2 July 1794, Sheridan presented it entirely free of all house charges as a benefit in aid of the dependants of the British sailors killed in Admiral Howe's hard-fought victory. The climate of national emotion in which the piece was given can be gauged from the fact that the benefit night, according to Charles Beecher Hogan, took 'by far the largest amount known for a single performance at either Drury Lane or Covent Garden at any time between 1700 and 1800: £1,526. 11s'.[15]

Plays now came thick and fast to celebrate the gallant deeds of Jolly Jack Tar. Naturally enough the actual savagery and horror of life between decks in the men-of-war were submerged beneath a romantic gloss, but part of the fascination for the seamen themselves of the nautical dramas that they thronged to see must have been that they had — so far — survived the real thing. The nautical genre in the drama of the nineteenth century is sufficiently well documented for it not to need rehearsal here.[16] Equally, there is a general understanding of the way in which the nautical drama of this time relates to the broader perspective of the Napoleonic wars. Consistent victories were won by the British navy, in actions large and small, during a period of twenty-five years. (The army's record was not so good.) In an age without television or film, and with a journalism capable of being read only by the literate minority and very inadequately illustrated if illustrated at all, the stage played its part in attempting to put on show the exciting current events that audiences were eager to hear about and see. Theatres had a 'news-reel' function.

This was not the only purpose served by drama in a marine setting. The contribution made by economic factors to the response of theatres and audiences to sea-faring issues must also be recognised. In the early part of the century, when water drama really came to the boil, British ships carried half the world's trade. The figures are staggering. During the eight years of massive expansion between 1803 and 1811 the British merchant fleet increased from 17,516 bottoms to 19,725 with another 3,450 registered as sailing out of the colonies,

94

and the Royal Navy spread during the same period from 105 line-of-battle ships and frigates to 244. In the one year of 1811 the number of ships of all nationalities and of all types and on all errands outward from London, the busiest port in the world, was 15,211.[17]

Side by side with a national glorification of successes in war and trade, there was a cultural reaction against materialism that led to the gothic revival and the work of the Romantic poets. The anti-classical landscapes of such painters as Richard Wilson became popular during the Regency period. The rediscovery by the Romantic movement of the delights of wild or unimproved nature was avidly taken up by the theatre. Ravines, ruins, windswept and misshapen trees, grottoes, caves, pools, meandering streams, waterfalls, were the fashion, almost the obligation, on the painted scenery of appropriate melodramas and pantomimes.[18]

It was, then, to a stimulus on the one hand of the Romantic 'back to nature' school, and on the other of patriotic and materialist considerations focused on unceasing naval glory and a mercantile economy that serviced the movements of an average of more than eighty ships into or out of the Port of London every day of the year, that Charles Dibdin the younger responded. He reconciled these different pressures in one stroke of showmanship by turning Sadler's Wells into 'The Aquatic Theatre'.

To deal first with the plumbing, a large tank, ninety feet long, was installed in the theatre at Sadler's Wells in place of the existing stage and cellar-work during the winter of 1803–4. (At this period Sadler's Wells, like most minor theatres, was dark in the winter and opened at Easter for the summer season.) Dibdin says that the tank was 'in breadth, at the widest part 24 foot; and at the narrowest 10 foot', with a length of 90 feet (*Memoirs*, p. 60). Dimensions given elsewhere, for example in the advertisements placed in the newspapers to herald the launching of the tank, suggest a width of 30 feet, a width of 40 feet, a length of 90 feet and a length of 'nearly 100 feet'.[19] These discrepancies imply that the width of the tank, narrower at one point than at another, was not easy to measure by eye, but that the tank's length was more easily reckoned up, and probably utilised the full extent of stage-depth. (In production, no doubt, scenery or drops forward of the back wall could be used to shorten the vista.) The exact shape of the tank can only be guessed at. Reference to Pugin's picture of Sadler's Wells Theatre interior in Ackermann's *Microcosm of London* (see illustration) indicates that an angled bay came forward under the proscenium arch. This narrowing of the tank at the front

A scene using the Sadler's Wells water tank. Pugin and Rowlandson cartoon from Ackermann's *Microcosm of London* (1809). Reproduced by permission of Islington Council.

end, or a possible narrowing of the tank towards the back of the stage, or both, could account for the variation in Dibdin's breadth measurement. Apart from the bay-front, Pugin shows no angles. It seems fair to surmise, then, that the tank was more or less coffin-shaped, with the 'head' end, as it were, towards the audience, being at its widest at the shoulder position, and eventually narrowing away upstage toward the 'foot'. There is no proof for any such tapering effect as I have suggested for the main upstage stem of the tank, though sightlines would seem to make some tapering desirable. Nor is there proof for the hypothesis that the main stem upstage followed the centre line symmetrically.

Two side channels or cuts, 'about 3 or 4 feet in width', led off from the sides of the tank (not precisely opposite each other). These gave floating access to and from the wings. One presumes that in performance appropriately painted shutters masked the cuts. In two somewhat conflicting items of evidence Dibdin indicates firstly that the cuts extended to the '[side] Walls of the Theatre', and secondly that there was a practice of 'going round the extremity of the Cut'

(*Memoirs*, pp. 60, 63). Perhaps the cuts were bridged over at the far ends, or possibly they shelved. I suspect that the proprietors imposed a theatre ruling, or even railed the cuts off, following Dibdin's accidental immersion in one of the cuts during the first night of the tank's operation: 'On this night, . . . many more of the people of the Theatre than were intended, went into the water, and among them myself' (*Memoirs*, pp. 62–3).

The tank had three feet of vertical depth. The inconsistent measurements bedevil any attempt to calculate the capacity of the tank with any accuracy, but the spectrum of the dimensions seems to make more likely a capacity of between 7,200 and 8,000 cubic feet (45,000–50,000 gallons) than Dibdin's own figure (1800 barrels, or 64,800 gallons). This was still a fair weight of water — at the lowest estimate, two hundred tons.

Dibdin is also tantalising about the problems of water control, other than that water was gained from the New River adjacent. At first this was done by troughs fed from an 'Archimedes' wheel', leading to the 'Edge of the back part of the Tank' (*Memoirs*, p. 63). Denis Arundell finds that it took twelve men twelve hours to fill the tank, working in teams of four.[20] Subsequently the tank was connected to the New River Main. This would have made feeder-pipes necessary. Their siting and dimensions, when installed, would remain a mystery but for Robert Wilkinson's engaging information printed in 1819:

Leather hose, 4 inches calibre, that can be conveyed to any part of the theatre with the greatest ease. The water is always on the main, from which a large bore is laid from the steam-engine, which fills the tank in twenty-six hours, and rises a perpendicular 37 feet, to the top of the house.

(*Londina Illustrata*, II, 75)

I take the steam-engine to be a pumping-engine appertaining to the New River Head, that is to say, the pool and service area immediately to the south-west of the theatre at which the New River proper terminates and the Main begins. (The site is still operated by the London Water Authority.) The water was changed periodically, though not frequently enough for the Sadler's Wells doorkeeper of the day, one R. Wheeler, whose sometimes acerbic recollections are annexed by George Speaight to Dibdin's *Memoirs*: 'Full houses were the reward of having a leaden tank full of putrid water — for it was not renewed but once in two months' (*Memoirs*, p. 163). There is an absolute, and perhaps ominous, silence on the matter of the tank's outlet.

One can only trust that it discharged into the sewer system and not back into the New River Main.

To facilitate 'real waterfalls', a supplementary tank was installed in the roof. This was some time after the main tank first came into operation, though quite when is not clear. The roof-tank must certainly have been in place for the season of 1808, as a 'Grand Cataract of Real Water' was advertised in this year. Dibdin says that the roof-tank was 'fifteen feet square, and five foot deep' (*Memoirs*, p. 60) – therefore holding over 7,000 gallons. If all this was released, it meant that there were thirty-one tons of water to find a home for. It comes as no surprise to find Dibdin implying that the tank sometimes overflowed (*Memoirs*, p. 123).

Waves must have been caused by the action of the 'water-boys' at times, and may have been prone to spill over the edges of the tank if it was full. The water-boys formed Dibdin's team of boys and young men who, wading or swimming, operated the practicable model ships, water-chariots etc., and set the scenery of the littoral. They were well clad for their parts out and in. Dibdin says that he gave them 'thick duffil trousers' and a glass of brandy before and after their immersion. One imprudent water-boy and one consumptive sceneman who in any case 'had a predisposition to Decline' were all the fatal casualties suffered by the company in fourteen consecutive years, so Dibdin claims with some pride (*Memoirs*, pp. 78, 80).

The water-scene was the final sensation of a full evening's entertainment. What preceded it was played on a wooden stage laid over the tank. This stage took twenty minutes or more to remove in Dibdin's time, the hands working feverishly behind a front-drop. Under the subsequent management of Egerton in 1823 apparatus was installed to raise the stage mechanically so as to avoid such a long delay. Seventy-five years later Clement Scott described this operation, though whether with complete authenticity seems open to doubt:

Previous to these water scenes the drop-scene was let down for the last act of the piece. In the interval the audience could plainly hear the water run into the tank, while gusts of air strongly agitated the act-drop, which was after a few minutes partly drawn up to allow the first edge of the rising platform free action upwards, as the great tank extended to within six feet of the foot-lights.[21]

The scenery associated with the water was often spectacular. Unfortunately, its technical provision is nowhere described. We can only postulate that the scenery was made up from some combination of independent items at the edge of the water or islanded in it, and shutters in the groove-and-shutter system that ran offstage into the wings from the sides of the tank, and drop-curtains (painted or otherwise).

For his first aquatic production, *The Siege of Gibraltar* (1804), Dibdin seems to have used built-up scenery at one side only of the stage. The setting for the battle scene 'discovered to public view . . . a Sheet of Water . . . with a representation of the Rock and fortress of Gibraltar on one side and the mimic ocean spreading itself on the other' (*Memoirs*, pp. 61–2). Dibdin put only the last scene fully on the water. The whole thing contained a variety of scenes and songs and was surprisingly close in character to the dramatised documentary, with lyrics, of today's expository or political theatre. The playbills and advertisements for *The Siege of Gibraltar* drew attention to 'Real Ships' of sixty-four, seventy-four and one hundred guns, which

work down with the wind on their starboard beam, wear and haul the wind on their larboard tacks, to regain their situations . . . The floating batteries take fire, some blowing up with a dreadful explosion, and others, after burning to the water's edge, sink to the bottom; . . . the gallant Sir Roger Curtis appears in his boat to save the drowning Spaniards, the British tars for that purpose plunging into the water.[22]

Dibdin boasts of the employment of Woolwich Dockyard shipwrights to make the working models 'in exact imitation . . . even to the slightest minutiae', while the sight of

the boats by which Sir Roger Curtis is recorded to have preserved the lives of many of the drowning Spanish sailors, suddenly darting from the side branches of the water into the heart of the mimic ocean with children for the sailors, picking up other children, who were instantly seen swimming and affecting to struggle with the waves

caused 'the enthusiasm of the audience' (and, clearly, Dibdin himself) to exceed 'all bounds' (*Memoirs*, pp. 60, 62).

There was, supposedly, no dialogue in these minor theatre confections. Dibdin published the 'Book of Songs' of this, however, and of some of his later aqua-dramas and harlequinades. In his valuable study of early-nineteenth-century pantomime, *Harlequin in his Element*, David Mayer counts eight surviving libretti by Charles Dibdin the younger and analyses the contribution of water to the scenic effects as follows:

These libretti provide considerable evidence of the use to which the tanks of water were put. They seem to have permitted four possibilities: the water might be used for effect. A jet or cascade might harbor a benevolent agent or work some magic. More often the water ornamented and lent verisimilitude to an already attractive setting. And, almost invariably, the water figured in some splendid last scene augmented by novel hydraulic effects.[23]

The 'Book of Songs' of *The Siege of Gibraltar* gives only modest information beyond the lyrics.[24] From the heading given for each scene, however, the reader can gain some idea of how this piece, and later aqua-dramas, were patched together.

Scenes 1 and 2 are on the stage's wooden boards, being entitled 'Camp at St Roque' and 'Interior of the Mole at Gibraltar'. Scene 3 shows that part of the wooden stage was dismantled, giving what was presumably a limited, downstage, scene on the water in front of a painted drop: 'View of the Rock of Gibraltar from the sea; part of the stage REAL WATER.' The stage direction shows that an English sailor and soldier row on, 'having escaped from the enemy', and sing:

> *Sailor*: The foe on one string always strumming, boys,
> Declare to attack us they're coming, boys,
> But I fancy they're only humming, boys,
> What say you? (*to Soldier*)
>
> *Soldier*: Let 'em come, let 'em come, if resolv'd to attack,
> The best way to come they their brains needn't rack,
> They'd much better study the way to get back,
> What say you? (*to Sailor*)
>
> *Sailor*: I say so too —
> *Soldier*: And so do I —
> *Both*: Let 'em come, let 'em come, we their force defy,
> Then strike hands (*join hands*) for together we'll conquer or die.
> Tol derol derol liddle lol, &c.
> Cheery my hearts, yo! yo!

There is a further stanza. The awfulness of the song must have been made worse by the fact that the singers were sitting (standing?) in a practicable boat on a narrow strip of water and had no opportunity for action. There is nothing happening in Scene 4 beyond the lowering of a majestic drop, which the audience admire while the band plays and the scenemen remove the rest of the boarded stage behind the curtain: 'Scene IV: Grand Drop, measuring nearly Nine Hundred square feet, representing the BRITISH GRAND FLEET going to the RELIEF OF THE GARRISON.' The scenic artist was R. C. Andrews, the theatre's scene-painter and Dibdin's fellow-proprietor. This 'very beautiful Drop Scene . . . completely filled up all the Area of the proscenium (which by mechanism was enlarged in width 7 or 8 foot)', says Dibdin, implying that the theatre was using some system of false proscenium for earlier, normal scenes (*Memoirs*, p. 61). Furthermore, we may assume that the drop-scene was footed not by the wooden stage but by the waters of the tank, which had (I take it) been disclosed downstage for the previous scene, thus adding to the drop's effect. Then at last the final scene is ready. There are no more lyrics, but all is business. Here is Dibdin's description of it from the 'Book of Songs':

Scene V: GRAND AQUATIC SPECTACLE, THE WHOLE OF THE STAGE REAL WATER Containing nearly Eight Thousand Cubic Feet of Water; On one side, the Garrison of Gibraltar, on the opposite the Combined Fleets of France and Spain. GRAND AND MEMORABLE ATTACK, with real Ships and Gun Vessels, regularly built and rigged; blowing up the Spanish Floating Batteries, &c, &c with a real representation of the Humanity of the English in saving their Enemies' drowning Sailors from Destruction by the exertions of that meritorious Officer Sir ROGER CURTIS! and the curtain drops at the moment of BRITISH VICTORY.

The lubber public flocked. So did the seamen. Sadler's Wells Theatre already had a strong nautical following, even before 1804, which Denis Arundell ascribes to the theatre's having achieved the patronage in 1800 of the Duke of Clarence, 'Sailor Bill'.[25] Grimaldi, who was the other great attraction at this theatre at the time, speaks in his memoirs of the Wells in 1807 as 'a famous place of resort with the blue-jackets, the gallery being sometimes almost solely occupied by seamen and their female companions'.[26] In the early days of the tank-drama the proprietors had trouble with the 'unreflecting Sons of Neptune': until threatened with the watch-house, they developed a habit of shinning down the sets of pillars all the way from the gallery to plunge into the tank's mock sea (*Memoirs*, pp. 64–5).

Amongst the continuing fare of harlequinades, melodramas, and spectacles of all kinds, Dibdin now put on one, two, or three new or revived aqua-dramas every year. At first he had substantial success, but recognised the need to keep straining after some further novelty. The gothic and picturesque taste made its contribution in the tank's second year. The advertisements for Dibdin's *An-Bratach* (1805) show that this Celtic piece concludes with a view of 'Fingall's Cave, in which the Spectre will arise from the immense body of real water'.[27] The perpetrator describes how, in this exciting scene,

the principal female character in the piece (personated by Madame St Amand) was, by the tyrant who persecuted her precipitated into the Real Water and rescued by some boatmen, a sight so unprecedented, that the stimulus to public curiosity which it excited, doubled the profits of the preceding Season. That

101

we were neither ungallant nor cruel enough to throw a lady into the Water nor the Lady weak enough to consent to such a violence, will naturally be supposed; but the deception was so adroitly managed, and the substitution for the Lady of a slim boy, dressed in every particular exactly like her, so instantaneously and deceptively made, that it was impossible for the most lynx eyed observer among the auditory to detect the imposition. *(Memoirs, p. 66)*

A piece to celebrate the victory of Trafalgar was presented in 1806, followed by *The Invisible Ring, or Water Monster and Fire Spectre*, with a volcano erupting beside the 'lake' in whose waters it was reflected. A large Newfoundland dog rescued an infant (for which at the last moment a doll was substituted) from the waters in *The Ocean Fiend* (1807). The waterfall was inaugurated, so a study of the advertisements suggests, in *The White Witch, or the Cataract of Amazonia* (1808). In addition to various aquatic harlequinades, such novelties were offered in the following years as an 'illuminated revolving aquatic temple' (1810), the 'Lake of the Grotto' (1811), a single-ship engagement between 'two ships, as large as our tank would allow the disposal of' (1813), a 'grand conflagration' reflected in the water (1814), and a ship-launching (1815).

The end of the Napoleonic wars in 1815 coincided with the decline of Dibdin's management. Indeed he makes a statement that 'Theatres (in London, at least) prosper most during War . . . As soon as the Peace was announced, our receipts suddenly fell off to a very serious degree' *(Memoirs, p. 119)*. The Dog Bruin came briefly to the rescue in 1816. Full houses returned for what has become perhaps Dibdin's best-known aqua-drama, *Philip and his Dog, or Where's the Child?* The culminating rescue by the excellent and sagacious Bruin was to jump into the water and save a drowning child. In the next season even the Dog Bruin failed to appeal to the jaded Regency appetite. During the last three seasons before Dibdin gave up the management in 1819 the tank was only used sporadically.

While the period between 1804 and 1816 at the Sadler's Wells 'Aquatic Theatre' was undoubtedly the crest of the wave for water drama in the English theatre, there were repeated attempts in the years that followed to catch an audience with tank plays and hydraulic effects of one sort and another. A few examples can suffice.

Dibdin's successors at Sadler's Wells maintained the water tradition for a few years. Howard Payne presented in *Albert and Elmira, or the Dumb Boy and his Horse* (1820) an equestrian and aquatic melodrama in which there was a fight on horseback in the water. Egerton in 1823 put on at least three water-shows, one being based on the 'Bounty' escapade and another introducing the 'evolutions' on the water of an Eskimo and his wife.[28] The impact was fading, though. *The Theatrical Magazine* reviewed *The Brazen Water-Tower* of 1824 with disappointment:

The last scene represented a lake of real water, but we think this scene as now managed is not near so effective as Mr Dibdin used to make it during the time he had the management of the house: his foaming cascades, cataracts and waterfalls were indeed 'most refreshing', as Leigh Hunt would express it.[29]

After this it seems that the tank in this theatre fell into disuse. It may have been instrumental in the favourite hydraulic effect of real fountains which flowed in *Giselle* at Sadler's Wells in 1841.[30] Henry Crabb Robinson, going to see Samuel Phelps's *Pericles* during the Wells's next cycle of grandeur, thought in 1854 that the tank was still there, even if neglected: 'After taking my tea I went to the Theatre which still seemingly has real water.'[31]

Hydraulic demonstrations continued in popularity during the nineteenth century, and featured in entertainments given by one R. Morris (for some years Dibdin's property-man) and others at the Lyceum and Astley's as well as Sadler's Wells between 1803 and 1805. At Vauxhall Gardens there was a Hydraulic Temple in 1821 with revolving columns and chains of buckets. There were further displays in 1823 by Morris, whom Charles Dibdin, writing in 1830, describes as 'now attached to the establishment at Vauxhall Gardens' (*Memoirs*, p. 67), and in 1828 by Cocks who gave an 'Hydroptic Exhibition'. At the Coburg in 1828 Morris presented hydraulics displaying 'jets d'eaux of real water, Chinese and horizontal fountains', and also stars and feathers. In 1829 Clarkson Stanfield's diorama of *Virginia Water* at Drury Lane included 'hydraulic apparatus' apparently capable of discharging thirty-nine tons of water.[32]

Morris and Clarkson Stanfield came together for Moncrieff's ineffable *Cataract of the Ganges*, lavishly presented by Elliston at Drury Lane in 1823. Stanfield's Indian architecture and costume gained full credit. Morris's cascade was praised, though one reviewer expressed a minority opinion: 'It was something like the pouring of a good teapot, only flatter . . . We ourselves could have walked up the fall in pumps, and not have wetted the upper leathers.' The incline needed to be reasonable for the sake of the horse which nightly made its way up the cataract. Public opinion and most reviewers were enthusiastic. After all, in the words of Elliston's recent biographer, '*The Cataract* has one of the best *deus ex machina* finales since

Medea. An exit on horseback up a cataract, with fire raging all around, is a tough one to beat.'[33]

The Cataract of the Ganges seems to be the cascade play which made the most mark. It was as popular in the provinces as in London. If they had not already installed water facilities, provincial houses put them in for this play. Kathleen Barker describes how the water for the Bristol Theatre Royal's *Cataract of the Ganges* was provided by the Sun and Norwich Union Fire Brigades. Provincial theatres continued to present occasional 'real water' shows. From Miss Barker again we learn that 'Professor Johnson, the Man-Fish' toured with a swimming display in the 1880s. At Bristol in 1890, also, amongst the elaborate water effects advertised for *Saved From the Streets*, 'A portion of the Stage converted into a Huge Tank' is taken almost for granted.[34]

Aquatic plays, and displays, continued to be given in theatres up and down the country until the outbreak of the First World War. Then the rise of film took the extravagance out of theatrical illusion. Even so, tank plays have made occasional appearances up to the present day. *Pyjama Tops* at the Whitehall Theatre during the early 1970s showed that 'real' water drama is with us still. Ship-shape it may not be, any more; but Bristol-fashion it demonstrably is.[35] Yet for a long time critics have found it difficult to take real water seriously. A satirical note was already creeping into reviews in the latter part of the nineteenth century. Here is the critic in *Fun* for 11 August 1866 (was it W. S. Gilbert?): 'Often as real water has been introduced into stage scenery, it has never been introduced more successfully than in the new Alhambra ballet, *The Sports of Diana*. The effect is really lovely, and should be seen by everyone who takes pleasure in washing his hands and face.' George Bernard Shaw announced to the world in January 1896:

I have lived to see *The Colleen Bawn* with real water in it . . . The real water lacks the translucent cleanliness of the original article, and destroys the illusion of Eily's drowning and Myles na Coppaleen's header to a quite amazing degree; but the spectacle of the two performers taking a call before the curtain, sopping wet, and bowing with a miserable enjoyment of the applause, is one which I shall remember with a chuckle while life remains.[36]

Shaw's clarity of perception helps us to identify the dramatic ineffectuality of over-doing the 'realism' on stage. Theatre is an art, and works through artifice. It seems necessary not only for the actors but also for the scenery to partake in an act of mimesis. Though no one would deny that it can create its own range of diverting

spectacles, the introduction of real water on stage appears to dispel
rather than enhance the essential dramatic illusion. Perhaps the
final word should be that real water in the theatre may be fun, but
it is not theatre.

NOTES

1 H. W. Fairman, *The Triumph of Horus* (London, 1974), pp. 35, 47–50.
2 *Enciclopedia dello Spettacolo* (11 vols., Rome, 1954–68), s.v. 'Naumachia'
   (vol. 7).
3 Richard Southern, *The Medieval Theatre in the Round*, 2nd (rev.) edn
   (London, 1975).
4 Two versions exist of Hubert Cailleau's coloured frontispiece for the Valenciennes play, both in the Bibliothèque Nationale. The two versions may be
   seen, respectively, in Cesare Molinari, *Theatre through the Ages* (London,
   1975), p. 95, and Bamber Gascoigne, *World Theatre* (London, 1968),
   pl. X. The vessel afloat on 'la mer' is differently rigged in each case.
5 [Robert Laneham], *Captain Cox, his Ballads and Books*, ed. F. J. Furnivall
   (London, 1871), pp. 6–7, 33–5.
6 David M. Bergeron, *English Civic Pageantry 1558–1642* (London, 1971),
   passim; W. W. Greg *et al.* (eds.), *Collections vol. III*, Malone Society Re-
   prints (Oxford, 1954), p. xxvii; David H. Horne, *The Life and Minor Works
   of George Peele* (New Haven and London, 1952), pp. 74n and 214–19.
   Extravagant water-pageants took place on continental Europe at this time;
   see, for example, A. M. Nagler, *Theatre Festivals of the Medici* (New Haven
   and London, 1964).
7 G. C. D. Odell, *Shakespeare from Betterton to Irving* (2 vols., New York,
   1966), vol. 1, pp. 175 and 193.
8 Fred Majdalany, *The Red Rocks of Eddystone* (London, 1959), pp. 33–4
   and 68.
9 W. J. Macqueen Pope, *Theatre Royal, Drury Lane* (London, 1945), p. 216.
   See also Charles Beecher Hogan, *The London Stage Part Five, 1776–1800*
   (3 vols., Carbondale, 1968), vol. 3, pp. 1638 and 1643; and Oscar Sherwin,
   Uncorking Old Sherry (London 1960), pp. 267–8.
10 James Boaden, *Memoirs of the Life of John Philip Kemble* (2 vols., London,
   1825), vol. 2, p. 123.
11 *Professional and Literary Memoirs of Charles Dibdin the Younger*, ed. George
   Speaight (London, Society for Theatre Research, 1956), p. 59. Mr Speaight's
   meticulous edition of Dibdin's memoirs (hereafter cited in the body of the
   text as *Memoirs*) is the major source for information about aqua-drama at
   Sadler's Wells Theatre. Research for this paper has included reference to
   the Sadler's Wells material in the Finsbury Public Library, Islington (where
   I have been much helped by the Assistant Librarian, Miss Dawson), and in
   the Percival Collection in the British Library.
12 The uncurtailed paper presented by the writer to the Kent Conference in
   1977 goes into more detail on this topic. A copy of the original paper has
   been deposited at the Finsbury Public Library (reference section).

13 V. C. Clinton-Baddeley, *The Burlesque Tradition in the English Theatre after 1660* (London, 1952), p. 77.

14 Cecil Price (ed.), *The Dramatic Works of Richard Brinsley Sheridan* (2 vols., Oxford, 1973), vol. 2, p. 475.

15 Hogan, *The London Stage Part Five*, vol. 3, p. 1570.

16 Michael Booth, *English Melodrama* (London, 1965), pp. 99—117. See also Clinton-Baddeley, *The Burlesque Tradition*, pp. 98—107; George Rowell, *The Victorian Theatre: a Survey* (Oxford, 1956), pp. 47—50; and Edward J. Dent, *A Theatre for Everybody* (London, 1945), pp. 15—16.

17 Richard Armstrong, *The Merchantmen* (London, 1969), pp. 33—4 and 47—8.

18 Some indication of the growth of 'romantic' scenery, including water-scapes, at this time may be found in the toy theatre scenes; a selection is reprinted in George Speaight, *The History of the English Toy Theatre* (London, 1969). Collections of designs by the original scene-painters are held in the British Theatre Museum and the British Library. Less well-known but commendably accessible is the 'Grieve Collection', a fascinating hoard of designs by the Grieve family of scene-painters in the Senate House Library of the University of London (secondary strong room).

19 Robert Wilkinson, *Londina Illustrata* (2 vols., London, 1819), vol. 2, p. 75; Percival Collection relating to Sadler's Wells Theatre, vol. 3, folios 164—7 (British Library, pressmark Crach. 1. Tab. 4. b. 4).

20 Denis Arundell, *The Story of Sadler's Wells* (London, 1965), p. 72.

21 Clement Scott, *The Drama of Yesterday and Today* (London, 1899), vol. 2, p. 177.

22 Cuttings in Percival Collection, vol. 3, folio 164.

23 David Mayer, *Harlequin in his Element: English Pantomime 1806—1836* (Cambridge, Mass., 1969), p. 96.

24 Charles Dibdin the Younger, Ωκεανξια, *or The Siege of Gibraltar* (London, 1804) (British Library, pressmark 11602.ff.24 (6)).

25 Arundell, *Sadler's Wells*, pp. 61—2.

26 *Memoirs of Joseph Grimaldi*, ed. Boz, rev. Charles Whitehead, 2nd edn (London, 1846), part 2, p. 10.

27 Percival Collection, vol. 3, folio 171.

28 Arundell, *Sadler's Wells*, pp. 98, 101.

29 Cutting in the Finsbury Library Collection relating to Sadler's Wells Theatre (press-cuttings etc., box 13).

30 R. Mander and J. Mitchenson, *The Theatres of London* (London, 1975), p. 275.

31 Eluned Brown (ed.), *The London Theatre 1811—1866* (London, Society for Theatre Research, 1966), p. 199.

32 I am indebted to Miss Sybil Rosenfeld for supplying most of the information in this paragraph.

33 Christopher Murray, *Robert William Elliston, Manager* (London, Society for Theatre Research, 1975), pp. 103—4.

34 Kathleen Barker, *The Theatre Royal, Bristol, 1766—1966* (London, Society for Theatre Research, 1974), pp. 95, 173.

35 Mr Paul Raymond's topless lady-aquabats in *Pyjama Tops* have given the

1970s look to the stage-tank. Another aspect of the tradition is that of the flooded arena. John Carthew has told me how thrilled he was as a boy in the early years of the Second World War to see an enactment of the *Graf Spee* affair in the flooded ring of the Blackpool Circus. Clive Barker has tales to tell of the flooding of the stage of the Sunderland Theatre. I am informed by George Speaight that the annual Blackpool Circus still floods the ring for a hydraulic performance as the climax to the show.

36 George Bernard Shaw, *Our Theatres in the Nineties* (London, 1932), vol. 2, p. 28.

Equestrian drama and the circus

Antony D. Hippisley Coxe

The term 'equestrian drama' means a play enacted by horses and
riders, usually presented both in the ring and on the stage of a
permanent amphitheatre. It is basically a bastard entertainment, the
result of a misalliance between the theatre and the circus, two types
of spectacle whose fundamental principles are very different. The
offspring did enlarge the base line of the theatre although, in this
country, I submit it actually inhibited the development of the
circus. But before we consider this naive, colourful, melodramatic
and, above all, popular entertainment, I would like to deal briefly
with the basic characteristics and relevant history of the parent
spectacles, particularly those concerning the circus. Whereas the
underlying principles of the theatre have been discussed ever since
Aristotle set out his Unities, few have attempted to analyse the
attributes of the circus. One, however, who has published a critical
comparison of stage and ring spectacles is Pierre Bost,[1] whose study
fifty years ago led me to try to develop the basic principles he laid
down.

In the traditional theatre the audience is confronted with make-
believe on the stage. The spectacle is seen against a representational
background. Go backstage and the illusion is lost; all you will see is
the plain, ungilded, reverse side of the proscenium and unpainted
canvas. It is like looking at the back of a picture. In the circus there
is no scenery, no backstage; the spectacle can be seen from all sides,
like sculpture. Because the audience holds the spectacle in its midst,
there are eyes all round to see that there is no make-believe.

The theatre is interpretative — and therefore an art; the circus is
demonstrative — and simply a craft. I think it fair to say that the
theatre is a spectacle of illusion, and the circus a spectacle of actuality.
After all, jugglers *actually do* keep six clubs turning in mid-air, and
a flyer *really does* turn three somersaults between leaving the bar
of his trapeze and reaching the hands of his catcher. One could call

the circus a spectacle of reality; but that word has metaphysical overtones which might complicate a very simple concept.

The ring is an ideal place to demonstrate physical skills and prowess — agility, dexterity, strength and balance — because the encircling audience can be assured that a difficult feat really has been accomplished. So when in the eighteenth century the London fairs went into a decline,[2] showmen and fairground performers, such as acrobats, jugglers, strong men and rope-dancers, found the circus ring a better place in which to perform than their own booths.

The ring was invented when a trick-rider found that by making his horse gallop in a circle, while standing on its back, he could use the centrifugal force to help him keep his balance. Philip Astley (1742—1814) is usually credited with this innovation in 1769, and his amphitheatre, on the Surrey side of Westminster Bridge, is usually recognised as the birthplace of the circus. One of his company, Hughes, set up a rival establishment, the Royal Circus (afterwards the Surrey Theatre), nearby. Competition was fierce, each striving to introduce new attractions, such as *ombres chinoises* and fireworks, to draw the crowds. In 1782 Hughes added a stage alongside his ring. Two years later Astley followed suit. From then on most London circuses — the Rotunda at Vauxhall, the Holborn Amphitheatre, right down to the Hippodrome — combined ring and stage, placing the two different types of spectacle in uneasy proximity. Not one of these buildings lasted. They failed as circuses, because the proscenium prevented the audience from surrounding the spectacle; and they became either proper theatres, music halls, boxing clubs or cinemas.

It was, however, this combination of stage and ring that led to the rise of equestrian drama.

The earliest *scenes played*, as distinct from *feats presented*, in the circus ring were comedy riding acts, such as *The Tailor Riding to Brentford* and *The Flying Wardrobe*. Many readers will have seen in some circus an apparently tipsy yokel insisting on trying to ride. His ridiculous antics gradually give way to an accomplished routine, and, having divested himself of numerous waistcoats, he eventually stands on the horse's back in all his sequined glory, the principal rider in the show. Andrew Ducrow (1793—1842) developed such acts into straight scenes on horseback. In *The Sailor's Return or the British Tar*, for example, he stood on the back of a horse dressed up like a battleship, with gunports along its flanks and anchors at its neck, and he enacted leaving home, being drilled in a training ship, enjoying his first cruise,

110

climbing the rigging, heaving the lead, fearing an approaching storm, piping all hands to quarters, taking part in a naval engagement, loading and firing a gun, carrying a wounded mate to the cockpit, celebrating victory over the enemy, grieving over the death of his mate, committing his body to the deep, receiving orders for home, arriving in port, being paid off, buying trousers for his son and a pinafore for his daughter, and, finally, taking a coach for home — all this as the animal cantered round the ring (see illustration).

Similar scenes were built round *The God of Fame, The Chinese Enchanter, The Indian Hunter, The Greek Chieftain, The Yorkshire Foxhunter* and many others. In *The Carnival of Venice* he played six different characters on the back of his horse. Only one of his many acts is still seen in the circus today: *The Courier of St Petersburg*. I believe that the reason it alone has survived is simply because it requires more equestrian skill and less histrionic talent than the rest.

Such numbers became very popular during the first half of the last century. People became accustomed to seeing performers acting

Ducrow in *The Vicissitudes of a Tar.* From the author's collection.

on horseback. At first, performances on the stage and in the ring had been kept separate (except for spectacles such as pony races at Astley's); but it was not long before the two spectacles blended, although dialogue was forbidden and words had to be sung, mimed or displayed on banners.

In 1800, Astley presented *Quixote and Sancho, or Harlequin Warrior*, in which, for the first time, two squadrons of horse appeared on the stage. Astley's rival Hughes, at the Royal Circus, was determined to go one better and in *The Magic Flute, or Harlequin Champion*, an equine actor tore down a banner because it was an insult to his master. The horses in *The Tailor Riding to Brentford* had lain down, jumped through windows and pushed actors through doors with their noses, but this, one feels, was merely an act built around their ordinary tricks. *The Magic Flute*, on the other hand, contained stage 'business' for which a horse had to be specially trained. It must have been very useful to include action by a dumb animal when speaking lines were forbidden.

Harlequin Mameluke, or the British in Egypt points the way to the military spectacle, and it is here that equestrian drama really comes into its own.

The Afghan War, The Burmese War, The Conquest of Magdala, The Destruction of the Bastille, The Invasion of Russia, The Siege of Sargossa, The Storming of Delhi, and battles galore from Alma to Waterloo were just a few of these military spectacles. Equestrian drama had recreated actual events on several occasions since 1789, when *The Storming of the Bastille* was reenacted on 5 August, barely three weeks after the event. The Crimean War came when equestrian drama at Astley's was riding high on the wave of popularity. And here we find it again almost taking on the role of the news-reel. The actual battle was fought on 20 September 1854; Cooke was reenacting it at Astley's on 23 October with 400 extras, and for the production ring and stage were joined not merely at each side as had become customary, but as A. H. Saxon has pointed out[3] all the way across. In fact, the ring had become a sunken apron. This spectacular production ran for four months.[4]

Even grand opera was played on horseback. Several of Shakespeare's plays were turned into equestrian drama, including *Macbeth*, *Othello* and *Henry IV*. In *Richard III*, White Surrey stole the show. Horses did tend to get rave reviews; human actors were summarily dismissed. An excerpt from a press notice of *Timour the Tartar* reads: 'The exertions of the horses have a wonderful effect. The white horse which carries the heroine (Mrs H. Johnson) plays admirably. He kneels, leaps, tumbles, dances, fights, dashes into water and up precipices, in a very superior style of acting, and completely astonished the audience.'[5]

Timour the Tartar was one of the three most popular equestrian dramas, the others being *The Battle of Waterloo* and *Mazeppa*. Altogether over 250 different pieces were produced in France and England, mostly in the capital cities, but sometimes in permanent or semi-permanent amphitheatres in provincial towns. W. and G. Pinder, for instance, presented *Thalaba, the Destroyer*, in Middlesborough in 1868. It had first been produced at the Coburg in 1823. I doubt that the circus production was anything like the original. The Pinders billed it as *Thalaba, the Destroyer, or the Princess of Mingrelia*, and that alternative title belongs to *Timour the Tartar*. Maybe neither production kept very closely to Southey's original poem; neither Mahareb nor Zohak appears in the circus list of characters. In such productions one suspects that plays were spatchcocked and untold liberties taken with the text to ensure that there was plenty of action and scope for the horses. Writing was not important. When *The Conquest of Magdala* was produced, the author was accused of taking his previous piece, *The Battle of the Alma*, and merely turning the Russians into Abyssians.

The construction of *The Battle of Waterloo*, first produced in 1824, is perhaps typical of equestrian drama. Act I presents Napoleon reviewing his troops and ends in a bloody skirmish at Ligny to capture a bridge. The French are successful but Blucher has his horse shot from under him. In Act II, Wellington reviews his army, and we witness the Battle of Quatre-Bras, a victory for the Allies. Score, one all; so the scene is set for Act III, the Grand Finale. Such is the bare outline, but it is festooned with romantic and comic sub-plots. A Prussian lady, with her small son, follows her husband to the front. Mary Cameron, disguised as a soldier, joins her sweetheart who is serving in the 71st Highland Regiment. On the French side there is a foppish hairdresser, Maladroit (originally played by Amherst, who wrote the piece), and on the British side there is an Irish biddy of a camp follower called Molly Malone.

The delightful absurdity and ingenuity of equestrian drama can be seen in the story concerning a revival of *The Battle of Waterloo*, when even horses were in such short supply that Wellington appeared in Act II riding the same animal that Napoleon had ridden in Act I. There was a shout from the gallery of 'Where did you get that horse?'

113

When Napoleon next appeared to address his troops he was on foot, but ended his exhortation with these unscripted words: 'But what I am most proud of in ye is that by the prowess of your glorious arms, you have rescued from the hated thraldom of the blood-thirsty British soldiery my favourite charger, who has, on so many occasions, carried me — and ye — to victory.' And the same old horse was led in.[6]

Mazeppa is chiefly remembered because of Adah Isaacs Menken, although there were plenty of greater performers in the title role, mostly men, but sometimes women, both before and after. These were seen not only in England and American but in France and Italy as well.[7] Yet to most people *Mazeppa* still means Menken. Her appearance in public and her private life caused a scandal, although much of it was a well-engineered publicity stunt.[8] In these full-frontal days it seems extraordinary that a woman whose legs were not only covered in fleshings but also by a tunic 'which descended towards the knee', should have been considered shocking; but then she also *smoked in public*. The play was originally based on Byron's poem which describes how Mazeppa, a page at the court of the King of Poland, falls in love with the young wife of an elderly Polish Count, who finds out and punishes Mazeppa by strapping him to the back of a wild Ukrainian stallion which is then set loose. The horse spends two nights and two days galloping through forests, up rivers, over mountains and across deserts, pursued by wolves at one point, and, towards the end of the poem, dies of exhaustion, with Mazeppa still strapped to its back, under the hovering wings of a vulture. However, Mazeppa is rescued by a band of Cossacks and eventually leads an attack on the old Count and destroys his castle. Of course the story was adapted and embellished almost out of recognition for equestrian drama, but the wild ride remained, the horse zigzagging up a series of inclined planes, pursued by cut-out wolves, while a property vulture dangled on a piece of string overhead.

When Lord George Sanger and his brother John took over Astley's in 1871, they did not fall into the same trap as William Cooke, who lost £40,000 in seven years by presenting Shakespeare and grand opera on horseback. They steered equestrian drama towards zoological pantomimes. In one production the cast included three hundred girls, two hundred men, fifteen elephants, nine camels, and fifty-two horses as well as ostriches, emus, pelicans, kangaroos, reindeer, hog deer, acis deer, brahma bulls, water buffalos, chamois, ovdod

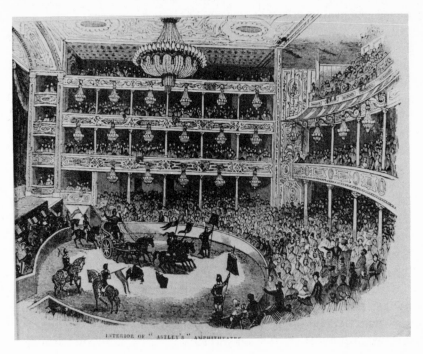

Astley's Amphitheatre. From the author's collection at the Theatre Museum, London.

moufflons and two lions on leads. Sanger gleefully added that all this completely hid the whole of the scenic artist's work.[9]

In this they were following the pattern of the circus proper. The history of the circus to date has been marked by three distinct influences: first, that of the horse; then, following Leotard's invention of the flying trapeze and Blondin's exploits on the high wire, an increasing influence came from acrobats and gymnasts; which in turn was partially eclipsed by the wild animal acts, which followed Hagenbeck's gentling system of training. Neither acrobats nor wild animals, however, completely usurped the horse and rider in the ring.

But there were those who deplored the waning of the influence of the horse on stage. Dutton Cook wrote in 1876,

The noble animal is to be seen occasionally on the boards, but he is cast for small parts only, is little better than a four-footed supernumerary . . . Plays are not now written for him. He is no longer required to evince fidelity and devotion of his nature by knocking at street doors, rescuing a prisoned master,

115

defending oppressed innocence or dying in the centre of the stage to slow music.[10]

So true equestrian drama faded away. It had contributed greatly in keeping Astley's Amphitheatre the centre of popular entertainment in London for more than sixty years. It might well have lived longer had it followed the same path as its French equivalent.

In France the circus developed along lines very similar to those found in England. Rowdyism led to the decline of the Paris fairs. But here the protectionist attitude of the patent theatres extended to the acrobats and rope-dancers. When Astley tried to include feats of agility and balance in his programme, he was told that all his performances must take place on horseback. So he built a platform which was supported on the backs of a number of horses. Here his acrobats performed 'on horseback'.[11]

It was not long before a real stage appeared alongside the ring in the circuses of Paris. This, however, did not last. By the middle of the last century circuses had reverted to their purest form without a stage, so that the seating encompassed the ring and was broken only in the lower tiers by the ring doors. This was the pattern for Le Cirque d'Eté, Le Cirque d'Hiver (which still survives), Le Nouveau Cirque, Le Cirque de Paris and the enchanting Cirque Medrano which lasted until the 1960s. Here the true circus developed more surely and was better appreciated for being unencumbered.

It was popular with all classes, income brackets and age groups. It became as fashionable as the opera, and, what is more important, it was taken just as seriously. There is a story of how one clubman asked another if he yet seen Caroline Loyo, a brilliant equestrienne, riding her new bay. 'No, not yet', was the reply, 'You see, I've been away in Forence, visiting the Pitti Palace.' This brought forth a stern rebuke. 'Sir! When Caroline rides a new horse, one does not go gallivanting off to Italy to look at Pitti Palaces!'[12] That continental circus patrons showed a subtler appreciation of the finer points of circus techniques than we did can be seen from the number of English performers who left England to work in Europe, particularly riders and clowns.

Of course the French enjoyed equestrian drama; but they soon realised that one does not go to the circus to see a play, or to the theatre to see a circus. As neither stage, nor ring — nor, indeed, both together — provided a suitable setting for this kind of production, they built hippodromes with vast arenas where hippodrama could be

116

produced on an epic scale. All together, from 1845 to 1907, Paris
could boast of a succession of five hippodromes and two suburban
arenas. In 1847, at the Hippodrome de l'Etoile, *The Field of the Cloth
of Gold* was presented in an arena 104 metres long and 68 metres
wide, with an orchestra of 100 musicians, before an audience of 12,000.
The Hippodrome d'Alma arena was smaller, 84 metres by 48 metres,
but it could be covered by a sliding roof. Here the stage machinery
and production facilities were remarkable. In the production of *Joan
of Arc*, the arena was surrounded by a semi-transparent 'wall', painted
to represent the Old Market Place in Rouen. This was so lit that the
spectators could see through the 'wall' immediately in front of them,
but not through that which lay on the opposite side of the arena.[13]
Even this production was surpassed by *Nero*, in which Christians
appeared to be thrown to live lions. The audience was protected
from these beasts by a cage 4.5 metres high and 185 metres in diameter.
It weighed 32,000 kilograms and cost 200,000 francs. It was set in
position by sixteen lifts in exactly one minute. That production had
a cast of 396 men and 158 women; and every performance ended
with 'Rome in Flames'.

Unfortunately it was not until true equestrian drama had disappeared
that we in England built arenas on anything like the same scale. Its
successors were *Buffalo Bill's Wild West Show* and Frank Fillis's
Savage South Africa, which were presented in arenas like Olympia.
The billing for the latter might well have referred to one of Sanger's
pantomimes at Astley's. 'Five hundred zulus, ten families of boers,
400 basuto ponies, 80 buck, lion, tigers and elephants.

One has only to see the Royal Tournament at Olympia today to
realise how splendid *The Battle of Waterloo* would be in a large
arena. To my mind the hybrid building of the amphitheatres did a
disservice to equestrian drama as well as to the circus. Flamboyant,
heroic, gaudy, but naive and direct in its appeal, so full of bravado
and derring-do, so much larger than life itself, equestrian drama
needed an epic setting — something much bigger than a 42-foot ring
and adjacent stage. How magical a C. B. Cochran production of
Mazeppa at Olympia could have been.

Or should one, perhaps, go to the other end of the scale? After
all, the characters which appear in *Timour the Tartar* and *The
Battle of Waterloo* are still to be seen with all their stylised gestures
and naive charm, cut from the 'penny plain, tuppence coloured'
sheets of juvenile drama. And there also does magic lie.

117

NOTES

1 Pierre Bost, *Le Cirque et le Music-Hall* (Paris, 1931).
2 M. Willson Disher, *Fairs, Circuses and Music Halls* (London, 1942). This author's history of Astley's Amphitheatre, *Greatest Show on Earth* (London, 1937) is also of considerable interest.
3 A. H. Saxon, *Enter Foot and Horse* (New Haven and London, 1968). This excellent history of hippodrama in England and France is both invaluable and unique.
4 See J. S. Bratton 'Theatre of War', this volume.
5 *European Magazine*, May 1811.
6 Errol Sherson, *London's Lost Theatres of the Nineteenth Century* (London, 1925). In this case, the author is quoting Arthur W. Beckett, *Green Room Recollections* (Bristol, 1896).
7 Marian Hannah Winter, 'Popular Theatre and Popular Art', in *Western Popular Theatre*, ed. David Mayer and Kenneth Richards (London, 1977).
8 Bernard Falk, *The Naked Lady: or, Storm over Adah* (London, 1934).
9 'Lord' George Sanger, *Seventy Years a Showman* (London, 1908).
10 Dutton Cook, *A Book of the Play* (London, 1876).
11 Philip Astley, *Astley's System of Equestrian Education*, 7th edn (London, 1802).
12 Baron Charles M. de Vaux, *Les Ecuyers et Ecuyères* (Paris, 1893).
13 Paul Adrian, *Histoire Illustrée des Cirques Parisiens* (Bourg-la-Reine, Seine, 1957).

Theatre of war: the Crimea on the London stage 1854-5

J. S. Bratton

War is a major subject of popular art; its connotations and associated values — the notions of heroism, daring, stoicism, acclaim, victory, comradeship, patriotism — are created, and reinforced, between the sword and the song. When Percy wi' the Douglas met, the job of the singer who reported and immortalised the conflict was comparatively simple. His public expected the details of the fight, and those he gave them were in the expected form, carrying the expected assumptions, and they were accepted as a record of facts. The function of the reporter was not separate from that of the artist: he delivered and shaped reality. When the broadside writer and afterwards the equestrian dramatist created the Battle of Waterloo for public consumption, little had changed. Hard news was brief, or forbiddingly couched in official despatches, and the myth of Napoleon was a much stronger power in the minds of the British public than any desire for dry truth. The voice of the people was still that of the balladeer who wrote 'Not a drum was heard, not a funeral note', rather than that of the *Times* correspondent who failed to report after the Battle of Corunna that Sir John Moore had been killed.

In the middle of the nineteenth century, however, the advent of accurate and fast news reporting affected popular art profoundly. In 1854 the outbreak of the first real war for forty years showed up very sharply the extent and nature of the effect of newspapers upon the older forms, broadside ballads, songs and plays. War was still the province of all popular art; but the role of the balladeer was now fragmented. This paper attempts to record what happened when the advent of the special correspondent and the photographer at the front, and of the electric telegraph, dispelled the illusion of apparently factual reporting created by the popular artist. The balladeers and their successors in the theatres and music halls could not compete with the press in fullness, accuracy or speed of transmission of events; but the concentrating, simplifying lens of popular

119

art was still needed to transmute the war for its audience, and the audience for the war.

During 1854 and 1855 at least twenty-five plays dealing in some way with the war with Russia were produced at, or licensed for, ten London theatres, chiefly Surrey-side or East End houses.[1] At first the plays differed considerably from each other. During the summer of 1854 there was a shift from predominantly comic to predominantly heroic treatments. This seems to be because comedy could more easily be mounted, but also because there were shifts in public feeling about the war, and the progress of events provided varying subject-matter. There was a reciprocal relationship between events, public mood, and theatrical presentation. The diversity of responses continued from the declaration of war, on 28 March, until the Battle of the Alma in September. This was a period of what would now be called phony war: little was happening, and preparations and diplomacy were not enough to catch the popular imagination, though the press and the music hall singers had been trying all year to be thrillingly patriotic about the first British war of the reign. Nothing was now happening, and entertainers cast round for some way of expressing and making capital out of the public interest. They fell back upon existing theatrical modes, both traditional and new-fangled. In the West End the panoramas and magic lantern dissolving views were busily occupied with quasi-informative displays of the seat of war and picturesque representations of Turkish scenery and cities. At the Egyptian Hall the Grand Moving Diorama of Constantinople was now accompanied by a lecture on the war by J. H. Stocqueler, who was later to write the *Battle of the Alma* for Astley's Amphitheatre. Admission to this was one shilling, however, and the minor theatres offered their patrons better value by adapting both the matter and the medium to dramatic ends, in the ways that were expected of them. Spectacular Eastern scenery, whether or not presented by diorama, could be used to make battle-pieces with historical plots vaguely topical, like *The World's War*, presented in April at the Victoria, where the rather deceptive title in fact covered a play about Richard I and the Crusades. At the Surrey, exotic settings were habitually used for stories of freedom fighters defeating tyranny, so there was no difficulty in producing a polished piece called *Iran Safferi, or the Sultan and the Czar* as early as mid April, using the name of a real rebel leader for their usual picturesque hero and his revolutionary adventures.

Attempts to bring the war nearer home were rather slower to develop, since British heroism had not yet had much chance to show itself. One of the first pieces to try it appeared at the Standard, Shoreditch, early in June, and is a clear instance of a theatre falling back upon traditional models. Throughout the century British heroes had been sailors and so the play is not about the East at all, but about the fleet which had been sent, under Sir Charles Napier, to attack the Russians in the Baltic. It was called *The Storming of Hango, or the Baltic Fleet*. Napier's force had done little that was dramatic, and had certainly not stormed the fortress of Hango; the play is entirely fictional, a compilation of commonplaces which shows signs of very hasty construction, or possibly of a playwright having difficulties in matching his means to his subject: it begins with a young officer in love with his admiral's daughter, but ends with the burning of an unnamed fort, without ever resolving the love interest. Bombast, slapstick shipboard comedy, sturdy tars and a spectacular finale are offered in a mixture which does not differ substantially from any nautical piece of the previous decade, except for some very clumsy speeches attempting to fit in reference to current events.

These presentations profited by the interest in the war, rather than attempting seriously to come to terms with it; so it is fitting that the longest running war play of these months was a burlesque which opened at the Adelphi in April, called *The Overland Journey to Constantinople, as undertaken by Lord Bateman, with interesting particulars of the fair Sophia*, which was about the war in the theatre rather than the war in the East. It begins with a very funny introduction about the panoramas as a managerial device for avoiding 'Keeping troops extensive, Who come on Saturdays and come expensive . . .'[2]

As involvement in the war gathered momentum, the theatres still dealt with the subject, using existing techniques of presentation and according to the conventions already established, with little regard for actual events. Spectacle and exotic settings were turned to comic ends or backed up the familiar plot and character patterns of domestic and nautical melodramas. The central issue was often the fate of the heroine, between a Russian villain and an officer hero; the comic members of the company took on the roles of cheerfully invincible sailors and various other existing types, however improbable in the context. There are several examples of comic Londoners involved in the fighting, such as Peter Poppleton, a salesman who in *The War in Turkey* at the Britannia Saloon vanquishes various Russians with the cry 'Whitechapel needles for ever!', and Sam from Smiffield who sells

121

weal and kidney pies and gets immured in the dungeons of Cara Bey in *The Lion of England and the Eagle of France* at the Victoria. An indispensable and often a central figure is the Irish soldier who, as a *Times* reviewer noted, is in 'every . . . military melodrama . . . the chief representative of the valour and humour of the three king-doms'.[3] The use of this central figure is a significant feature of these plays. Dramatically it is of course necessary to use individuals to focus the action; and it is axiomatic that on the popular stage they should be Other Ranks rather than generals.[4] In this concern for the impact of events upon the humble individual the drama is within the tradition of popular art inherited from earlier forms. The plays were adopting the method of the broadsides which continued alongside them: H. Such printed a ballad called 'The Battle of the Alma'[5] in which a single stanza about the conflict itself is used to set the scene for the story of a soldier's wife and child and their attempts to return home after he dies on the field. The first plays were building apparently topical dramas out of such materials, not only from a lack of new ideas or methods, but because their function in relating the war to their audiences was to put it into terms which could be recognised and to provide, through characters who would be welcomed and identified with, ways to understand and participate in the events. For this purpose they had a cast of Irish batman, Scottish sergeant, superhumanly strong and cheerful Jack Tar, cunning non-combatant cockney, faithful wife with children and shrewish woman sutler, directly drawn from or closely based upon familiar types. For the newspapers, reporting of events was the first priority; but for the popular artist, events could be invented, or more or less ignored. What mattered was the response to the idea of the war and its effects on people.

The new material did create certain difficulties and new demands, however, and put the established forms and stereotypes under pressure. At first this was destructive rather than creative: the awkward relation-ship between fact and fiction in *The Storming of Hango*, for example, makes for a weak and shapeless play. But gradually the theatres came to terms with what they conceived of as the important aspects of the new subject-matter, and new formulae of plot and character, formed according to the old priorities and by the old processes, came into being. How little this process owed to individual inspiration and how clearly it was a function of the whole of popular drama can be seen from the way in which the same issues appear in all the plays, the same selection of events is dealt with, and the same new scenes, routines and characters appear, often practically simultaneously.

There were from the outset certain modifications which obviously had to be made to the established popular attitudes, to meet the new circumstances of war. The most pressing of these was the revision of the character of the French, who, it was constantly pointed out, were now our Allies for the first time for four hundred years. There was a whole play, *The United Service of England and France*, at the Strand in July, about how difficult it was to shed ingrained attitudes to people whom forty years ago one was taught to think of as cannibals. The new situation is thought of as progress, however; in this play a character reflects that 'the railways and steamers have done this for us' as he contemplates the new alliance. In *The Storming of Hango* one is even less convinced when Boatswain Ben, a typical xenophobic Jack Tar, asserts 'I always had a sort of sneaking kindness for mount-seer'; but play after play rehearses the lesson that all victories are Allied victories, and that the French have a new national character, and are lively, bold and dashing, their officers romantic and kind to horses. The *vivandière* was a useful character in this, being a new phenomenon and useful for love interest and national dance routines. A recurring scene was one in which a Scot and an English or Irish soldier drunkenly swapped uniforms with a Frenchman. Occasionally a Turk was also included, newly introduced to the good fellowship of drink.

The establishment of a national stereotype for the Russians was less emotionally difficult than the rehabilitation of the French, but it had less material to go on. At first the only recourse is a joke about their infantry and their prisoners being fed on candles and train-oil; the Cossack, an erstwhile ally, is presented as the respected enemy. There is a tendency to avoid the problem by presenting instead of Russians members of various subject races, especially Poles and Circassians, as eager to escape the oppression of Russia for the liberation of England and France; there is even a repeated suggestion that all Russians except the Tsar and his agents are oppressed and forced to fight under the knout. The women in the enemy camp, including in some cases the wife of Prince Menshikov, are often presented as being on the side of the Allies. Gallant Russian officers with names like Romanoff express their faith in 'England's rule to offer a home to all who seek it in the hour of peril' (*The Storming of Hango*) or are rescued wounded from the field by British officers who turn out to be their brothers-in-law (*The Battle of Inkermann*, by Dibdin Pitt, at the Pavilion, December 1854.) The characteristics eventually fixed upon as expressive of the evil enemy were first the vice of skulking behind ramparts and refusing to come out and fight, and then that of lying. Prince Menshikov became Mendaciakoff or Mendaxikoff, who falsified all news of encounters with the enemy including the retreat of the French from Moscow in 1812, and his officers were pompous asses with comic names such as Stroganoff or Gruffenough.

The reports of Russian falsification of news came through the columns of *The Times*: and in several other ways the stage drew upon aspects of the conflict stressed by the press. There were scenes in several plays which both demonstrated and spelt out the need for soldiers' wives and children to be cared for, which was a cause taken up by the press and the fashionable world immediately the troops had embarked; and later the appeal started by *The Times* for money to fund the hospitals in the Crimea and at Scutari was written into plays. As a dramatic framework for dealing with the events of the war began to be worked out, the plays proved to be surprisingly sensitive and adaptable to changing public mood, and to new circumstances reported by Russell in *The Times*. At the beginning of October, for example, *The Times* described the erratic efforts of the post office at the seat of war, and by 11 October Astley's had submitted a play to be licensed in which a character mentions 'the postal arrangements, so much complained of'. The theatre even seconded certain of the complaints of the press about the conduct of the war, as these emerged: there is a scene in both the war plays licensed for Astley's in 1855 in which British Other Ranks complain about the difficulty of getting promotion, and in one a Russian is congratulated on being so fortunate as to be in an army where he had been promoted on merit: 'If you had been in some countries I could name, you would have continued a Subaltern unless an old Aunt had died and left you a few hundred — family interests and old age are the grand qualifications on the other side' (*Fall of Sebastopol*). The inclusion in Astley's plays of this grievance, which is essentially part of the middle-class attack upon the inefficient aristocratic control of the army revealed by the war, suggests the broadness of the base of the popular audience.

Much had obviously been learnt, between the staging in April and May of plays like *The Storming of Hango* and *The War in Turkey*, pretending to deal with the current conflict but in which dramatic effect comes from the evocation of old responses by the old means, and the coming of plays in which the old methods were significantly adapted and brought to embody the events of the war in dramatic form, so that detailed references to current preoccupations can be accommodated with no sense of strain. The plays which succeed best in this were staged in the last quarter of 1854 and early in 1855. Other factors beside the rapid learning by experiment of the previous months contribute to their superiority. After the months of waiting for something to happen, during which public interest in the war was fluctuating and uncertain, the embarkation of the Allied troops for Sebastopol early in September stirred the attention of Britain, and anticipation of action reached a high pitch before the news of the Alma broke. After that victory, tension increased rather than relaxed for the rest of the year, as daily expectation of the fall of Sebastopol was intensified by news of increasingly desperate battles.

The rapid ways in which the tidings of war were carried back to Britain added greatly to the sense of urgency, and also to a curiously wide-spread self-consciousness on the part of the waiting public. This manifested itself in the repeated use of dramatic metaphor by commentators and reporters, which in turn stirred a complexity of feelings, including guilt as well as fervour. Interest was keen, sympathy and patriotism were whipped up by first-hand reports and photographs of the camps and the battles, but that very interest was in some sense felt to be shameful. Earlier in the summer it had resulted in a rage for Alma polkas and Turkish gallops, and the press had savagely castigated young ladies for dancing amid the bones of the dead. The apparently equally heartless theatrical metaphor was irresistible in their own reporting, however: the *Times* leader of 12 October 1854, for example, speaks of the British public as onlookers at the spectacle of war, a drama so far rather tedious but about to come to its catastrophe. Russell was conscious of his role as creator of fictional characters: looking back he said that he had not at first grasped 'the fact that I had it in my power to give a halo of glory to some unknown warrior by putting his name in type'. When he realised the effect of his reporting he tried to use it justly, but he was aware of the theatrical dimension of the war he relayed: speaking for instance of the behaviour expected of generals, he asked rhetorically whether they should always be 'shouting "Follow me!" to their legions, or taking snuff à la Gomersal and Napoleon, in extreme military crises in front of their battalions'.[6] The news that Russian ladies from Sebastopol watched the battles like a show was greeted in England with revulsion, but British trippers went out East in private yachts to get a better view of the conflict. A cartoon in *Punch* combined the rising tide of concern about the lack of provisions for the troops with the notion of the war as a spectacle. It shows a group of soldiers with a large trunk of food before them, sitting looking down upon a plain, and is captioned 'The Theatre of War. A Private Box for England's dear boys before Sebastopol!' (vol. 27 (1854), p. 252). It would seem that all the modern problems about the interrelation of wars and the reporting of wars were present in embryo in the Crimea; it is perhaps no coincidence that, as M. Van Wyk Smith suggests,[7] the war produced one of the last great heroic battle-poems in English before the ramification of mass communication made that vision impossible to sustain. News reporting was eventually to render stage military spectacles obsolete; but at this juncture, as its recurring metaphors of the stage suggest, it stimulated demand for them. The public read of the spectacle of war, and saw lavishly produced pictures of it: the *Illustrated London News* published pictures of battles, officers, nurses and places as well as maps and diagrams and floods of patriotic songs and pieces for the piano. During 1854 people had grown familiar with these images and with the new stereotypes of national characteristics which were embodied in the reporting as well as in the plays. The suspense, and the speed of events from September 1854 onwards, held them in a state of emotionally charged attention. Material and audience were ripe for the entry into the ring of the theatre whose technical capacity far exceeded in resources, experience and expertise that of all who had so far tackled the subject of the war. Astley's was about to mount its first Crimean spectacle.

At Astley's the minor theatre tradition of domestic and nautical melodrama was subordinate to the cultivation of specifically equestrian, military spectacle. The stage, measuring 75 by 101 feet, was one of the largest in London, and accommodated the horses who acted in elaborate dramatic pieces as well as going through circus routines in the ring below. The traditions of the establishment, and its large and expert audience, demanded that if London was to see in the flesh, living and moving, the Crimean battles presented to them in stills by the newspapers, Astley's was the place for it. In *The Times* on 8 September 1854 a reviewer hinted at the possibilities when he asked, 'shall we never have another equestrian classic like *Mazeppa*, or a military spectacle like *The Battle of Waterloo* — something that may effectively employ the really superb stud of Astley's for purposes of

dramatic illustration?' Astley's spectacles took time to mount
and were too expensive to run for a day or two to see if they caught
on, as other theatres did; but as the reviewer wrote, Cooke, the
manager of Astley's, was planning the amphitheatre's entry into
the field of battle. It was in the Crimean plays which he staged that
the specific myths of this war took their dramatic shape, and the
scenes and characters evolved from the old stock were finally fitted
together into a particularised and integrated representation of
events.

The build-up to the Battle of the Alma was almost as confused
and tense at Astley's as in the Crimea. Contradictory accounts of
events in the East are accompanied in the newspapers by contradictory
announcements of plays at the amphitheatre, where Cooke was
attempting to match the speed of the electric telegraph in presenting
the expected victory to the British public, and at the same time to
outdo the most detailed written reports from the scene of the
battle in vividness and impact. He announced his imminent production
of a war play on 24 September, when news of the first effect of the
Allied expedition was hourly expected. The play announced was to
be *The Siege of Silistria* by Nelson Lee, based on a French piece
which had already been playing at the Paris Hippodrome for some
weeks. Its outstanding features were to be four hundred auxiliaries,
and a rearrangement of the interior of the amphitheatre, with a broad
ramp joining circle and stage to give one large area for the enactment
of battles. This too was copied from the Hippodrome, which had
built a stage with a connecting ramp to the ring for the purposes of
the play. On 28 September the text was submitted to the Lord
Chamberlain's office; it seems remarkably unlike the French play,
and contains none of the 'allusion . . . to the pending struggle with
the Autocrat' which the *Era* reporter confidently expected. It was
to be staged on 2 October. On that day, however, *The Times* reported
the Battle of the Alma and (mistakenly) the fall of Sebastopol.
Obviously Cooke could not bring out his battle-piece with no reference
to this; so *Silistria* did not open that night. Apparently to avoid
again being overtaken by events, Cooke next advertised *The Fall of
Sebastopol*, but by the time the advertisements and the posters
appeared, 8–9 October, this was known not yet to have taken place.
On 11 October Cooke fell back on *Silistria* and sent in an entirely
different text with that name to be licensed for 16 October. What
seems to have been the final scene from this text was actually advertised as a conclusion to the evening, as a 'Grand Entrée Amicale

127

of England and France', from 9 October. The second text, probably by William Thompson Townsend, really is based upon the French piece; from the advertisements for *The Fall of Sebastopol* it seems likely that Cooke's intention was to add on a scene of action to this *Silistria* text, after it had been licensed, to represent whatever it was that was happening out there. On 15 October his advertisement for the forthcoming spectacle leaves it without a name, since the last one proved to be a mistake. He had also changed his mind about opening on 16 October, which may indicate that he was hoping for a completely new play, material for which was now available in profusion: the *Era* collected enough from *The Times*, the *Gazette* and other sources to give away a supplement on the Battle of the Alma with its issue of 15 October.

The metamorphoses of the stage directions and some of the scenes of this prospective piece furnish us with an interesting example of how Astley's dramatists and stage managers handled the material for their equestrian spectacles. The first version of *The Siege of Silistria* submitted for licensing on 28 September had appended to it two extra scenes, which were to be substituted for scenes four and five of the second act. They concern two contrasting incidents entirely unconnected with the plot. In the first the heroine Zuleika, the Aga's daughter, and her attendant Fatima ride in on a peasant cart and are captured by Cossacks. Comic business follows in which the Russians discard vegetables from the cart and eat candles, the ladies are rescued by the hero and the Cossacks beaten with their own knouts. (These are Cossacks because they are at Astley's and all possible scenes must include riders.) The second scene shows a fight (in the circle) between Turks and Russians, after which the Russians are given permission to bury their dead and do so to the strains of the Dead March. The British officer hero and a Turk exchange rather disjointed heroic platitudes about freedom and deathless renown, concluding with the injunction 'Be vigilant be wary'. A further battle and a tableau of dead and dying conclude the scene. The two episodes would sit very awkwardly in the place assigned to them in the text, but they do at least involve the known characters of the play.

The second *Siege of Silistria* submitted to the censor on 11 October may well have been put together by a different writer;[8] it was certainly the result of Cooke's initiative in sending to Paris for information, and borrows the chief scenes of spectacle from the Hippodrome. The stage directions in this text make very clear the use of stage and ring

128

in concert: for example, at the end of Act I 'The procession marches down the L.H. into the circle right round — making their exit R.H. Circle Entrance — To keep up the Action on the stage — Turkish Male and Female inhabitants and Children appear on the Bridge and Stage waving Turkish flags as the Act curtain descends.' Between the borrowed scenes of spectacle the comic business with the cart reappears, this time involving Lady Erol and the heroine Josephine, the latter dressed as an officer. The same business ensues. After an attack from the circle to the stage in the next scene the routine of burying the Russian dead is introduced, and this time the injunction 'Be vigilant be wary' and the platitudes about the honourable dead pass between the governor of the city and Henry, the hero, this time a private soldier.

In the final version of the play, *The Battle of the Alma*, submitted on 23 October, the comic scene is noted in the licenser's text simply as 'here enter Cart — Comic Business'. This plot, however, has no heroine to whom the events can happen; the *Punch* review reported that it befell 'Some Crimean market-women (who, by the way, looked far above their station)'. They were presumably dressed as Lady Erol and the heroine from the earlier pieces. Such a chain of evolution goes a long way towards explaining the often criticised failure of Astley's pieces to maintain a coherent plot. Obviously what the management wanted of the three writers who composed and borrowed and rewrote this piece was a mere framework for action; in the theatre a comic routine with a cart was no doubt in rehearsal from mid September and was quite unaffected by the total transformation of the drama in which it took place. The second scene, of the Russian collection of their dead, disappeared under the pressure of events; in this case, though, while the action went, a part of the dialogue, the catch-phrase 'Be vigilant be wary', was too good to lose and was preserved in performance.

When *The Battle of the Alma* reached the sawdust and the boards at Astley's Cooke had lost the chance of being first in the field. The Victoria opened on 16 October with *The Lion of England and the Eagle of France*. This is a war play of no special interest, though it does draw details from newspaper reports; but the title page shows that between copying on 30 September and licensing on 5 October a third act was added, called 'The Battle of the Alma, or, the Fall of Sebastopol'. The Victoria's play however, presented no real threat. None of the resources of the house matched what Astley's could do. Not only was the Victoria without the space, the horsepower, ordnance or extras for staging a battle, but also *The Lion of England* fails to provide an effective vehicle for one. The emotional effectiveness of *The Battle of the Alma* was the result of a skilled combination of staging, acting and writing. It opened at last on 23 October, employing not only the four hundred supers but also detachments of the '1st Royal Fusileers and the Band of the Coldstream Guards',[9] and donating £60.10.6d to the benefit of the fund for the sick and wounded. All rivals were eclipsed. The audience response was almost hysterical; the press reports ecstatic.

The points of reference used by reviewers to express their sense of the play's success are interesting: they felt that the excitement of the audience was so great, from the first scene onwards, that they were responding to the presentation of events as if to the events themselves; and they also felt that this production marked an era in Astley's history to be compared with the great landmarks of *The Battle of Waterloo* and *Mazeppa*. On those occasions too, and especially with *Waterloo*, the triumph of the drama had been its sense of actuality, its presentation, in a way which somehow transcended fiction and illusion, of the popular vision of the people and events portrayed. Sophisticated observers of the Astley's Napoleon had scoffed at the simplicity of mind which made Colonel Newcome and his like exclaim how like the General Gomersal was;[10] now they laughed at the cheering multitudes who had to be restrained from joining in the mock defeat of the Russians. But this excitement, generated not by realism, for the tinsel theatricality of the effects could very easily be demonstrated by those who cared to do so, but by the creation of an image of the event which became its reality in the popular imagination, was precisely what Astley's was about. For its audience, Gomersal speaking words by Amherst had been Napoleon; and this, for them, was the Battle of the Alma.

The first act opens with the embarkation at Southampton. Such scenes had appeared in several plays already, embarkations having been a regular feature of the war so far. This was a very polished and effective example, and impressed the *Times* reviewer by its use of the combined ring and stage, so that multitudes of troops seemed to be 'rising, as it were, from the midst of the audience' to march up to the ships. The effect was clearly to excite a sense of participation, and the speeches of the scene are directed as much to the audience as to the other actors, calling for cheers for the soldiers, their wives and children, the Allies, and the ladies of England who are sending medical aid to the troops. The traditions of English arms and

130

Astley's spectacles are invoked by an old man who reminds his sergeant sons, 'Your Uncle fought at Waterloo.' The scene ends on a sub-Shakespearean couplet: 'Away to Turkey — let the Russians feel the Frenchman's bullets and the British Steel.' The reference to the greatest English military dramatist may not be conscious — most melodramatists fell very easily into fake Shakespeare in moments of high emotion — but the ensuing scenes in which national types are introduced and handled comically make use of conventions of characterisation which go back to the chronicle play. The stereo-types drawn here had been firmly established in the preceding months. Praise of the French no longer needed to be so careful, and a Scotsman curses the French as the enemy and then apologises to the cuirassier whose uniform he is in fact wearing. The Turks call their Allies 'pic-turesque eaters of unclean animals', but show good will by producing a troupe of Circassian dancing girls. There is some play made with specific items of news, including an incident in which a soldier falls choking, and has to be released from his stock, so that the grievance about the ridiculous uniforms of the infantry regiments can be aired, and immediately redressed by the news of permission to leave off stocks and grow moustaches. The act ends with exhortations and Grand Manoeuvres.

Act II is full of incident, building to the climactic battle, and alter-nating scenes which draw upon real events, fitting them into their places in the drama, with scenes in which the representative figures can be tested and displayed in action. The first scene, for example, is the infamous bivouac in the rain which took place on the night of the Allied landing, and was represented in reports as the final straw in the story of delay and inefficiency in getting to grips with the enemy; each of the group of central characters reacts to it in his own way. One is reminded, however distantly, of *Henry V*. The third scene, by contrast, is fictional, inserted to show them off at their best, un-daunted by the weather, fighting off Cossacks, rescuing and kissing peasant girls, and amicably singing, eating and getting drunk together. This is another episode which had become conventional, as had the capture by the Russians, which gives an opportunity for comic and defiant exchanges and clever escapes, and which here makes up Scene 5. Against the scenes of Allied *esprit* and heartiness are set episodes in the Russian camp which show their tension, self-importance and moral inferiority. The Russian ladies are used to underline these points, scolding the officers for their cowardice and inefficiency, and ghoulishly assembling on the heights to watch the battles. Harry

131

Hawser, a gallant tar momentarily captured in this scene by the Russians, has the last word before the battle itself is staged: Prince Menchikoff asks if the audience for his glorious victory is assembled, and Hawser roars out that it is: 'Already I hear them shouting "Why don't you begin? Play up Nosey!"' This must be an Astley's audience slogan as old as *The Battle of Waterloo* — 'Nosey' is of course the Duke of Wellington.

Thus in the thick of the fiction, the audience is referred to, and drawn in to participate in the action of the final scene. This opens with 'The crowning *tableau* of the Heights of Alma, where the whole extent of the theatre is revealed . . . [with] sloping platforms to the very flies at the back, whilst the assailants emerge from the level ground of the circus, and fight their way up to the extreme verge of the rocky heights above them.'[11] At first only the gorgeously arrayed Russians are on the stage, ranged on the heights so that the spectators confront them alone and no doubt work themselves up like hounds held in check, until the music changes to 'The British Grenadiers'. The instructions for the battle are detailed:

the French and English troops enter the arena — the Rifles and Chasseurs leading in *open order* and firing upon the retreating Russians — then the Cavalry — the Line — the Artillery — then more of the line — after a few manoeuvres they are formed and the Battle begins — the whole advance in line — firing as they go — the Russians come down again — a Grand Struggle between the Cossacks and Cavalry — the Cossacks are driven back. As the English and French advance — the wounded are brought to the rear — the women and sailors attend them — bind up their wounds and carry them off — a Horse dies — a caravan is dismounted — in fact all the incidents of war must be observed — Finally the British commander appears to consult with the French General and one Grand Charge is ordered up the heights which are carried and cleared, and the English and French colours hoisted amidst loud cheers and God Save the Queen.

The characters involved in the campaign are the expected array: Sandy the Highlander; Paddy, who eventually manages to get into the 93rd too; Harry Hawser, who serves successively on all ships of any note including the *Tiger*; an anonymous representative Frenchman, a Turk, and Prince Menchikoff, small and blustering with yellow epaulettes as big as birdcages and a nagging wife. To them has been added Montague Quillet, the Crimea Correspondent of the *Illustrated Blood and Thunder Penny Herald*. He is equipped with a notebook and a skeletal umbrella; Paddy calls him a 'little hairy gent', and an officer says he is a 'silly villian' (instead of a civilian). He offers to translate for the troops, on the strength of his French, 'considered

very good by the Manager of the Horsleydown Theatre', but, as the
Times reviewer was pleased to note, he finally acquits himself bravely
in a tussle with the Cossacks, and fights them off with his umbrella.
He is indeed the rescuer of the ladies in the final version of the
scene with the market cart. Russell of *The Times*, the man who had
appropriated the role of commentator and interpreter of this war,
had already been taken to the heart of the public, and his accounts
of himself at the front were as eagerly read as his accounts of the
battles. To accommodate him within the conventions of the play
he has been given a stage persona adapted from one which already
figured in earlier pieces, that of the non-combatant cockney opportunist. The correspondent, who from this point onwards appears
in most of the dramas, is also always on the lookout for a profit,
and is often ludicrous and selfish until put to the test; he takes on
the ambivalence of the earlier figure, and his joker's role in the
story, with the additional dimension of literary humour. It is, I feel,
a mark of the vitality of the form that the military spectacle could
not only compete with the popular press but even find a way of
appropriating the good will felt towards Russell and incorporating
him as a comic/heroic type in its version of events.

Once the various strands of the Crimean spectacle had been
pulled together by *The Battle of the Alma* other theatres were able
to make use of the conventions it established, and work variations
upon them. Focus could be shifted, picking out whatever elements
suited the house. *The Soldier's Wife* at the Strand in November had
no battles, but made much of the correspondent as a romantically
inclined literary figure. *The Siege of Sebastopol* at the Britannia in
February shifted to a largely tragic, and very traditionally popular,
view of war as the scene of personal heroism and tragic death. In
this play, subtitled 'The Horrors of War', and in *The Battle of Inkermann* staged at the Pavilion in December 1854, the heroic protagonist
dies in the battle at the end of the piece, and figures are introduced
which contrast with the heroic stereotypes, even qualifying their
effect. The Pavilion's play includes a traitorous British sailor, who is
of course the object of execration, but at the Britannia the ambiguous
cockney jester becomes in this play an avowed coward. He evokes
the theatrical metaphor once again, by wishing that he were not a
soldier but a 'per' — a supernumerary soldier in the theatre, and so not
in danger. His devout cowardice and nostalgia for the London pubs
is contrasted, comically but by no means unsympathetically, with

the bloodthirsty enjoyment of slaughter shown by Ben Block, who wants to take a newly severed Russian head home as a souvenir for his girl.

Alongside this very deep-rooted popular figure, who provides the parodic counterbalance to the heroics of the piece in a way also found in, for instance, the music hall, this play also responded to the tide of feeling and of events by introducing a different kind of heroism, that of Florence Nightingale. She became, of course, a figure of great power in the story of the war which was evolved by writers of drawing-room ballads and popular histories: her heroism compensated for the damage done to the national pride by the angry recognition that stupidity and mismanagement were causing greater suffering than the arms of the enemy. Many of the pantomimes of 1854 and 1855 include a comic scene in which mismanagement of the war is attacked, followed by a scene in which Florence Nightingale is introduced (often by means of a pun or a visual trick of some kind), treated with great respect, and despatched to solve the problems of the nation and the army.[12] In the Britannia play she is called 'Miss Bird', and we are informed that although she will not escape calumny, 'In that young lady we behold true heroism — the heart that beats in her bosom is capable of any heroic deed.' The oracular announcement underlines the importance of her function in the popular eye: she is the triumphant underdog, the mere woman who rescues the nation's honour, at the risk of her own.

At Astley's too the drama evolved as the months went by, reflecting new events: in February 1855 an additional act 'Illustrating the Battles of Balaclava and Inkermann' was presented complete with the heroic stand of the Thin Red Line and the charge of the Light Brigade. When Sebastopol finally capitulated in September 1855 a new piece was mounted. *The Fall of Sebastopol* includes, besides a response to the rising tide of specific complaints about the conduct of the army mentioned above, a new sharpness of expression and even cynicism about its own heroics. Men wrapped in motley rags — a detail taken straight from the pictures and photographs of the war that were reaching England[13] — complain not only of the cold, but of the fact that 'There's not a pig stye in the United Kingdom that wouldn't be clean compared with Balaclava.' Their officers speak of their patient endurance, and Miles the navvy, a new figure in the plays introduced because of the building of the railway to transport material from the coast, feels called upon to assure the audience that anyone who has seen the soldiers suffering would not grudge the taxes needed to support them. The invincible tars are obliged, in the last scene, to haul guns by hand because the horses are weakened by bad provender; they undertake it with cheerful pluck, but the implied criticism of a system that makes use of the mythic hero Jack Tar by turning him into a beast of burden is felt quite strongly. Even Paddy's comic inanities take on an edge: he remarks on how busy Victory must be rushing from man to man, so that all the British can die in her arms. Sergeant Campbell, to whom he addresses the observation, replies that she no doubt has assistants to see to the Other Ranks, reserving herself for the officers — a dig which backs up the insistent attack in this play upon the British army system of purchase and promotion, its unfairness when compared not only with the French, but even with the Russians. At the end they cut the cackle, and come to the victory; but the prevailing tone of the piece reflects the less euphoric public mood, and at the same time as dealing with current news and events, asserts the perpetual preoccupations of popular art.

In the whole series of Crimea plays, but particularly in those staged with all the resources of men, horses, writers, audiences and traditions that Astley's could command, one sees vividly exemplified the flowering — perhaps the last flowering — of the nineteenth-century popular art of theatre. In these plays the conventions of popular drama responded fully and effectively to the demands of the situation and the expectations of the audience. The dramatists and managers made use of the changing circumstances of their day, manipulating the huge influx of information and of images of the war transmitted by the emerging mass media to assert their own superiority in bringing the war to the people. Reciprocity between the press, the stage and the public mood resulted in the creation of a myth of the war which, while it dealt with new kinds of information from the scene of war, much of it shocking and profoundly anti-heroic, nevertheless cast it into forms consonant with the old heroic models. The flexibility of the stage, in providing such models as the comic cockney coward and the larger-than-life Jack Tar, helped in this evolution and preserved a place for itself at the same time. By the time of the next major war, the Anglo-Boer War in the nineties, conditions in the theatre and in the field had changed, and the days of the military spectacle were over.

NOTES

1 This count includes plays dealing directly with events in the Crimea and

also some obviously staged to take advantage of the interest in military subjects and eastern settings. It does not include the many pantomimes in 1854 and 1855 which had comments on the war in their comic scenes, some aspects of which are discussed below. There must have been many similar dramas staged at provincial houses; a few have come to light in the course of research for this discussion, and one is mentioned below, note 9.

2 This and all subsequent quotations from plays are taken from the copies in the Lord Chamberlain's collection, housed at the British Library.

3 *The Times*, 24 Oct. 1854, p. 10 (reviewing Astley's *Battle of the Alma*).

4 Treatment of British and French leaders in the theatre was circumspect. Most plays present no one above the rank of captain, often using a junior officer as hero, and depicting him as supported by invulnerable soldiers and sailors. Astley's dramas, however, never baulked at depicting greatness, as Gomersal's Napoleon witnessed, and the Crimea plays there included exchanges of pleasantries between French and English leaders 'brilliantly equipped' and calling each other 'My Lord' or even 'Your Highness', to suggest H.R.H. the Duke of Cambridge. In the additional material added to *The Battle of the Alma* in February 1855 to represent Balaclava and Inkermann, the stand of the Thin Red Line of Highlanders is commanded in dumb show by an officer 'supposed to be Sir Colin Campbell' whose white hair and hat without a feather are specified in the text. Campbell was, however, a sort of folk hero, the son of a Glasgow carpenter who made his way in the army without money or influence, and he would no doubt have had a great appeal for the Astley's audience.

5 Copy in the Crampton collection, vol. 3, p. 74, held by the British Library.

6 Quoted in Elizabeth Grey, *The Noise of Drums and Trumpets* (London, 1971), pp. 80 and 236.

7 *Drummer Hodge* (Oxford, 1978), p. 12.

8 The Lord Chamberlain's copies rarely include writers' names for spectacles of this kind, and bills and advertisements are equally reticent, unless, as in the case of Stocqueler, some claim for authenticity or erudition can be made by using the dramatist's reputation. On 1 October a letter from William Thompson Townsend appeared in the *Era* claiming that he and not Nelson Lee was the writer of *The Siege of Silistria*. On 24 September the paper had reported that the forthcoming piece was by Lee. It seems likely that Townsend was actually writing the second script when he wrote to the paper, and Lee's script was the one submitted on 28 September.

9 The use of real soldiers at Astley's was another old tradition of the house, dating from Philip Astley's beginnings as a breaker and trainer of horses for Colonel Elliot's 15th Dragoons. Other entrepreneurs attempted to mimic the Crimean spectaculars and sought to employ the same means. In Bury, Sam Wild, proprietor of a large travelling theatre, decided to 'keep pace with the times' in January 1855 and mounted his own Alma show with 'a genuine British sergeant and twenty-four genuine British soldiers lent by a friendly local Colonel'. Every night they marched amidst cheering crowds from barracks to theatre and stormed 'a series of stage rocks', travelling 'a distance of at least thirty feet'. However, despite the fact that they were 'the smartest and cleanest fellows' Wild ever saw, they terminated their

engagement prematurely by getting drunk on Wild's payments to them and failing to get back to barracks. After that Wild stuck to exploiting the war by the display of two genuine 'War Camels from the Crimea'. Real soldiers in mock fights were hazardous in several ways: at Wild's as at Astley's the battles generated dense smoke, and spectators and combatants lost sight of each other for minutes together. Injuries were not uncommon, and according to Willson Disher the guardsmen employed at Astley's on this occasion let the management in for large sums in compensation by holding their fire until they saw the whites of the supernumerary Russians' eyes, and so injuring them considerably with flying gun wadding. Sam Wild, *Old Wild's* (Halifax, 1888), pp. 117–18, 120–1; M. Willson Disher, *The Greatest Show on Earth* (London, 1937), pp. 211–12.

10 Thackeray has his Colonel visit Astley's in *The Newcomes*, and his response was not novelist's licence, for many real soldiers including the Duke of Wellington enjoyed *The Battle of Waterloo* and visited it repeatedly when first staged and at its revivals. The sceptical observers had included a mordant comic periodical, *Figaro in London*, which had an especial dislike for Ducrow and all he did at Astley's, and mocked Gomersal's interpretation of Napoleon, which featured, they said, the very genteel habit of taking snuff and wiping the fingers on the inexpressibles.

11 Review in *Era*, 29 October 1854, p. 10.

12 In 1854 Florence Nightingale figured in the pantomimes at, for example, the Theatre Royal, Birmingham, Drury Lane and the Surrey — the latter demonstrating the general failure to understand her new conception of nursing by equipping her with 'six old women hobbling with sticks' as her nurses. In 1855 she was shown at Sadler's Wells, the Royal Standard and the Strand, amongst other places. The targets of pantomime satire were also those of the literary responses to the war: in *Harlequin Puss in Boots*, at Sadler's Wells in 1855, a sequence in which Clown drills some awkward soldiers and then bayonets one and puts him in a box labelled 'A Soldier ready drilled' is followed by Clown going to a 'Government office' and being cheeked by a 'Lazy clerk . . . reading a newspaper and covered with red tapes', whom he tips into another box containing 'The best uniform for the civil service — uniform politeness.' In the same month the first part of *Little Dorrit* was published.

13 See Pat Hodgson, *The War Illustrators* (London, 1977), p. 44, where she reproduces one of a series of lithographs drawn by artists at the front for publication in a series called *The Seat of War in the East*; it is by William Simpson, and shows 'huts and warm clothing for the army', consisting of a bedraggled train of men in sheepskins and blankets driving thin beasts laden with planks. Roger Fenton the photographer was in the Crimea early in 1855 and took photographs of officers and men in camp wearing layers of ill-assorted oddments.

Popular drama and the mummers' play

A. E. Green

I

For the folklorist, debate over the definition of popular drama has an uneasily familiar ring; for 'popular culture' read 'folk culture' and many of the principles adduced are identical, as is implied in the old-fashioned terms 'popular antiquities', 'popular traditions' and 'popular ballad', and even more clearly in William Thoms's successful move to replace them all with the term 'folklore'. In 1846 all that was required was a letter to *The Athenaeum*; would that matters were still that simple.[1] Not, of course, that the semantic field of the term 'popular' has not widened considerably in response to the advent of mass-culture; the creation and continuous revision of a majority taste by powerful commercial institutions – and not only among manual workers – has widened the gap between art that is popular by desti-nation and art that is popular by origin, so that folklorists at least, being nothing if not sensitive to the inadequacies of their working vocabulary, have on the whole abandoned the concept of popularity as too unspecific to be useful. But it is still striking how much of the terminological debate in popular drama would have fallen gently into place in a folkloristic symposium of the late 1960s or early 1970s.

Seductive as *Dreiheit* is to the Western academic mind, let me venture this suggestion: that, sub-divisions and quibbles aside, 'popular' can mean three things. First, it may advance a quantitative proposition, that such a work of art is to the taste of the majority of a given population as expressed in the crude statistics of box office, record sales, viewer ratings and library borrowings. Second, it may be pol-emical: such a work of art is about and generally sympathetic to working-class life and experience and employs techniques and images known or supposed to be favoured by working-class artists and audi-ences. (Ironically, two opposing political and aesthetic arguments can

139

be based on this all-purpose premise — the one built into our educational system through the curriculum, that such art is unworthy of notice, being as crude and narrow as the social life from which it springs, the other that favoured by fringe theatre, and radical 'folk singers', that such themes have a high moral purpose which is most effectively expressed through techniques of enduring vitality and proven appeal.) Third, it may connote a particular relationship between artist, audience, and opus which is not in the first instance based on a common interest in art but rather on ties of kinship, friendship, neighbourhood, and work. Several quite different notions of art itself lie behind these definitions: that at best art is for art's sake and at worst art is for profit's sake (and it is devilish hard to distinguish between the two); that art is for art's sake or that art is for ideology's sake (roughly corresponding to which side of the political fence you sit on); that art is for community's sake (community here signifying not some splendid abstraction which can be invoked to justify a contribution to spiralling house-prices in a dying Oxfordshire village, or to explain to the man from *Down Your Way* why Castleford is such a nice place to live in, or to dignify the dealings of a shabby little customs union; but a group of people who by common habitation, intermarriage, frequent face-to-face contact, shared economic interests, and similar experience, have developed for good and ill a life style which is identifiable both subjectively and objectively. Historical continuity is self-evidently a crucial aspect of this.)

Only the last of these referents makes any sense. The first is superficially appealing in the same way that anything is that can apparently be counted. But it serves to disguise the power which commercial and even educational institutions have to shape and reshape taste to such an extent that the *populus* has little to do with it. The second — sympathetic as I am to its manifestations in left-wing theatre and song, as a matter of personal taste — suffers from the built-in ambiguity already alluded to; worse, hard as it may try, the work built upon this polemical foundation is invariably divorced from working-class audiences, even when the effort is made to perform for them in pub or club or factory canteen — it cannot only be me that shudders at the well-meaning attempts of middle-class actors to mimic the dialect of the manual workers watching and listening to them. In the end, preaching to the initiate is what all this is about, or whistling in the dark — or for the next Arts Council grant. And as a well-cushioned employee of the state, who am I to complain?

140

It is my contention, then, that only theatre which grows out of
and exists for little aggregations of people — whether a rural village
or a city street — can ever be popular in any useful sense. I have no
programme for creating it — presumably, on the model of worker-
priests, we need worker-directors (in more senses than were dreamed
of in Lord Bullock's philosophy), and worker-actors — but I can
describe historically, with particular reference to one of the handful
of surviving examples, a form of British working-class theatre which
fulfilled these conditions over, to our certain knowledge, roughly
a century and a half. That form is the mummers' play, and the
example on which I shall concentrate is the Soulcaking Play, performed annually at the Hallowe'en season by men of the Cheshire
village of Antrobus.[2]

II

In referring to the mummers' play as 'British working-class theatre',
I do not mean to imply that analogues or derivative forms do not
exist or have not existed elsewhere. The extension of British culture
into the New World has produced similar plays and allied manifestations — though it is not without interest that mummers' plays as
such, i.e. performances involving *dramatis personae* with their proper
dialogue, as distinct from perambulatory house-visits by disguised
people, are rare in the folkloristic record of the North American
sub-continent, in contrast to other genres such as the Märchen and
the narrative-ballad, both of which have on the whole lasted longer
there than here — and comparable forms of drama are of course
known in mainland Europe and indeed elsewhere.[3] Rather, the
description is used to suggest an historical and analytical focus
quite different from that usually applied to the mummers' play —
or to be precise, mummers' plays, since within the British Isles alone
it is possible to distinguish with reasonable certainty at least six
types, generally known as the Hero-Combat Play, the Wooing Play,
the Sword Dance Play, the Old Tup Play, the Old Horse Play, and
the Robin Hood Play.[4] The Antrobus play belongs to the first type,
which also happens to be the most common and widespread; it is to
this type that all subsequent remarks are addressed.

Brecht may be right in his assertion that the folk play cannot
be revived,[5] though the point is arguable; but what must be understood is that in no sense can the Hero-Combat Play be regarded as
a relic of the distant past, fragmentary in form, corrupt in meaning,

divorced from its natural frame of reference, and consequently devoid of function — roughly the view taken by most students of it up to and including Brody. All the evidence points the other way.

Records of this (or any other) type of mummers' play before 1800 are extremely scanty; during the nineteenth century they multiply a hundredfold. Of course the argument from silence is a dubious one, and the multiplication of records as the nineteenth century progresses derives in part from a growth, among the learned and the middle class more generally, of interest in folklore as such — the very coinage of the word is evidence enough, deriving as it does from that Romantic and post-Romantic fascination with peasant culture which is so widely documented as to need no elaboration here. But, we are bound to ask, if Hero-Combat Plays were common before the nineteenth century (their existence is not in itself in doubt), why did those recorders of 'all old strange things', Stubbes, Aubrey, Grose, Brand and Strutt,[6] make no mention of them? We know that the Hero-Combat (or something like it) was in existence by c. 1737, as Brice's textual fragment (the earliest extant) shows;[7] and it is possible that it existed at the end of the previous century, if a doubtful source purporting to refer to Cork City in 1685 is reliable.[8] However, even eighteenth-century references are rare, and do not occur where we might expect to find them. It is a fair inference, then, that the growth in the number of references during the nineteenth century broadly reflects a growth in the number of local plays (albeit variants of a small number of main types); the more so when we consider two important points.

First, many descriptions and allusions derive not from the more isolated and conservative areas of the British Isles, but from major centres of population such as south Lancashire and the industrial West Riding.[9] This does not suggest a rural tradition, receding under the onslaught of industrialisation, but either a new tradition, or one that is expanding in response to demographic change and the foundation of new modes of livelihood and living.

Second, it can be no accident that the increase in scholarly and casual references coincides pretty exactly with the growth in numbers of cheap printed texts and of printers producing them. For while the relationship between these chapbooks and mummers' performances is an intricate one, which is yet to be worked out, it is unquestionable that play-texts are produced so that plays can be acted, and that, if they are not acted, the publishers, who are in it for the money, stop producing them. Since in fact this line of business flourished like the vine, as far as the evidence yet shows, there can only be one conclusion about performances of mumming plays: that they became more frequent during and after the industrial revolution, not less.

Hence, British working-class theatre: even when rural in provenance, these plays are the property, and their performance the expression, of an agrarian proletariat, not a peasantry;[10] and their provenance is just as often the small town or the industrial village. This is what the evidence shows; and whatever the mummers' plays were, or whether they even existed in substantial numbers before 1800, is obscure and likely to remain so. It seems sensible to place the weight of the argument where the weight of the evidence is.

Here I must again enter a *caveat*, and an apology. The detailed social history of mumming in the nineteenth century has yet to be written, and I am in no position to write it. Most of my concern with the phenomenon has focused upon problems of fieldwork in contemporary England; and to extrapolate back a century may be as dangerous as to extrapolate back a millenium. The foregoing remarks, then, were designed mainly to shift the balance of interpretation, and should not be read as implying that the analysis of a particular local play based on fieldwork in 1970 would hold good in all particulars for that same play in 1870 (supposing it existed), or that the mummers' play in the twentieth century is, at last, a survival in culture, with no referent other than the social conditions of one hundred years ago. It is easy to show, with reference to any of the few remaining traditional plays, that the second point, at least, is not true. At the same time, there are grounds for the suggestion — provided that it be not elaborated into a definitive thesis — that the frame of reference of the mummers' play is in some important respects a nineteenth-century one. Again, these grounds are both external and internal. Externally, it is undeniable that most local plays have died out in the twentieth century, partly no doubt because of the pressure of other modes of entertainment, but also, it must be supposed, because of loss of meaning. The internal grounds we shall come to in due course. First it is necessary to look at a text.

III

Here follows the text of the Antrobus play recorded by the Leeds University Television Service at the Wheatsheaf Inn, Antrobus, on 12 November 1974. The Antrobus gang vary their lines to some degree from one performance to another, so that neither this nor any other transcript should be seen as definitive. At present, it is possible to offer only tentative comments on the history of this text. Internally, it shows some similarities to chapbook texts printed in the north-west during the nineteenth century; externally, there is evidence in the form of local oral testimony to suggest that it is a result of the collation of at least two local texts, which took place under the aegis of the late Major A. W. Boyd,[11] who was centrally involved in the revival of the play at Antrobus after the First World War, the tradition having been discontinued for the duration of hostilities, like so many other seasonal festivities.[12] But firmer conclusions must await the completion of the work of Smith, Smith and Preston on the chapbook texts.

THE ANTROBUS SOULCAKING PLAY

(*Opening Song outside pub*)
Here comes one, two, three, jolly good hearty lads and we're all of one mind;
For this night we come a-souling good nature to find;
For this night we come a-souling, as it doth appear,
And it's all that we are souling for is your ale and strong beer.

O the next that steps up is Lord Nelson you see,
With a bunch of blue ribbons tied down to his knee,
And the star on his bosom like silver doth shine,
And I hope you will remember that it's soulcaking time.

O the next that steps up is the miser you see,
He wears his old rags to every degree,
And when he does sell them he sells them so dear,
That no one will buy them until this time next year.
(*A knock at the door. Enter* LETTER-IN)
LETTER-IN:
Good evening, ladies and gentlemen.
Make a fire and strike a light,
For in this house tonight there's going to be a dreadful fight
Between King George and Black Prince.
I hope King George will win.
But should he win, stand, fight, or fall,
We'll do our best to please you all.
Now if you don't believe these words I say,
Step in King George; just clear the way.
(*Enter* KING GEORGE)
KING GEORGE:
In come I, King George, the champion bold,
I won ten thousand pound in gold.

144

'Twas I that fought the fiery dragon and brought it to a slaughter,
And by these deeds won the King of Egypt's daughter.
I've travelled the whole world round and round,
And never a man of my equal found.
    If you don't believe these words I say,
    Step in, Black Prince, and clear the way.

(*Enter* BLACK PRINCE)

BLACK PRINCE:

In comes I, Black Prince of Paradise, born of high renown,
This night I've come to bring King George's life and courage down.
If that be he that standeth there
That slew my master's son and heir,
If that be he of royal blood
I'll make it flow like Noah's flood.

KING GEORGE:

Mind what thou sayest.

BLACK PRINCE:

What I say I mean.

KING GEORGE:

Stand back thou black Moroccan dog
Or by my sword thou'll die.
I'll pierce thy body full of holes
And make thy buttons fly.

BLACK PRINCE:

How canst thou pierce my body full of holes,
Make my buttons fly?
My body's made of iron,
Head and sword they're made of steel,
Even my fingers and toes are double jointed.
I challenge thee to yield. Prepare!

(*They fight.* BLACK PRINCE is killed. *Enter* OLD WOMAN)

OLD WOMAN:

Oh! King George, King George, oh what have you done?
Oh dear, dear, dear, dear, dear
Oh thou'st gone and slain my only son
My only heir;
See how he lies dead and bleeding there.

KING GEORGE:

Well, Mary, he challenged me.
Better to fight than to die.
Five pounds for a doctor, ten for the quack
That can raise that man from off his back.
    If you don't believe these words I say,
    Step in, Quack Doctor, and clear the way.

(*Enter* QUACK DOCTOR)

QUACK DOCTOR:

In comes I that never cometh yet.
I am the best Quack Doctor that you can bet

Why, straight from the continent I came
To cure this man King George here's slain.
OLD WOMAN:
  How camest thou to be a doctor?
QUACK DOCTOR:
  By my travels.
OLD WOMAN:
  Travels: Oh, where has thou travelled?
QUACK DOCTOR:
  I've travelled through the land of Icky Picky, France, Spain,
  Three times to the West Indies,
  And now, Mary, I return to Old England again.
OLD WOMAN:
  What can you cure?
QUACK DOCTOR:
  I can cure all sorts.
OLD WOMAN:
  Eh?
QUACK DOCTOR:
  All sorts.
OLD WOMAN:
  Oh. What's all sorts?
QUACK DOCTOR:
  I can cure the 'ump, the gump, the gurr and the gout,
  The pain within and the pain without;
  Why, if a man has nineteen devils in his heart
  I'll cast twenty-one of 'em out.
  Now, in this bag here there's crutches for lame ducks,
  There's plasters for broken-backed earwigs,
  And there's bottles of pickled frog's eyelashes.
OLD WOMAN:
  What is thy fee to cure him, Doctor?
QUACK DOCTOR:
  My fee, Mary, is five pounds.
OLD WOMAN:
  Oh dear, dear, dear, dear, dear! Oh I can't afford all that.
  No, no, no, no, no.
QUACK DOCTOR:
  But Mary, you're such a decent old woman,
  I'll just charge you ten.
OLD WOMAN:
  Oh that's better.
  Will you have a cheque?
  Come on, cure him, come on.
(DOCTOR *produces wooden mallet from his black doctor's bag*)
OLD WOMAN:
  Oh, you can't use that, what's that?
QUACK DOCTOR:
  Anaesthetic, Mary.
(DOCTOR *sharpens knives and carries out examination with stethoscope*)

146

QUACK DOCTOR:
Aye, Mary, he's dead.

OLD WOMAN:
(*Screaming and crying*) Oh dear! Oh dear, dear, dear, dear, dear, dear, dear.

QUACK DOCTOR:
Here John, you take three sips this bottle
Down thy thrittle throttle
And you arise and fight thy battle.

OLD WOMAN:
Oh, you silly man, as green as grass,
The dead man never stirs.

BLACK PRINCE:
Oh! My back.

OLD WOMAN:
Oh, what ails thy back, my son?

BLACK PRINCE:
My back is broken,
My heart is confounded.
Knocked out of seven senses into fourteen score;
That's never been known in Old England before.

OLD WOMAN:
Oh, what have you, what have you done?

QUACK DOCTOR:
Mary, I quite forgot,
I've taken the wrong cork off the right bottle,
Or the right bottle off the wrong cork.
Never you mind, I've got another bottle here
In my inside, outside, round-about-my-back-side pocket.
Now my father brought me this from Spain;
This'll bring dead men to life again.
Now, John, you take three sips of this bottle
Down thy thrittle throttle
And you arise and fight thy battle.

(BLACK PRINCE *rises. He and* KING GEORGE *fight again.* LETTER-IN *intervenes*)

LETTER-IN:
Lay down those swords and rest;
Peace and quietness is the best.
He that fights and runs away
Will live to fight another day.
    Now if you don't believe these words I say,
    Step in, little Dairy Doubt, just clear the way.

(*Exeunt all except* LETTER-IN)
(*Enter* DAIRY DOUBT)

DAIRY DOUBT:
In comes I, little Dairy Doubt,
With my shirt lap hanging out,
Five yards in and ten yards out,
And out goes little Dairy Doubt.
    If you don't believe these words I say,
    Step in, Beelzebub, and clear the way.

(*Exit* DAIRY DOUBT. *Enter* BEELZEBUB)

BEELZEBUB:

> In comes I, Beelzebub!
> On my shoulder I carries my clog,
> And in my hand, my dripping pon,
> And I reckons misen a jolly owd mon.
> With a rin tin tin and a bottle of gin,
> I'll sup a pint pot down with any owd mon.
> If you don't believe me, try me.

(BEELZEBUB *steals beer from nearby member of audience, and downs it in one*)

> 'Twere early Monday morning —
> Or were it late on Sat'day night? —
> I stood ten thousand mile ahead
> And saw a house just out of sight.
> The walls projected back'ards,
> And front be round at back.
> It stood alone between two more,
> And walls was white-washed, black!
> I just done six months up in Walton Jail
> For making a whipcrack out of a mouse's tail.
>
>> And if you don't believe these words I say,
>> Step in Wild Horse, and clear the way.

(*Enter* WILD HORSE *and* DRIVER)

DRIVER:

> Hey, Ho, Hey now, stand still.
> Oh, he's a bugger tonight.
> Whey, whoa, stand still now! Whoa.
>> Have you done? Whey!
> Good evening, ladies and gentlemen. —
> In comes Dick and all his men —
> Why, we've come to see you once again.
> Once he was alive, but now he's dead,
> And nothing left but a poor old horse's head.
> And as you know he's getting quite old
> We've put this sack on to keep him from the cold.
> So stand round Dick and show yourself.
> Hey now, stand still. Stand still.
> Now, ladies and gentlemen, just look around
> And see if you saw a better class beast stand on England's ground.
> Why, he's double-loined, sure-footed, works well in any gear;
> But, my God, ride him if you can.
> He has an eye like a hawk, a neck like a swan,
> A pair of ears made from an old lady's pocket book.
> So read 'em if you can.
> Every time he opens his mouth, his head's half off.
> Every tooth in his mouth stands rink, jink and jank,
> Like a regiment of pickled onions.
> Tell you what, if you look down his mouth you can see holes in his socks.

Hey, whoa, stand still.
He has as many jinkles and wrinkles in his forehead as there are furrows in
    an acre of new ploughed land.
He's a very fine horse, he's very fine bred;
On Antrobus oats this horse has been fed.
He's won the Derby and the Oaks
And finished up pulling an old milk float.
So stand round, Dick, and show yourself.
Whoa now! Stand still!
And now, ladies and gentlemen, this horse was coming down Frandley Brow
    here
the other day, he saw a caravan parked on
the side of the road, and what did he do?
He ran into it, knocked a wheel off, broke
one or two mahogany fire irons, and a glass
wheelbarrow what they bring sticks in with;
but that's not all this horse's career, my God, no!
Why, ladies and gentlemen,
This horse, he's travelled high, he's travelled low,
He's travelled both in frost and snow.
He's travelled Asia Minor, Spain, Antrobus, China;
He's travelled the whole world round.
He's even travelled in the land of Icky Picky —
That's North Germany.
Where there's neither land or city,
But where houses are thatched with pancakes,
Walls are built with dumplings,
Streets are paved with penny loaves,
And black puddings grow on apple trees
They pluck 'em just when they want them —
Little pigs run about with knives and forks stuck in their back
Crying out, 'Who'll eat me?'.
I said, 'One', and my horse, 'Another'.
So stand round, Dick, and show yourself.
Whoa now, stand still! Whoa!
And now ladies and gentlemen,
This horse was born on Antrobus Moss;
Now round here you all know that's where crows fly tail first.
Oh not again!
(WILD HORSE *farts and defecates.* BEELZEBUB *collects the turds in his pan,*
begins to chew one himself, and offers the others to the audience)
BEELZEBUB:
    We're frying tonight!
DRIVER:
    It can only come twice; second time we apologise.
    As I say, that's where crows fly tail first.
    And just before he was found
    They shot its mother to save it being drowned.

149

He was fed night and day with a spoon
And at one time could dance to any tune.
But now you see he has but one leg,
And with that he's forced to beg.
Alright, I've told 'em.
All he begs it is but small
But that's obliged to serve us all.
So now all you kind ladies and gentlemen,
I'm going to ask you to open your heart;
We're collecting for Dick a new spring cart;
And it's not one for him to draw, it's one for him to ride in.
And if you don't believe these words I say,
Ask these chaps out here;
They're bigger liars than me.
Stand round, Dick, and show yourself.
Whoa now, stand still.
Now Dick make your obeisance to your best friend,
That's it; lovely. Now stand still.
(GANG *re-enters and stands in group to sing:*)
And now our play is ended and we can no longer stay,
But with your kind permission we will come another day.
But before we go we'll have you to know, we'll have you to understand,
We're a credit to Old England; we're the boys of the Antrobus Gang.
(*The* GANG *unmasks. A collection is taken up in* BEELZEBUB's *pan, and the* GANG *mingle and drink with the audience*)

IV

It is evident from this text alone that we are dealing with a highly stylised form of drama. Two songs bracket a performance in which prose mingles with metrically flexible rhymed verse and dialogue alternates with direct address. A passage of narrative is interrupted by a *deus ex machina*, and followed by a pageant of individual characters. Stylisation is even more evident in performance. The acting area is as much space as the gang can clear in a village pub; there is no set or special lighting, and the play is given in the round. The boundary between players and audience is insecure: Beelzebub steals beer from whoever is nearest, and offers horse-droppings in return, while the Horse makes forays into the audience, snapping his jaws and knocking over glasses; after the closing song, instead of retiring into the darkness, the actors unmask and move among the audience, renewing old acquaintances and making new ones, accepting and buying drinks; Beelzebub takes up a collection, and the Horse is stood against the wall.

The costumes and make-up are representational, but not natu-
150

ralistic. King George wears an approximation of the British soldier's
former dress uniform: red tunic, blue trousers, and peaked cap
adorned with a Flanders poppy. Black Prince has a black uniform
and a spiked helmet of uncertain provenance, suggesting rather than
reproducing a German helmet of the Great War; he is blacked up.
Both are armed with a wooden sword. The Old Woman wears a wig
and veiled hat, shawl, long skirt and bloomers — beneath which pro-
trude a man's hairy legs and shoes — and carries a handbag. The Doctor
is dressed in black frock-coat and top-hat; bespectacled, false-nosed
and false-whiskered, he carries an instrument-bag and sports a huge
wrist-watch. Dairy Doubt appears as an overgrown school boy in
round peaked cap, striped tie, and trousers rolled above the knee;
his cheeks are rouged and his shirt-tail hangs out beneath his jacket.
Beelzebub looks like a tramp, in boots, slouch hat, and old over-
coat tied with string; he too is heavily false-whiskered, and carries a
bed-roll, a clog, and a battered frying pan. The Driver wears the
livery of a local hunt, and has a black moustache marked in with
crayon. The Wild Horse is made of a real horse's (or possibly donkey's)
skull, painted black, red and white, with articulated lower jaw, and
mounted on a short pole; a canvas drape hangs from below the head
to cover the man operating it, who bends from the waist and holds
the pole in both hands. The overall effect is of a creature with a well-
defined skeletal equine head, an amorphous body, and three legs.

Only the Letter-In's costume is not representational, in the sense
that it has no dramatically relevant referent in real life — though, of
course, it represents his part in the play no less than any other
character's dress. In keeping with his role of presenter, his clothes are
formal but without any semantic weight. He wears black top-hat and
tails, carries a stick (which he uses to separate the protagonists during
their second duel), and is in principle the only character without
facial make-up.[13]

Thus the costumes and make-up are designed for maximum immediate impact: a stereotype of each character is created from the
moment of his appearance — these men are clearly soldiers, this man
is evidently a tramp, and so on. Yet nothing is quite right. King
George may look like a British soldier, but he is improperly dressed
because of the poppy in his cap, and his sword is a child's toy. Black
Prince may appear to be a member of the Kaiser's army, but his face
is black. Beelzebub is dressed naturalistically; but why is he carrying
a frying pan and, more mysteriously, a single clog on a piece of
string? And why does this person with a falsetto voice and old woman's

151

The Antrobus Soulcakers, 1976: 'We're a credit to Old England; we're the boys of the Antrobus Gang' (photograph by John Murray, University of Leeds).

dress have big feet and hairy legs? Similar points could be made about the other characters. The principle is clear: the colourful general-isation of each design is undercut by the use of precise and bizarre detail. In the case of the Wild Horse, this principle is carried to surreal lengths. That he is a horse seems beyond doubt, for that magnificent head is manifestly the real thing; but it is also a death's head, and, to complicate matters further, a decorated death's head. What is more, his body contradicts his head, for there is nothing equine about it, and two of his three (three?) legs are apparently human while the third is wooden. Here the disintegrative effect of clashing connotations threatens the unification of the broad, vulgar design.

Stylisation, then, is apparent in the text, in the visual appearance of the actors, and indeed in the acting, which is declamatory and employs·large gestures. Granted the varying technical skills of the actors, and occasional whims and idiosyncrasies, all this is absolutely consistent. It is necessary to emphasise this because most descriptions of mumming, in so far as they have anything to say about it as a

152

theatrical event, tend to speak condescendingly of corrupt and
nonsensical texts, eclectic costumes, and crude acting, invoking –
usually tacitly – a definition of drama (prose, naturalistic, fourth
wall, technically elaborate) which, powerful as it is in the history of
the professional Western theatre, is local, recent and utterly inappropriate. The mummers' play does not attempt the detailed
imitation of reality; it is an imagistic theatre whose effects lie in
holding real and unreal worlds in a precarious balance. The setting
is normal – a public bar – and no attempt is made to transform it
into anything else, yet Letter-In knocks before entering. The verse
is metrically irregular, its stresses following natural speech rhythms,
but it is rhymed. That horse cannot be real, in the sense that it
looks like nothing on earth, but it knocks over real glasses and
real liquid stains real trousers. Beelzebub is obviously somebody
dressed up for a show, but his misbehaviour is real enough, and of a
kind that would usually occasion an angry or even violent response,
for the beer-stealing is not prearranged. The play cannot quite be
contained within an agreed space, and any member of the audience
runs the risk of finding himself an involuntary participant in it. At
its conclusion, the actors unmask and become once more Jim, Bernard, David and so on, familiar faces, friends, neighbours, relations,
who behave exactly as you would expect them to, drinking recipro-
cally, inquiring after someone's health, cracking jokes, talking gardens
and bemoaning the price of beer.

What then are these very ordinary men doing in taking up this
extraordinary position somewhere between jest and earnest? The late
Wilfred Isherwood, in 1974 Letter-In and the gang's senior member,
offers us the grounding of an analysis:

Yes, well, it's our belief really. Family tradition, that's all. My father used to go,
it was his belief as well. My father, my great-grandfather, great-great-grandfather.
Well it might seem funny to watch, but we don't think we're funny, we don't
think we're funny, we're only doing the part. It's showing people that – like
television today – it's letting 'em see the people that was actually on it, see.
They're all supposed to be ghosts. So people could see – they can see an image
there, as they know what they're talking about, which they couldn't tell 'em.
And that's what we're supposed to be: we're supposed to be ghosts of the forefathers. I'm not ashamed of my father, I'm not.[14]

In a volume of this kind it is not necessary to labour the point
that Mr Isherwood was a dramatic theorist of some sophistication,
within his experiential limits – more than some writers on mumming
plays have been, for that matter. The passage is a useful corrective to

the outmoded view, still all too prevalent among folklorists and historians of drama, that mummers do not know what they are about and engage annually in a meaningless activity out of some kind of atavistic folly. Certainly consciousness of the past is manifest in Mr Isherwood's words, but that is precisely the point: consciousness, not unthinking conservatism. It is this consciousness — which is also evident in the conversation of the other soulcakers — that is the intellectual foundation of the play's popularity, in the sense outlined above.

Mr Isherwood's account of his motives emphasises four things: the underlying seriousness of a broadly comic entertainment; the inherited obligation to perform; the demonstrative nature of the play; and the importance of its characters as such — all of whom are representatives of the past — in what they are, primarily, rather than what they do. As we shall see, this last notion provides us with an understanding of the play's structure, but for the moment I want to concentrate on the nature of the characters, along lines proposed in 1972 and taken up by Susan Pattison in her recent article.[15]

As already suggested, the Letter-In is exceptional, in that he is purely a functionary. He introduces the play, remains on the edge of the acting area throughout, watching the action, and thus mediates between actors and audience. He also intervenes to prevent King George and Black Prince from fighting again after the latter is resurrected; his speech at this point, which ends the play's narrative and introduces the pageant which constitutes its second half, is a statement of general principle which ironically combines moral precept with pragmatic advice. The other characters, except one, apparently a miscellaneous bunch, have in common the fact that they are peripheral to the village community: two soldiers, an itinerant mountebank, a widow, a village idiot, a tramp, and a lackey of the gentry.[16] None of them is engaged in productive work, none of them has an unambiguous social role. Their peripherality of course differs in its expression. The soldiers, the Doctor, and the tramp Beelzebub are all wanderers. Beelzebub is a solitary who can support himself only by begging and stealing, he has the diabolical name of one who is beyond the pale, and his eccentricity and unreliability are stressed by his entering unexpectedly through the pub's back door. The Doctor is a self-confessed quack, whose verbal fluency and elegant sleight of hand are merely a professional pitch. The two soldiers are boastful, mischancy, and violent; though Letter-In initially deceives us into thinking we are to witness the just battle of a national champion

154

against a foreign villain, in which no doubt the righteous will prevail, his final condemnation of violence includes King George as well as his adversary, and reduces a heroic duel to a pub brawl.

The other three human characters live within the village, but are not fully of it. The groom, as an employee of the Tarporley hunt, spends his time in the maintenance of a gentlemanly luxury, and his social loyalties are therefore open to question. Dairy Doubt is mentally subnormal, 'the village simpleton that hung around the dairy', as his name was glossed by David Burne who played the part in 1974, physically an adult but incompletely socialised and unable even to keep his clothes in order. The Old Woman has a referent that is sociologically more complex but no less clear. Most societies regard the old and indigent as a problem, and there is usually tension between the principle that age demands respect and the practical difficulty that the aged are inconveniently de-pendent upon the young. Since women tend to outlive men, and to marry men older than themselves, this tension focuses particularly upon widows, and in Britain is possibly bound up historically with problems of inheritance, the more so where agricultural land is involved. In short, the cognitive field of the Old Woman's role is probably wider and more elaborate than I am yet in a position to show. What is self-evident is that, both now and in the past, the old tend to depend on their children for support, and that this was much more the case before the institution of the old age pension in 1908, i.e. the period from which most of our evidence about the mummers' play derives. It seems not unreasonable to connect this fact with the Old Woman's repeated emphasis that King George has slain her only son. Further, in any male-dominated society, the widow is an anomaly. She is a sexually mature and, in theory, fertile woman who has lost the highest status that society has to offer her, that of wife and mother. She cannot be sexually active without departing from an important social norm, and she has long since lost and cannot revert to the pre-sexual status of maiden. If anything, then, she is asexual — a situation from which she can only escape through remarriage, which has to be undertaken with the greatest circumspection if the gossip of neighbours and the alienation of children is not to be incurred. Finally, at the death of her husband she must either find another man to support her (whether second husband, son, or son-in-law) or support herself, which is a male role. This complex of social facts is made manifest in the sexual ambiguity of the Old Woman.[17]

The only character not so far discussed in these terms is the Wild

Horse, but what I have had to say already about his appearance will
have implied my view of his role. To describe an animal as peripheral
to the village community would be tautologous. The point about this
animal is that he is peripheral to everything. He is not human, but
neither is he a satisfactory horse. He has two names: one of them, the
familiar 'Dick', is used by the Driver to represent him as domesticated;
the other, the soubriquet by which Beelzebub introduces him, tells
us that he is 'wild'. His behaviour reflects both: he is equally ready
to make an obeisance and to attack the audience. Everyone else
speaks, but he is silent. He is an outsider among outsiders.

This brings us to the play's structure, which is at first glance in-
coherent. An opening song introduces two characters (Lord Nelson
and the Miser) who do not appear, and none of the characters who
do. There follows a simple and satisfactory plot in which two men fight
and one is killed, mourned by his mother, and revived by a miracle-
working doctor. But, not content with this outcome, the two protagonists begin to fight again, only to be arbitrarily interrupted by
the presenter, who separates them and packs them off stage. Enter
next a natural, who departs before we have a real chance to appreciate
his presence, ushering in a tramp who appears from another direction
entirely, to evoke a universe of paradoxes in which time and space
are distorted, to confess to a surreal crime, and commit a real one.
By now, any expectations of narrative unity, already frustrated by
Letter-In's intervention and thrown into confusion by Dairy Doubt's
fleeting appearance, are utterly confounded. But the play has another
ace up its sleeve. For instead of another single character following in
succession, we are confronted with a strange double-act — a horse
who does not talk, and a man who talks only of his horse. The
Driver's account of Dick's career echoes the characteristics, experience,
and imagery of the other *dramatis personae*. He has been a champion
in his day; he has suffered bereavement, death and resurrection; he
has travelled in strange lands and inhabits a topsy-turvy world where
birds fly backwards and wheelbarrows are made of glass; he is unruly
and unreasoning. Just as his physical appearance carries the costume
design to its logical conclusion of fragmentation, and his actions
threaten more consistently than any other character's to violate the
frontier between actors and audience, so his biography epitomises
everything that has gone before.

Finally, the gaff is blown. The Driver declares that the whole
performance has been a pack of lies, the enactment of a tall story.
The analogy is precise. Just as the art of the lying tale is to win the

156

listener's confidence before proceeding to ever less plausible events, so this play sets up expectations of narrative unity which it will not fulfil. The only possible conclusion is deference towards those who have been hoodwinked, and a public declaration of the liar's essential respectability.[18] Hence the closing song, which balances the opening song not only formally but because it replaces disinformation with plain statement. The players doff their hats while singing, in a gesture of courtesy that is also an unmasking, and normality reasserts itself.

If, however, the play is constructed to destroy one kind of unity, it replaces it with another, the unity of image and theme. Visual paradox echoes verbal paradox, the pageant characters reflect and heighten the disorder which is in the nature of the narrative characters, and the Wild Horse and his Driver integrate the narrative and the pageant into a Cockayne-like universe which is then shattered before our eyes. Interestingly enough, the clarity and power of the play's internal logic is perhaps most convincingly demonstrated by a detail, namely the irrelevant content of the opening song. Folklorists are inclined to say about such things that they are the result of borrowing, and this is part of the truth. This particular song is a short variant of one commonly associated with pace-egging in nearby Lancashire and Yorkshire, where it occurs sometimes within a Hero-Combat Play and sometimes independently, sung by a group of perambulating mummers disguised as the characters which its verses describe.[19] A borrowing, then, beyond doubt. But why, at some unknown date, should a group of mummers have borrowed a song that was irrelevant to their purposes? Plainly, because it was not irrelevant. On the contrary, not only did it enable them to tell their first lie right at the beginning, without making it obvious, it also reflected obliquely the two main sub-types of human personality with which their play was to deal, the threat from outside and the threat from inside. We cannot know, obviously, whether these motives were ever articulated, but nor do we need to know. All art-forms, and working-class art-forms no less than any others, have their own pattern by which their creators and interpreters are guided, and innovations within traditions may often illuminate that pattern most clearly. This too is part of what is meant by community.

It is clear then that this play is about outsiders of two kinds, the stranger who beats down the door and the neighbour who does not fit in. It is an annual restatement, through a medium which is particularly powerful because it uses visual effects and music as well as a verbal message, of a small community's self-definition. This is why the past is so important in it, and why different ways of presenting the past are so tightly interlocked not only in the play itself as a spectacle, but in the set of ideas held by its performers. They generally put it simply, as in the words of David Goulborn (Black Prince): 'My grandfather did it; my father did it; I did it.' Each succeeding generation takes up the obligation of the last. The characters are ghosts: a peculiarly telling metaphor for a group of men performing a play which their dead ancestors performed, and at the same time one that places the characters themselves in the past. It is no accident that most of their talk is of what they have done, not of what they plan to do. And what is the play's central event? A death and resurrection. Once more, the dramatic image is a reflection of social reality, both immediately (the gang is a resurrection of earlier gangs) and in broader terms (the continuous regeneration of Antrobus as a human community). Again, the Horse is all important, and the players all recognise this. They refer constantly to its dramatic effectiveness, to the fact that it provokes most response from the audience. They hide it during the twelve months between performances, and guard it closely during the post-performance drinking. Earlier this century, when more than one village in the neighbourhood had a souling gang, rival groups meeting on the road would fight for possession of each other's Horse, and gleeful anecdotes are told of how the present head was won in a fracas with the men of Hatton, half a century ago. The gang say that it is very old — figures of one hundred and fifty and two hundred years are given — and its age validates for the players the antiquity of the play itself.[20] In this as in so many other ways the Wild Horse is a metaphor of the tradition.

The sense of community which the play and its metafolklore invokes, then, consists of a moral continuity across the generations as well as a system of relationships in the present. This accounts for the now residual idea of good and bad luck which surrounds the play but is ascribed by the gang to a previous generation which performed in farm-kitchens as well as pubs. The soulcakers are luck-bringers, but their play can blight as well as bless, just as its content is a mixture of good humour and threat. A positive, welcoming, hospitable response brings luck to the audience for the coming year; a negative response produces negative effects. As Edward Isherwood, Old Woman and Wilfred's son, put it: 'You go to these farms and that . . . if they was up in bed they'd come down, let you in you see, otherwise used to think they'd have a bad year. They used to think it was bad luck.' To reject the play is to reject the communality which it represents and celebrates, to refuse both contemporary and historical obligations.

All this is true, I believe, but a little solemn. The element which requires final reintegration into the analysis is the play's comedy. Didactic it is, but not with the explicit moralising of a sermon or the gravitas of a tragic ballad.[21] The play deals in the grotesque, the rowdy, the absurd; it offers for our inspection an inverted and perverted version of reality, and a highly selective one. Positive values are stated only once, in the Letter-In's speech of intervention, and even that defies unequivocal ethical interpretation. For the rest, the watcher is invited to laugh at and judge the eccentric, the villainous, and the wild. These people are not, in the end, our forefathers; they are lay figures who invite our laughter at their expense, while keeping us on our toes by constantly changing the artistic premiss, and just occasionally hinting that if they were real they would be dangerous. Reality is here, among our neighbours and relations; what we have seen is a play, where that other world which lies outside and must be resisted can be controlled and made mock of.

V

Such then is the complex of traditions which we call the Antrobus Soulcaking Play, but which contains memorat, folk etymology, anecdote, ghost-lore, and belief about luck, as well as the play itself. The plays of different communities would almost certainly require their own detailed interpretations, though it is likely that my general remarks about community, the sense of past, didacticism, and comedy, would hold good. The importance of outsiders will likewise be true of all Hero-Combat Plays, by virtue of their *dramatis personae*, which, though they vary in name or detail, invariably show the same general characteristics. Father Christmas, with his strong seasonal connotations, may replace Letter-In where the play is performed at Christmas; Black Prince may be replaced by Turkish Knight or even the wonderfully named Turkey Snipe (merely the garbling of uneducated peasants, mutter those folklorists who like to pass off their own ignorance on the people they study[22] — as if the average five-year-old wouldn't understand the words 'Turkish' and 'Knight' — yet another example of comic paradox and innovation within the prevailing logic, say I);[23] Jack Finney (a traditional name for an Irishman) may join the pageant characters; and the drunkard

159

Tosspot may take up Beelzebub's twin roles of wild man and money collector; but all are variations on the same theme of marginality.

Following the lead of Melvin Firestone, whose excellent paper at a St John's seminar in 1963 provided the initial stimulus for Halpert and Storey's volume,[24] a number of the contributors to the New-foundland book explored the idea of the stranger, and that of identity, as central features of the cognitive complex motivating Christmas house-visiting in the province. Not that the mummers' play, as such, is extant on the island, though there are historical records of it; but the essential idea that neighbours disguise themselves as strangers is common to the play and the house-visit. In so far as the volume has a unifying historical thesis, it is that the preoccupation with strangers stems from the peculiar history of Newfoundland: settle-ment was illegal until 1824, and actively discouraged by punitive visits from the Royal Navy, trouble was to be expected from Indians and from the French, the Old World hostilities of Catholic and Protestant resulted in segregated communities, and all the little fishing villages scattered around the coast were (and perhaps still are) subject to exploitation by foreign entrepreneurs and political opportunists.

The package may be unique to Newfoundland, but obviously enough its features, taken one by one, could be reproduced else-where. It is my contention that the need to define insiders and out-siders, and normality and abnormality among the insiders, was just as pressing for the Englishman of the late eighteenth and nineteenth centuries as for his Newfoundland contemporary. Again the argument here is potentially a long and elaborate one; but its main outlines are already well established. Almost all our evidence of the mumming play coincides with the agrarian and industrial revolutions, axiomati-cally a period of social upheaval and demographic change. As changes in agricultural practice brought with them the need for a different kind of labour force, the old rural village with a long and relatively settled genealogy had to accommodate itself to the seasonal migration of groups of workers — gipsy pea-pickers, harvest workers (the 'July barbers') from Ireland, itinerant gangs of sheep-shearers and steam-threshers. A little later, after the coming of the railway — itself constructed, like the canals, by gangs of men on the tramp — it increasingly had to face trippers too, on cheap excursions from the manufacturing centres. The railway, of course, had deeper implications: not only was it an image of a nation on the move, it was the mechanism by which agrarian micro-economies were tied into a larger system. The children and grandchildren of men and women who had seen the land

160

taken from them and engrossed into estates and big farms during the enclosures, now saw the produce of the land leaving the railway station for destinations unknown. Whatever little degree of control over local resources and local products had existed, it was fast disappearing into the hands of strangers. The industrial towns grew in size and economic power, attracting a new population of migrants from rural Britain and Ireland; the villages on the coal measures were turned over to mining, and new ones created; and those on the fringes of the urban centres were industrialised, or suburbanised as the manufacturing bourgeoisie abandoned the inner city that its factories had rendered uninhabitable by decent people. It can be argued that the need to define the community, and to restate that definition regularly in a vivid, provocative, and festive way, had never been stronger, whether in the old agrarian settlements which were undergoing the effects of a massive change which they had neither invited nor agreed to, or in the new industrial towns and villages where people were struggling to adapt themselves to a startlingly novel way of life based not on the seasons and the land but on the clock and the machine, and the sense of neighbourhood and belonging had to be created more or less from scratch. Time and place were being reorganised — obviously so in the manufacturing districts, but no less profoundly in the countryside, where deliveries of grain and milk were no longer determined by the spoken wishes of a man whom you could at least identify but by the railway schedule, and the hedges and walls of enclosure had broken up the broad terrain into little patches. And all this at the behest of people that the farmworker or the millhand never saw. Small wonder if the mumming play is full of strangers, if time slips out of gear and place becomes a fantasy which can be changed at will; perfectly reasonable that the man who collects the money is a free-range ruffian who bears the devil's name.[25]

The appeal to the past is thus put into proper perspective. As any sensible folklorist or social anthropologist knows, newly founded or changing communities need a sense of continuity so badly that they will sometimes attribute yesterday's innovation to their great-grandparents' day in order to achieve it.[26]

VI

Much work remains to be done, on the Antrobus play in particular and on the Hero-Combat and other types of mumming play in general. Specifically, rather than merely assume and assert a link with the

161

more or less distant past (fair game for mummers, not for students of mumming), we need to know precisely what kind of continuity is represented by such apparent links with the middle ages as the Cockayne theme and the figure of Saint/King George. For those ingredients may, or may not, have come down to the Hero-Combat as we know it through repeated dramatic expression of some kind. Our understanding also needs to be brought up to the present, in a way that has not been attempted in this paper. As a pointer, I will merely record that all but one of the 1974 gang were born in or near the parish of Antrobus, that all but one (the same one) were manual workers as their fathers had been and had no other dramatic experience, and that by 1974 the majority of them had left Antrobus to live and work in neighbouring towns as the mechanisation of agriculture took away jobs and the cost of housing in prime commuter-country went up. The similarity to the nineteenth-century experience is superficially attractive at least, and the differences probably rewarding of study.

But my intention here has been merely to shift the focus of attention to the period from which most of our records of the mumming plays came, and which, by reasonable inference, saw their diffusion and proliferation at least, and possibly their crystallisation into their present form. Further, it is clear that the Antrobus play and in all probability other mumming plays fulfil the criteria of popularity laid down. If Britain has ever had an authentically popular drama, this was and is it.

NOTES

1 Ambrose Merton [William Thoms], *The Althenaeum*, 22 August 1846, pp. 862–3.

2 My observations are based largely upon the research of a former student, Susan Pattison, who has recorded her findings in her unpublished MA dissertation, 'The Antrobus Soulcaking Play' (University of Leeds, 1975), and in 'The Antrobus Soulcaking Play: an alternative Approach to the Mummers' Play', *Folk Life*, 15 (1977), pp. 5–11. In addition, this essay draws upon introductory notes provided by Ms Pattison and myself for the accompanying booklet to the film *Soulcaking at Antrobus*, made by the Leeds University Television Service for the Institute of Dialect and Folk Life Studies. This film was shown at the Kent Conference on Popular Drama in September 1977.

It should not be assumed that what I have to say about the Antrobus play will apply in detail to any other mummers' play, living or dead. The legacy left us by folkloristic research based on Sir Edward Tylor's concept of 'survival in culture' (it still goes on, itself a survival in culture if ever there was one) is a number of grand historical generalisations, none of them properly substantiated and few of them tenable; and a scattering of insights into contemporary meaning. Detailed microstudy has only recently begun, and Susan Pattison's article is the first published result, as far as the British Isles are concerned. In the Leeds Institute and the Sheffield Centre, there exists a growing body of unpublished and continuing research, which I know quite a lot about, especially where my own students are concerned; but it would be improper to pre-empt publication of the findings, hence my concentration on Antrobus. At least, notice of the existence of this research may be of interest.

3   See Herbert Halpert and G. M. Storey (eds.), *Christmas Mumming in New-foundland* (Toronto, 1969); Roger D. Abrahams, '"Pull out your Purse and Pay": a St George Mumming from the British West Indies', *Folk-Lore*, 79 (1968), pp. 176—203, and 'British West Indian Folk Drama and the "Life Cycle" Problem', *Folk-Lore*, 81 (1971), pp. 241—5; Leopold Schmidt, *Le Théâtre populaire européen* (Paris, 1965); and *Drama Review*, 18: 4 (December 1974), *Indigenous Theatre*.

4   This is not the place for a discussion of these types and their geographical distribution. The first three are dealt with by Alan Brody, in *The English Mummers and Their Plays* (London, 1971), a work lacking in imagination and not always accurate in detail, but not without usefulness as a general handbook. For the Robin Hood Plays see M. J. Preston, 'The Robin Hood Folk Plays of South Central England', *Comparative Drama*, 10 (1976), pp. 91—100. As yet no good discussions exist of the Tup and Horse Plays. For examples see P. S. Smith, 'Collecting Mummers' Plays Today', *Lore and Language*, 1 (July 1969), pp. [5]—[8], and Rory Greig, 'We Have a Poor Old Horse', *Lore and Language*, 9 (July 1973), pp. 7—10; and for further information see E. C. Cawte, *Ritual Animal Disguise* (Cambridge, 1978).

5   'Notes on the Folk Play', in *Brecht on Theatre*, ed. John Willett (London, 1964), pp. 153—6.

6   Phillip Stubbes, *The Anatomie of Abuses* (London, 1583), ed. F. J. Furnivall (London, 1877—9); John Aubrey, *Three Prose Works: Miscellanies, Remaines of Gentilisme and Judaisme, Observations*, ed. John Buchanan-Brown (Fontwell, Sussex, 1972); Francis Grose, *The Antiquarian Repertory* (4 vols., London, 1807—9) (Grose died in 1791); John Brand, *Observations on the Popular Antiquities of Great Britain*, ed. Sir Henry Ellis (3 vols., London, 1890) (this edition, which appeared in the Bohn's Antiquarian Library series, is an enlarged version of the work which Ellis first issued in two volumes in 1810; the preface to Brand's manuscript is dated 1795); Joseph Strutt, *The Sports and Pastimes of the People of England*, ed. William Hone, 3rd edn (London, 1830; 1st edn 1801). All these works offer information on a range of traditional festivities, including various kinds of mumming and guising; but none of them describes anything remotely resembling a Hero-Combat Play.

7   Alexander Brice, *The Mobiad* (Exeter, 1770), p. 90; the relevant passage is reprinted in *Notes and Queries*, 2nd Series, 10 (15 December 1860), p. 464.

8 The alleged 1685 reference actually occurs in a manuscript of *c*. 1800. See Alan Gailey, *Irish Folk Drama* (Cork, 1969), p. 8, and Halpert and Storey, *Christmas Mumming*, p. 59.

9 See E. C. Cawte, A. Helm, and N. Peacock, *English Ritual Drama: A Geographical Index* (London, 1967).

10 It is only fair to add that full consideration of the Irish evidence (not yet undertaken) would perhaps produce a more complicated picture.

11 See his *A Country Parish* (London, 1951).

12 This text is given here by permission of the Antrobus Soulcaking gang. The law of copyright and performing rights is obscure in its application to traditional texts; but as a matter of courtesy, permission to reproduce, quote from, or perform this text should be sought of the Soulcakers themselves, who can easily be contacted c/o The Wheatsheaf Inn, Antrobus, Cheshire. I trust that this notice will be taken seriously: the Antrobus gang, like many traditional performers, is jealous of its play — in which it has indisputable moral rights, whatever the legal position — and has permitted the printing of the text only on the grounds of its educational value and scholarly interest. Further, a folkloristic fieldworker is entitled to advise readers without his particular experience that breaches of trust always damage rapport built up by hard work over a long period, and can do irreparable damage to folkloristic research.

13 In 1974, King George wore no make-up, as a matter of personal choice. Though mutual criticism is not thought proper and rarely if ever voiced within the gang, the fact of participation and their sense of unity being more important than details of technique and presentation, it was possible to elicit by interview the general opinion that all the players except the Letter-In ought to be made up.

14 From the film mentioned above, and its accompanying booklet, *Soulcaking at Antrobus* (Leeds, [1975]), pp. 14—15. This quotation is not actually a continuous passage of Mr Isherwood's conversation; the constraints of film-making required the cutting together of excerpts from recorded interviews, but this was done with careful attention to context, and the result was approved by each man involved, so that the likelihood of distortion is slight. The excerpt is used here because it is a useful condensation of Mr Isherwood's main ideas about soulcaking, as they emerged over several discursive conversations, recorded and unrecorded.

15 See A. E. Green, 'Review of Alan Brody's *The English Mummers and their Plays*', *English Dance and Song*, 34: 3 (Autumn 1972), pp. 118—9.

16 In so far as these interpretations are not obvious, they derive from interviews with the gang.

17 This argument is potentially a long and complex one which would require another paper (at least) to do it justice. Specifically, the question of conflict over inheritance, particularly where productive land is involved through either ownership or tenancy, needs detailed attention. Historical anthropology is still in its infancy, and there is much that we do not know about the history of the family in Britain. Indeed, when it comes down to local variation in customary law, which may have been considerable before Hardwick's Marriage Act of 1753 (prior to which there was no civil law

on marriage in Britain) and may have continued to exercise an influence after it, we are in almost total ignorance. The above generalisations are based largely on Peter Laslett, *The World we have Lost* (London, 1965), Ivy Pinchbeck, *Women Workers and the Industrial Revolution 1750–1850* (London, 1930), Margaret Hewitt, *Wives and Mothers in Victorian Industry* (London, 1958), Edward Shorter, *The Making of the Modern Family* (Glasgow, 1976), Paul Thompson, *The Edwardians: The Remaking of British Society* (London, 1975); on a number of works on the sociology of twentieth-century Britain, many of them usefully digested in Josephine Klein, *Communities in Britain* (2 vols., London, 1965); and finally on that first-rate index of areas of social tension, the accusation of witchcraft, in which widows and other solitary women figure highly among the accused. There is a vast literature on this last subject; most useful in the present context is Alan McFarlane, *Witchcraft in Tudor and Stuart England* (London, 1970). It is interesting that the idea of the solitary woman as witch is canvassed by some members of the gang in conversation, though it is nowhere present in the play.

18 For a good recent study of the tall story see Gerald Thomas, *The Tall Tale and Philippe D'Alcripe* (St John's, Newfoundland, 1977).

19 For a close variant see James Henry Dixon, *Ancient Poems, Ballads and Songs of the Peasantry of England*, Publications of the Percy Society 17 (London, 1846), pp. 196–9.

20 In our introductory notes to the film, p. ix, Susan Pattison and I upset some members of the gang by seeming to imply that we did not believe in the head's antiquity. This was not our intention, and it is good to have the opportunity to withdraw the offending remarks.

21 For the moral content of ballads see Herbert Halpert, 'Truth in Folk Songs — Some Observations on the Folk-Singer's Attitude', in John Harrington Cox, *Traditional Ballads from West Virginia*, ed. George Herzog and Herbert Halpert (New York, 1939), pp. ix–xiv; A. E. Green, 'McCaffery: A Study in the Variation and Function of a Ballad', *Lore and Language*, 3 (August 1970), pp. 4–9, 4 (January 1971), pp. 3–12, and 5 (July 1971), pp. 5–11; and John Ashton, 'Truth in Folksong: some Developments and Applications', *Canadian Folk Music Journal*, 5 (1977), pp. 12–17.

22 See Brody, *English Mummers*, p. 47. He is not the first and probably, alas, will not be the last.

23 Not only is the man a bird, he is two birds. Not only is he two birds, he is half a barnyard fowl, and half a game bird. The possibilities for chasing this idea through the labyrinth of folk taxonomy are extensive; as a starting point, see E. R. Leach, 'Anthropological Aspects of Language: Animal Categories and Verbal Abuse', in *Mythology*, ed. Pierre Maranda, (Harmondsworth, 1972), pp. 39–67.

24 'Mummers and Strangers in Northern Newfoundland', in Halpert and Storey, *Christmas Mumming*, pp. 63–75.

25 For acute comment on the role of the collection, and a just stricture on the 'tired saw' that it is a sign of degeneration in the folk play, see Norman Simms's perceptive review of Richard Axton's *European Drama of the Early Middle Ages*, in *Parergon*, 13 (December 1975), pp. 51–6.

26 See John Greenway's editorial introduction to *The Anthropologist Looks at Myth* (Austin, Texas, 1966); Venetia Newall, 'The Allendale Bonfire Festival in Relation to its contemporary social Setting', *Folk-Lore*, 85 (1974), pp. 93–103; and Roy Willis's review of Cawte's *Ritual Animal Disguise*, in *The Times Literary Supplement*, 14 July 1978, p. 800.

PART TWO

POLITICS AND PERFORMANCE
IN TWENTIETH-CENTURY DRAMA AND FILM

Introduction

David Bradby

The first part of this book demonstrated that nineteenth-century
popular theatre forms were a great deal more varied and more vital
than is often thought. Far from offering nothing but escapism, the
theatre of the period was able to speak to a popular audience about
the things that affected it in ways that seemed urgent and relevant.
Moreover, this theatre was sufficiently flexible to allow for the inclusion of all forms of popular entertainment, some of which, like
equestrian drama, were not obviously associated with social or
political themes. The strength of many of these theatre forms, especially of melodrama, lay in their ability to elaborate a complex
system of visual signs, thus creating a theatre language that was more
than the mere words of the texts. If these are facts that critics are
just beginning to discover about the last century's theatre, they correspond to ideas that have long been clear to writers trying to produce
popular theatre today, as will be seen from the conference discussions
given on pp. 297–314 below.[1]
   In the years following the Russian Revolution, Meyerhold and
Eisenstein adopted a wide range of nineteenth-century theatre forms
in their experimental work towards a new kind of drama. Nick Worrall's
paper shows their vigorous search for a new and enriched sign system
that would enable them to speak to a popular audience not merely
in verbal argument, but in powerful visual images as well. This concentration on visual language led them naturally to take an interest
in film and their work exemplifies the close links existing at that
time between research in theatre and in cinema; it shows, too, how
film was seized upon with enthusiasm as an art-form well suited to
making positive ideological statements. Today, the question of how
ideology is articulated in film no longer seems so clear. One of the
chief difficulties involved in understanding a popular genre like the
disaster movie (as Nick Roddick's paper shows) is to unearth the

different layers of ideological communication contained within the complex processes that go into the making and receiving of a film.

Most of the papers in this part of the book are concerned with the 1920s and 1930s, a period that saw a profusion of attempts to create a political theatre. A production like that of *Tarelkin's Death* (analysed by Nick Worrall) took place against a background of experimentation with popular theatre techniques unparalleled by anything before or since. In Russia, during the post-revolutionary years, experiments were made with every conceivable form of political theatre, from mass performances like *The Storming of the Winter Palace*, with thousands of participants, to the small-scale work of Terevsat groups or the animated posters of the Russian Telegraphic Agency, whose function was to transmit the latest news, with suitable comments.

In Weimar Germany there were similar experiments, though fewer in number, and the same range could be found, from the massive to the intimate. Piscator's production of Toller's play *Hoppla, We're Alive* (analysed by Martin Kane) can be taken as a contribution to a continuing debate about ways and means, uses and abuses of popular drama. The German Socialist parties tended to favour mass spectacles and had commissioned Toller to write the scripts for three such monster shows, performed at their annual Trades Union Congress. The Communist Party, on the other hand, favoured small-scale agit-prop work, not employing professionals, but written and performed by workers for workers.

This division between the type of work favoured by the Socialists and the Communists can be traced back to the immediate post-war period, when the theatre was dominated by two mutually contradictory tendencies: the Dada movement, believing in audience aggression and the death of all existing forms, ranged against expressionist plays calling for national regeneration, but often in the vaguest terms. Piscator avoided expressionism; he involved himself in Dada activities for a short time and then went on to a more positive revolutionary activity, founding his Proletarian Theatre in a working-class district of Berlin in 1920. Here he claimed that 'any artistic intention must be subordinated to the revolutionary purpose of the whole'.[2]

In the course of the twenties, Piscator's attitude developed: while seeing the dangers of mass theatre, he became convinced that small-scale agit-prop was not the only appropriate form and that the most technologically advanced resources of the modern stage could and should be used to put across a revolutionary political message. (Recently Edward Bond made a similar point in the less revolutionary context of the National Theatre: 'We use technology to make our bread and to farm the fields. There ought to be occasions when we use advanced technology to create the image of people on stage.')[3] Martin Kane's paper shows how the revolutionary tradition of Piscator's theatre practice, going back to his Proletarian Theatre, was able to alter the meaning of Toller's play, which had been written in the expressionist tradition.

In Weimar Germany the development of political theatre was decisively influenced by professionals, among whom Piscator and Brecht are the best known. Their contributions appear to have helped to strengthen and invigorate various kinds of popular and political theatre without weakening its message. Raphael Samuel's paper shows a very different picture emerging from the history of the British Workers' Theatre Movement of the 1930s. Here it seems that the involvement of professionals put an end to the performance of plays with any abrasive qualities. This is chiefly to be explained by the political circumstances, which were very different from those of Germany or Russia in the 1920s. Comparison with similar developments in France and the United States (as analysed by myself and Stuart Cosgrove) suggests that the emergence of popular front governments or movements helped to sap the ideological purity and to dissipate the vigour of much earlier agit-prop work. As Tom Thomas has written, 'the new popular front line didn't lend itself easily to popular theatre. In theatre terms, it's much more difficult to present an argument for a constructive line, like building a united front against fascism, than to write satires and attacks on the class enemy.'[4] The temptations of mass theatre reasserted themselves, especially in France, where the government of Léon Blum commissioned *Birth of a City*, a mass performance reminiscent of those put on at German Trades Union festivals in the 1920s.[5]

The intervention of Moscow certainly influenced developments, especially in France. For the French Communist Party to come out of its isolation and join in a popular front election campaign was a major change of direction. Not surprisingly, the party felt that the types of propagandist art that it supported must also undergo a significant transformation. In Britain, where nothing resembling a popular front government emerged, the realignment of political forces had the same effect: the Workers' Theatre Movement gave way to Unity. Raphael Samuel suggests that the WTM was literally sacrificed to the

need for building a broad popular left-wing alliance, and Stuart
Cosgrove shows that in 1935, when the New Deal administration
established the US Federal Theatre, the American agit-prop movement, which had been very strong in 1933, had almost entirely
disappeared again.

It is significant that the Kent conference was offered no paper on
Brecht. Ten years ago, a conference of this kind might have been
devoted entirely to Brecht. Today there is a sense in which his work
is known; it is referred to in a number of the papers and it arose
naturally in the course of conference discussions. From these discussions, Brecht's concern to establish a different relationship between the stage and the auditorium emerged as the most important
aspect of his work for subsequent practitioners of popular drama. The
whole purpose of 'Epic Theatre', as he began to develop it in the
late twenties and thirties, was to prevent the spectator becoming a
passive consumer. Instead, Brecht wanted to turn him into a detached
observer, while at the same time arousing his power of action.[6] His
attempts to prevent the wrong kind of audience identification and
his concern that from each scene a 'social gestus' should emerge, were
both governed by the search for a new form of active participation
by the spectator.

Indeed, the French critic Bernard Dort has made Brecht's attitude
towards his audience the basis of a fundamental contrast between
Brecht and Piscator. Dort argues that Piscator's methods (though
admired by Brecht for their attempts to show the real complexity
of social forces) remained within the framework of a traditionally
authoritarian actor—audience relationship: the audience was still
being told what to think. Brecht, on the other hand, wanted the
audience to do some of the work; instead of telling them what to
think, he wanted to put them in a position where they were forced
to think for themselves.[7] Brecht's work stressed the fact that an
act of theatre is always an encounter between people and that the
terms of this encounter are as important as the contents of the
play.

Another aspect of Brecht's work that has proved particularly
important in the context of the rediscovery of nineteenth-century
theatre practice was the fact that his plays do not stand on their
own: their full realisation can only be achieved in production. For
Brecht the work of staging was as important as the work of writing.
Every prop, every gesture, every movement was a significant element
in a stage language more comprehensive than that of the spoken word

alone. Indeed the action in a play by Brecht is frequently designed to contradict the words that are being spoken, to show that their meaning is just one element in a complex situation whose total significance is quite different. It is because of this that *Modellbücher* were published, setting minute-by-minute photographs of the stage action alongside the written text. Because Brecht has forced us to reassess gesture, costume, music, settings, etc. as significant elements of the stage vocabulary, it has been easier to understand their importance in nineteenth-century stage practice.

But these reflections on Brecht's work also suggest one of the difficulties involved in discussing popular and political theatre today. The absence of a paper on Brecht reflects a situation in which not only is his work known, but the theoretical issues that it opened up have been seized on and developed in directions not exclusively concerned with the theatre. Some of the most interesting discussions have taken place in the film journal, *Screen*. It is difficult to say what, in English theatre practice (as opposed to theory) has replaced the central focus provided ten years ago by Brecht. There are a number of groups, each of whose work would go some way to qualify them for this role, but no one of them seems able to cope with the range of work that characterised Brecht's practice.

One group that has made a consistent effort to develop the implications of Brecht's work across the whole range, from agit-prop to adaptations of the classics, is the French Théâtre du Soleil. The film record of their play about the French Revolution, *1789*, was chosen to open the conference, and traces of the problems it raised about how and where an authentic popular theatre may occur can be seen in all the different forms of popular theatres analysed in this collection of papers. To pick out just one such problem: the difficulty of how to put the audience into a different relationship with the actors was met by the Théâtre du Soleil by planning *1789* so that it would fit the simplest playing space that any small French town would possess: a basketball pitch.

Many other groups have made experiments with taking theatre into spaces not specifically designed for it. Unlike popular theatre between the wars, recent theatre groups have not, on the whole, been sponsored by any one party or performed for party meetings. While continuing to do agit-prop work when the opportunity has arisen, they have more often looked for neutral playing spaces, like the basketball pitch, not necessarily associated with theatre, but where a popular audience may be reached. This in turn has led them to

171

have recourse to forms of entertainment such as clowning, conjuring or acrobatics, and this provides one clear example of how modern popular theatre is linking up with the heterogeneous nineteenth-century practice. It is in the rediscovery of that flexible theatre vocabulary, combined with the astuteness and imagination required to use it in given political circumstances, that the most exciting developments are possible.

NOTES

1 See, for example, Trevor Griffiths's comments on p. 307.
2 See *Erwin Piscator* (London, n.d.), published for an exhibition in 1971.
3 *The Observer*, 6 Aug. 78.
4 Tom Thomas, 'A Propertyless Theatre for a Propertyless Class', *History Workshop*, 4 (Autumn 1977), pp. 113—27.
5 See below, pp. 234—5; it is impossible to gauge how far mass theatre was adopted in the second half of the 1930s because it seemed the appropriate form for the expression of unity or how far it was consciously attempting to counter the brilliantly stage-managed mass rallies of the Nazis.
6 See Brecht's notes on *Mahagonny* (Berlin, 1955), especially the passage on pp. 88—9.
7 See 'La Vocation politique', reprinted in Bernard Dort, *Théâtre Public* (Paris, 1967), pp. 362—47.

Meyerhold and Eisenstein

Nick Worrall

When the Bolsheviks seized power in October 1917, few major
Russian artists committed themselves unhesitatingly to their cause.
Outstanding among those who did were Meyerhold and Eisenstein.
In 1917 they were unknown to each other personally although
Eisenstein, the younger by nearly twenty-five years, had changed his
choice of career from engineering to the arts partly under the influence
of Meyerhold's production of Lermontov's *Masquerade*, which he
had seen in Petrograd before the revolution. Eisenstein's work as a
designer for Red Army travelling agit-theatre groups at the front
during the civil war can be seen as a further consequence of this
change of direction. After designing and directing productions at
the Proletkult Theatre in 1920, he became a student at Meyerhold's
Directors' Workshop in Moscow and, between 1921 and 1922,
attended rehearsals and performances of *Nora* (Meyerhold's version
of Ibsen's *A Doll's House*), Crommelynck's *The Magnificent Cuckold*
and Sukhovo-Kobylin's *Tarelkin's Death*, acting as personal assistant
to the director in the case of the last-mentioned production.

Meyerhold's personal influence on Eisenstein was profound as
was, although more indirectly, his artistic influence. By 1924 Eisenstein had abandoned both Meyerhold and the theatre for the 'higher'
form of the cinema just as, in 1902, Meyerhold had abandoned his
own teacher, Stanislavsky, and the latter's naturalist theatre for the
'higher' theatre of non-representational form. However, both men
retained a life-long feeling of veneration for their respective 'masters'
and, in a posthumously published essay, Eisenstein expressed an
admiration amounting to hero-worship for his own teacher.[1] He
recalled the most intensely exciting moments of his life as those
involved with a few days' rehearsals of *Nora* and, in a letter to his
friend the actor Maksim Shtraukh, described Meyerhold as the
greatest actor he had ever seen.[2] Certain Soviet commentators tracing
Eisenstein's supposed obsession with Meyerhold's personality have

even theorised that the model for Ivan the Terrible was none other than Meyerhold himself.[3] However, interesting as these biographical details are, the purpose of this paper will be to trace and emphasise the more significant social, historical and artistic factors mutually, although separately, affecting these major creative figures.

Of the two, Eisenstein was the more intellectually self-conscious. There is relatively little in the two volumes of Meyerhold's writings on theatre which has the theoretical rigour of Eisenstein's thought as it is applied to the technical means and signifying practice of film. By comparison, Meyerhold emerges as an almost purely instinctive artist, leaving little in the way of a legacy of theory or, indeed, much consideration for the future of the theatre as such, bequeathing the legend of his personality and the memory, sometimes scantily recorded, of his extraordinary productions. However, by 1917, Meyerhold's artistic personality was already formed and there is enough in his pre-revolutionary writings and a sufficiently adequate published record of his post-revolutionary work to facilitate the tracing of a theoretical core to his theatrical practice and to suggest parallels with the theory and practice of Eisenstein.

Eisenstein acknowledged that his concept of 'typage' went back to the 'types' of Commedia dell'Arte. Similarly, Meyerhold's concepts of *cabotinage* and the *balagan* also had their origins in the Commedia form.[4] The appeal to both artists lay in the emphasis on a limited range of theatrical archetypes, as opposed to the unlimited range of 'naturalistic' dramatic types identifiable less by an historically authenticated typicality than by a whole range of ephemeral 'true-to-life' mannerisms. In his early years especially, Meyerhold frequently identified himself with the figure of Pierrot, while Eisenstein always had a close sense of identification with the image of the clown.

The circus appealed to both men. Its form was traditional as well as popular, and its structure anti-naturalistic. Its means tended to emphasise physical action, rather than emotional self-indulgence, and it combined the melodrama of danger with the farce and pathos of clowning, to which were added the flair and skill of acrobatics and gymnastics. Here was a grammar of collective, external gesture opposed to internal, individualistic feeling. Furthermore, where the form of naturalist staging was adjusted to a linear continuum with a corresponding emphasis on narrative structure, the episodic nature of circus 'attractions', combining a heterogeneous series of independent episodes, seemed more in contact with a world demanding to be understood either scientifically, in terms of its molecular structure, or dialectically, in terms of its conflict of opposites.

Eisenstein's early essay 'Montage of Attractions'[5] which accompanied, by way of explanation, his approach to a production of a nineteenth-century classic drama — Ostrovsky's *Enough Stupidity in Every Wise Man* — throws a lucidly clear light on Meyerhold's comparatively untheoretical approach to Ostrovsky's *The Forest* prepared in the same year, 1923. The scientific basis of Eisenstein's 'montage' of Ostrovsky's play, staged as a series of circus 'attractions' in an arena, also shows evidence of the scientific theories of Pavlov. The audience was calculatedly exposed to a series of stimuli, or 'shocks', and the production as a whole was seen as a utilitarian exercise in the training of socially useful conditioned reflexes with a specific ideological orientation. Meyerhold's own debt to Pavlov, among others, is at the basis of his post-revolutionary approach to a non-naturalistic, non-individualistic system of acting, a theatrical 'means of production' based on the human body as technical equipment — a bio-mechanical apparatus trained and powered by the scientific principles of reflexology.

Apart from Commedia dell'Arte and the circus, other popular and folk traditions which affected the theory and practice of both Meyerhold and Eisenstein, especially in the immediate post-revolutionary period, are the *lubok* or satirical broadside with verse and caricatured illustrations, first introduced into Russia in the sixteenth century; the fairground entertainment associated with the *narodniye gulyan'ya* or 'public merrymaking' of the holiday seasons, which included travelling theatres and sideshows, puppet shows, pantomime and harlequinades;[6] mystery plays; religious festivals with their processions, and the mass theatre of the streets and public parks which were extremely popular in the nineteenth century when jingoistic episodes from Russia's imperialist past and present were reenacted and which, after 1917, became the basis of such mass spectacles as *The Hymn to the Freeing of Labour* and *The Storming of the Winter Palace*, both enacted in Petrograd in 1920.[7] Eisenstein's interest in the direction of mass scenes and Meyerhold's staging of similar episodes in the theatre are both deeply influenced by this last popular form.

A shared debt to foreign popular theatre forms is apparent in the influence of Japanese and Chinese theatre, in particular Kabuki. Meyerhold's acquaintance with the form dates from as early as 1909 when a troupe visited Russia for the first time. Eisenstein's debt

175

was more theoretical, deriving from his knowledge of Japanese, his love for the work of the artist Sharaku, and his recognition of a kinship between the Japanese ideogram and his own theory of montage. More important, possibly, than any eclectic derivation from oriental theatre on a formal level was the appreciation by both artists of the manner in which its characters and imagery were centrally rooted in the concept of the grotesque. At the heart of the work of both Meyerhold and Eisenstein lies a life-long fascination with this notion of the grotesque. Apart from oriental theatre and Sharaku, other influences range from Commedia dell'Arte to E. T. Hoffmann through Hogarth, Daumier and Callot. In estimating the importance of the grotesque in their work, it is interesting to establish a link with the effects of significant anti-naturalist movements in the arts, in particular cubism and formalism, as well as with the development of film.

Victor Shklovsky, himself a famous formalist literary critic of the 1920s in the Soviet Union, has described the fragmentary nature of the post-revolutionary world inherited by Eisenstein and his fellow artists and the delight with which they seized the shattered fragments of this old world, re-assembling the pieces in a wilfully arbitrary order as part of the artistic celebration of that world's overthrow.[8] The source of that fragmentation may be seen as implicit in the way in which the grotesque seizes on the perfection of appearances, the smooth continuity of surface reality, and distorts that perfection and smoothness with its own quality of disharmony; poisons beauty with ugliness and shatters perfection of form with its own unshapeliness, disturbing the calm of the surface with a hint of what lies below. The grotesque contains the essence of contradiction, the dialectical principle in embryo and is, formally, a perfect exemplification of montage in action. Similarly, cubism is the art of fragmentation, stemming from the duality inherent in the artist's vision (e.g. Cézanne) and, finally (as in Picasso), collapsing the naturalistic world of painted, organic appearances into the grotesque fragments of non-representational form. The deliberate absence of coherence in cubist form has the logical effect of shattering its confining frame and anticipates the manner in which the anti-naturalist theatre was to shatter the picture frame of the proscenium arch stage, demystifying its form and re-establishing dramatic action in the real world, pointing the connection between its economic productive base and its ideological superstructure. Likewise, formalist poetics dispensed with the inheritance of a logically sequential word order,

176

the tyranny of cause and effect, while engaging in the artistic effort of re-assembly as part of an attempt to see the world anew and to freshen our perception with the shock of its verbal reformulation. Its central technical effect of a *priyom ostraneniye*, or alienation device, was taken up later by Brecht in a workman-like way after the explosive delight expressed by artists working in this playground of fragments had subsided.

On the question of film, there is little doubt that Eisenstein's attraction to the cinema lay not only in the closer proxomity to the real world of its method and the total permeation by technology of its means, but in the palpable negotiability of its filmic substance. Film captures reality in its flux but is susceptible to 'distortion' and 'fragmentation' in the process of re-assembly. Inherent in the control which the artist can maintain over that process is a conscious possibility, not merely to reflect the world in its fragmentation, but to re-form it, ideologically, whilst affecting the consciousness of an audience as part of the effect of reconstruction. Compared to the possibilities of the film in this respect, the theatre appeared primitively inflexible to Eisenstein.

An important figure in this history, especially as it extends to include writers like Brecht, is Sergei Tretyakov. Tretyakov collaborated closely with both Meyerhold and Eisenstein, rearranging the Ostrovsky play as a 'montage of attractions' for Eisenstein, rewriting Martiné's *La Nuit* for Meyerhold as a revolutionary agit-play and introducing the concept of 'speech-montage' as part of its dramatic method. Tretyakov went on to write two original agit-plays for Eisenstein and Proletkult: *Are You Listening, Moscow?!* and *Gas Masks*, the staging of the second of which in an actual gas-producing plant so impressed Eisenstein with the essential falseness of theatricality in a realistic milieu that it caused him to 'drop out of the theatre and into the cinema'.[9] Meyerhold's production of *La Nuit* as *Earth Upreared* (*Zemlya Dybom*) in 1923 was his own attempt to permeate the theatre with the substance of revolutionary reality. To this end he introduced a real threshing machine on to the stage as well as an army lorry and military motor cycles. He also used detachments of the Red Army in parts of the action. In addition, he attempted to stage the play as a mass spectacle on the Lenin Hills in Moscow involving participants and spectators numbering several thousands. In this respect it is worth remarking that, to Eisenstein, the 'events themselves', like the introduction of an actual boxing match into his early production of Jack London's *The Mexican* (1920), always seemed a purely cinematographic element, as distinct from 'reactions to events', which he considered a purely theatrical element. Tretyakov went on to write the agit-prop play, *Roar, China!*, for Meyerhold's theatre, based on an actual revolt against British imperialism in China, which in its theatrical form and in the manner of its staging bears an interesting relationship to *Battleship Potemkin*, for which Tretyakov wrote the linking titles.

After *Strike* (1924), Eisenstein can be seen to move further and further away from the theatre and theatricality until, with unexpected dramatic force, these elements reappear in *Ivan the Terrible*.[10] By contrast, at least until 1926, Meyerhold can be seen to move closer and closer to the cinema, especially in a formalist sense. In *Give Us Europe!* in 1924, he may be said to have tried to cinefy the theatre, speeding up the action and obtaining the effect of a cinematic chase sequence by playing rapidly flickering lights over screens moved on castors; effecting rapid transformation scenes, of both milieu and character, in a manner which sought to breach the limits of conventional theatrical possibility. As in an earlier production, *Lake Lyul* (1923), he used screens, projections and titles. This search for a dynamic of action in the post-revolutionary period, closely associated with the Russian futurist movement, was directly opposed to the contemplative and static forms of earlier non-representational kinds of staging linked with the symbolist movement, and its energy was a direct challenge to what was seen as the neurotic introversion of Moscow Art Theatre realism. Conversely, in *Bubus the Teacher* (1925), Meyerhold cinefied the action in the reverse direction by playing everything in slow motion to piano accompaniment, deadening stage sound with carpeting and enlarging gesture to the point of the melodramatic grotesque while depicting the European bourgeoisie in its death throes. In connection with this melodramatic element, an additional debt common to both Meyerhold and Eisenstein is identifiable in the boulevard grand guignol — linking *Earth Upreared* (described by Tretyakov as an 'agit-guignol'), *Gas Masks*, *Are You Listening, Moscow?!*, *Give Us Europe!*, and *Roar, China!*, with *Strike*, *October* and *Battleship Potemkin*.

The term 'montage', while directly referring to cinematic practice, can usefully serve to define the effects which Meyerhold sought to achieve in many of his most important productions, particularly as the term affects an analysis of a central device of his work — the calculated discrepancy between form and content. For example, Ostrovsky's *The Forest*, a realistic nineteenth-century drama, was

played out in the context of an almost bare stage with the addition
of items of setting variously suggestive of a fairground, an amusement
arcade and a giant slide. An additional 'montage' structure was
integrated into the use of the setting with action proceeding either
simultaneously on two different stage levels, or with scenes following
each other in rapidly contrasting succession. Familiar characters
were presented unfamiliarly, and the content of the play, and the
audience, were subjected to a series of 'shocks'. Finally, the 'given'
trajectory of the action, which is downwards towards static irresol-
ution of an unalterable condition, was flighted upwards towards a
positive sense of liberation. To this end Meyerhold rewrote the
destinies of the youthful characters, Petya and Aksyusha. He became
the self-styled 'author of the production' (*aftor spektaklya*), exercising a degree of control over the 'film-strip' of the play as would a
director in the cutting room. Something of this effect can be seen in
the way in which he cut the five-act structure of the play into thirty-
three clips, or episodes, while more or less retaining the original
sequential order. Likewise, in his version of Gogol's *The Government
Inspector* (1926), he cut the play into fifteen sections, re-ordered
sequences, wrote in sections from Gogol's other works, edited out
sections, collapsed a series of scenes into one (as in the bribe scene)
and, in a continuous montage effect, stressed the universal nature of
the corruption by removing the play from its familiar spot on the
rural periphery of nineteenth-century Russian society and setting
it down in its luxuriant, cosmopolitan centre — St Petersburg. He
performed a similar operation on another nineteenth-century Russian
classic, Griboyedov's *Woe from Wit* (*Gorye Ot Uma*), in 1928.

A central notion in Eisenstein's theory of montage derived from
his work as a student of Meyerhold's acting classes. The notion is
that of the *otkaz*, or 'gesture of refusal, or negation'. Common to
the acting exercises, especially those in bio-mechanics, was the
theory that contradiction lies at the root of every stage action, that
every thesis has its antithesis. Eisenstein was impressed by the
proximity of this theatrical law within bio-mechanics to Engels's
materialist version of the Hegelian dialectic as well as with its relation
to Lenin's tactical theory of 'one step forward, two steps backward'.
Its theatrical apotheosis was represented for Eisenstein by the actor's
entrance in Kabuki theatre along the 'hanamichi', where his slow
progression was a precise mirroring of that pattern. A whole series
of his acting classes in the thirties was based on this central principle
of the *otkaz*.[11] The notion of 'the negation of the negation' in

dialectics finds expression in the structure of both Eisenstein's films and Meyerhold's productions.

Another common principle of their work relates to Eisenstein's concept of the synecdoche, connected with his use of the close-up, where a part is made to stand in place of the whole and is capable of evoking a sense of the whole in the perception and feelings of an audience. There is an interesting correspondence between this idea and Meyerhold's twin formulations, *veshestvennoiye oformleniye* and *igra s veshchami* (acting with stage objects and properties). In the former concept the formal trappings of stage naturalism, or any kind of stage clutter, are replaced by items of stage furniture, either representational or non-representational (as in the constructivist setting for *The Magnificent Cuckold*). Meanings then arise from the manner in which this minimal stage furniture is used, or the way in which it is lit, evoking specific recognition in the spectator in an actively creative, rather than a passively receptive, sense. The method has the effect of converting the spectator into an active participant in the creation of the production's meanings, just as the thesis and antithesis of a filmic montage collision become converted into a higher synthesis in the minds of a cinema audience. The stage objects are chosen for their typifyingly representative nature and this is frequently emphasised by a corresponding over-enlargement, which becomes the theatrical equivalent of the cinematic close-up — focusing of attention on a 'typical' part abstracted from the whole. In the second concept of 'acting with stage objects', properties take on meaning and significance from the way they are handled, or assume in their inanimacy an importance equivalent to the animate characters of the play or film. Objects come to function as characters, like the bread and salt of Mayakovsky's *Mystery-Bouffe* (1918), or to represent them, like the doctor's pince-nez in *Battleship Potemkin*, chairs in *The Forest* and *Give Us Europe!*, bicycle wheels and harps in *October*, a cream separator in *Old and New* (*The General Line*), skittles in *Tarelkin's Death*, hats and coats littering an abandoned conference room in *October*, to mention only a few examples. The selection of actors like properties resembles the selection of properties as actors and, as in Chinese theatre, the multiplicity of possible meanings stems from a dependency on use — the purposive creation of significance. Meyerhold may also be described as having used symbolic montage (in the manner of Pudovkin) where the spectator actively completes the synthesis of connected shots, or, in stage terms, brings the aggregate of symbolic theatrical elements together. For example,

180

in a scene from *The Forest*, the concept of Aksyusha's innocence was evoked not only by the expression on her averted face but by the whiteness of her apron, white sheets hanging on a line and white doves in a cage. In another scene from the same production a fishing rod held by one character and the carefully arranged cloak of another evoke the concept of a river, and so on.

Writing in 1929, Eisenstein stated that content had to do with the principle of organisation aimed at the class-cultivation of the spectator, and he emphasised the production-based inseparability of combined form and content that makes an ideology. An audience, he declared, is an abstraction until it becomes flesh and blood through the creative temperament unifying its pulse to give to formal arbitrariness the clarity of ideological formulation.[12] And, according to Jean Mitry, writing of Eisenstein's production of *Wiseman*, 'under the cover of buffoonery here is a collection of motifs which "react" on each other and whose sense becomes strikingly evident through these reactions. The idea was not in the facts nor in the dramatic expression of their consequences, but in the relations between them. It was "montage" before the word came into use.'[13]

To relate these points of theory to actual practice, the remainder of this paper will be devoted to a brief discussion of Meyerhold's 1922 production of Sukhovo-Kobylin's *Tarelkin's Death* and to a consideration of a single still photograph, very widely reproduced, of the interrogation scene in Act III. The special relevance of this production stems from the fact that it stands as a unique example of the mutual collaboration of Meyerhold and Eisenstein on a single work.

The play itself is permeated with a sense of the omnipotence of evil and gives vent to a sense of horror in farcical form, its predominant feeling deriving from a use of animal imagery emphasising predatoriness, as well as from images of death, decay and violence. Meyerhold and his co-director Eisenstein sought to liberate the play from its nineteenth-century legacy by investing the grim farce with the playfulness of Commedia dell'Arte, coupled with the dynamic energy of the gymnasium and the clown show.

The key to their conception of the production and their decision to present it in its particular constructivist form appears to have resided in the meaning of the Russian word *proizvol*, incorporating the dual sense of arbitrariness and dictatorship. Insofar as the play as written includes as part of its subject-matter the consequences of autocracy in the arbitrary arrest of citizens on the one hand and in

181

Drawing of stage props for Meyerhold's 1922 production of *Tarelkin's Death* (layout for Act I).

the fraud, bribery, scheming and suspicion in the social world at large on the other, its theme could be described as 'the consequences of tsarism'. The notion of an arbitrariness — of justice, morality and of social behaviour in general — which stems from an all-embracing autocratic arbitrariness, was conveyed by the directors in stage terms through the danger and ambiguity which underlay everything in these conditions.

The world presented through the stage objects was a society of cages and traps, each item resembling a contrivance placed in the blackness of a cellar to catch rodents. As if in ironic counterpoint to this suggestion each item was painted white, and brilliantly lit with constant lighting on a bare stage. The bare brick wall which was exposed by the absence of a cyclorama could be imagined as that of a cellar or prison. The constructions were made out of wood slats to represent chairs, cages, boxes, swings, instruments of torture, etc. The slats ran vertically like prison bars or like stripes on institutional uniforms or hospital pyjamas. It was the world presented as part-prison and part-hospital with these motifs taken up and carried over into the costuming. The society shown as an institution was paralleled by the revelation of the characters as institutionalised.

Arbitrariness and danger in the environment, signalled by shots and explosions, were built into the stage furniture as if these elements were a condition of existence. During the course of the action, specially designed wooden stools would either spring upwards, collapse or explode when sat upon (the noise being made by a cartridge in the stools' spring mechanism). This built-in arbitrariness was

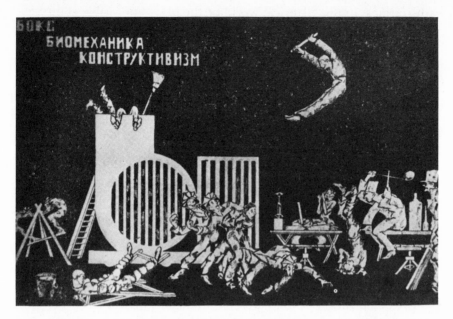

Sketch by I. Makhlis of Meyerhold's 1922 production of *Tarelkin's Death*.

redoubled by the fact that, in practice, a stool built to spring up would collapse and one made to explode would remain stable or silent. The levels of 'danger', for which adequate response could never be prepared in advance, meant that the actors needed to be in a permanent state of 'emotional excitation', of muscular pre-paredness, which would enable them to respond on motor-impulse to whatever situation they were suddenly confronted with. At one level, the stage implements were extensions of Rasspluyev's sense-less firing into the audience while insanely shouting 'Entrrrrracte!' (at the end of Act II), signs of a general arbitrary violence. At the same time, the stage furniture presented actors with the everyday dangers of twentieth-century living. The analogy was with a machine-oriented society and man's relative position within it as producer and controller. The kind of physical control, alertness, skill and familiarity brought to bear in working on an assembly line in the process of industrial production also needed to be brought to bear on the ordinary process of living. Thus, in responding with animal-like alertness to the explosions and collapsing furniture around them, the actors were demonstrating a process of control over the exigencies of a present world acted out in terms of a wild, uncontrollable

arbitrariness in the historical world of the play. The visible ability
to cope with this situation on the stage became the source of a
liberating laughter which rendered the danger and the arbitrariness
of the enacted history both distanced and subject to control.

The interesting feature of Meyerhold and Eisenstein's staging
of the interrogation scene in Act III (see illustration) is its susceptibility
to analysis as a 'montage of attractions' involving a dynamic structural
grouping which has the effect of revolutionising the social order
within the play. Rasspluyev, seated on a stool, is cross-examining
an apparently semi-literate witness, Pakhomov (standing behind him).
To help the witness present his testimony, Rasspluyev has a police
thug (Shatala) stand behind Pakhomov and jog his memory, if
necessary, by punching him in the back of the neck. When this
system fails to work efficiently, he incorporates a second thug
(Kachala) as the starting handle of a human 'interrogation machine',
in which the interrogators submit to being the dehumanised cogs of
a vicious and brutalising mechanism.

The composition of this carefully arranged still is built up of
structured 'chords' of tension and focus, and changes of stress
and direction within each chord. Shatala's position is a 'diminuendo'
of Kachala's, where the energy stems from the braced feet and the
tension in the raised arm. Shatala's position is a modified version
of this, the knees slackly bent and with no tension in the arm — a
'negation' of the other stance. The figure of Pakhomov completes
the chord, stated as a series of tensions, but continues the structural
line through the angle of his head. He appears to absorb the energy
represented by the invisible threat behind him and to transfer it
through the dynamic of his own stance on to the seated figure of
Rasspluyev in front of him. It is as if Pakhomov were waiting for
something to happen to Rasspluyev rather than anticipating a blow
in the back of the neck. This air of expectancy which surrounds
Rasspluyev appears to derive from two sources and is engendered by
his confidence. The external signs of that confidence registered in
the splayed position of the legs and arms and in the smiling face
are as if deliberately composed to be undermined. Then we see
that there is, in fact, a 'mine' under him. He sits at ease as if in a
comfortable chair when we know him to be sitting on one of the
stools which, during the course of the play, have been collapsing,
springing up and exploding. It is as if he were literally sitting on a
barrel of gunpowder. However, the sense of threat which hangs over
Rasspluyev and the system he represents extends beyond the mere

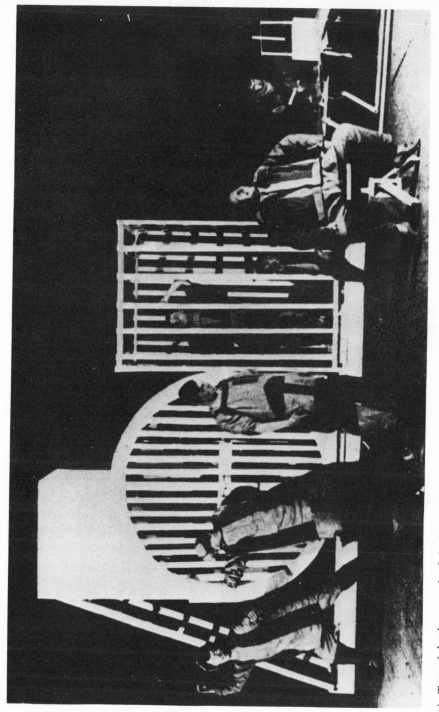

A. Temerin's photograph of the interrogation scene from Act III of Meyerhold's 1922 production of *Tarelkin's Death*.

instability of his seated position and is built into the whole design of the scene as well as into the production in general.

The assault which Pakhomov makes on Rasspluyev in the play at this point is the direct result of a blow which, as it were, launches him at the seated figure. In Sukhovo-Kobylin's play this is not presented as a conscious attack, but the sense of attack is, nevertheless, implicit in a situation in which some men dominate others, who then retaliate. The real threat stems less from the stool than from the alienated, mechanised function of Rasspluyev's own subordinates. How is this suggested? The stripes on the uniforms of Kachala and Shatala are precisely re-echoed in the bars of the constructions behind them. They fit into their environment. Running counter to this are the stripes on Pakhomov's costume, which contradict the pattern by running crossways. Additionally Kachala and Shatala are made to fit into the pattern by being mechanised. In submitting as functionaries to being reduced to dehumanised working parts of a 'mechanics' (as Rasspluyev calls his interrogation machine), their complete alienation is apparent in their having become an exact reflection of the working parts of the machine behind them, the circular shape of which couples the impression of a torture chamber with that of a treadmill. We are presented with an image of society, apparently stable, in fact at a point of crisis. The social components are the alienated and those whom the system actually imprisons, in the shape of the two in the cell, whose expressions of hope seem to centre on Pakhomov. (Brandakhlyusova's position, sitting half in and half out of the cage, registers both hope and anticipation.)

The key figure is Pakhomov. The character becomes the polemical centre of the composition. His stance, while relaxed and firmly balanced, has a potential aggression in the intensity of the angle of the head and in the flexed position of the hand. The sleeves are rolled up and the pattern of the costume is that of the ordinary worker's overall. The blow, when it comes, does not simply propel Pakhomov helplessly forward as part of a general mêlée, but is more like the kick of a starting handle, launching him forward in active aggression. The confused entanglement on the floor, which the play records, becomes in production a metaphor for revolt when played as active assault and struggle. The structure is built of a series of statements and counter-statements, registered in the full dynamics of pose and movement, activated by a process of montage, where meaning takes off from a groundbase on which thesis and antithesis, image and counter-image collide.

186

It has been said of Eisenstein's *October* that its 'formal development *enacts* the overthrow of one sign system by another, the abstract and alienated relationships and static time of the provisional government being replaced by the functional, personalized relationships and dynamic time of the bolshevik revolution'.[14] Substantially the same can be said of all Meyerhold's productions conceived in the hectic burst of creative energy which affected Soviet artists following the revolution and the successful culmination of the civil war. Meyerhold and Eisenstein, both products of a bourgeois background, were energised by this fervour and, across the divide of revolution, were not content merely to contemplate with satisfaction the collapse of an old order but, out of its death throes, attempted to express in artistic terms the dynamic of a new society and a new way of seeing.

NOTES

1 S. Eisenstein, 'Iz Avtobiograficheskikh Zapisok', in *Vstrechi s Meyerkhol'dom* (Moscow, 1967), pp. 219–24.
2 L. Kozlov, 'Gipoteza o Nyevyskazannom Povyashchenii', *Voprosy Kino Iskusstva (Moscow)*, 12 (1970), pp. 109–33.
3 *Ibid.*
4 V. E. Meyerhold, 'The Fairground Booth', in *Meyerhold on Theatre*, trans. and ed. E. Braun (New York, 1969), pp. 119–42.
5 S. Eisenstein, 'Montage of Attractions', trans. D. Gerould, *Drama Review*. 18: 1 (March 1974), pp. 71–6.
6 E. Kuznetsov, *Russkiye Narodniye Gulyan'ya* (Moscow, 1948).
7 V. Vsyevolodsky, *Istoriya Russkovo Teatra*, 2 vols., (Leningrad/Moscow, 1929), vol. 2, pp. 307–74.
8 V. Shklovsky, 'Sergei Eizenshtein', in *Zhili-Byli* (Moscow, 1966), pp. 466–514.
9 S. Eisenstein, 'How I Became A Film Director', in *Notes of a Film Director*, trans. X. Danko (New York, 1970); and 'Through Theatre to Cinema', in *Film Form*, trans. and ed. Jay Leyda (New York, 1949).
10 P. Wollen, *Signs and Meaning in the Cinema* (London, 1969), pp. 19–73.
11 S. Eisenstein, *Izbranniye Proizvedeniya*, vol. 4 (Moscow, 1966), pp. 81–9.
12 S. Eisenstein, 'Perspectives', in *Film Essays*, trans. and ed. Jay Leyda (London, 1968).
13 J. Mitry, *S. M. Eisenstein* (Paris, 1961), p. 27.
14 D. Bordwell, 'Eisenstein's Epistemological Shift', in *Screen*, 15: 4 (Winter 1974–5), p. 46.

Erwin Piscator's 1927 production of
Hoppla, We're Alive

Martin Kane

Erwin Piscator would probably have disliked the term 'popular theatre' — at least in its most obvious German version, 'Volksdrama' or 'Volkstheater'. As a director whose ambition was to create a revolutionary, class-conscious theatre which aimed at 'agitation with scenic means',[1] these expressions would have had an innocuous and anachronistic ring. The Berlin Volksbühne, for instance, founded in 1890 to bring serious drama within the reach of the working masses, had ceased by the 1920s to reflect their political and social interests and, as Piscator put it, 'had lost its last vestige of aggressiveness and been swallowed up and absorbed into the sphere of the bourgeois theatre'.[2] Piscator's own early experiments led him to realise that any hope of building up a truly proletarian theatre movement was not possible in a society devoid of the necessary political and economic prerequisites. After some half dozen productions mounted between 1920 and 1921 in various assembly halls and workers' pubs in Berlin, he was forced to develop his ideas within the framework of the conventional theatre, including the Volksbühne about which he had been so disparaging. Three politically tendentious productions there between 1924 and 1927 led to a clash with the management who objected to the word 'Volk' in the name of their institution being equated with the 'radical working classes'.[3] Piscator was obliged to look around for an alternative home for his dramaturgical ideas and, thanks to the wealthy connections of the actress Tilla Durieux, was able to take over the Theater am Nollendorfplatz.

The connection with the Volksbühne was not severed entirely, however. The new Piscatorbühne functioned as a 'special department' of it ('an outlet for the Bolshevist leanings of the Volksbühne' was the way it was described by one newspaper),[4] and attracted a subscription of 16,000 members (mostly, according to Piscator, young workers) who committed themselves to five forthcoming productions.

Piscator had originally intended to launch his new venture with a play on the Russian Revolution commissioned from Wilhelm Herzog. But when, in July 1927, Herzog presented his play, it was nothing more than a lifeless, loosely cobbled together string of historical documents. With the opening of his new theatre only weeks away this left Piscator in something of a predicament. Ernst Toller's new play, *Hoppla, We're Alive*, the first he had written since being released from prison in 1924, offered a way out. Piscator had already seen a draft of the play in February and, despite reservations about its over-lyrical language, he accepted it for performance.

In a letter to the press the previous year, Toller showed that he had begun to absorb some of Piscator's theories. 'I have tried', he wrote, 'to find a new form for a collective drama, since I believe it is not possible to give shape to the internal profile and the external atmosphere, as well as to the ups and downs of a great modern mass movement, with the usual means of dramatic formulation.'[5] The collaboration on *Hoppla* would demonstrate that in their concept of popular political theatre an enormous gap still separated the two men. Toller's blithe comments about 'collective drama' would ring very hollow in retrospect when he realised what this could mean in practice for the text of his play. Some years later in Manchester he recalled how he had entered the theatre while *Hoppla* was being rehearsed to suddenly hear totally unfamiliar dialogue and to be told by Piscator, 'I decided yesterday to introduce a new scene. I've had it written by my theatre collective.'[6]

Toller's play explores the fate of Karl Thomas, a revolutionary of 1918–19 who, after eight years in a mental institution, is released into a totally changed world with which he can establish no point of contact. Although 'the play takes place in many countries eight years after the suppression of a people's uprising',[7] this attempt to lend it universal significance is contradicted by the nature of the main characters who clearly mirror the broad spectrum of political opinion in the Weimar Republic. The lines of demarcation are drawn from the prologue in which we see a group of prisoners who have been condemned to death for their part in an abortive revolution. In the young, romantic revolutionary Karl Thomas, the class-conscious worker Albert Kroll, and the *petit bourgeois* socialist Wilhelm Kilman are represented the main factions of the left in Germany in 1919 — the Independent Socialists, the Communists and the Social Democrats. As the death sentences are commuted to terms in prison at the end of the scene, Kilman is left alone with the aristocrat Baron Friedrich, in a prefiguration of the alliance of Social Democrats and

190

the traditional ruling elite which would form the basis of the new
governing order in Weimar.

Even at this stage we can see both the appeal and the shortcomings
of the play for Piscator. He approved of its characters which were
'sharply contrasted in terms of class',[8] but his alterations to the text
show how he radically pruned the language of the play to make its
emphasis less ambiguous. A good example of this is provided by
Karl Thomas's speech on revolutionary motivation:

Look around you at those who rush to support an idea in a revolution or a
war. One is running away from his wife for making life hell for him. The other
can't keep up with life and limps along until he finds a crutch which looks
wonderful and makes him feel like a hero. The third can no longer stand his own
skin and thinks he can change it overnight. The fourth is looking for adventure.
It's always very few who do it out of inner necessity.

Only the first and last sentence of this speech were retained, a change
which subtly alters Toller's original conception of his hero. The
intellectual revolutionary given to cynicism and abrupt changes of
mood becomes a less extravagant figure. Piscator reinforced this
change by choosing Alexander Granach, a specialist in sturdy proletarian roles, for the part, and thereby avoided what he called 'the
typical Toller hero'[9] — the lyrical idealist.

The unexpected reprieve which comes at the end of the prologue
proves too much for Karl, who becomes severely unbalanced and is
confined to a mental institution. To indicate the passage of time
before his release in 1927 a film interlude was devised. The effort
and care invested in the research for this footage, which in actual
performance lasted only seven minutes, demonstrated the enormous
lengths Piscator was prepared to go to in order to achieve a particular
dramaturgical effect. From a manuscript comprising roughly 400
items of political, economic, cultural and even sporting and fashion
news, and by using a mixture of documentary material, as well as
3,000 metres of film shot for the purpose, a cinematic distillation of
the most crucial events between 1919 and 1927 was arrived at.[10]
Shots of Karl Thomas in asylum uniform were followed successively
by film of the Versailles Treaty; stock exchange unrest in New York;
fascism in Italy; hunger riots in Vienna; inflation in Germany; the
death of Lenin; Gandhi in India; fighting in China; and finally by
the hands of a clock which moved at ever-increasing speed.

Karl Thomas takes the first steps towards reconstructing a life
for himself in the Germany of 1927 by renewing his acquaintanceship
with former comrades. Successive uneasy meetings continue the

pattern established in the prologue and are made the means of exploring the different paths that German socialism had taken since the melting pot of 1919.

In the first act we see how Kilman has blossomed to a position of power by softening his socialism. We are at first reminded of George Grosz's cartoon of Friedrich Ebert, 'From the Life of a Socialist', as we see him taking measures to crush a strike and in cahoots with old guard aristocrats who can scarcely conceal their contempt for the parvenu beneath the ministerial facade. And yet there is an equivocalness in Toller's text which makes us hesitate to condemn Kilman. When, for instance, Karl accuses him of betraying his former beliefs, Kilman replies with arguments which reveal him as something more than a cynical opportunist: 'You see nothing but armed struggle, hitting out, wounding, shooting. To the barricades, to the barricades O workers! We reject the notion of struggle by brute force. Unceasingly we've preached that we want to be victorious by means of moral and spiritual weapons. Violence is always reactionary.'

Although, as the more soberly restrained style of this play shows, Toller had shed the extravagantly idealistic elements of his early expressionist dramas *Transfiguration* and *Masses and Man*, his view of political theatre was still far less radical than that of Piscator. He had left prison in July 1924 severely disillusioned by the rigid inflexibility of the KPD, the German Communist Party, and with a concept of art which attempted to assert a humanitarian conviction free of the restraints of party ideology. This view was expressed in a speech made in Magdeburg in July 1927 when he declared that 'presentation of class struggles does not mean a dramatic form in which all the good is on one side, and all the bad on the other'.[11] This was complete anathema to a director such as Piscator whose art had clear-cut political aims. It is apparent from the *Regiebuch*, as well as his comments in *Das Politische Theater*, that his text deletions, additions and overall direction for *Hoppla* were designed to polarise the political ideas in the play, and to cancel the balanced presentation of not only Kilman, but also the student who murders him, which we can find in Toller's text. His cryptic instructions, for instance, as to how Kilman's defence of his political philosophy should be delivered destroys any credibility it may have. They read: 'Apes the melody maliciously — heavy contempt.' This is just one of the many examples where Piscator's interpretation eliminates Toller's recognition of political complexities, and his reluctance to make an unambiguous stand in favour of one position or another.

The beginning of Act II demonstrates the change which has come over another of Karl Thomas's cell mates. Eva Berg, a timid and frightened girl in the prologue, has toughened politically and emotionally, and developed into a communist activist whose severely rational view of life and politics is totally at odds with Karl's absurd escapist fantasies:

Karl Thomas: Eva come with me. We will go to Greece. To India. To Africa.
There must be somewhere where men still live like children, who are, just are.
[In whose eyes the reflected heavens and the sun and the stars revolve and shine.]
Who know nothing of politics, who simply live, and are not always having to fight.
Eva Berg: *You want to abandon the cause?* You're disgusted with politics? Do you imagine you could break away from them? Do you imagine that a southern sun, palm trees, elephants, colourful clothes, would make you forget the way mankind really lives? The paradise you dream about does not exist.[12]

While Karl is still rooted in the now anachronistic revolutionary aspirations of 1919 and belongs to a 'generation which has disappeared', Eva, a feminist who has developed Nora Helmer's awakening into a political life style, has moved on to control her own destiny as a woman and to grapple with the political realities of 1927.

Toller generates considerable intensity from the gulf which has opened up between Karl and Eva. In the previous act the dramatically appetising knowledge that the meeting between Karl Thomas and Kilman was one of former comrades now separated by an embarrassing change in personal circumstances was almost swamped by the development of the confrontation into a clash of disembodied political standpoints. Now, in the scene with Eva, the political and temperamental aspects of the divide between Karl and his co-revolutionaries of 1919 become fully and painfully integrated:

Karl Thomas: What have you been through in these years to make you so hard?
Eva Berg: You're using expressions again which no longer hold good. I admit that I was a child. But we can no longer allow ourselves to be children. The clear-sightedness and knowledge we have gained can't be cast aside like toys we've outgrown. Experience? — yes I've experienced a good deal. Men and situations. For the last eight years I have worked as formerly only men worked. For eight years I have had to decide for myself about every hour of my life. That's why I am what I am . . . Do you think it's been easy for me? Often, in one of those hideous furnished apartments, I've flung myself on the bed and cried as if heartbroken. I felt I could no longer go on living . . . Then came work. The Party needed me. I clenched my teeth and . . . Be reasonable Karl. I must go to the office . . .

The historic specificness of the play is reinforced by the election setting in a workers' pub in Act II, Scene 2. The victory announced at the end of the scene of a right-wing aristocrat, von Wandsring, over Kilman and the communist candidate Bandke, closely parallels the presidential election of 1925 when Hindenburg polled 14.6 million votes to narrowly defeat the Volksblock candidate Marx with 13.7 million votes, and the communist Thälmann who polled 1.9 million. In his dramatisation of voting irregularities and disturbances — workmen disqualified on technicalities, ineligible students on the electoral lists, intimidation — Toller has also caught the fraught atmosphere of the 1925 campaign. The *Kölnische Zeitung* of the day reported that the campaign was characterised by the 'americanisation' of its methods, and by a lack of proper political ethos in which social and ideological differences split the electorate into two hostile groups — those who saw Hindenburg as an out-and-out Junker militarist and monarchist, and those who regarded him as a saviour who could guarantee peace and the social order.[13]

It is just these tensions which Toller draws on in the election scene to provide the backdrop to Karl Thomas's increasing alienation. Piscator, however, intervenes once again to subtly modify the nature of this alienation. When Karl reproaches Albert Kroll (his former cell mate and now a member of the Election Committee) with having betrayed his revolutionary ideals to 'a pack of electoral *petits bourgeois*', Kroll replies, 'You seem to expect the world to be a sort of firework display got up for your benefit, with rockets and Catherine wheels and battle cries.' Piscator cut this speech, with the effect that Karl Thomas is still politically naive and bewildered by the world of 1927 (see later in the scene his exchange with Kroll: '*Karl Thomas*: What pleasure can you find in votes? Are they a deed? *Albert Kroll*: Deed, no. A spring-board to deeds'), but his egotistical and romantic motives for rejecting the painstaking spade-work of the political process have been considerably toned down.

In the third act, the set, which was one of the most remarkable features of the production, came fully into its own. Designed by Piscator and built by Traugott Müller, it was basically a tiered scaffold structure on a turntable which, in addition to the stage itself, offered eight separate acting areas and could also be used for film and slides projected from front and rear. The diagram, taken from Piscator's *Regiebuch*, shows the arrangement for Act III, Scene 2, set in the Grand Hotel where Karl has taken a job as a waiter (the information in the top left and bottom right segments refers to a telephone conversation between Count Lande and the Chief of

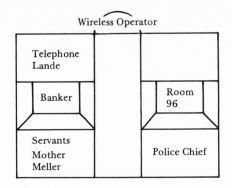

Diagram of the set for Act III Scene 2 of Piscator's 1927 production of *Hoppla, We're Alive*

Police which is not in Toller's text, but is inserted in type-written form in the *Regiebuch* as part of Act IV Scene 2). This technically elaborate structure was the perfect vehicle for the rapid, graphic insights into the heartlessness, corruption and decadence of Weimar society suggested by the sequence of cameo scenes in Toller's text. The private room in which the banker sets up dubious deals with Kilman; the office and sordid servants' quarters; room 96 in which Count Lande is closeted with the lesbian Lotte Kilman; the wireless room perched at the apex of the set. Speedy intercutting between these scenes by the use of spotlights which moved from space to space as the action required, leaving the rest of the structure in darkness, accompanied by garish effects (jazz music which swelled to a crescendo as the scenes changed, the penetrating ring of cash registers), all built up a sense of frenzied pace and of an environment in which Karl was being gradually crushed. Dashing frantically from room to room, the climax of his anguish is reached when, through the messages pouring into the wireless room, he is confronted with the miseries of the world of 1927.

Piscator trimmed down Toller's original scene here and supplemented it with a mixture of film, slide and sound to emphasise the political and economic context. To a background 'cacophony of voices' a loudspeaker quoted share prices in English 'in a vulture-like screech', while film projected from the rear onto the central panel of the scaffold showed shots of the stock exchange, a six-day bicycle race, and of American warships leaving port followed by scenes of starving women and children in Romania. The high point and most spectacular moment of this scene, however, was a wire-less request for help for a passenger who had suffered a heart attack aboard a plane flying between Paris and New York. The sound of heart beats reverberated throughout the auditorium, while pictures of an aeroplane over the ocean, an X-ray of a human heart and a film depicting 'the human machine' were projected. Piscator's belief in the liberating power of technology which was symbolised in this scene was somewhat contradicted by Karl Thomas's des-pairing comment on man's inability to use it to transform himself and the world in which he lived:

Karl Thomas: How wonderful all this is! And what do men do with it! They live like sheep, a thousand years behind the times!

His decision to shoot Kilman, the symbol of the betrayed ideals of 1918—19, is a melodramatic expression of this despair. As he is about to fire, however, the student we had seen plotting with Lande at the beginning of the act shoots first and Kilman falls dead — a clear echo of the murder of the German Foreign Minister Walther Rathenau in 1922 by right-wing, nationalist students.

The ensuing scenes in which first Pickel (the provincial *petit bourgeois* who has wandered in and out of the play with no apparent motivation other than to provide the comic counterpart to Karl Thomas's anguished bewilderment), and then Karl, are arrested for the murder were drastically reshaped by Piscator. He wrote in a telephone conversation between Lande and the Chief of Police, accentuated the comic side of Pickel's mistaken arrest, and cut entirely the long third scene in which an investigating judge questions Karl, Mother Meller and Eva Berg. These changes are salutory. As the scene stands, showing blatantly prejudiced judicial attitudes which can lead to only one verdict, it creates the feeling that the play must inevitably fade away, its end a foregone conclusion. By removing it, Piscator also spared the audience an embarrassingly sentimental display of defiance in the face of class justice from Eva Berg.

The Piscator production moved directly from Karl's arrest to his second confrontation with the psychiatrist Ludin. Played at a 'fast, frantic pace', this scene works up to a fine climax in which Ludin, interested initially 'only in motives', is unmasked as a fascist whose mission in life is to eliminate anti-social elements such as Karl. The dialogue between the two sees Ludin becoming increasingly frenzied and is dramatically counterpointed by scenes of financial collapse and disaster from the Grand Hotel, and a semi-surrealistic chorus of asylum inmates whose chant of 'Normal!' raises Ludin's replies to Karl's litany of misery and corruption to a hideously mocking leit-motif. The sense of a catatonic world on the brink of disaster was reinforced by Piscator's introduction at the end of the scene of a ballet interlude in which female figures bathed in ultra-violet light and dressed in fluorescent, skeleton costumes danced a frenetic Charleston.

Piscator's most extensive remodelling of Toller's text occurred in the brief fifth and final act, where his preoccupation with technical effects almost entirely usurped the function of actors and dialogue. The opening scene with Mother Meller, Albert Kroll and Eva Berg once again behind bars began with projections of prison windows cast from the front onto the transparent gauze in front of the scaffold construction, while the prison wall from Act I, Scene 1 was projected from the rear onto the middle section, and shots of cells appeared on the top left-hand and right-hand segments (see diagram). After film of

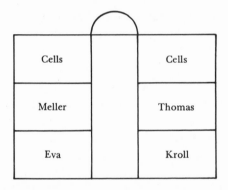

Diagram of the set for Act V of Piscator's 1927 production of *Hoppla, We're Alive*.

Eva Berg and the warder Rand, Piscator produced the most spectacular effect of the whole play. Doing away with the spoken text except for two interludes (an exchange between Rand and Kroll, and a despairing outburst from Karl), communication between the prisoners was conveyed by text projected onto the gauze screen and made to run horizontally from right to left in turn. The revamped text and Piscator's notes read:

from bottom right to bottom left 'Who are you'? Returning from bottom left to bottom right: 'Eva Berg'. Again from bottom right to bottom left: 'What

197

do you know about the others?' Back: 'House searches everywhere, arrests because of Thomas.' Across to the other side: 'Did he do it?' Back: 'Of course.' Across: 'Is he already here? Be careful.' Film stops.

Later in the scene the text was made to run vertically and then horizontally at the height of the prisoners on the second level of the structure. Accompanied by the rhythmic knocking of the prisoners the moving script left a deep impression even on those who were critical of the play as a whole. One critic wrote that it was the most poignant rendering of human misery since Chaplin's hunger scenes in *The Gold Rush*.[14]

This mixture of spoken and projected text continued into the dramatic final scene of *Hoppla*. The news that Kilman's real murderer had been caught and that the prisoners were to be released was flashed across the gauze, while the discovery that Karl had hanged himself in his cell was enacted by the warder Rand, Eva Berg, Albert Kroll and Mother Meller. Piscator attempted to counteract Toller's defeatist ending by giving Mother Meller the last, rousing word: 'Damn the world. It's got to be changed!' As the final curtain fell, this revolutionary appeal provoked what Piscator called 'the proletarian youth' among the audience to a spontaneous rendering of the Internationale.[15]

The first production of the new Piscatorbühne on 3 September 1927 had been witnessed by a packed house whose widely different social status was reflected in dress ranging from 'dinner jackets to the open neck shirts of the hard up'.[16] Graphic testament to the appeal of radical Weimar art to chic sophisticates as well as to the politically conscious proletariat. Critical reaction to the play also revealed the turbulence which sprang from the point where the culture and the politics of Weimar Germany met.

The response was not along simple right—left lines. The nationalist critic Erich Metzger predictably dismissed this first offering from Piscator's 'Bolshevist Temple of Art' as 'dripping with arrogantly deceitful political tendentiousness',[17] but there was also harsh criticism of Toller (his role in the Munich Soviet Republic of 1919 had not been forgotten) from the Communist Party's *Rote Fahne*. Typical was Frida Rubiner's remark that Toller offered no solution to the problems he raised — an unavoidable consequence as she saw it of a life spent 'vacillating between revolution and social democratic pacifism'. She concluded that 'Toller's drawing-room communism will not satisfy a single revolutionary worker; not even in Piscator's production, a work of genius.'[18]

198

This distinction between Toller's play and the actual production was typical of many other reviews. Piscator's original reservations about the text proved to be justified. Ideal in concept, with 'the possibility of giving social and political outline to a whole epoch',[19] Toller's own interpretation of Karl Thomas's fate as a personal rather than a historical tragedy made for a basic incompatibility of purpose which Piscator, despite his substantial alterations, was never completely able to eliminate from the play.

Piscator nevertheless created one of the theatre events of the decade and also took German political theatre an important step forward. Despite technical imperfections and inadequate rehearsal time (the final film sequence was still being run through for the first time as the audience began to trickle into the theatre), Traugott Müller's set in conjunction with the elaborate film and stage effects was the perfect vehicle for Piscator's artistic and political aspirations. In 1929 he described it as an example of a 'Marxist stage construction' which arose from the attempt 'to link every single scene with universal social events, and to give it its heightened historical significance'.[20]

NOTES

1 Erwin Piscator, *Das Politische Theater* (Hamburg, 1963) p. 64 (my translation).
2 *Ibid.*, p. 57.
3 *Ibid.*, p. 100.
4 *Ibid.*, p. 121.
5 'Das neue Drama Tollers', *Die Volksbühne*, 15 Aug. 1926.
6 'The German Theatre Today', *The Manchester Guardian*, 17 Feb. 1934, p. 13.
7 Note after list of characters in Ernst Toller, *Hoppla, wir leben!* (Potsdam, 1927). This and all subsequent translations from the play are my own.
8 The comments on Piscator's alterations to the published text are made on the basis of the *Regiebuch* for the 1927 production of *Hoppla* which is in the Akademie der Künste der DDR, Berlin, and was kindly put at my disposal by Dr Hannelore Köpping-Renk. Piscator, *Das Politische Theater*, p. 152.
9 Piscator, *Das Politische Theater*, p. 148.
10 *Ibid.*, p. 150.
11 Ernst Toller, 'Rede auf der Volksbühnentagung in Magdeburg', *Das Tagebuch*, 2 July 1927, p. 1075.
12 Square brackets indicate passage deleted by Piscator. Passage italicised was inserted by him.
13 Walter Hubatsch, *Hindenburg und der Staat* (Gottingen, 1966), p. 75.
14 Arthur Kurschner, 'Berliner Notizbuch', *Das Theater*, 8: 18 (Sept. 1927), pp. 440–2.

15 Piscator, *Das Politische Theater*, p. 154.
16 P. Fechter 'Eröffnung der Piscatorbühne', in *Deutsche Allgemeine Zeitung*, 5 Sept. 1927.
17 Erich Metzger, 'Piscator's Gluck und Ende', in *Kreuzzeitung*, 417 (5 Sept. 1927), p. 2.
18 Frida Rubiner, 'Zur Toller-Aufführung bei Piscator', *Die Rote Fahne* (7 Sept. 1927). Reproduced in *Die Rote Fahne*, ed. Manfred Brauneck (Munich, 1973). Other *RF* reviews of *Hoppla* are included here, pp. 273—87.
19 Piscator, *Das Politische Theater*, p. 146.
20 Erwin Piscator, *Schriften* (2 vols., Berlin, 1968), vol. 2, p. 51.

Prolet Buehne: agit-prop in America

Stuart Cosgrove

Unlike Germany during the 1920s, America had no apparent need for
an active agit-prop movement. The United States had not been beaten
in the war and for the time being seemed prosperous and secure. As
a decade, the twenties was radically different in Europe. It was characterised by the inadequacies of a failed capitalist system and punctuated
with the resultant class conflict. In these circumstances an orientation
towards Marxist politics and thus Marxist cultural forms is inevitable.
However, the excessiveness of twenties America completely obfuscated
the need for such a culture. Throughout the decade which produced
Piscator's agitational revues, the revolutionary experimentation of
the Soviet *Lef* group, particularly Mayakovsky and Eisenstein, and
the coalescence of the Blue Blouse movement, America formulated
little or no Marxist-based theatrical culture. Besides the limited appeal
of the New Playwrights Theatre and the predictable realism of workers'
club performances, American theatre was devoid of political commitment.

In 1926 there was nothing to distinguish the Prolet Buehne from
New York's other European immigrant groups. They were the official
dramatic wing of an *arbeiterbund*. The Prolet Buehne's function was
to provide a dramatic outlet for German immigrant workers and
promote theatrical activities in New York's predominantly German-
speaking Yorkville area. With the arrival of Hans Bohn from Germany
in 1928 the group soon became independent of their *arbeiterbund*
and assumed a determinate, activist policy. Over a period of five
years Bohn (who anglicised his name to John Bonn) and Ann Howe
guided the Prolet Buehne to the vanguard of American revolutionary
theatre. Their contribution to the radicalisation of the American stage
has been ignored or understated ever since.

Bonn's arrival in America was closely followed by the Wall Street
collapse of 1929. The slump proved to be the most important contributory factor to the upsurge of American agit-prop. It created the

201

severe social and economic situation in which Marxism thrives, and
for the time being questioned America's individualist mythology. It
was inevitable that Marxism would spread more forcefully from
Europe than it had in the twenties and present a viable alternative
to disillusioned Americans. Since every major philosophy has its
own cultural and artistic forms it was equally inevitable that Marxism
would be accompanied by its particular cultural forms. Agit-prop
was an essential Marxist theatre form of the twenties and thirties.
In the same way that Miracle cycles had acted as a convenient vehicle
for celebrating and propagating Christianity, agit-prop suited all
the requirements of Marxism. It had broad, proletarian appeal.
It presented class issues in a clear-cut, indisputable manner and
simplified political theory for an audience who were often illiterate
or uneducated. Having been created as an instrument of communist
propaganda in Russia it was understandable that agit-prop would
accompany Marxist ideology to the United States. Once established
in America, agit-prop maintained close links with Europe but also
went through a clear process of Americanisation. John Bonn's Prolet
Buehne were instrumental in preserving those links and precipitating
that process.

Bonn's personal theatre history helps explain the dynamic way
in which he radicalised the Prolet Buehne and re-emphasises the
European origins of agit-prop. His university education at Berlin,
Cologne and Leipzig and his subsequent education at the Reicher
Theatre School provided an adequate basis for his theatrical work
in Germany. He worked with the State Theatre in Berlin as dramaturg
and assistant director, with the Chamber Theatre in Leipzig as director
and produced his own political revue, *Was Uns Fehlt*. Despite his
apparent peripatetic character Bonn was almost certainly an active
theatre director in Berlin between 1923 and 1928 when he was
undoubtedly familiar with the work of Erwin Piscator. It is safe to
assume that Piscator's agitational revues such as *Revue Roter Rummel*
(1924), *Trotz Alledem* (1925), and *Hoppla, wir leben!* (1927) were a
crucial influence on Bonn's radical ideas for a non-bourgeois, activist
theatre. Besides Piscator's experimentation, Bonn lived through the
growth of the German agit-prop and Sprechchor movements which
culminated in the visit to Germany of the influential Soviet Blue
Blouse group. It is reasonable to assume that a committed KPD
(German Communist Party) communist like Bonn would have seen
the Blue Blouses and have absorbed their phenomenal fusion of
satire, music, jazz-gymnastics, acrobatics and propaganda.

By 1930, the Prolet Buehne were gaining a substantial reputation. Their lively performances at street corners, picket lines and on New York's waterfront earned them a sizeable working-class following. Together with the Workers' Laboratory Theatre (WLT) they formed the nucleus of New York's expanding agit-prop movement. The Prolet Buehne's most popular plays of this initial period were *Tempo, Tempo*,[1] *Scottsboro*,[2] and *Vote Communist*.[3] The first two were German-language agit-props but there is evidence to suggest that *Vote Communist* was performed in both German and English.

As the title suggests, *Tempo, Tempo* is reliant on agit-prop's theatrical sense of rhythm and syncopation to achieve its dramatic effect. It is an archetypal agit-prop script complete with an obese, capitalist stereotype who demands harder and more diligent work from his overtaxed workforce. The police are characteristically portrayed as defenders of capitalist property and enemies of workers' power. The eventual dénouement of *Tempo, Tempo* is the collectivisation of the oppressed workers and an implied rejection of capitalism. *Tempo, Tempo* therefore has a clear Marxist structure. It uses agit-prop's penchant for conflict and dialectic methodology to achieve its purpose. Workers are shown in opposition to the capitalist and the policeman and Soviet workers' 'Tempo' is seen to conflict with capitalist 'Tempo'. The synthesis or final outcome is the awareness that Soviet collectivisation is more advantageous to the proletariat. *Tempo, Tempo* is therefore a typical European agit-prop which could have been performed anywhere — there is no evidence to suggest any Americanisation of form or content (see p. 315).

However, the Prolet Buehne's other agit-props were not so rigid in their adherence to European standards. The *Scottsboro* recitation, despite being performed in German, dealt with a purely American subject, albeit in a style which was reliant on the syncopation of early European agit-prop. The recitation attacked the wrongful arrest of nine black teenagers accused of raping a white girl aboard a train en route to Scottsboro, Alabama. Besides unemployment and poverty, the Scottsboro case became the most important issue in the eyes of America's left-wing activists. The Prolet Buehne were therefore dramatising an American issue in a twofold attempt to politicise their audience and win support for the Scottsboro boys' release. By dealing with a negro case, the Prolet Buehne were bringing racial issues into a form which normally concerned itself with straightforward class conflict. Until the Scottsboro affair, agit-prop, particularly in Europe, had had no apparent need to relate racial issues to the overall class superstructure. The *Scottsboro* recitation was soon replaced by agit-prop scripts which dealt more conclusively with racial issues. The best examples are *Newsboy*[4] and Langston Hughes's agitational play *Scottsboro Ltd*. Both of those agit-props end with the unification of oppressed blacks and communists in an attempt to overthrow the system responsible for their respective grievances.

The contribution agit-prop made to American theatre history is perpetually undermined. In their eagerness to criticise agit-prop's simplistic and dogmatic style, theatre historians rarely mention its progressive outlook. The New York agit-prop groups were the first to make a concerted effort to introduce black actors and writers into a theatre tradition which was entrenched in white taste.

The Prolet Buehne's contribution to election campaigns in the early thirties was confined to an excellent and uncompromising agit-prop, *Vote Communist*. Despite its patently un-American title, *Vote Communist* is the most American of the early agit-props. The sketch sets out to reveal the major American political parties as defenders of capitalism. Systematically, the liberal veneer of the Democrats and the contrived honesty of the Republicans are torn away and they are revealed as friends of capital. The capitalist is characterised with all the abstractions we expect of agit-prop. A top hat, a correlative dollar sign and a money bag are his symbols. Each time a Democrat or Republican begins to make an election address their name signs are torn away to reveal the ubiquitous dollar sign. By portraying Democrats and Republicans as defenders of the 'dollar-ego', the Prolet Buehne were deliberately putting their beliefs into an American frame of reference. But the Americanisation goes deeper still. They were not merely criticising a generalised concept of capitalism but capitalism as it has always manifested itself in American mythology. The Prolet Buehne were not concerning themselves with generalisations like greed but with 'Cash Nexus', 'Rags to Riches' and 'Rugged Individualism'. *Vote Communist* uses contemporary American references to explode a peculiarly American myth.

Second Worker: The Rugged Individualism of Rockefeller to massacre miners.
First Worker: The Rugged Individualism of Ford to fire on starving workers.
Third Worker: Rugged Individualism is the backbone of capitalist exploitation.

The Prolet Buehne had not abandoned the megaphones and matching shirts they borrowed from Europe but they were clearly reassessing the content of their work to suit an American proletariat.

As the thirties progressed, the Prolet Buehne's material was becoming more adventurous and was presented to an ever-increasing audience. In a letter to the Marxist cultural magazine, *New Masses*, in 1930, John Bonn describes the group's fifth season.

On Friday, October 24th, the Prolet Buehne, German Revolutionary Workers Theatre Group of New York, opened its fifth season of activity with a revue *Fest der Neuen Massen* attended by about 700 workers and their families at the Yorkville Casino.

Most of these were newcomers, attracted to the affair thru poster displays and ticket sales directly in the streets.

The program was built of a revue, specially made lantern slides in caricature with accompanying monologue (very popular), and a mass recitation Vote Communist written by Hans Bohn (Bonn), and led by 65 workers seated thruout the audience and in all parts of the hall.[5]

The Prolet Buehne were obviously not confining themselves to standard agit-prop. The *Fest Der Neuen Massen* with its caricature and assembly-hall atmosphere is more akin to Piscator's agitational revues than *Tempo, Tempo*. Bonn's letter also mentions that the revue was repeated in Brooklyn, Philadelphia and numerous cities around New York. The Prolet Buehne were clearly fulfilling the demand that agitational propaganda must go to the masses and not wait for the masses to go to it. Portability has always been the essence of agit-prop and as a result a whole movement of portable groups grew up with the Prolet Buehne. The early thirties saw the birth of the Workers' Laboratory Shock Troupe, the Hungarian Workers' Shock Brigade and John Bonn's anti-fascist Die Naturfreunde, all in New York. The groups used their feet, cars or subways to reach their audience and provided a stimulus for a national agit-prop movement which included the Rebel Players of California, the Red Dust Players of Oklahoma and the Chicago Blue Blouse Group.

Perhaps the most important event in the unification of an American agit-prop movement was the birth of *Workers' Theatre Magazine* in April 1931. Under the joint editorship of the Prolet Buehne and the Workers' Laboratory Theatre, the magazine grew from being a few inconspicuous mimeographed sheets to a campaigning organ with a multiplicity of purposes. It provided a platform for discussing the problems of form and content confronting the revolutionary theatre. Each issue contained a new agit-prop script in an attempt to ameliorate the groups' relatively slim repertoire. But most of all, the magazine was instrumental in preserving links with European theatre developments. By translating articles from the German *Rotes Sprechchor*

The Federal Theatre Portable Theatre Caravan erected during a performance in Crotona Park, New York (*c.* 1938). Reproduced by courtesy of the Federal Theatre Research Centre, North Virginia.

and reporting on the work of the Soviet Blue Blouse groups, *Workers'* *Theatre* was establishing an internationalist policy. This international outlook was shared by *New Masses*, who relieved *Workers' Theatre* of some of the tremendous burden of keeping in touch with theatre abroad. The report of the International Conference of Revolutionary Workers' Theatre Groups, held in Moscow in 1930, which appeared in *New Masses* in November of the same year, had a strong influence on American agit-prop. The US groups were made aware of the potent satirical content in European agit-prop (particularly in the work of the Berlin group Kolonne Links) and set about injecting more satire and burlesque into their own performances.

Since *Workers' Theatre* was Marxist orientated it soon developed a clear-cut campaigning policy. Its major aim was to revolutionise American theatre. The magazine saw Broadway as its political and theatrical enemy and aimed the brunt of its venom at Broadway's

206

escapism and commercialism. *Workers' Theatre*'s attack on Broadway was at its most vitriolic when it raised the issue of 'the negro on Broadway'. It pointed out that the usual practice was to caricature blacks on stage and discriminate against them in the audience. *Workers' Theatre* urged its readers to write and produce plays involving black themes and highlighting black problems. It called upon all worker's groups to make every possible effort to make the revolutionary theatre a multi-racial theatre.

By the end of 1931 over 200 agit-prop groups were known to exist in the United States. Part of this phenomenal growth rate is attributable to *Workers' Theatre Magazine* but in the main it was due to the worsening economic situation. The sharp rise in unemployment and the resultant confrontations between the workers and the police increased the need for organised Marxist propaganda. In 1930 four million were unemployed, by 1931 the figure had doubled to eight million and by 1933 unemployment had reached thirteen million. The dole queues and picket lines were the audiences agit-prop sought most. As the audience grew, so the number of agit-prop groups increased to meet the demand. The Prolet Buehne were by this time performing to mass audiences and regularly extending their repertoire. In his capacity as chairman of the dramatic section of the Workers' Cultural Federation, John Bonn wrote to *New Masses* describing workers' events in August 1931. The letter confirms the Prolet Buehne's commitment to collective effort and their insistence on audience participation.

The first activity of the dramatic section was the anti-war mass pageant, given on August 1st at the Union Square demonstration in New York and repeated on August 2nd at the picnic of the Trade Union Unity League in Pleasant Bay Park. The play was written, directed and organized collectively by the dramatic section. The Workers Laboratory Theatre, the Prolet Buehne, (German) and Artef (Yiddish) participated as groups. Members of the International Workers Order, Hungarian Workers Dramatic Club, the Young Communist League, the International Labor Defense and the Womans Council were among the 40 worker-players who took part in rehearsals. At the performance workers from the audience were drawn into the play. Even the bourgeois press had to admit the success of the performance and its enthusiastic reception by the audience of 15,000.[6]

Although Bonn's description of the New York anti-war pageant falls short of the mass spectacles staged in Moscow in the early twenties, there are distinct parallels. Both were collectively organised, both had overt political content and both were aimed at a mass proletarian audience. However, the Prolet Buehne had no real opportunity to stage events as spectacular as *The Storming of the Winter*

Palace. The mass spectacle demands civic co-operation and that was unlikely to be granted to a revolutionary theatre group. The Prolet Buehne differed in a simple but important way from their Soviet counterparts. Whereas Soviet agit-prop was designed to propagandise the work of the political party in power, the Prolet Buehne were concerned with denigrating the government and overthrowing capitalism.

In order to achieve their respective ends, Soviet groups and the Prolet Buehne were aware that agit-prop was not exclusively an urban genre. Marxism applies to the farmer and miner as well as to the city dweller, and thus agit-prop must convert the rural and small town community too. Bonn's letter to *New Masses* comments on the New York groups' work outside the metropolis.

The dramatic section also sent two of its members to the Pennsylvania coal strike and the Paterson silk strike to organize Agit-Props groups. Alfred Sachs [sic] did some excellent work with the miners' children in Pennsylvania. In Paterson, Bernard Reines directed a children's play which was presented at a mass meeting and was enthusiastically received.[7]

By virtue of taking theatre to the mass meeting, the picket line and the farms, agit-prop was seen as the antithesis of legitimate theatre. In its early years, American agit-prop had no desire to learn from the bourgeois stage. Being a proletarian form, it seemingly had more in common with indigenous, popular entertainment than with the status quo. Historically agit-prop had always borrowed from popular culture. Mayakovsky had used the circus and Piscator had used cabaret technique. It was inevitable that American agit-prop would borrow from a domestic popular form. Vaudeville proved to be the most convenient source of influence. It shared agit-prop's direct, immediate knockabout style. This fusion of vaude-ville and agit-prop was the final stage in the Americanisation of revolutionary theatre and was a testament to the maxim that propaganda and entertainment must be inextricably linked.

The Big Stiff[8] exemplifies the successful fusion of the two styles. Its format is taken from an old vaudevillian doctor's skit which was adapted for propaganda by Red Vaudeville, a faction of the Workers' Laboratory Theatre. In many ways it is the most American of the extant agit-prop scripts. Not only does it borrow from vaudeville but it concentrates on depression poverty and sets out to attack the inadequate Hoover administration. The central symbol of *The Big Stiff* is the invalid 'Uncle Sam'. He is not the healthy old man of army recruiting posters but a dying hospital patient who symbolises

208

the weakness and tiredness of Western capitalism. *The Big Stiff*'s burlesque approach to politics made it a favourite with New York's militant groups, but it never approached the popularity of *Newsboy*. Adapted from a poem by V. J. Jerome, *Newsboy* became the most successful American agit-prop. It was ultimately performed throughout America and was adapted for production in London. *Newsboy* is archetypal Marxist art. It is concerned with the conversion of a newsboy from inaction to committed communism and presents the conversion by a series of conflicts. At the beginning of the play he is happily working for the reactionary Hearst Press, who violently opposed organised labour, communism or any attempt to radicalise the theatre. The opening lines of *Newsboy* parody the escapist journalese of Citizen Kane's papers. 'Evening paper, read all about it. Love nest raided on Park Avenue. Extra! Marlene Deitrich insures leg for $50,000 . . . Yanks take Dodgers 3—0 . . . Getcha paper here.' As the newsboy sells his papers the realities of depression America parade in front of him. He sees breadlines, pan-handlers and people reduced to fighting over a dime. Ultimately a racist attack on an innocent black affects the newsboy. The event is a political epiphany and he becomes attracted to communism. *Newsboy* ends with the hero selling copies of the *Daily Worker* and a passer-by encouraging the audience to join in the struggle. It is no longer the pro-Soviet exhortations of earlier scripts but a reminder that the genre has come to terms with its own domestic popular culture: 'Get yourself a trumpet, buddy, a big red trumpet. And climb to the top of the Empire State Building and blare out the news — Time to Revolt.'

Having begun in Europe and gone through a process of Americanisation it was inevitable that agit-prop would ultimately be influenced by legitimate theatre. Until the National Spartakiade of Workers' Theatres in April 1932[9] there had been no significant change in the movement's anti-bourgeois standpoint. The Spartakiade was advertised as 'A mobilization of all workers against the bourgeois theatre for the workers' theatre', but despite drawing a large entry it was severely criticised by the Marxist press. Even the winning entry performed by the Prolet Buehne did not escape unscathed. Nathaniel Buchwald, the director of the Yiddish Artef group, reviewed the winning entry, John Bonn's *Red Revue*, in *Workers' Theatre*. His criticism is applicable to most of the work of the period.

In general, the work of the Prolet Buehne, though outstanding in the field of Agit-Prop theatre, leans too heavily on direction and delivery of lines and too little on the dramaturgical shaping of its plays. The Prolet Buehne players speak their lines with a ringing galvanic forcefulness, and the director marshals them up on the stage in perfect rhythm and in a variety of group patterns, with changing tempi building up to a spectacular climax. But the plays themselves are frequently devoid of effective theatrical form and the vocabulary leans to the conventional propagandist jargon.

Bonn immediately responded to this criticism and repudiated his long-held rejection of bourgeois theatre. The propagandist theatre groups were now to learn all they could from the legitimate theatre. Thus in April 1932 a new period in the American workers' theatre began. They appealed to the skilled craftsmen of the Professional and Little Theatre movements for artistic and technical aid. Workers' Theatre Schools were established with professionals participating as tutors. Prominent members of Group Theatre like Harold Clurman, Lee Strasberg and Clifford Odets held special classes on theatre technique. In the Spring of 1933 a regional Spartakiade was organised. The event underlined the new direction in which agit-prop was moving. There was to be no outright rejection of bourgeois drama. Entries were accepted under three clearly defined groupings — 'Naturalism', 'Symbolic Review' and 'Militant Symbolism' (the new-wave term for agit-prop).

The collaboration of agit-prop and the social stage was a major step towards the foundation of a progressive people's theatre in the United States. In September 1933 *Workers' Theatre* became known as *New Theatre Magazine* and sought a 'popular-front' readership comprised of communists, socialists and Democrats united by their anti-fascist beliefs. The magazine carried articles from most of the important figures of New York's social theatre movement. Under the jurisdiction of the League of Workers' Theatres, *New Theatre*'s policy seemed to be diffuse. It claimed to embrace anyone who was 'assisting the advancement of theatrical art'. However, its list of foreign editors included Piscator, Meyerhold, Tretyakov and Romain Rolland, which suggests that *New Theatre* was not relinquishing *Workers' Theatre*'s broad-based Marxist outlook.

By the end of 1933 there were over 400 agit-prop groups in America but it was not long before they were to disappear completely. As *New Theatre*'s circulation grew to 3,500 the demand was clearly in favour of social drama rather than 'militant symbolism'. To cultivate this demand the magazine initiated 'New Theatre Nights' at the Civic Repertory Theatre in New York and ran a successful playwriting contest. The contest was won by Clifford Odets's *Waiting for Lefty*,

which is the archetypal American protest play and the logical conclusion of the fusion of social drama with agit-prop.

At the end of 1934 there were very few agit-prop groups left in
the United States. They had vanished for a variety of reasons. The
Soviet non-realist stage which had proved such a potent influence
was being stifled by Stalinist 'Socialist Realist' dogma. Epic Theatre
was favoured in Germany as a more comprehensive form in which
to raise political issues. The use of projection or 'the cinefication
of the theatre' was growing rapidly and was obviously incompatible
with itinerant agit-prop. Over and above these 'theatrical' reasons
for the decline of agit-prop there was a major political reason.
Agit-prop was a less suitable form in which to discuss anti-fascist
politics than it had been with the more clear-cut issues of class
conflict.

After a relatively short but eventful lifespan, agit-prop disappeared
from the American scene, but it did not expire without influencing
subsequent American theatre. Besides *Waiting for Lefty*, its contribution to American theatre history is significant. The American
Epic Theatre, particularly Marc Blitzstein's *The Cradle Will Rock*

Agit-prop technique on the professional stage: the partnership scene in the
Federal Theatre Living Newspaper *Injunction Granted* (New York, 1936).
Reproduced by courtesy of the Federal Theatre Research Centre, North Virginia.

211

and the Federal Theatre Project's Living Newspapers, particularly *Injunction Granted*, borrowed its slogans, knockabout scenes and rapid transitions from agit-prop. The Federal Theatre's experimental policy was largely activated by project workers recruited from the agit-prop groups (John Bonn was director of the Federal Theatre's German unit in New York). Finally, the integration of the blacks into American theatre, which was precipitated by the Federal Theatre (particularly their Negro Unit), was initiated by the agit-prop movement.

It could be argued that agit-prop did not die in the thirties but merely retired. It was regenerated in the sixties when the Vietnam war and America's proto-imperialist policies created the ideal political climate. By this time the name agit-prop had become anachronistic and the term 'Guerilla Theatre' was invented. The name was new but the style and themes were time honoured.

NOTES

1 *Tempo, Tempo* appeared in the *Workers' Theatre Magazine* and is reproduced here in the appendix, p. 315.
2 The script of *Scottsboro* is contained in Karen M. Taylor, *People's Theatre in Amerika* (New York, 1972).
3 The script of *Vote Communist* is contained in *Guerilla Street Theatre*, ed. Henry Lesnick (New York, 1973).
4 Two extant versions of *Newsboy* are known to exist in print. The first version, to which I refer, can be found in Jay Williams, *Stage Left* (New York, 1974). The later version, which includes parodies of well-known American right-wingers, including Father Coughlin, Huey Long and Hearst, is more patently anti-fascist and can be found in Taylor, *People's Theatre in Amerika*.
5 *New Masses* (December, 1930).
6 *New Masses* (September, 1931).
7 *Ibid*.
8 *The Big Stiff* appeared in the *Workers' Theatre Magazine*.
9 A more extensive report on the National Spartakiade can be found in the *Drama Review*, 17:4 (1973).

Workers' theatre 1926-36*

Raphael Samuel

'Cultural Politics' in Britain is today very largely a preoccupation of
the New Left, and the proliferation of socialist theatre groups —
perhaps its most vigorous expression in recent years, and certainly
the one which has made most impact on the labour movement —
is peculiarly a phenomenon of the 1970s: 7:84, probably the best
known of the new theatre groups, was only founded in 1971, Red
Ladder in 1968, CAST (Cartoon Archetypal Slogan Theatre) around
1966. The new troupes are determinedly experimental, and insofar
as any lineage is recognised at all, it does not go beyond Unity
Theatre, which is vaguely associated with the 1930s, and remembered
only in its moribund later years, or Joan Littlewood's Theatre Workshop, founded (with Ewan MacColl) in 1945. Yet many of the
questions discussed today were burning issues for socialist theatre
workers in the 1920s, in now-forgotten movements like the Workers'
Theatre Movement (WTM), and the idea of a political theatre can be
traced back as least to the 1900s. It played an important, if subsidiary
role, in the early socialist movement (1880—1914), as also in the
suffragist agitation of the time, and it is possible that diligent research
may drive the frontier back still further. When — to take an instance
from trade union history — the operative stone-masons employed
on building the new House of Commons went on strike in 1841, they
hired the Victoria theatre for a benefit, and presented a dramatised

---

* Editor's note: the paper contributed by Raphael Samuel subsequently appeared as the
introduction to a feature in *History Workshop*, 4 (Autumn 1977), pp. 102—42. The
feature was entitled *Documents and Texts from the Workers' Theatre Movement (1928—
1936)* and consisted of the following: I Editorial introduction by Raphael Samuel; II 'A
Propertyless Theatre for a Propertyless Class' by Tom Thomas (1977); III Documents:
'The Market Quack in Hackney' — a monologue (1930); 'The Basis and Development
of the Workers' Theatre Movement' — a conference statement (1932); 'Solidarity Appeal
from the Proletarian Theatre Union of Japan' (1932); 'How to Produce *Meerut*', by
Charlie Mann (1933); *Their Theatre and Ours*, an agit-prop sketch for six performers
by Tom Thomas (1933).

version of their case. One of the strikers stood on the stage declaiming a long poetic argument which ended thus:[1]

> They would have made us slaves, nay worse; but then
> We struck to show them that we were still men.
> And all who value worth and manliness
> Have sympathised with us, except the Press —
> The Press! that engine to enlarge the slave,
> Can it refuse when truth and justice crave?
> Alas! Oppression sways the venal pen —
> Corruption backs the master — not the men!
> But time will come when these things will not be —
> When heaven will give success to honesty.
> And those who worked at Nelson's Monument,
> And Woolwich too — by slavery unbent,[2]
> Shall with their brethren raise a noble name
> That tyranny shall daunt, and treachery shame.
> Oh! may the members of the Houses be,
> as were the builders, foes to tyranny.

The main cultural thrust of the early socialist movement was in music, which for some forty years occupied a central place both in branch life and in open-air propaganda. Concert meetings, with both vocal and instrumental music preceding the propaganda address, were a staple fare of the Independent Labour Party (ILP), both at political demonstrations and Sunday evening lectures. 'Have singing at all the meetings', ILP branches were advised in September 1903. 'A good hymn puts everybody in good humour. If possible, have at every meeting a soloist, quartet or reciter.'[3] Massed singing was no less characteristic an activity for the Clarion League and the Co-operative Guilds; socialist choir movements were a major event in labour movement life down to at least the end of the 1920s. Even the Labour Party, culturally (if not electorally) the least ambitious organisation ever produced by the British Left, felt obliged, at least in its early years, to maintain a musical side. In 1925 the National Executive was sponsoring both a Choral Union — 'to develop the musical instincts of the people, and to render service to the labour movement' — and a Federation of Dramatic Societies, with Herbert Morrison, the up-and-coming machine politician, as its co-ordinator. In the London area there was even a Labour Party Symphony Orchestra. Morrison, 'one of the busiest members in the London movement', was the energetic master of ceremonies when the London Labour Choral Union held its second Musical Festival in 1925.[4]

The place of drama in the early socialist movement was more uncertain and it served as an adjunct to other activities rather than — as in the case of 'singing for socialism' — a spearhead. For some, like the Avelings, or the early followers of Bernard Shaw, it was a vehicle for advanced ideas, in the form of discussion plays (principally those of Shaw himself) and 'ethical' drama (Ibsen, Galsworthy).[5] For others, notably the co-ops, who in the 1920s sponsored hundreds of drama classes and theatrical troupes, it was primarily an arena for education and improvement. In the ILP, as also in the Social Democratic Federation (SDF), 'dramatic entertainments' were put on as a means of raising party funds, paying off branch debts, and livening up social occasions. The Socialist Sunday Schools and the Woodcraft Folk and Junior Co-op Guilds prepared dramatic tableaux for Labour's May Day, and staged performances at the summer galas and winter-time bazaars. Propaganda plays, before 1914, seem to have been comparatively few, but in 1912 the National Association of Clarion Dramatic Clubs set about forming a library of plays dealing with Labour and socialist subjects, and encouraging local authors to write for the central body. Among the plays available to them at that time were the expressively titled *Woman's Rights* by Sackville Martin, *Recognition of the Union* by Landon Ronald, and *Evolution* by Norman Tiptaft.[6]

One of the most impressive of these early socialist dramatic ventures, and certainly the most enduring, was the People's Theatre of Newcastle upon Tyne, which survives to the present day. (Its stablemate, the Gateshead Little Theatre, founded by the local ILP in 1914, has also had a long life and still exists.) The Newcastle Theatre started life in 1911 as a Clarion Club offshoot of the British Socialist Party (BSP), the successor of the SDF and one of the Marxist forerunners of the Communist Party. Its nucleus was made up from a family called Veitch: Norman, who was to be one of the leading actors for the following fifty years, Colin, who was also captain of the Newcastle United football team (at that time holders of the Football Association Cup), and his wife, who acted as financial secretary. The theatre ran in tandem with the BSP (later the Newcastle Socialist Club) from 1911—28, sharing the same premises. It was originally formed to raise funds for the BSP, but soon branched out into propaganda sketches and full-length plays on 'advanced' subjects. Nine of the first twelve plays were by Bernard Shaw, and it was the performance of Shaw which made the group's local reputation though they also put on some of the propaganda sketches of the Clarion League, and, in later years, the dramas of Toller and the brothers Čapek, as well as a more orthodox repertoire of amateur dramatics.[7]

The Workers' Theatre Movement (1928–36) was marked off from these early ventures in a number of ways, but above all, perhaps, by its sharp emphasis on class struggle. It belonged to the Communist rather than the Labour wing of the movement; it was concerned with agitation rather than entertainment, and addressed itself to specific issues rather than the 'social question' generally. Theatrically, it turned increasingly from 'naturalistic' drama to agit-prop, in the form of sketches, cabaret and revue, and attempted to exchange indoor performances for a theatre of the street.

The WTM was contemptuous of what it termed 'left centre' and ILP drama, but this was the soil in which it was originally nourished. The years after the First World War seem to have seen a large expansion in politically based drama groups (the Woolwich Labour Thespians and the Welwyn Garden City Labour Players are two of the names one comes upon),[8] and a considerable appetite, within the labour movement, for a more committed drama. The sharpening of class struggle and the increasing polarisation of British politics along class lines were reflected in its themes. There was a spate of anti-war plays — notably those of Miles Malleson (Henderson's Bomb Shop in Charing Cross Road reissued two of those which had been banned in 1916 as subversive)[9] and in 1926 the Labour Publishing Company began publishing a series of 'Plays for the People' which soon ran to some twenty titles.[10] As well as this there were also the efforts of worker-playwrights and literary-minded branch secretaries who turned their hands to writing propaganda scripts. In the ILP, according to the *Labour Leader* (1 June 1922) there was a 'great rush' to put on sketches and plays. In Edinburgh the local ILP packed the Melbourne Hall for their propaganda sketch *This Way Out*, written by the branch secretary, and in Glasgow the Shettleton ILP were no less successful with their sketch *What Tommy Fought For*. 'This makes the fifth Sunday this season that the branch propaganda party have filled the Sunday Evening meeting', wrote the *Labour Leader* in February 1922. 'Branches finding a difficulty in maintaining an attendance at their weekly meetings should try this method, for as much propaganda is given in the sketch as is often supplied by our ablest Socialist speakers.'[11]

The Plebs League, and the National Council of Labour Colleges

(NCLC) — the syndicalist and Marxist breakaway from Ruskin
College, and rival in adult education to the Workers' Educational
Association — were also fostering propagandist drama in these
years, with class struggle, rather than pacifism, as their central theme.
One of their early productions (staged in association with the *Sunday
Worker*) was Upton Sinclair's *Singing Jailbirds*, a play about the
Californian seamen's strike of 1923 which had earned its author a
spell in jail, and which was later to figure in the early repertoire of
the WTM.[12] Jack and Alice Loveman, who played with the Greenwich
Red Blouses and the Streatham Red Front in the early 1930s, remember performing this with a south-east London Plebs group about
1924 or 1925, using Wobbly songs to heighten the drama of the
readings.[13] It was from the NCLC that the most systematic case
for class struggle drama was to come — Ness Edwards's *The Workers'
Theatre*. In this little book the author, a Labour College tutor at the
time, and later a miners' agent in the Rhymney Valley (S. Wales),
dismisses every species of legitimate theatre as either irretrievably
class-biased (Shakespeare is accused of dignifying royalty, and
making his plebeian characters figures of fun) or else — like West End
marriage dramas — sterile and superannuated. He pays tribute to Ibsen
and Shaw ('radical social drama'), but argues that the new workers'
drama, corresponding to the movement and the spirit of the age,
must present problems in class rather than personal terms.

The Workers' Drama is an agitational force. It is propaganda by a dramatisation
of facts.

What the drama was able to do for the Catholic Church, the Guilds and the
ruling classes, it can be made to do for the working class. No longer will it be
confined to a professional clique, no longer will it be merely an entertainment.[14]

A less tangible, though ultimately perhaps more potent, influence
was that of post-war German expressionism, with its predilection
for montage, and evident rejection of bourgeois art-forms. This was
the movement to which Brecht owed his artistic formation and its
drama came to England via 'little' theatres, like the Everyman, Hamp-
stead, and the Gate in Covent Garden, as well as by the publication
of individual scripts. Ernst Toller's dramas made by far the greatest
impact on the labour movement, to judge by their reception in the
socialist press, and their effect was heightened by the fact that
when the first translations appeared the author was still serving time
in jail for his support of the Bavarian Soviet in 1919. As early as 1922
the *Labour Leader* was hailing Toller's work as the most brilliant

217

poetic product of 'revolutionary pacifism' (15 June 1922) and in 1924 *Plebs* was producing a special cheap edition of *Masses and Man* for its readers.[15] In *The Workers' Theatre* Ness Edwards had this to say about *Machine Wreckers*, Toller's verse-drama about the Nottinghamshire Luddites: 'This play is a real workers' drama. It depicts the class struggle, the class problem; it exposes the working class weaknesses, arouses class emotions, and endeavours to carry its audience with it to make Lud's prophecy become a living fact.' Another play to have a big impact, as an attack on machine civilisation, was Karel Čapek's *R.U.R.*, first produced in 1926. It is a kind of stage equivalent of *Metropolis*, a nightmare vision of capitalism in which cheap work machines, or robots, replace the working class. Čapek's *R.U.R.* was one of the first WTM productions, and Toller's *Masses and Man* and his *Machine Wreckers* were among the very few full-length plays to keep their place in the WTM repertoire when it had turned, for the most part, to cabaret and revue.[16] (Another to survive was an earlier German play, Hauptman's *The Weavers*; Kaiser's expressionist drama *Gas* also enjoyed a high reputation among socialist theatre workers in these years.)

The WTM was preceded by – and should be understood in the context of – a whole series of local and national initiatives. At Bowhill, in the Fife coalfield, a group of players formed around Joe Corrie, the miner-poet, presenting dramas of mining life in the pit villages which, in the 1935 election, were to return Britain's first Communist Member of Parliament.[17] In Woolwich, Labour's earliest citadel in South London, the Trades and Labour Council set up a workers' theatre at the Plumstead Radical Club, to offset the 'anti-working class dope' of press, pulpit, school, cinema and radio, and to propagate the Co-operative Commonwealth. Tom Mann opened the first show, which was made up of a comedy on the housing question – *Mrs Jupp Obliges* – and a political farce on general elections.[18] At Levenshulme, Manchester, under the auspices of the local Labour Party, a workers' theatre was developed out of the dramatic section of the National Council of Labour Colleges, performing its first play in October 1927. 'Ultimately', wrote the *Co-operative News*, 'the theatre may become similar in outlook to the Moscow Arts Theatre, and present plays under conditions which will make community drama possible.'[19]

The Hackney Labour Players – the original nucleus of the Workers' Theatre Movement – evolved rather differently. They staged their first performance in the weeks before the General Strike, but at the

218

start they seem to have been intended more as a way of livening up branch social nights than as a means of propaganda. The group, however, moved steadily to a more committed theatre, concentrating first on slice-of-life dramas, then — in association with other theatre troupes — evolving towards cabaret and revue.[20] The Lewisham Red Players grew out of a hard core of what one of them has described as 'Old SDF families'. Two of them had played with the Plebs League, and also taken part in 'Red Concerts' and the Deptford Labour choir. Another was a teacher who had been recruited from the Lewisham Labour Party dramatic group.[21] Others were taking part in dramatic performances for the first time, though they would have been used to public speaking, since most of them were members of the Young Communist League. The Salford Red Megaphones evolved from a group of Clarion Players, some of them — like the Lewisham Red Players — from old SDF families, and when the group established an indoor theatre in 1934 it was at the old headquarters of the South Salford SDF.[22] The London WTM groups (reflecting, perhaps, the peculiar composition of the metropolitan Communist Party and Young Communist League) seem to have been drawn quite largely from clerks, school teachers and out-of-work young people, together with a substantial complement of East End Jewish proletarians. The northern WTM groups were more working class. The Bowhill Players were miners, mostly drawn from a single village street,[23] while Ewan MacColl remembers the Salford Red Megaphones as being made up of two weavers, a miner, a motor mechanic (himself) 'and the rest were unemployed'.[24]

The rise and extension of the Workers' Theatre Movement was closely associated with the 'Left' turn in the Communist International (1928–34), and its translation into terms of 'class against class' in Britain. Though developing, in many cases, out of a pre-existing tradition of Labour drama, it mirrored the sharp break which took place between Labour and Communist in these years. The WTM stepped zestfully into this breach:

It rejects decisively the role of raising the cultural level of the workers through contact with great dramatic art which is the aim of the dramatic organisations of the Labour Party and the ILP . . . the task of the WTM is the conduct of mass working class propaganda and agitation through the particular method of dramatic representation.[25]

The rupture was fully in line with Party feeling, and it had the notable endorsement of two of the leading Communist intellectuals of the day. Palme Dutt denounced ILP drama as 'reformist',[26] while

Maurice Dobb was no less scathing about the 'so-called socialist' plays of Miles Malleson, 'whose "labour" hero is so much at home with a baronet's daughter in a Mayfair drawing-room, and whose *Fanatics* discuss the "sex problem" as though . . . the class struggle did not exist'.[27] There was a parallel development in music when Rutland Boughton (a leading composer, and for many years an indefatigable worker in the socialist cause) left the London Labour Choral Union and formed a new choir devoted to revolutionary mass singing: for too long, it was claimed, Labour choirs bearing socialist labels had been singing nothing but 'Annie Laurie' and 'Aberystwyth'.[28]

The WTM linked its work, wherever possible, to specific agitations. The sketch *Gas Masks*, for instance, served as a prologue to anti-war meetings, and those on the means test to rallies of the unemployed. In Sheffield, the WTM was reformed by a group of younger members who wanted to pursue a more activist course: during a local strike of newspaper sellers they wrote a sketch about it and played it on the streets, while the strike was proceeding, 'with very great success'. The Becontree Reds, at Dagenham, East London, wrote a sketch about an eviction and were able to perform it outside the house where the actual eviction was threatening, 'thus contributing very effectively to the fight to defend the workers' homes'.[29] 'Grim drama', as the *Daily Worker* rightly remarked, marked a WTM performance of *Murder in the Coalfields* in the Rhondda: the troupe had hardly finished putting on the first performance of the play, at Treherbert, when news was brought to the hall that eleven miners had been killed in a terrible pit explosion at Llwynypia.[30] The WTM also played an active part in raising funds for strikers. One of their early efforts was in support of the twelve-week strike for union recognition at Rego's, a tailoring factory in North London: in the course of it seven students from the Central Labour College were expelled for singing for the Rego girls at a WTM strike benefit.[31] In Lancashire, during the 'More Looms' agitation of 1931–2 (a series of rolling strikes in which hundreds of thousands of workers were involved), the WTM members — mostly unemployed young workers - made fund-raising their central activity. As Ewan MacColl, a member at the time of the Salford Red Megaphones, recalls:

It became a question of going and performing on every street of a town, putting on a show lasting about four minutes, collecting contributions, and then moving on to the next street. You took a barrow with you, or a hand-cart, and collected food, and bundles of clothing, and money, and it all went into the strikers' relief fund.[32]

The WTM also came to occupy a definite place in Communist Party life. They would be used as crowd-drawers at street-corner meetings, or to hold the fort until the speaker had arrived. They would perform from the back of lorries at the larger demonstrations, or in street-corner work with planks and trestles as the stage. They were also widely used on social occasions, very much as the Clarion Players had served the ILP. Harry Pollitt found their May Day Show in 1931 very impressive, but 'got the impression that the comrades were apt to be concentrating on getting too much propaganda across of rather heavy character'. Characteristically he called for more wit and colour. 'In all their shows they should remember that there are many humourous incidents both in the workers' lives and the capitalist class social life that can most effectively be portrayed, and, at the same time, a political message can be conveyed.'[33] The most hazardous work was in the open air. Like other Communist activity at that time it involved a cat-and-mouse relationship with the police. Ewan MacColl recalls:

If we were due, say, to go to Wigan, in the bus on the way we'd write the sketch and we'd try it out for about half-an-hour, and then put it on at the market place by the stalls. We'd maybe be there for ten minutes before the police arrived in a van, and we'd scarper, say, to the steps of the public baths, and put it on there. Or we'd go to a factory, and occasionally we'd manage to get through a few satirical songs outside the factory gate before the police came and moved us on.[34]

The WTM had an ideology — a definite theory of what theatre was about. All art was propaganda and the theatre itself a splendid weapon of struggle, both as a means of consciousness-raising and of dramatising specific issues. They rejected what they called 'the theatre of illusion' and instead put forward a theatre of ideas. They were equally opposed to 'naturalism' ('a mere photographic view of things as they appear on the surface') and counterpoised to this what Tom Thomas called 'Dialectic Realism' — 'the X-ray picture of society and social forces'.[35] They performed not full-length plays, but sketches and satires, or montages of mime and song. Instead of individualistic characterisation ('the basis of the bourgeois stage')[36] they concentrated on types, and employed the simplest possible devices as signifiers. 'If you wanted to represent the boss you put a top hat on, and if you wanted to be a worker you put a cloth cap on.' The WTM used no costumes, except for dungarees, and no make-up: when Prolet, the WTM's Yiddish-speaking group in East London, used a judge's wig in one of their sketches, a heated controversy followed

221

and a special meeting was called at which they were threatened with expulsion for making use of props.[37] Words were kept deliberately simple, partly to cut down on the need for elaborate rehearsals, partly to avoid individualistic self-boosting, but chiefly in order to get the message across. Charlie Mann, of the Lewisham Red Players, devised a particular method of choral speaking, and made his actors clip their words so as to avoid the risk of any of them being slurred. He also went in for half-repetition (suitably disguised), to heighten audience concentration, and make sure that nothing was lost.[38]

WTM troupes had nothing in the way of a stage beyond a bare platform. They built up their visual effects not by scenery, but by rhythm, gesture, and pace. In the *Meerut* sketch, a short piece about the jailed trade union agitators in India, the sketch opened with the statement: 'In every state in British India, troops and police are out to crush the rising tide of revolt.' But the tension was built up not so much by words as by a tightly disciplined choreography. The actors came on with broomsticks — three vertical, two horizontal — which they clasped together to indicate a prison. Each of the prisoners then told his story and ended by stretching his arms through the bars. 'The secret was to start on a sombre note and then intensify', Charlie Mann recalls, and his directions show how meticulously the gestures were planned. In *Rationalisation*, a sketch about unemployment in industry, the players were introduced with a song ('Speed up, speed up, watch your step — Hold on tight and show some pep') but the drama of the action lay in the mime. 'The speed up was introduced and then one [worker] dropped, and another dropped out, until only one was left.'[38]

Many of these techniques were adapted from the agit-prop theatre in Germany, then in the most brilliant, if tragic, phase of its development, on the eve of fascist power. They made an enormous impact on the WTM troupe who toured the Rhineland in 1931, as Tom Thomas testifies, and the impact was enhanced by the German 'contacts' who were sent to England to give advice and instruction to the WTM.[39] Nevertheless the evolution in the direction of sketches and cabaret was an indigenous British development, which preceded the movement's contact with Germany, and so too were such sketches as the Hackney Market Quack monologue, with their peculiar mixture of the colloquial and the didactic, the music hall and Shaw. The rejection of 'slice-of-life' or naturalistic drama also seems to have preceded the WTM's German visit. Gorky's *Lower Depths* and Sean

O'Casey's *Juno and the Paycock* were being dismissed as 'pessimistic' by English Communists in 1926, while Upton Sinclair's *Singing Jailbirds* was expelled from the early WTM repertory as 'defeatist'.[40] The idea of a street theatre seems to have been mainly due to the German example, though the Hammersmith WTM troupe had already adopted it in the spring of 1931,[41] and so too was the extremely disciplined choreography exemplified in the *Meerut* sketches. Montage too may have been adopted from Germany, though *Their Theatre and Ours* shows that it was possible to naturalise it in a thoroughly English setting.[42]

The WTM was uninhibitedly — even, one might say, exuberantly — sectarian. Parliament was 'the gashouse show' and the three main parties were treated as one and the same. The troupes sported the hammer and sickle, and their message was openly revolutionist. As the Lewisham troupe put it in their group chorus:

> There is a word you mustn't say — revo-lution
> All the same it's on the way — the workers' revolution
> Every day the world turns round — revo-lution
> A few more turns, it will resound, to the workers' revolution.
> It's coming here, it's coming there — revo-lution
> The ground it's tumbling everywhere — the workers' revolution.[43]

How then, in a country where communism was comparatively weak, did the WTM win a following in the labour movement? How, even more problematically, did they get a hearing on the streets? In some cases it was because of their association with particular agitations. In others it was because their sketches were speaking to central and familiar experiences. In the case of the *War Memorial* sketch, for instance, it did not require any particular Communist sympathies to respond with anger at the memory of the First World War generals who had sent millions of soldiers to their deaths;[44] and listeners to the Hackney monologue knew well enough that pallor and undernourishment were associated with low pay. 'The whole thing was to get down to the audience familiarity', Charlie Mann says, recalling his troupe's performances in Lewisham High Street; he speaks too of the invisible support of class feeling:

> At that time — it doesn't apply today — there was a sort of working-class loyalty against the powers that be. It wasn't exactly socialist, but there was this feeling of brotherhood among working people. We'd get more than fifty per cent of the audience with us — some just looking because it was something to watch. Sometimes ten per cent would be hostile, but these would be generally shouted down by others. We always got respect from the audience — on the whole they were sympathetic and prepared to listen.[45]

The WTM, like other theatres of its kind, depended on real-life agitations for its sustenance, and was peculiarly susceptible to changes in the political atmosphere. The movement was at its height in the period of the third National Hunger March — the largest mobilisation of the unemployed in inter-war Britain — and the 'More Looms' agitation in Lancashire. It was brought to an end in 1936 as a result of a radical realignment of class forces.

The demise, or virtual demise, of the WTM in 1936, after a vigorous life of some seven or eight years, corresponds to a much more general change in the cultural and political climate. Very summarily and crudely one may suggest that the WTM was a casualty of the Popular Front, and the change in the Communist Party line from 'class against class' to that of the broad 'progressive' alliance — the eventual response of British Communists, like those in other lands, to the rise of Hitler's Germany. The Popular Front marked the end, or the partial end, of the revolutionary epoch in European communism; artistically it was associated with the rise of 'socialist realism' in the Soviet Union and a decisive rupture between communism and experimental art. In theatre it was accompanied by the destruction of agit-prop, along with every other species of socialist and communist activity, in Nazi Germany. At home the WTM was irretrievably associated with what now came to be regarded as sectarianism; its exuberant revolutionism was an embarrassment; its attacks on the Labour Left, out of place, while its very name was an obstacle to building the broad alliance. It is possible that there were other less immediately political causes at work, sapping its cultural energies and undermining its appeal — the partial stabilisation of British capitalism in the mid thirties, the falling off in the industrial struggle, at least in the old manufacturing areas, and the decline in the number and even more strikingly the mass activity of the unemployed.

Another tendency, closely related to the rise of fascism, was the quite widespread recruitment of professional people — among them actors — to the ranks of the British left, a phenomenon which was to find its apotheosis in the mass membership of the Left Book Club. As early as 12 December 1933 the *Daily Worker* comments on one or two theatre people who were beginning to take an interest in the WTM and to offer their professional services. There was, it seems, consternation when the first of them — a well-known London producer — appeared, and after much discussion it was decided to assign him to the Rebel Players, 'a troublesome and difficult group in East London'.[46] But by 1935 at least four WTM groups were under pro-

224

fessional producers, and when Unity Theatre was founded in March 1936 the leadership of professional directors was accepted without question. Outside the WTM the Westminster Theatre was putting on plays of 'social significance' (among them were two by 'the well-known revolutionary poet' W. H. Auden),[47] while the Embassy, Swiss Cottage, was experimenting with mass spectacle, notably in the anti-war play *Miracle at Verdun* (André van Gyseghem made his reputation there as one of the most brilliant directors in London, before moving on to Unity Theatre in 1936). The appearance of a 'West End' theatre left was also marked by the formation, in April 1934, of an organisation called Left Theatre, which put on Sunday performances at the Phoenix theatre, and took its shows to Labour and Co-operative halls. It was composed exclusively of professional actors and actresses, and among those who appeared for it were Ina de la Haye, an artiste 'frequently heard on the wireless', and Anita Sharpe-Bolster, who gave entertaining sketches of village ladies.[48]

Within the WTM there seems to have been a growing demand for more professional standards of performance, and there were also a number of moves towards the establishment of indoor theatres. The West Ham United Front troupe were proudly announcing in March 1935 that they now had their own hall ('with a properly equipped stage, and an electric light outside').[49] Theatre Action in Manchester set up in a permanent home, and they were followed by the Rebel Players in London, who in 1936 established themselves, as Unity Theatre, in a converted mission hall in Goldington Square. In Manchester (according to snippets which appeared occasionally in the *Daily Worker*), there seems to have been a deliberate attempt to break out of the WTM's theatrical isolation. In February 1935 the WTM was pleased to record that the Rusholme Repertory Company had called on it for assistance in providing a crowd of workers who actually looked like workers ('this sort of operation means a big step forward for the WTM and it should become universal', the *Daily Worker* approvingly commented); and it followed this up by sending out a questionnaire to actors, critics and authors with a view to forming a 'United Front' of theatre progressives.[50]

In art as in politics the epoch of the Popular Front made revolutionary perspectives an embarrassment.[51] Unity was the watchword of the day, and in the theatre it found its most extreme expression in the formation of the New Theatre League. The League was intended to subsume the Workers' Theatre Movement in a larger, umbrella organisation, which would link all amateur dramatic groups with 'progressive' ideas and also obtain the co-operation of professional artists. At the inaugural meeting there were performances by the Dance Drama Group, the Labour Choral Union, Theatre Action of Manchester, and the Battersea Players, and the speakers included Gillian Scaife of the Westminster Theatre, William Armstrong of British Actors Equity, and the Earl of Kinoull, who spoke on 'peace plays'.[52] No WTM names appear among the speakers, and when Unity Theatre was opened some three months later, the opening ceremony was performed not by an agit-prop troupe, but by Dr Edith Summerskill, the victorious peace candidate in the Fulham East by-election and in later years a well-known cabinet minister.[53]

The founding of Unity in 1936 marked a partial breakaway from agit-prop, and a return to legitimate, conventional theatre. It was under the firm direction of professional producers, even though its actors were part-time, and amongst the actors themselves there was a good deal of traffic with the West End stage (Alfie Bass, Bill Owen and Ted Willis are three of the well-known theatre people who first made their name at Goldington Square). Unity Theatre productions were widely reviewed in the capitalist press, and the notices pinned up for members to see in the club-room. It also won favourable notice in the world of amateur dramatics, and in 1939 carried off the prizes at the annual festival of the British Drama League (the WTM, by contrast, confined its competitive efforts to the international olympiad of revolutionary theatre groups in Moscow). Artistically Unity made few innovations, and for the most part was content with a fairly simple naturalism. Politically, too, its aims were comparatively modest, and though it prided itself on the 'social significance' of its plays ('Sing me a Song of Social Significance' was a pre-war Unity hit tune), the main thrust of its work lay in the direction of finished staging and accomplished performances.

The WTM was dead set against the entire paraphernalia of the theatre, whether in its West End, repertory or amateur dramatic forms. Unity, on the other hand, was much more ambiguously placed, and on many of the artistic issues of the time found itself facing both ways. Yet one should not exaggerate the rupture. *Waiting for Lefty* — the play which made Unity's reputation — is a play which breathes a revolutionary spirit, and dates from an earlier period (it had already been performed by two WTM groups in 1935). The trade union leaders are the villains of the piece (the play is about a taxi drivers' strike in New York), and it ends with a tremendous appeal to the 'stormbirds of the working class' which has not lost its theatrical,

226

or political, force today; the 'mass speaking' by the audience which follows — a minor theatrical sensation in its day — was precisely the same device as the Hackney Labour Players had used to conclude their 1928 production of *The Ragged Trousered Philanthropists*. The Living Newspaper, another of Unity's early theatrical coups, had been widely used by the Proletkult groups in early 1920s Russia, and was staged in England by the Holborn Labour Party players as early as 1926.[54]

The relationship of left theatre in the later thirties to its predecessors is difficult to characterise, and awaits a critical and historical account both of the Unity Theatre movement (there were Unity Theatres in the provinces, as well as the London one in Goldington Square) and of the Left Book Club Theatre Guild, which in 1938 had some 250 different groups.[55] It is clear, though, that the spirit of the WTM was very far from dead. Many of the new groups played the Labour and Co-operative halls, very much as the WTM had done, and the pageants they took part in had much in common with the mass speaking which the WTM had pioneered. In Manchester, the Theatre of Action, led by Joan Littlewood and Ewan MacColl, was developing a combination of theatre and song and mime which, like many of the WTM sketches, was to draw heavily on popular idiom. Unity Theatre itself, at least in its early years, kept strictly to group ideals and, until the war, the actors' names did not even appear on the programme.

The WTM's work is difficult to evaluate unless you have seen it performed, and even when it is possible to rescue a few of the texts it is impossible to recreate the original circumstances in which they were staged.[56] No runners would appear bringing news of a pit disaster, as happened to the WTM troupe at Treherbert, nor would there be hunger marchers to assess the truth, or otherwise, of the message. One context which has vanished, and which must have done a great deal to give the street theatre its force, is the open-air meeting, which, for more than a century, served as a very cockpit in the battle of ideas. Another is that of a labour movement which offered — or attempted to offer — to its members an alternative cultural universe. On the other hand, the questions raised by the Workers' Theatre Movement, both about the contents of a socialist theatre and its form, are live issues for many theatre workers today, and their experience, if it is brought to bear on history, could do a good deal to illuminate the record of the past, as well as to bring enlightenment and perspective to the present. The cultural dimension of politics is one which historians of the modern labour movement have consistently ignored. We hope this feature will prompt some of them to undertake the work before the materials on which it should be based are irretrievably thinned.

NOTES

1 W. S. Hilton *Foes to Tyranny* (London, 1963), p. 82. 'The Vic' was a great proletarian theatre in the days before it was anaesthetised by the Coffee Taverns and Lilian Baylis.

2 For the solidarity strikes at Nelson's Monument and Woolwich Dockyard, see Rodney Mace, *Trafalgar Square* (London, 1976), p. 96.

3 *ILP News* (September 1905), p. 6. The 'hymns' referred to are Labour anthems such as Edward Carpenter's 'England Arise'.

4 *Co-operative News*, 9 May 1925, p. 11; *Clarion*, 21 Aug. 1925, p. 7, 25 Dec. 1925, p. 2, 13 Aug. 1926, p. 2, 29 Oct. 1926, p. 1, 27 Nov. 1926, p. 4; *Sunday Worker*, 31 May 1925, p. 10, 1 Nov. 1925, p. 8; B. Donoghue and G. W. Jones, *Herbert Morrison* (London, 1973), pp. 70–3.

5 'Drama with a Purpose' was *Clarion*'s description of Galsworthy's *Silver Box* (*Clarion*, 7 Aug. 1925, p. 3), while the *Co-operative News*, reviewing a performance of it by the Holyoake Players at Eccles, Lancs., claimed that it 'probes beneath the fickle surface of society' (6 March 1926, p. 9).

6 Norman Veitch, *The People's* (London, 1950), pp. 14–15.

7 See Veitch, *The People's*, pp. 1–12, 18–19, 29–31, 41, 70–5, 88–90, 102–3, for the long but difficult association of theatre with the Newcastle socialist movement. See *Clarion*, 31 March 1911, for the foundation of the theatre.

8 W. Barefoot, *Twenty-Five Years ... Woolwich Labour Party* (Woolwich 1928), p. 40; *Clarion*, 23 Jan. 1925, p. 8.

9 *Clarion*, 13 Feb. 1925, p. 2. Henderson's was the predecessor of Collet's bookshop, Charing Cross Road.

10 The twentieth volume was a primer called *Play Production for Everyone* by Monica Ewer, drama critic of the *Daily Herald*. It carried an introduction by the actress Sybil Thorndike, who was a lifelong supporter of left-wing causes. Leonard A. Jones, 'The Workers' Theatre Movement in the Twenties', *Zeitschrift für Amerikanistik und Anglistik*, 14 (1966), writes that 'Plays for the People' started in 1920. But the *Sunday Worker*, 15 Nov. 1925, writes of it as a new series. There was an earlier but different series called 'Plays for the People', printed by C. W. Daniel Ltd and published by an organisation called 'The People's Theatre Society'. Its first play was Douglas Goldring's *The Fight for Freedom*. See *The Worker* (*Huddersfield*), 3 Jan. 1920.

11 *Labour Leader*, 16 Feb. 1922, p. 8, 6 April 1922, p. 8.

12 *Sunday Worker*, 27 June 1926, p. 8, 4 July 1926, p. 8, 25 July 1926, p. 8. For some Plebs playwrights, see *Plebs*, 16: 363 (Sept. 1924), 21: 234 (Oct. 1929).

13 Richard Stourac and Kathleen McCreery, interview with Jack and Alice

Loveman, July 1977. 'Wobblies' was the nickname of the American working-class socialist organisation, the International Workers of the World.

14 Ness Edwards, *The Workers' Theatre* (Cardiff, 1930), pp. 39—52, 79, 27—31. Although the Miners' Library copy of the book is dated 1930, the book appears to have been written in 1926. Do any readers have further information about the circumstances of its publication?

15 *Plebs*, 16: 9 (Sept. 1924).

16 Tom Thomas papers, 'List of Plays now available . . . ' (1934?).

17 *Daily Herald*, 3 Jan. 1928, p. 7; *Sunday Worker*, 8 Jan. 1928, p. 8, 29 Jan. 1928, p. 8. I would be grateful to hear from any reader who knows more about this group. At one stage they worked with the Glasgow Orpheus choir. They may have provided the original nucleus for the Cowdenbeath WTM. Joe Corrie became a prolific playwright on Scottish subjects. His numerous scripts, which continued to be published until the early 1960s, can be found in the British Library.

18 *Sunday Worker*, 10 Jan. 1926, p. 8, 11 Jul. 1926, p. 8; 2 Feb. 1927, p. 8. Sean O'Casey sent good wishes for the opening show. *Mrs Jupp Obliges* was one of the 'Plays for the People' produced by the Labour Publishing Company.

19 *Co-operative News*, 29 Oct. 1927, p. 9. The Labour Club had been opened in December 1925, with William Paul, editor of the *Sunday Worker*, giving a song-recital on 'Music and the Masses'. *Sunday Worker*, 6 Dec. 1925, p. 8.

20 For some press notices of the Hackney group, see *Daily Herald*, 26 Jan. 1928, p. 9; *Sunday Worker*, 8 Aug. 1926, p. 8, 23 Dec. 1928, p. 6, 14 July 1929, p. 7.

21 Raphael Samuel, interview with Charlie Mann, 30 June 1977.

22 Raphael Samuel, interview with Ewan MacColl, 13 Aug. 1977; Ewan MacColl, 'Grass Roots of Theatre Workshop', *Theatre Quarterly*, 3:9 (1973); Eddie and Ruth Frow, 'Manchester WTM', *History Workshop Journal*, forthcoming.

23 *Sunday Worker*, 25 Sept. 1927, p. 8.

24 Raphael Samuel, interview with Ewan MacColl.

25 Tom Thomas papers, memorandum of resolutions dated July 1930.

26 R. Palme Dutt, 'Notes of the Month', *Labour Monthly* (Aug. 1926).

27 Maurice Dobb, 'The Theatres', *Plebs*, 21: 54 (March 1929).

28 *Sunday Worker*, 14 July 1929, p. 7, 1 Dec. 1929, p. 5.

29 Tom Thomas, 'The Workers' Theatre in Britain', *International Theatre* (1934), pp. 23—4.

30 *Daily Worker*, 29 Jan. 1932, p. 6; for the disaster, see *ibid*, 27 Jan. 1932, p. 1.

31 *Sunday Worker*, 23 Dec. 1928, p. 1. Three of the expelled students were from the South Wales Miners' Federation, two from the National Union of Railwaymen, and two were on TUC scholarships.

32 MacColl, 'The Grass Roots of Theatre Workshop', pp. 59—60.

33 *Daily Worker*, 5 May 1931, p. 11.

34 MacColl, 'The Grass Roots of Theatre Workshop', p. 59.

35 *Daily Worker*, 8 Feb. 1930, p. 11.

36 *Ibid.*, 3 Jan. 1931, p. 4.

37 Ray Waterman, 'Prolet', *History Workshop Journal*, forthcoming. Richard Stourac and Kathleen McCreery, interview with Philip Poole.

38 Raphael Samuel, interview with Charlie Mann.
39 The first German 'contact' spoke at a WTM weekend school in June 1930. He spoke of the 'brilliant work' of the Hamburg 'Riveters' and criticised 'the mistaken attempt' of the WTM 'to wed decadent and erotic jazz tunes to the revolutionary message'. *Daily Worker*, 11 June 1930, p. 5.
40 *Sunday Worker*, 1 Dec. 1929, p. 4; 24 June 1928, p. 8; *Daily Worker*, 8 Feb. 1930, p. 11.
41 *Daily Worker*, 1 March 1931, p. 3.
42 A script by Tom Thomas (1932) reprinted with stage directions in *History Workshop*, 4 (Autumn 1977), pp. 137–42.
43 Raphael Samuel, interview with Charlie Mann.
44 A copy of the *War Memorial* sketch is in Tom Thomas's papers.
45 Raphael Samuel, interview with Charlie Mann.
46 Richard Stourac and Kathleen McCreery, interview with Philip Poole.
47 *Daily Worker*, 27 April 1935, p. 8.
48 *Ibid.*, 9 April 1934, p. 4.
49 *Ibid.*, 26 March 1935, p. 4.
50 *Ibid.*, 19 Feb. 1935, p. 4, 14 April, 1935, p. 4.
51 'Although it is not possible to draw many actors together on a pre-socialist basis, it is possible to get them on an anti-Fascist basis.' John Allen, 'The Socialist Theatre', *Left Review*, 3 (Aug. 1937), p. 418.
52 *Daily Worker*, 31 Jan. 1936, p. 7.
53 *Ibid.*, 22 Feb. 1936, p. 6.
54 *Sunday Worker*, 14 March 1936, p. 9.
55 'A Real Workers' Theatre Movement', *Discussion* (March 1938), p. 42.
56 Of the WTM sketches to survive, apart from the two reprinted in the Autumn 1977 issue of *History Workshop Journal*, 'Something for Nothing' and 'Love in Industry' will be found in *Red Stage* (April–May 1932), 'Speed up' in *ibid.* (June–July 1932); 'Means Test Murder' is in *Storm, Stories of the Struggle* (April 1933). There are no copies of *Red Stage* in the British Library, but the Frows 'Working Class Movements' Library has a file, as also some copies of *Storm*. There is one issue of the *Bulletin of the WTM* (no. 3) in the Marx Memorial Library. *History Workshop Journal* would be glad to hear from anyone else who has WTM materials, and would also urge them to have xerox copies made and copies sent to any of those libraries. *Something for Nothing*, a brief sketch on redundancy, has certainly not lost its point to-day and theatre groups might like to consider giving it new life. Tom Thomas's adaption of *The Ragged Trousered Philanthropists* is in the British Library; so too is *International Theatre* (the journal of the international workers' theatre movement) and Ness Edwards's *The Workers' Theatre*. There is an extract from *Malice in Plunderland* in Jones, 'The Workers' Theatre Movement', which also has a lively description by Mark Chaney of the reception given to Tom Thomas's *The Ragged Trousered Philanthropists* in town hall tours.

The October Group and theatre under
the Front Populaire

David Bradby

The Front Populaire government that came to power in June 1936,
and lasted for nineteen months until January 1938, was the first
French government since the revolution to promote the use of
theatre for political purposes. Because of this, the development of
different styles and forms in this period is particularly interesting
for the history of popular and political theatre.

Cultural policies

The government, composed of Radicals, Socialists and Communists
under a Socialist Prime Minister, Léon Blum, was a coalition of
political forces that a mere six years earlier had been fiercely opposed
to one another. After the sixth Communist International Congress in
1928, Western Communist Parties had agreed on a policy of refusing
to co-operate with Socialist or Radical parties, denouncing social
democracy as the first step on the road to fascism. This extremist
line was adopted with enthusiasm by writers like Aragon: in his
poem *Front Rouge* (1931), which earned him a five-year prison
sentence (suspended), he wrote

> Descendez les flics . . .
> Feu sur Léon Blum
> Feu sur Boncour Frossard Déat
> Feu sur les ours savants de la social-démocratie[1]

But the failure of the German Communist Party to contain the
rise of Nazism and the threat of a new war in Europe caused a
rapid change in such violent attitudes: politicians and writers of
East and West alike realised the importance of closing ranks against
fascism. Between 1932 and 1935, as the threat from the right in
France increased, Communists and Socialists joined forces once again.
The way to political union was shown by the numerous intellectual
and cultural organisations which were founded, grouping Communists

231

and Socialists of all shades, for example in 1932, the AEAR (Association des Ecrivains et des Artistes Révolutionnaires) and in 1934 the CVIA (Comité de Vigilance des Intellectuels Antifascistes).

This rapid reconciliation of former enemies was made possible by the enthusiasm of the Communist leader Maurice Thorez. He was determined to bury the old Bolshevik image and to present the Communists as the party of National Union. In place of the scorn frequently poured on nationalism and patriotism by Communists of the twenties, Thorez decreed the adoption once again of the *tricolore* flag and the *Marseillaise*. The politician was supported by the intellectuals, especially Paul Vaillant-Couturier and Louis Aragon, both of whom now changed course, abandoned the aggressive stance, and put their weight behind the policy of union, or *rassemblement*. It was under the influence of Thorez that the AEAR was founded, with Vaillant-Couturier as its secretary-general and Aragon, Nizan and Malraux among its most active members. In July 1933 the AEAR started a monthly journal, *Commune*, with a directing committee of Barbusse, Rolland, Gide and Vaillant-Couturier (only the last was active in policy making) and edited by Aragon and Nizan.[2]

Through this journal, which attracted contributions from every important left-wing writer, the *frontiste* enthusiasm of Thorez was developed. In its political articles, this entailed justifying and promoting the pact between Communists and Socialists, signed in 1934, and which was to lead to the Front Populaire victory in 1936. In its cultural policy, it lead to a frenzied appropriation of every French literary giant, ancient or modern, as part of the great popular cultural heritage. The doctrine which said that 'high' culture was tainted with bourgeois values was reversed and a new doctrine was proclaimed, which insisted that culture was 'one and indivisible' and that it was all to be seen as 'the inalienable property of the masses'.[3] In this changed atmosphere culture became inflated to the point where it subsumed every other aspect of traditional Communist policy, including the class struggle. Vaillant-Couturier wrote in *Commune* in 1935 that 'the class struggle to-day has become the equivalent of the struggle for culture'.[4]

Front Populaire policy on theatre

Thus for the period of the Front Populaire the gap separating revolutionary politics from the politics of Union was papered over; the potential clash of opposed tactical methods was resolved by abandoning

232

the call to violent struggle. A similar clash of opposed methods was apparent in the theatre, where there was also an attempt to cover it up. In the theatre it can be described as the clash between small-scale agit-prop theatre and mass spectacular theatre.

In the twenties there had been little political theatre; but in the early thirties an increasing number of workers' theatre groups were formed and in 1932, under Communist auspices, a national organisation was formed, the Fédération des Théâtres Ouvriers de France. Its tendencies were fairly militant and increased with Hitler's rise to power and the consequent arrival in France of many people who had been active in the very large German workers' theatre movement. Like its German counterpart, the Fédération encouraged agit-prop work in streets, factories or working men's halls and favoured the use of mass chant or spoken chorus.

But in 1936 with the coming to power of the Front Populaire government, the Communist Party's attitude towards workers' theatre was brought into line. The Fédération underwent a change of name: it was transformed into a Union of Independent French Theatres (Union des Théâtres Indépendants de France) and Aragon made an impassioned speech at its annual congress on the central theme of union.[5] He adopted as his watchword a phrase of Romain Rolland, who had spoken at a recent writers' congress of the 'indivisibility of peace'. Aragon in turn spoke of the 'indivisibility of culture, as of peace', and went on to say, 'that implies that its defence, like the defence of peace, can only be guaranteed by union, by collaboration among theatre people and among the people as a whole'. He concluded with a call for 'a Peoples' theatre such as Romain Rolland dreamed of, in which the virtues, heroism and gaiety of the French people will give birth to a new poetry . . . a poetry as international as the *Marseillaise*, which was the song of the Russian Revolution of 1905 in which the Soviets were invented'.

Theatre patronised by the Front Populaire

The kind of theatre patronised by the Front Populaire in accordance with this programme included almost anything except agit-prop. The first play sponsored by the new government was Rolland's *Danton*, performed at the Alhambra theatre on 14 July 1936. This performance of a play already creaking with age (it had first been performed in 1902) was received with unnatural enthusiasm. Critics wrote of the 'astonishing contemporaneity of every line and every

233

situation' or exclaimed that 'the Bastille was really taken that night'.[6]
These curiously inappropriate reactions to a play with a conservative
message and a patronising attitude towards the proletariat certainly
seem to show, as J.-P. A. Bernard has suggested, the unwillingness
of people at the time to analyse their real situation and their preference
for riding on the tide of enthusiasm.

But there were more up-to-date attempts at creating the new theatre
that Aragon had called for. The pretext in a number of cases was the
1937 Paris International Exhibition. For the opening of the exhibition,
the government commissioned a massive composite show of fourteen
scenes with musical interludes entitled *Long Live Liberty*, 'inspired
by the history of the French People'. It was performed in the fashion-
ably exclusive Théâtre des Champs Elysées and so could hardly be
said to have appealed to a popular audience.

A more coherent attempt to realise the idea of a theatre of union
and popular celebration was the performance of Jean-Richard Bloch's
Naissance d'une Cité (Birth of a City) at the Vélodrome d'Hiver. This
vast sports stadium imposed on Bloch a special style of writing, which
he defined as 'Un grand spectacle *total*':

since the dimensions of the stadium imply the presence of a vast crowd of
spectators, we made it our rule to try to draw in, around a central action that
was simple, progressive and lively, the principal desires and habits of the modern
masses. What are these habits? What are these desires? We shall find *dance, music,
sports, competitions, athletics, social life, corporate action, public meetings*, that
is to say a mixture of real preoccupations and of movements towards 'escape'.[7]

Since the size of the stadium made dialogue inaudible, the two
principal elements were to be action and music: 'The play must, of
necessity, explain itself through actions. These actions will consist
of very simple, clear-cut mass movements . . . The musical score
is very important. This will be a genuine popular opera, at once
sportive, social, industrial, gymnastic, legendary.'[8] *Naissance d'une
Cité* was directed by Pierre Aldebert (who was later to become
director of the Théâtre National Populaire) with movable sets by
Fernand Léger, music by Roger Desormières, Jean Wiener, Darius
Milhaud and Arthur Honegger and choreography by Tony Gregory.
It ended with a genuine *fête populaire*, which included trapeze artists,
a wrestling match, clowns and a running race, as well as singing and
dancing.

The problem of sound was overcome by having three announcers,
a cross between radio newscasters and sports commentators, who
introduced and commented on the action as it progressed. The

problem of size was solved by two teams who performed the same actions at opposite ends of the stadium. The stylisation of the play, its attempts at solving the difficulty of representing the 'mass man' of the modern industrial age, recalls the work of the German expressionists. The crushing representation of everyday life in a factory and the sense of bewildering confusion of modern times expressed through spoken choruses is similar to German examples.

The plot of *Naissance d'une Cité* is simple: it begins with an evocation of the life of the industrial workers, and moves on to show how they are affected by an international political crisis. Just as they are about to be plunged into war, they realise that they have no reason to fight one another and lay down their arms. Together they vow to construct the city of honour and comradeship. Their liberation is vividly enacted as all unzip the uniformly grey overalls they have been wearing, and step out to reveal clothes of gay colours. They board ship and sail to an island in the Atlantic which they colonise as a collective. But their happy life is cut short by a surprise oil strike: within hours the major powers are carving up their land. The play has two alternative endings, which sum up the tragedy of the Popular Front and all European hopes for peace in the late thirties. One ending, pessimistic and only too prophetic, shows the gradual oppression of the free workers by the major powers, culminating in a war which forces the workers once again to fight against one another. But for the 1937 Exhibition an optimistic ending seemed necessary, so there was a *deus ex machina* in the form of a declaration from the League of Nations to the effect that the earth's natural resources would in future be used only for the benefit of all mankind. The major powers roll up their barbed wire and go home leaving the arena free for the *fête populaire*.

Aragon wrote that Bloch did not believe in this 'happy end' any more than Molière believed in the *coups de théâtre* with which his plays so often conclude. By 1937 the League of Nations was already discredited in left-wing circles, and it seems probable that Bloch meant his ending to be deliberately fantastic so as to point the message that something stronger than the League would be needed to prevent the outbreak of war.

What interested contemporary critics about this production was its congruity with the political line of the Front Populaire. This kind of total theatre, in which all the different forms of expression combine, suggested the birth of a new universal art-form, synthetic and all-englobing, unlike the analytic and divisive style of agit-prop.

Agit-prop theatre: October

If we now turn to agit-prop theatre, we run into difficulties. The
major difficulty is lack of documentation. Isolated reports exist,
showing that agit-prop groups were active. For example, a group
called the Theatre of Peace performed a play entitled *Freedom, Dear
Freedom!* to striking workers on the steps of the Galeries Lafayette
on 13 May 1935, causing a commentator in the right-wing paper
Volonté to remark that it was better that strikers should have
recourse to comedies than to cannons. The Theatre of Peace was
typical of a number of small groups who travelled around, sometimes
putting on informal performances in any available hall, sometimes
acting in theatres. But most of the researching and cataloguing of
the work of such groups still remains to be done.

The only itinerant agit-prop theatre group whose scenarios survive
from this period is the group which came to be known as October (Le
Groupe Octobre), which originated from a group rather poetically
entitled Prémices (i.e. First Fruits or Early Beginnings). In March
1932, this group split, one half wanting to perform good plays for
the masses, the other wanting to do 'shock theatre' and calling themselves Le Groupe de Choc Prémices. In the same year, Léon Moussinac
introduced members of this group to the Prévert brothers, at that
time just beginning their career in the cinema.

After preliminary discussions with the group, Jacques Prévert wrote
and took part in a satirical sketch on the role of the press in a capitalist
society entitled *Vive la presse* (Long Live the Press). This used a deliberately schematic formula: the *dramatis personae* consisted of caricature figures, each representing one of the French dailies, and the
text was composed almost entirely of genuine quotations lifted from
these papers. The sketch is lucid, witty and economical; most of its
points are made by simply juxtaposing quotations from different
papers, and the concluding spoken chorus is incisive and ironical.
Vive la presse marked the beginning of a close association between
Prévert and the group that was to last until 1936.

During the next four years, the group evolved a simple performance
style, using unisex overalls as costumes and the minimum of props
and sets in order to be as mobile as possible. Their work consisted
mainly of putting on short sketches at cafés or workers' meetings,
though they occasionally gave a complete evening's entertainment,
often including the screening of a film as well as the performance of

plays, mime dramas and spoken choruses. One of Prévert's sketches was specifically written to be performed in the same programme as a screening of *The Battleship Potemkin*.

In his essay on 'The Author as Producer', Walter Benjamin contrasted large- and small-scale theatre: 'The theatre of complex machinery . . . Its position is a lost one. Not so the position of a theatre which, instead of competing against the newer means of communication, tries to apply them and learn from them – in short to enter into a dialogue with them.'[9] This precisely describes Prévert's approach to the theatre, from his first play about the press onwards. Benjamin's contrast was neatly summed up when the two halves of the original Prémices group changed their names: one became Masses and the other October.

One of the distinguishing features of October's work was its topicality; it remained close to the tradition of the Living Newspaper, mounting sketches on important current events with minimum delay. *L'Avènement d'Hitler* (The Coming of Hitler), with Prévert in the role of Hitler, was put on thirty-six hours after the news that he had taken power was announced. They did sketches on the trial of the nine Scottsboro negroes condemned to death for alleged violation of prostitutes, on the Reichstag arson trial, on the Citroën company for some of their workers who were on strike, and on a number of worker and peasant problems.

But the other feature that characterised this group, differentiating them quite clearly from most of the work of the German workers' theatre, was their emphasis on humour. Prévert, when questioned on workers' theatre, invariably answers that the main thing is for it to be funny. Although the didactic intention was clearly present in their work, October's predominant desire was to share with their audience a spirit of scorn for capitalism. It was not so much a call to arms, more a call to the power of laughter. Because of this approach, they tended to exploit the *play* element more effectively than most agit-prop groups.

The year 1933 saw the first Moscow workers' theatre olympiad, which attracted groups from more than twenty countries, including Japan and America. A distinguished French committee was set up, including Gémier, Vildrac, Nizan, Moussinac, and Autant-Lara; they selected October and the Bobigny Blue Blouses to represent France. The plays performed by October were *La Bataille de Fontennoy, Citroën*, and the play about the Scottsboro negroes. They carried off the first prize and achieved a glowing write-up in *Pravda*, despite the displeasure of the French Communist Party, who felt that their whole approach lacked the necessary seriousness.

In the sketches written by Prévert and performed by the group in the following year, the traditional methods of folk theatre were frequently used. For example, in *Le Palais des Mirages* (The Palace of Mirages) the old device of the wax-works was used. Doumergue, an old-style radical who had been called out of retirement to patch over the nation's troubles as Prime Minister by a 'dictatorship of the smile', was shown taking the place of his own wax-work in the Musée Grévin in order to discover what people thought of him. Inevitably, he heard far more than he wanted to, which proved an excellent means of introducing political discussion in a farcical manner.

Some of the themes of Prévert's later poetry were already present in these sketches, notably the satires of family life and, most persistent of all, the attacks on the war-mongers. *La Bataille de Fontennoy*, which takes the latter theme, is a near-perfect example of the short political play for workers' theatre groups. Its brevity and simplicity make it easily stageable and readily transportable. But though short, it is condensed, rich in allusions and varied in appeal. It was October's most successful production, written early in 1933 and put on for the delegates of the second congress of the Fédération des Théâtres Ouvriers de France. The text of this play, as well as several other scenarios by Prévert, was published after the war in 1949 by Gallimard in a volume entitled *Spectacle*.

Despite the simplicity of its staging (it only requires a raised stage and some chairs), *La Bataille de Fontennoy* effectively exploits not just the political but also the very theatrical nature of such performances by the device of the play within the play. Rather than attempting to turn the performance into a political discussion meeting, it presents an audience of spectators who have come to watch a battle: they applaud when the fighting is fierce, boo when it stops, and bring the curtain down with shouts of 'encore'. The 'Battle' is not an attempt at historical reconstruction, but a disguised version of the First World War. The legend which recounts that the Battle of Fontennoy was opened by the gallant French commander crying 'Messieurs les Anglais, tirez les premiers!' is cleverly used to achieve two comic effects. One is achieved through the impatience of the bloodthirsty spectators, who simply want the two sides to get on with it, and the other through a demonstration of the General's

238

hypocrisy: he is as eager as anyone for the battle, but has become embroiled in his own fine words. Prévert suggests that the French politicians of all parties who pretended they did not want to start the war in 1914 were in a similar position of duplicity.

The imbecility of a consenting population is attacked in the form of a mother refusing to hide her son who has run from the horror of the trenches, merely crying out: 'You wretch, you'll ruin your sister's marriage.' Despite his attempts to hide beneath her skirts, she hands him over for execution to an old man, who turns out to be Clemenceau, 'The Tiger', who enters with growls and roars.

The arms merchants, one of Prévert's favourite targets, are satirised in one of the best scenes, between Schneider, Krupp and Poincaré:

Krupp & Schneider: Monsieur le Président,
Nous sommes désolés,
Mais les munitions,
On les a mélangées,
Ça va faire mauvais effet!
Poincaré: Mais non, ça ne fait rien. Les obus français et les obus allemands sont de la même famille. Vous n'avez qu'à partager.[10]

Prévert's instinct for the telling theatrical effect and his sense of the stage are visible in the other play from October's repertoire which is printed in *Spectacle*: *Le Tableau des Merveilles* (The Scene of Wonders). This piece by Cervantes was discovered by Barrault, who staged an adaptation of the play in his actor's co-operative Le Grenier des Augustins in 1935. Inspired by this, Prévert wrote a revised adaptation for the group which was performed a number of times in 1936 with Barrault in the leading role.

The play tells the story of a gipsy, his wife and orphan child, who come to a small town to put on a travelling show. They tell the public that only chaste girls and honest men can see their wonders. These are, like the Emperor's New Clothes, non-existent, but everyone of course claims to see them.

Both these plays are striking for their witty demystification; they also demonstrate Prévert's playful use of puns and permanent attention to the humorous possibilities of language. This sort of thing is quite untranslatable, but lends Prévert's language much of its appeal.

In June 1935 the group turned its attention for the first time towards the problems of the provinces, with a show called *Suivez le Druide*. This contrasted the tourist image of a jolly folksy Breton people with the real conditions in what then was and still remains an underprivileged area of France.

The year 1936 was a very successful one for October. They performed *Le Tableau des Merveilles* a number of times, including a performance at the large Paris Mutualité hall on 1 July with 500 free seats for the unemployed, and they gave performances during strikes at various department stores. But towards the end of the year they ran into severe financial difficulties, and since Prévert was spending more of his time on film scripts the group broke up.

One contemporary critic remarked on 'This fierce, biting humour of Jacques Prévert . . . his irony, so difficult to get across to a popular audience, draws on the real things they suffer from: egotistical "morality" "liberating labour", inhuman production methods.' The effectiveness of Prévert's theatre work lies in this use of ironic humour. Like Brecht, he distrusted mass theatre and believed instead in an intimate theatre where the actors could establish a particular relationship with their audience, asking them not just to consume, but to think. Writing of Prévert's use of humour, Bazin said that 'in the Prévert brothers' films the gag is always an idea whose visualisation comes *a posteriori* in such a way that it only appears funny after a mental operation; you have to move from the visual gag to its intellectual intention'.[11]

The agit-prop scenarios written by Prévert show a constant awareness of Benjamin's 'dialogue' between the media. This is hardly surprising, for during the four years of October's activity Jacques Prévert scripted ten important films (as well as a dozen other shorts or projects which did not reach completion). Members of the group were also involved in most of these films and the whole group took part in the masterpiece of the period, *Le Crime de M. Lange* (scripted by Prévert and directed by Renoir). The music for this film was written by Joseph Kosma, who found in Prévert's work a similar lucidity and humour to that of Brecht. He said,

When I first met Prévert I knew exactly what I was looking for. The 'songs' of Bertolt Brecht had fascinated me and I had become familiar with Brechtian aesthetics. But I did not want to produce an imitation: I was looking for something written in a similar spirit but a different form — especially since my music bore no relation to that of Kurt Weill or Hans Eisler. I set Jacques Prévert's poems to music without changing a comma.[12]

Conclusion

All the comments made by contemporaries about October's demise

240

suggest that it failed for lack of money. Clearly there were other reasons as well. From the Préverts' own point of view, the film was the more attractive medium; Pierre Prévert had been working as director and assistant director on a number of films and had never taken a very large part in the activities of October, and in 1936 both brothers were in heavy demand. But the agit-prop form itself failed to fit the dominant cultural mode. It was opposed to the mass art of Union that was the Front's official policy; it was too combative and too intellectual, demanding too much of the kind of work that Brecht demands of his audiences.

But the mass political spectacle was in fact doomed to extinction. Although some of Bloch's contemporaries felt that they had seen the birth of a new art-form in *Naissance d'une Cité*, it did not, in the event, lead on to anything significant. It might seem, therefore, that the theatre policy of the Front Populaire was a total failure. But in one important respect, the *frontiste* emphasis on the totality of culture and the cultural heritage has born fruit. In 1936 the Minister for Education, Jean Zay, commissioned a report on the decentralisation of the theatre from Charles Dullin, who recommended the establishment of artistic centres throughout France to lead to the development of a regional popular theatre movement. The Front Populaire collapsed before the report could be implemented, but it is largely the recommendations of this report that have been acted upon by successive post-war governments.[13] When, in 1968, the leftists protested against the liberal ideology of the Maisons de la Culture, they were in fact reopening the battle between revolutionary politics and the politics of Union that had been abandoned on the cultural barricades of the 1930s.

NOTES

1   Shoot down the police . . .
     Fire on Léon Blum
     Fire on Boncour Frossard Déat
     Fire on the trained bears of social democracy
2 For further information concerning *Commune* and the AEAR, see D. Caute, *Communism and the French Intellectuals 1914–1960* (London, 1964) and J.-P. A. Bernard, *Le Parti Communiste et la question littéraire 1921–1939* (Grenoble, 1972).
3 Louis Aragon, speech given 13 April 1936 and reprinted in *Commune*, 33 (May 1936), pp. 1147–53.
4 'La Défense de la culture', *Commune*, 23 (July 1935), p. 1262.
5 See note 3. *Commune* also gave a brief account of the annual congress.

6 Cited by Bernard, *Le Parti Communiste* pp. 198—9.
7 'Quelques indications de l'auteur pour la représentation de *Naissance d'une Cité*', *Toulon et autres pièces* (Paris, 1948), pp. 294—7.
8 *Ibid.*
9 Walter Benjamin, *Understanding Brecht* (London, 1973), p. 99.
10 *Krupp & Schneider:* Mister President,
                 We regret
                 The Munitions
                 Have got mixed up,
                 It will make a bad impression!
   Poincaré: No, no, that doesn't matter. French and German shells are of the same family. Just share them out between you.
11 André Bazin, *Qu'est-ce que le cinéma?* (Paris, 1975), p. 42.
12 Cited in *Les Préverts*, ed. Gérard Gillot (Paris, 1966), p. 135.
13 For a history of the decentralisation movement see D. Gontard, *La Décentralisation théâtrale en France 1895—1952* (Paris, 1973).

Only the stars survive: disaster movies in the seventies

Nick Roddick

'Disaster movies' were a phenomenon of the early and mid 1970s, and for a time it looked as though they might prove an enduring feature of the world movie market: they had done extremely well at the box office in both the United States and Britain,[1] and a definite cycle of films could be identified. The cycle, however, seems to have terminated early in 1977 with the second sequel, *Airport '77*, to the movie that apparently started it all at the beginning of the decade.[2] Since then, there has been the occasional echo — in, for instance, the ill-fated *Cassandra Crossing*, some scaled-down TV movies (*Flight to the Holocaust*, *Smash-up on Interstate Five*), and a sequence or two in the otherwise straightforward thriller *Rollercoaster* — but it is certainly no longer possible to speak, as it was in 1974–5, of a flourishing cycle of films. Disaster movies, in other words, are now a part of cultural history. Their narrative strategies and devices, on the other hand, are still very much current: they exemplify a trend in popular — or 'dominant' — cinema.

The term 'disaster movie' needs some definition: though never a true generic label like Western or Horror movie, it was nevertheless in fairly current use and endowed for a time with a definite if imprecise meaning by the cinema-going public. Someone going to see a disaster movie knew by and large what she or he was going to get. Irwin Allen, producer of *The Poseidon Adventure*, pointed to at any rate some of the essential characteristics of that meaning in a 1972 interview with *Hollywood Reporter*, the American film industry's main trade paper: 'We have a perfect set-up of a group of people who have never met before and who are thrown together in terrible circumstances. In the first six minutes, 1,400 people are killed and only the stars survive.'[3] Why this should be regarded as 'a perfect set-up' is obviously an interesting question. For *The Poseidon Adventure*, though not the first movie of the cycle, was nonetheless the film which confidently established its basic narrative model: a

243

random collection of people centred around a small group of what *Variety* calls 'topflight thesps' (stars), caught up in a spectacular disaster and, despite a reduction in numbers — minimal for the topflight thesps, massive for everyone else — overcoming apparently impossible odds in order to survive. This pattern held true throughout the cycle: *The Poseidon Adventure* and the movies which followed it show a remarkable consistency in terms of themes, narrative structures and, above all, ideological content. It is this which makes it possible — as well, I hope, as useful — to consider them as a single group, and thus to draw certain conclusions about the cycle.

It is obviously interesting to speculate — though I suspect one can do no more than that — as to why such a cycle of movies should have emerged in the mid seventies. The simple answer — the 'trade' answer — is that they were profitable: the runaway success of *The Poseidon Adventure* prompted the 1974 batch of *Juggernaut, Airport 1975, Earthquake* and *The Towering Inferno*. But none of these flopped, and three out of four were in fact major box office hits. This is in itself remarkable: it is very rare for Hollywood in recent years to have struck oil with quite such regularity by offering variations on the same formula (cf. the string of violent anti-war movies which tried unsuccessfully to cash in on the success of *The Dirty Dozen* in 1966, or the even more catastrophic batch of 'youth movies' which tried to recapture the audience of *Easy Rider*). For the disaster formula to have succeeded quite so regularly and quite so well implies that the cycle met some basic need in the mass audience. One doesn't need to be a structuralist to observe this fact, and innumerable unsupported explanations have been put forward to account for it: a sort of post-Watergate depression, a national inferiority complex after the Vietnam debacle, or even a 'bread and circuses' attitude caused by 'the erosion of democracy and the Western materialist way of living'[4] — all of which are both a little too obvious and wholly impossible to substantiate. Popular culture is not simply a matter of cause and effect: needs do not arise clearly and cultural products do not materialise expressly to fulfil them. But some conclusions can be drawn from a closer look at the disaster movies themselves. A number of articles, mainly in French film journals,[5] did, at the height of the cycle and with varying degrees of success, investigate the broad outlines of historical precedent, narrative structure and political content. This paper has three main aims: (i) to locate the mid seventies' cycle of disaster movies within the overall context of a long tradition of screen catastrophe, indicating

244

what is peculiar to the most recent batch; (ii) to arrive at a working definition of the cycle in narrative and thematic terms; and (iii) to examine its latent ideology more carefully and consistently than has so far been done. Because if disaster movies from *Airport* (1968) to *Airport '77* have met certain of the needs of the mass audience, it is clear from a closer look at the movies themselves that the fears and feelings which attracted moviegoers to them, rather than being calmed or assuaged, were being consistently channelled in a particular direction. The relationship between popular culture and socio-economic forces is, of course, complex and above all dialectical. Movies create a demand as well as satisfying one. Since this is an area in which the term 'manipulation' is bandied about with equal enthusiasm by both left and right,[6] it is obviously foolish to make assertions about intent (on the part of the producer) and effect (on the minds of the audience). Nevertheless, the remarkably consistent ideological 'direction' of a number of different movies provides an interesting and instructive example of one of the chief apparent functions of mass-produced culture: to pose a very real contemporary problem in dramatic terms, and to provide a compelling fictional solution which can be readily translated into a practical (political) one. I am not, of course, proposing a theory of conspiracy: disaster movies are no more 'dangerous' than most modern mass culture. What they do provide, however — and what makes them a particularly rich field of study — is an exemplary demonstration of one of the more elusive processes of that culture. The movies are worth studying in detail because they give clear indications of how a cultural industry reacts to a period of economic and political crisis in capitalist society, and how culture can become ideologically active. Disaster movies are 'reactionary culture' par excellence. And 'in each period, reactionaries are as sure indicators of its spiritual condition as dogs are of the weather'.[7]

The present cycle and its predecessors

Most of those who have written on disaster movies to date have indicated that there is nothing new in the phenomenon: disaster 'has *always* been box office', and the present cycle is basically 'the resurrection and refurbishing of old models, stereotypes, gimmicks, etc.'.[8] David Annan, in his glossy survey of catastrophe in the cinema, sees the disaster movie as being occasioned by a twin fear: 'the primeval fear that the earth and heaven will destroy us all, or the paranoiac fear that a conspiracy of our own invention will put an end to us'.[9] The development of late, claims Annan, has been very much in the direction of the second fear. But if we are to characterise the recent cycle of movies adequately, something a bit more specific is obviously necessary. *Earthquake*, *The Towering Inferno* etc., do have their forerunners, but they differ from them in quite important respects. Also, the recent cycle occupies a fairly narrow part of the general spectrum of cinematic catastrophe over the past sixty years. These variations and this narrowing of focus are, as will be seen, of considerable significance as far as the recent spate of films is concerned.

What, then, is a disaster movie? Clearly it is not just a movie with a disaster in it: it must be 'about' the disaster. But not just any disaster. Almost all science fiction, horror and war movies have elements of disaster: Tokyo ravaged by Godzilla (the quality of the special effects apart) ends up looking pretty much the same as Los Angeles ravaged by *Earthquake*, and the number of lives lost or threatened in *The Poseidon Adventure* is negligible by comparison with, say, *The Longest Day* or *All Quiet on the Western Front*. But the films just mentioned are clearly not disaster movies, any more than are biblical epics: *The Ten Commandments* contains enough spectacular catastrophes (in either version) to fill half a dozen disaster movies, but that does not mean that it *is* one. The kind of disaster with which disaster movies are concerned has a number of basic requirements. It must be diegetically central; factually possible; largely indiscriminate (in that it could happen to all sections of the population and is not restricted to certain professional groups, e.g. soldiers);[10] unexpected (though not necessarily unpredicted); all-encompassing, in the sense that potential victims cannot simply opt out of it;[11] and finally, ahistorical, in the sense of not requiring a specific conjuncture of political and economic forces to bring it about. At this stage, then, it is possible to exclude one whole category of disaster-ridden movies: those involving monsters from space. Disaster movies are an essentially earthbound form: they operate, almost by definition, within the realm of the possible. People must believe 'it' could — indeed, very well might — happen to them. This rules out even such relatively sober visions of an inter-galactic future as *2001 — A Space Odyssey*, *Earth II* and *Silent Running*.

A working definition of a disaster movie would be a film in which the central pivot or impulse of the narrative was provided by a natural or man-made disaster occurring, either without warning or after unheede warnings, in a setting or environment close enough to the audience's experience for identification to be possible. Such identification is, of course, encouraged: disaster movies operate within a basically realist mode of representation. Any attempt to establish a definitive list of disaster movies is far beyond the aims (or even inclinations) of this paper. But it may be useful to draw up three basic categories. These are, of course, very broad, particularly where they come close to the boundaries of science fiction, and it must be stressed that they aim to define the main trends rather than to be exclusive. With these reservations in mind I would suggest the following categories.

1. A future world in which a disaster on a huge scale has already happened, happens during the course of the movie or is narrowly averted. The distance into the future varies — it may be 'tomorrow', it may be a thousand years hence — but it is crucial that the action is set 'in the future'. At the same time the basic social, political and moral structures of the world depicted closely resemble those of the period in which the film was made. The world is frequently over-populated and depersonalised (*Metropolis*, *Things to Come*, *1984*, *Alphaville*, *Fahrenheit 451*, *TXH 1138*, *Soylent Green*, *Zardoz*, *Logan's Run*), or else brutalised (*The Time Machine*, *Planet of the Apes* and its sequels, *The Omega Man*). Things are, more often than not, the way they are because of a nuclear disaster, and the films frequently present themselves as a kind of warning. The disaster is either threatened (*Dr Strangelove*, *Fail Safe*, *The Bedford Incident*), or else its immediate after-effects are depicted (*Five*, *Invasion USA*, *When Worlds Collide*, *The Day the World Ended*, *The World, the Flesh and the Devil*, *On the Beach*, *The Last Woman on Earth*, *The Damned*, *The Day the Earth Caught Fire*, *The Last War*, *Panic in the Year Zero*, *La Jetée*, *Crack in the World*, *The War Game*). The disaster movie comes closest to pure science fiction when it deals with mutations caused by nuclear radiation or other forms of 'tampering with God's creation'. Its narrative strategies are, in fact, basically identical to those of the monster movie, where man's scientific arrogance or commercial greed are the more or less direct cause of the disaster (Baron Frankenstein's experiments, or the pig-headedness of the oil company executive in the 1976 *King Kong*). But the movies listed here remain within the bounds of the present definition because of the explicit or implicit declaration to the spectator that such a disaster could happen as things now are (though needless to say such scientific pretexts are often wholly spurious). At all events, disaster has ensued from insufficiently controlled

nuclear experiments in the form of monster ants (*Them!*, *Empire of the Ants*), spiders (*Tarantula*, *The Giant Spider Invasion*), molluscs (*The Monster that Challenged the World*), octopi (*It Came from Beneath the Sea*), mantises (*The Deadly Mantis*), carnivorous mud (*X, the Unknown*), re-animated prehistoric animals (*The Beast from 20,000 fathoms*, *The Cyclops*, *Behemoth the Sea Monster*), resurrected corpses (*The Night of the Living Dead*) and mutated human beings of various shapes and sizes (*The Atomic Kid*, *The Incredible Shrinking Man*, *The Amazing Colossal Man*, *The H-Man*, *War of the Colossal Beast*, *The Most Dangerous Man Alive* and, most recently, the comic-book *Spider Man*). Fear of The Bomb was very much a folk nightmare of the fifties and early sixties, however, and with the exception of the giant spiders, more recent scientific mutants have been caused, predictably enough, by tampering with The Ecology. This has given us, among others, the giant rabbits of *The Night of the Lepus*, the murderously well-organised ants of *Phase IV*, the carnivorous worms of *Squirm* and the giant octopus of *Tentacles*.

2. Natural disasters or acts of God. The essence of a natural disaster in screen terms is that it should threaten an entire community. Even so, it is a great deal more specific than many of the disasters contained in the preceding group, which tended to threaten 'the whole world' or 'America as we know it' (i.e. two stars and a handful of contract players) in general, and therefore no one in particular. Earthquakes have devastated entire cities — in *San Francisco* and *Earthquake* — but only once have they threatened the world (a chain of them in *The Night the World Exploded*). Fire is more problematic: the burning of Rome is featured in the three versions of *Quo Vadis?* and in *The Sign of the Cross*, but could scarcely be said to be the central pivot of the narrative, any more than is the burning of Atlanta in *Gone with the Wind*. On the other hand, the great Chicago fire is very definitely the central pivot of *In Old Chicago*, and *The Towering Inferno* is unquestionably 'about' fire. Floods have been dealt with in *Deluge*, *Der Tunnel*, *Transatlantic Tunnel*, *The Rains Came*, *The Rains of Ranchipur* (a remake of *The Rains Came*) and in the final, cataclysmic *The Submersion of Japan* (also known as *Tidal Wave*). Volcanic eruptions have destroyed Pompeii with considerable frequency (*The Last Days of Pompeii* in at least ten versions to date), and a number of other places besides (*Volcano*, *Krakatoa — East of Java*). Hurricanes have also struck in *The Hurricane* and *Suez*. Populations have been threatened or destroyed by plagues of one kind or another in *The*

Omega Man (a virus), *The Naked Jungle* (ants), *The Birds*, and *Willard* and its sequel, *Ben* (rats).

3. Disaster occurring to or threatening forms of mass transport. What causes the disaster is in this case relatively unimportant. The disasters in this group of films are the most intimate, since even the largest ocean liner carries no more than the population of a small town. They also play more particularly on the idea of claustrophobia: the vessel is inescapable and the disaster must be faced up to. Trains that for one reason or another cannot be stopped or escaped from have provided the setting for *The Runaway Train*, *The Taking of Pelham 123*, *Silver Streak*, *The Cassandra Crossing* and *The Bullet Train*[12]. Requiring less narrative ingenuity, there has been a string of disaster-struck ships (*Atlantik*, *Titanic* — two versions — and *A Night to Remember*, all of course closely modelled on an actual disaster; *Lifeboat*, *The Last Voyage*, *The Poseidon Adventure*, *Juggernaut*), planes (*The High and the Mighty*, *Airport 1975*, *Airport '77*, *Survive!*) and airships (*Madame Satan*, *Zeppelin*, *The Hindenburg*). The whole thing has been splendidly parodied in *The Big Bus*.

The narrative structures of the modern disaster movie

When one comes to consider the modern cycle, it becomes clear that almost all the disasters are of a specific kind. They come almost entirely in category (3). They are neither extravagant nor, at any rate at first sight, apocalyptic. They are realistic, contemporary and happen in settings which, if not always everyday, are disturbingly familiar. Finally, they happen to *groups* of people — an all-star cast — rather than, as previously, to a star couple (e.g. *In Old Chicago*, *The Naked Jungle*). The cycle referred to appears to start in 1968 with *Airport*, though in most respects the film belongs more in the tradition of *Grand Hotel*[13] — the interaction of a number of separate destinies drawn loosely together in one setting — and it is not until *The Poseidon Adventure*, released in December 1972, that the cycle really gets underway. *Poseidon* was followed by *Juggernaut*, *Earthquake*, *The Towering Inferno* and *Airport 1975* (all 1974); more recently by *The Hindenburg* (1975) and *The Big Bus* (1976) and finally by *Airport '77* (1977) — which last, almost inevitably, has no more to do with airports than recent films in the Pink Panther series have had to do with the original 'Pink Panther' diamond.

In every film of the cycle, the narrative structure has been more or less the same, consisting of three parts: the world before the disaster, the disaster itself, and the world after the disaster.[14] Most of the constituent parts of the world before the disaster are to be found directly reversed in the world after the disaster: the immaculate, smoothly functioning machine (aircraft, ship, building or city) has been reduced to chaos, its elegant inhabitants to ragged primitives; on the other hand, a disparate collection of people has become a tightly knit collective, selfishness has been replaced by a sense of communal responsibility, tottering relationships have been stabilised, greed has given way to generosity and permissive liberalism to a disciplined hierarchy. Before examining the implications of this transformation, however, it might be just as well to look at the constants of the present cycle in greater detail, since they hold true for all the movies including, in parodic form, *The Big Bus*. With minor variations, the formula is as follows: as a result of a catastrophe which kills most of the people around them, a random selection of people assembled in a comfortable modern environment find themselves cut off from the outside world and threatened with death; after a more or less protracted initial period of chaos and panic, they are organised into a hierarchic collectivity by a natural leader and, through an ingenious and courageous response to the technology of their shattered environment, manage for the most part to escape. Individual movies in the modern cycle may give greater or lesser emphasis to details of the formula, but all stick fairly closely to it. What distinguishes the above definition from that suggested earlier for disaster movies in general is its emphasis on the group rather than the individual, and on the *reaction* to the disaster rather than — or as well as — the disaster itself (a characteristic which it shares with some of the nuclear disaster movies of the fifties). The modern disaster movie is not so much a spectacular entertainment, it is more a didactic form which plays on the latent guilt and *Schadenfreude* of the audience in order to indicate the need for a certain kind of societal reorganisation. Thus, what happens after the disaster — or, in the case of *The Towering Inferno* where the disaster is progressive, during it — occupies the major part of the narrative.

The constituent elements of the movies in the recent cycle come under the following headings.

Isolation

In all nine movies, the action takes place in an enclosed setting from

250

which normal means of escape have been rendered impossible. The passengers of the various aircraft, ships and buses are trapped in them as a result of in-flight damage (*Airport*, *Airport 1975*) or disaster (*The Poseidon Adventure*, *The Hindenburg*, *The Big Bus*, *Airport '77*). The passengers on board the 'Britannic' (*Juggernaut*) cannot be taken off because of mountainous seas. The guests in *The Towering Inferno* are trapped by the fire at a height way beyond the reach of existing fire rescue equipment.[15] The featured players in *Earthquake* are all trapped at various times — at the top of an office building, in an underground car park when the building above it collapses, in a flooded storm drain — and the city as a whole is sealed off from the rest of the world. The preference for aircraft is, in this respect, self-explanatory. Claustrophobia is also an important element, reaching its most acute in *Airport '77*, where the airliner also doubles as a submarine, and the passengers are trapped under water with a diminishing air supply and a hull unlikely to withstand the pressure for long.

Luxury

All the disaster-struck environments are luxurious in one way or another. The hyper-modern luxury of the airports is carefully detailed. The 747 in *Airport '77* is custom-built by a millionaire to fly his guests to a party: 'Is this airplane as amazing as the press says it is?' asks a wide-eyed Olivia de Havilland as she comes aboard, and she (and we) are treated to a tour of its gadgets and fittings. The ocean-going liners in *The Poseidon Adventure* and *Juggernaut* are, as the captain of the former remarks, not really ships but hotels 'with a bow and a stern stuck on'. Both *The Hindenburg* and *The Big Bus* are triumphs of twentieth-century technology, conveying mainly the rich and famous (the latter being nuclear-powered and on its inaugural, non-stop run from New York to Denver). *The Towering Inferno* is the world's tallest building, and we are invited to marvel at the luxury of its furnishings, the sophistication of its computerised control centre and the magnificence of its owner's house-warming party. *Earthquake* takes place in one of the richest cities on earth: the narrative devices it employs simply would not work if the quake had wrecked, say, Calcutta. This luxury has three basic functions. Firstly, it guarantees the expensiveness of the production: we built all this, and now we're going to flood it/burn it/blow it up. Secondly, the luxury is paraded before us as a kind of wish fulfilment, in the manner of an advertising film: we are drawn into a celebration of

251

the technological and economic marvels of the capitalist world. But thirdly, we find in retrospect that this luxurious wonderland was a dangerous delusion: peopled by sybaritic, self-centred beings totally reliant on a technology which they utilise without understanding and which proves incapable of resisting the basic elemental forces of earth, air, fire and water. Those living in such luxury are weakened and, ultimately, trapped by it.

A random gathering of people

The characters in a disaster movie have been assembled (they believe, temporarily) in a plane, ship, airship or bus, or on the top floor of a skyscraper. This narrative device has a number of advantages. Firstly, it is possible for the studio to fit in half a dozen stars without the slightest problem. Secondly, psychology can be reduced to an elementary level, since no single character occupies the centre of dramatic interest for long enough to be developed or to establish a relationship of any complexity with any other character. Thus disaster movies are peopled by archetypes who react to the given situation in function of their sex, class or profession and not in function of any individual identity. What is more, the archetypes are extended by the known personality of the star playing the part: in accordance with the usual formula, what we respond to on the screen is not someone called Stuart Graff (*Earthquake*) or Alan Murdock (*Airport 1975*), but someone far more substantial called Charlton Heston. This random gathering of people threatened by disaster has three main narrative functions: it comprises a microcosm of twentieth-century society, having what Olivier Eyquem[16] calls the 'exemplary banality' necessary for wide audience identification; it is at the out-set egotistical, divided and full of conflict, lacking the sense of corporate identity supposedly necessary in a smoothly functioning society; and finally, it is known to be at risk. This last is an important narrative element in the modern cycle of disaster movies where surprise, other than at relatively minor details, is not a feature. In most cases, the audience knows when it enters the cinema that it is going to witness a disaster; if it doesn't know already, it is quickly told, either by an opening caption (*The Poseidon Adventure*, *The Big Bus*) or by narrative information released almost immediately (*Juggernaut*). The audience is thus in a position to judge the behaviour of this random collection of characters before the disaster in full knowledge of its imminent arrival. This introduces both a kind of suspense —

252

which ones are going to die? — and a premonition of the societal model to be posited in the third part of the movie: we can easily decide who 'deserves' to survive, and we are usually right.

Cause and nature of the disaster

For the reasons suggested above (that it is with *reactions* to the disaster that the present cycle of movies is concerned), the direct cause of the catastrophe is of very little significance. Thus there is no definite model: in six of the nine movies, the disaster is directly caused by a human being (by a bomb in *Airport*, *Juggernaut*, *The Hindenburg* and *The Big Bus*; by pilot error in *Airport 1975* and *Airport '77*); in the remaining three it is an act of God, in the sense in which insurance companies understand the term (earthquake or fire). *Every* movie, on the other hand, has its villain — either criminal or criminally negligent — who can be held partly responsible for the disaster: the mad bombers; the wicked Greek, Linarcos, in *The Poseidon Adventure*; Simmons, the son-in-law of the builder of *The Towering Inferno*, who has installed inferior electrical equipment which allows the fire to get out of control; the director of the seismological institute and the Mayor of Los Angeles in *Earthquake*, both of whom, in time-honoured fashion, refuse to take the warnings seriously; the pilot of the light plane in *Airport 1975*, flying when in no fit state to do so, who crashes into the 747; and the hijack pilot in *Airport '77* who, through inexperience and incompetence, hits the top of an oil rig and crashes into the sea. The last two instances are particularly interesting, since in both cases the qualified expert — the *real* pilot — is absolved of all responsibility. Equally significantly, the character of Linarcos is an invention of the screenplay of *The Poseidon Adventure*. In the novel,[17] the decision to proceed insufficiently ballasted at full speed ahead is the decision of the Captain, a Greek on his first command and eager not to arrive behind schedule. In the film the Captain, transposed into an American, wants to slow down and take on ballast — the fact that it would make no difference to the disaster is not indicated — but is prevented from doing so by Linarcos, the owners' representative, whom he calls an 'irresponsible bastard' (while, however, continuing to do what he is told).

The implicit cause of the disaster, however, is generally quite different from its actual cause: it can be seen as an elemental endurance test imposed on a group of people. Disaster movies give central importance to elemental forces: the threats arise without exception from earth (*Earthquake*), air (*Airport, Airport 1975, The Big Bus* — which ends up hanging over a precipice), fire (*The Towering Inferno, The Hindenburg*) or water (*The Poseidon Adventure, Juggernaut, Airport '77*). The more ambitious movies combine several elements: in *The Towering Inferno*, for instance, fire threatens from below, people die from falling out of windows and, at the end, the survivors are threatened by a massive flood released from the rooftop water tanks in order to extinguish the fire. This fondness for the basic elements is taken even further by the TV spin-off disaster movies, two of which are called, quite simply, *Fire* and *Flood*. If *The Poseidon Adventure* is more or less alone in making explicit use of religious imagery,[18] the idea of the disaster as a primitive elemental test sent by God is strongly present in all the movies with the exception of *Juggernaut*. What is more, as Denis Lévy has pointed out, a recurring image in the movies is that of the rescuer appearing from on high like an angel. One final point should be made about the disasters themselves: although they are spectacular in terms of special effects and superlative in terms of stunt work, there is very little explicit suffering or violence in them.[19] Violent deaths are severely limited, and each movie seems to have rationed itself to one striking example (the man who falls to his death in the lighting installations in the inverted saloon of the Poseidon; Robert Wagner and Susan Flannery burned to death in the apartment in *The Towering Inferno*; one or two passengers and crew crushed by shifting cargo and fittings as the plane hits the water in *Airport '77*). In a cinematic climate dominated by *The Texas Chainsaw Massacre* and *Death Weekend*, such deaths can scarcely be described as graphic. The disaster movie is not concerned with blood and gore: it is aimed at a family audience.

Reaction to the disaster

This is the key section in nearly all the recent cycle of disaster movies, with the exception of *The Hindenburg* where, untypically — and, from a box office point of view, seemingly fatally — the disaster provided the climax to the film. Since it is in this section that the ideological significance of the movies becomes clear, I shall restrict myself here to outlining the narrative strategies and leave the implications for the concluding section. In narrative terms, three basic things happen as a result of the disaster. Firstly, chastened by it, the survivors overcome their internal divisions and form themselves into a self-regulating

Parody of the disaster movie: *The Big Bus* (1976).

collective, with the strong protecting the weak and the wounded, men protecting women and the group uniting to deal with threats to its survival. This tendency is weakest (though still present) in the first two *Airports*, where there is little that individual members of the group can do other than not panic and keep out of the way; and strongest in *The Poseidon Adventure*, *The Towering Inferno* and *Airport '77*. Secondly, a natural 'leader' emerges from within the group itself or, in a few cases, is brought in from outside (*Juggernaut*, *The Towering Inferno*, *Airport 1975*). This leader is invariably white (black characters appear in several of the movies but never adopt leadership roles), male[20] and, most significantly of all, wears a uniform of some kind to denote his function. Groups are led by pilots, navy officers (*Juggernaut*), policemen (*Earthquake*), fire chiefs, priests and bus drivers. In one case where no uniformed male is available — after the crash in *Airport 1975*, which kills one of the pilots and blinds the other — the leadership role is taken on a strictly temporary basis by the only other uniformed person, the stewardess, who pilots the plane until help (Charlton Heston) arrives. Two of the movies — *The Towering Inferno* and *Earthquake* — back up their uniformed heroes with a hero from the professional world, but in both cases the civilian hero is somehow tainted — by partial responsibility for the disaster in the case of Paul Newman's architect in the former movie, and by adultery (for which he is drowned) in the case of Heston's engineer in the latter. The leader averts the disaster or leads its victims to safety, always at the risk of his own life, and sometimes at the cost of it (*The Poseidon Adventure*). Having assumed control as of right, he amply demonstrates his fitness to exercise it. What is more, many of the natural leaders are men who have been prevented by a weak and foolish society from exercising their God-given functions, e.g. Hackman's positivist priest in *The Poseidon Adventure*, 'angry, a renegade, stripped of most of my clerical powers'; George Kennedy's cop in *Earthquake*, suspended for overzealousness; and, in the parody, Joseph Bologna's bus driver, the 'best in the business' but unable to get work after some nasty rumours about disappearing passengers following a crash in a remote mountain area ('You eat one lousy foot and they call you a cannibal!').

The third significant post-disaster feature is the resurrection of the technology apparently thrown into question by the disaster itself, but this time placed in the reliable and knowledgeable hands of the leader. It is not the technology that is at fault, but the use made of it by inexperienced laymen. In this respect, the heroes of the disaster

movies rejoin the heroes of the American frontier — men of great
physical and moral strength and men who, above all, are in tune with
their environment: they understand it and are able to adapt to it.
In exactly the same way, therefore, as the hero of the Western must
'know' the desert, Indian lore, horses, how to use his gun and so on,
the hero of the disaster movie must know the technological environment in which he and his flock find themselves adrift. Thus when
the normal solutions break down, he will be able to improvise fresh
ones on the basis of an extensive knowledge and an equally extensive
inventiveness. Knowledge on its own, of course, is not enough:
physical strength is also essential. The new super-hero — the initiate
in a technological environment — is not to be confused with the
scientist who, in Hollywood imagery, is either a dangerous fanatic,
a potential traitor liable to share his knowledge with 'the other side',
or, where he represents no direct threat to the community, a dotty
boffin devoid of all normal masculine[21] attributes (perhaps the
reductio ad absurdum of this image is the Jerry Lewis of *The Nutty
Professor* who has to go through an actual chemical transformation
before becoming a 'real' man). The new hero has all the attributes
of the old — muscles, good looks, sexual aggressiveness — but is a
hero for the technological age: Charlton Heston with a degree in
electrical engineering.

Disaster movies and the spectre of corporatism

The degree of consistency within the recent cycle points to a shared
ideological stance which, while not made explicit within the narrative,
is nonetheless central to it. At the simplest level, it can fairly be
asserted that the 1970s cycle of disaster movies both responded to
and exploited contemporary phobias, certainly as far as the USA
was concerned, and probably in the case of Europe too. If we are to
get beyond this level, it is necessary to go back to the tripartite
narrative model proposed earlier. The first part of the narrative —
the world before the disaster — is clearly and classically realist: a
representation of the world in which we now live, and a representation,
moreover, which reflects a wide-spread contemporary phobia that
traditional values are somehow threatened, if indeed they have not
already collapsed. The disaster itself (the second part of the narrative)
can thus be seen as an expiation of the guilt felt about this and a
punishment of the implied transgression. The social structure which
precedes the catastrophe is a schematised but supposedly accurate

257

picture of the contemporary Western world. It is a society which
has lost sight of 'frontier values', has grown weak through excessive
self-indulgence and total reliance on a protective shell of technology,
whose moral codes are threatened by liberalism and permissiveness,
and whose institutions have been diverted from their original purpose:
instead of protecting the collective and providing a firm foundation
for individual initiative, they now frustrate initiative and act as a
safety net for the weak, the incompetent and even the criminal.
The world before the disaster, in fact, is pretty much like the Cities
of the Plain, crystallised into an assemblage of stereotypes and
embodied by a group of stars who 'flesh out' the stereotypes with
the socially determined characteristics of their own images. This
microcosm is, *pace* Irwin Allen, allowed a certain amount of time to
establish itself — an average of about thirty minutes in all the movies
except *The Hindenburg* and *Juggernaut* — before being shattered.
The cause of the disaster is, as has been noted, imprecise and above
all ahistorical. In narrative terms, it functions as a catalyst, enabling
a transition from the first to the third stage of the narrative, and
justifying the societal transformation which is characteristic of the
third and final stage. In ideological terms, the filmic disaster stands in
for a series of possible real disasters (nuclear holocaust, population
explosion, destruction of the ecology, revolution or even energy
crisis), none of which is ahistorical: it is thus the *spectacle* of a
disaster, which can be presented as inevitable, total, inescapable,
retributive and, finally, therapeutic. The first and second stages of
the narrative correspond, therefore, to the spectator's perception
of the world and to his fear of the eventual outcome of present
trends. The statement that 'unless something is done *now*, disaster
will ensue' is made in one way or another in all the movies. But it is
the third part of the narrative — the world after the disaster — which
is the core of the modern cycle. If we set aside *Airport* as being a
prototype in which the narrative structure is as yet insufficiently
established,[22] we are left with eight movies (seven serious, one parody)
in which the only ones not to be runaway successes are those which
either do not examine the world after the disaster at all (*The Hindenburg*) or else do not do so systematically enough (*Juggernaut*). This
may be mere chance, but it does seem as though reassurance — some
indication of how the people involved *cope* with the disaster — is
an essential part of the cycle.

The end of a disaster movie posits, sometimes explicitly, sometimes
implicitly, a new world whose inhabitants have learned from the

mistakes of the old and from their experience of the disaster. There
is never any suggestion — as is fundamental to the Horror movie —
of 'getting back to normal'. True, the movies end on a positive note:
the plane lands safely and/or the passengers are evacuated, the bomb
is defused or the survivors philosophically survey the wreckage.[23]
But things are different: the new world into which the characters
emerge, at any rate symbolically, has been purged of certain things
and an alternative structure has been suggested. At the end of *The
Towering Inferno*, architect and fire chief stand in front of the
building and agree to work together in future, in an almost exact
reprise of enlightened capital and co-operative labour shaking hands
at the end of Lang's *Metropolis*. Significantly, the features that have
been purged from the old world are, generally speaking, those things
which were the targets of the corporatist demagogues of the thirties,
including America's own aspiring demagogue, Governor Huey P. Long
of Louisiana.[24] In this new world, whole categories of people have
been removed or transformed. The wicked are punished: Stella
Stevens's ex-prostitute is *not* one of the survivors of *The Poseidon*

Uniformed heroes and professional men: Steve MacQueen and Paul Newman
in *The Towering Inferno* (1974). Reproduced by courtesy of Columbia—EMI—
Warner Distributors Ltd.

Adventure; the sexually deviant National Guardsman (Marjoe Gortner) is shot in *Earthquake*, in which the bitch (Ava Gardner) and her adulterous husband (Charlton Heston) also perish; the publicist and his secretary having an illicit affair in the former's apartment in *The Towering Inferno* die in a particularly unpleasant way. Disasters are a highly moral affair, and though the wicked are not the only ones to perish, they rarely survive. This was perhaps to be expected. But the other groups of victims are less immediately predictable. First among these are the weak — or at any rate those who do not have the 'excuse' of being either infant, elderly or female — excluded from a Kingdom of God for which they are not prepared to fight: the passengers of the *Poseidon* who will not take their chance and follow Gene Hackman in a positive attempt to escape ('God loves triers'); the pilot of the light plane in *Airport 1975* who is unworthy of his machine and simply annihilated. In general terms, the problems faced by the survivors of the disaster are so enormous that the weak are quite simply purged out of existence: social Darwinism reasserts itself after being thwarted by a century of improved living conditions and welfare. Along with the weak go the criminal — the suicidal bomber in *Airport*, presented as more or less sub-human; the looters in *Earthquake*; the gang who try to take over the plane in *Airport '77* — all of whom are effortlessly eliminated. But it is not just society's marginals who must be removed: like corporatism, disaster movies aim their attack just as much at those who are in positions of responsibility for which they are not suited. A judgement of this kind — an actual or figurative stripping of powers — is implied or, more usually, meted out in every movie: e.g., against the purser and Linarcos in *The Poseidon Adventure*, the Government spokesman in *Juggernaut*, the director of the seismological institute and the Mayor in *Earthquake*, Simmons in *The Towering Inferno* and even the owner of the building himself, who refuses until it is too late to have the upper floors evacuated for a 'store-room fire'. Such men who in the normal, liberal, capitalist, democratic run of things have risen to positions of power through commercial enterprise or by due (or even undue) process of election are, it is implied, not fit to run society. Business acumen is no guarantee of leadership potential, and the mass electorate no judge of it. More efficient methods of selection are called for. Our leaders have been shown to be wanting at times of crisis. This fear, fuelled by Watergate and exploited by the 'super-cop' cycle, is evidently a very real one. And disaster movies respond to it in a typically demagogic

260

fashion: by portraying the transfer of power from the old, the incompetent and the corrupt to the new race of super-heroes, brave, morally upright and technologically brilliant. Behind them, the people can be united into a corporate identity, free from the divisions and the individual selfishness which characterised them before the disaster.

This is more than a merely thematic process: the narrative devices of the disaster movie actively encourage our allegiance to it.[25] In addition to providing a character for each member of the audience to identify with, the characterisation of the world in terms of archetypes may be seen as a tacit statement that the world is simple, easily organised and hierarchically structured. Complexity of motivation and a problematic social structure, it is implied, are products of degeneracy. Before the disaster, when the group is as yet unformed, parallel editing is necessary if we are to follow the destinies of the individual members of the future collective, whereas afterwards they can all be drawn together into the same scene or even the same shot. Disparate threads are drawn together into a single destiny both narratively and formally. Once the disaster has occurred we, too, quite literally follow the leader: his actions are what determine the advancement of the narrative. A hierarchical structure in which individual initiative leads to disunity, disunity leads to disaster, disaster is replaced by order and the individual becomes a passive follower, is as much a part of the movies' narrative strategies as it is of their ideological content. They open onto a new world in which stories can be told more simply and people behave more positively, a world in which, it is suggested, we will be fired with a new positivism and 'a pioneering, "head-for-the-stars" mood will pervade once more'.[26] The critics of the right are in no doubt about the message: for Michel Marmin in *Valeurs actuelles*, disaster movies 'call for a kind of reassessment of our values. In particular, they stress the incapacity of the masses to govern themselves alone, and the need for hierarchies and masculine supremacy.'[27] But disaster movies do more than simply stress this: they *act out* the coming disaster to show the changes which must occur. And in most cases they indicate, through the use of recognisable uniforms, that the elite who will lead us is already in existence. It will take over in a crisis and deserves to be given our full support. As the closing caption of *Airport '77* (the last image of the cycle) pointedly declares in a significant variation of the hallowed formula, 'the incident portrayed in this picture is fictional. The rescue capacities used by the Navy are real.' Disaster movies are undoubtedly, on one level, straightforward spectacular entertainment. But on another, operative only because of the first level, they are consistently and seductively the embodiment of a corporatist world view, a pleasingly simple solution to the troubling problems of our age within an effective narrative framework. These disasters may happen, they suggest; and if not these, very similar ones: when they come, you will know what to do.

NOTES

1   For American box office figures (USA and Canada), see the annually updated list of 'All-Time Film Rental Champs' published by *Variety*. In the 'top 40' of all films released up the end of 1976 (*Variety*, 5 January 1977), by which time the cycle was more or less complete, disaster movie placings were as follows: 8. *The Towering Inferno* ($55 million); 14. *Airport* ($45.3 million); 16. *The Poseidon Adventure* ($42.5 million); 20. *Earthquake* ($36.1 million); 36. *Airport 1975* ($25.7 million). British release details are taken from the much less detailed ratings in *Screen International and Cinema—TV Today* (January 1976). In 1975, the top six were: 1. *The Towering Inferno*; 2. *The Exorcist*; 3. *The Man with the Golden Gun*; 4. *Emanuelle*; 5. *Earthquake*; 6. *Airport 1975*.

2   For details of disaster movies referred to, see the Skeleton Filmography (pp. 264—9).

3   *Hollywood Reporter*, Wednesday July 5th 1972 ('Human condition stressed in Irwin Allen's "Poseidon" film', by Ron Pennington).

4   Cf. Art Ross, 'What is the True Meaning of the Disaster Film?', *Making Films in New York*, 9: 2 (April 1975), pp. 28—31, *passim*; and Adrian Turner, 'Quaking in the Stalls', *Films Illustrated*, 4: 44 (April 1975), p. 295.

5   Cf. in particular Olivier Eyquem, 'Sur fond d'apocalypse (à propos de 7 films-catastrophes)', *Positif*, 179 (March 1976), pp. 39—50; Ivailo Znepolsky (adapted by Marcel Martin), 'Films-catastrophes et contradictions de la conscience collective', *Ecran*, 50 (Sept. 1976), pp. 34—40; and a series of three articles (Joël Magny, 'Films catastrophiques, spectateurs catastrophés', Denis Lévy, 'Les Archanges du capital' and Stéphane Sorel, 'Catastrophique virilité') in *Téléciné*, 199 (May 1975), pp. 11—14. All the above are valuable, and this paper owes a debt to both Eyquem and Znepolsky. The two articles mentioned in the preceding note are also intermittently interesting (though not always for the right reasons), the former being an interview with a Dr Bennett Roth, Professor of Counsellor Education, NYU.

6   For a less vague discussion of the term 'manipulation', see Hans Magnus Enzensberger's essay, 'Constituents of a Theory of the Media', in *Raids and Reconstructions* (London, 1976), pp. 20—53.

7   Karl Marx, in an unfinished article for the *Rheinische Zeitung* (Marx and Engels, *Collected Works*, vol. 1 (London, 1975), p. 182).

8   Ross Pickard in *Photoplay*, 27: 3 (March 1976), p. 27; and Eyquem, 'Sur fond d'apocalypse', p. 40.

9 David Annan, *Catastrophe: the End of the Cinema?* (London, 1975), p. 40.

10 This effectively rules out a flourishing minor cycle (it is tempting to call it a sub-cycle) involving people trapped in submarines (e.g. *Run Silent, Run Deep*, *Ice Station Zebra* and, more recently, *Gray Lady Down*), since submarines are, after moon probes, the form of transport least accessible to the general public. To get a cross-section of stereotypes trapped on the sea bed requires the narrative ingenuity (and improbability) of *Airport '77*. It is worth noting, though, that *Gray Lady Down* ends with a caption virtually identical to that concluding *Airport '77*, pointing out that the US Navy already has the technology to carry out the kind of rescue shown.

11 I would also, therefore, exclude from the definition *Jaws*, often referred to as a disaster movie, since, after the initial attacks, the citizens of Amity have no obligation to go into the water: they can — and do — opt out of the disaster, and the film thereafter develops into a Melvillian personal confrontation between man and Leviathan.

12 I am, of course, excluding what are sometimes referred to as 'train movies', i.e. thrillers which take place on trains: *The Lady Vanishes*, *Night Train to Munich*, *The Narrow Margin*, *The Tall Stranger*, *Murder on the Orient Express*, to name but a tiny proportion. Train movies may share the claustrophobia of a disaster movie, but clearly have nothing much to do with disasters.

13 Arthur Hailey, author of the original novel *Airport*, has also written a novel along the lines of *Grand Hotel* called, simply, *Hotel*. It was filmed the year before *Airport* by Richard Quine. In the same vein, one could mention *Separate Tables*, *Ship of Fools*, *The VIPs* and *Voyage of the Damned* among many other films relying on the narrative device of separate but interwoven destinies.

14 Cf. Znepolsky, 'Films catastrophiques', p. 36.

15 Habitués of such buildings will be reassured to learn that McDonnel-Douglas have invented a system, based on a helicopter module, for rescuing people from burning skyscrapers. The report on the system in *New Scientist*, 77: 1090 (1978) specifically refers to *The Towering Inferno*.

16 Eyquem 'Sur fond d'apocalypse', p. 49.

17 Paul Gallico, *The Poseidon Adventure* (London, 1974).

18 As Stuart Kaminsky points out in a review of *The Poseidon Adventure* in *Take One*, 3: 10, p. 30, the characters who are saved are those who follow religion (Gene Hackman) as opposed to commerce (the purser) or science (the doctor). The film's imagery is more explicit. The journey to salvation is an inverted Dante's Inferno, from the hell of the upside down saloon, through the subsequent circles of galley and engine room ('Welcome to hell!', says Red Buttons as the others surface after their swim to the engine room), to the relative paradise of rescue. At the end, Gene Hackman explicitly sacrifices himself, Christ-like, for the salvation of the others: 'What more do You want of us?' he screams at God after the death of Mrs Rogo (Stella Stevens). 'We've come all this way, no thanks to You. Don't fight against us. Leave us alone! How much more blood, how many more lives? You want another life? Then take mine!' God does.

19 There is certainly none of what Philippe Mora calls 'macro-violence' ('Disaster

Films', *Cinema Papers* (*Australia*) (March—April 1975), p. 13); nor is it true, as claimed by Adrian Turner ('Quaking in the Stalls', p. 295) that 'these films' sole purpose is to provide death as graphically as possible, with a minimum of involvement'. Involvement is of the essence.

20 For an analysis of the role of women in disaster movies, cf. Sorel, 'Catastrophique virilité'.

21 The question of Hollywood's image of the female scientist is too large to go into here, though the implied point is pretty much the same as for a man: if she is a real woman she can't be a real scientist; if she is a real scientist, she can't be a real woman.

22 It has, for instance, at least three possible heroes (Dean Martin's pilot, Burt Lancaster's airport manager, and George Kennedy's troubleshooter), two entirely separate areas of action (the airliner and the airport) and at least three climaxes (the fight for and explosion of the bomb, the clearing of the runway, and the landing of the crippled airliner). It might be worth pointing out that, of the heroes, only Kennedy as Joe Patroni has any real possibility for heroic *action* (flying an aeroplane may require active heroism, but never really looks like it!) and, as a result, proves extremely durable, reappearing in a guest capacity in both *Airport 1975* and *Airport '77*.

23 The obvious exception here is *The Hindenburg*, though it might be argued that the destruction of this flying testimonial to Nazi technology is, in fact, positive: certainly the film's screenplay toys with this notion.

24 Cf. Thomas Harry Williams's definitive biography, *Huey Long* (New York, 1969).

25 For one reason or another, this essay has not specifically concerned itself with the narrative constraints of the disaster movie.

26 Dr Bennett Roth, quoted in Ross, p. 31.

27 Quoted by Sorel, 'Catastrophique virilité', p. 13.

A SKELETON FILMOGRAPHY

The following filmography contains the titles of those films which I have defined in the preceding essay as disaster movies. Obviously, it is neither complete nor definitive, and it gives only very basic information about the films: title, country of origin, date, production company (abbreviated to 'p.c.'), director (d.) and leading players (l.p.). A slightly fuller filmography which covers a parallel area and with which there is some overlap can be found in John Baxter's *Science Fiction in the Cinema* (London/New York, 1970).

English language films are listed here under their original release titles (i.e. American films under their American titles, British films under their British ones); alternative titles are given where known. Foreign language films are, with two exceptions (*La Jetée* and *Der Tunnel*), listed under their English titles, since to all intents and purposes these are the only ones under which an English-speaking audience will ever have heard of them. This may go against normal filmographical practice, but there seems to me little place in an essay on popular cultural forms for the kind of academicism which insists on *Bijo to Ekitai-Ningen* instead of *The H-Man*.

Airport. USA, 1968. p.c. Ross Hunter. d. George Seaton. l.p. Burt Lancaster,
   Dean Martin, Jean Seberg, Jacqueline Bisset, George Kennedy, Helen Hayes.
Airport 1975. USA, 1974. p.c. Universal. d. Jack Smight. l.p. Charlton Heston,
   Karen Black, George Kennedy, Susan Clark.
Airport '77. USA, 1977. p.c. Jennings Lang Productions (for Universal). d. Jerry
   Jameson. l.p. Jack Lemmon, Lee Grant, Brenda Vaccaro, Olivia de Havilland,
   Joseph Cotten, Christopher Lee.
Alphaville. France/Italy, 1965. p.c. Chaumiane (Paris)/Filmstudio (Rome).
   d. Jean-Luc Godard. l.p. Eddie Constantine, Anna Karina.
The Amazing Colossal Man. USA, 1957. p.c. Malibu Productions. d. Bert I.
   Gordon. l.p. Glenn Langan, William Hudson, Cathy Downs.
Atlantik. Germany, 1929. p.c. British International Pictures. d. E. A. Dupont.
   l.p. (English version) Ellaline Terriss, Franklyn Dyall, Madeleine Carroll;
   (German version) Fritz Kortner, Elsa Wagner, Heinrich Schroth.
The Atomic Kid. USA, 1954. p.c. Mickey Rooney/Republic. d. Leslie H. Martinson.
   l.p. Mickey Rooney, Elaine Davis.
The Beast from 20,000 Fathoms. USA, 1953. p.c. Warners. d. Eugène Lourié.
   l.p. Paul Christian, Paula Raymond, Cecil Kellaway.
The Bedford Incident. Britain, 1965. p.c. Bedford Productions. d. James B. Harris.
   l.p. Richard Widmark, Sidney Poitier, James MacArthur, Martin Balsam.
Behemoth the Sea Monster. Britain, 1958. p.c. David Diamond Productions.
   d. Douglas Hickox and Eugene Lourié. l.p. Gene Evans, Andre Morrell.
Ben. USA, 1972. p.c. Bing Crosby Productions. d. Phil Karlson. l.p. Joseph
   Campanella, Lee Harcourt Montgomery.
The Big Bus. USA, 1976. p.c. Cohen & Freeman/Phillips (for Paramount).
   d. James Frawley. l.p. Joseph Bologna, Stockard Channing, Lynn Redgrave,
   Ruth Gordon.
The Birds. USA, 1963. p.c. Universal. d. Alfred Hitchcock. l.p. Rod Taylor,
   Tippi Hedren, Jessica Tandy, Suzanne Pleshette.
The Bullet Train. Japan (original title: *Shinkansen Daibakuha*), 1975. p.c. Toei.
   d. Junya Sato. l.p. Ken Takakura, Shin-ichi Chiba, Akira Oda.
The Cassandra Crossing. Britain/Italy/West Germany, 1976. p.c. Associated
   General Films (London)/Compagnia Cinematografica Champion (Rome).
   d. George Pan Cosmatos. l.p. Sophia Loren, Richard Harris, Martin Sheen,
   Ava Gardner, Burt Lancaster.
Crack in the World. USA, 1965. p.c. Security Pictures. d. Andrew Marton.
   l.p. Dana Andrews, Janette Scott, Kieron Moore.
The Cyclops. USA, 1957. p.c. A.B. & H. Productions. d. Bert I. Gordon. l.p.
   James Craig, Gloria Talbot, Lon Chaney Jr.
The Damned. Britain, 1962. p.c. Swallow/Hammer Films. d. Joseph Losey.
   l.p. Macdonald Carey, Viveca Lindfors, Shirley Anne Field, Oliver Reed.
The Day the Earth Caught Fire. Britain, 1961. p.c. Melina. d. Val Guest. l.p.
   Janet Munro, Leo McKern, Edward Judd.
The Day the World Ended. USA, 1955. p.c. Golden State Productions. d. Roger
   Corman. l.p. Richard Denning, Lori Nelson, Adele Jergens.
The Deadly Mantis. USA, 1957. p.c. Universal-International. d. Nathan Juran.
   l.p. Craig Stevens, Alix Talton, William Hopper.

Deluge. USA, 1933. p.c. RKO. d. Felix Feist. l.p. Peggy Shannon, Sidney Blackmer, Lois Wilson.

Doctor Strangelove. Britain, 1963. p.c. Hawk Films. d. Stanley Kubrick. l.p. Peter Sellers, George C. Scott, Sterling Hayden.

Earthquake. USA, 1974. p.c. Universal. d. Mark Robson. l.p. Charlton Heston, Ava Gardner, George Kennedy, Lorne Greene, Genevieve Bujold.

Empire of the Ants. USA, 1977. p.c. Cinema 77 (for American International Pictures). d. Bert I. Gordon. l.p. Joan Collins, Robert Lansing, John David Carson, Pamela Shoop.

Fahrenheit 451. Britain, 1966. p.c. Anglo-Enterprise-Vineyard. d. François Truffaut. l.p. Oskar Werner, Julie Christie, Cyril Cusack.

Fail Safe. USA, 1964. p.c. Max E. Youngstein/Sidney Lumet. d. Sidney Lumet. l.p. Henry Fonda, Dan O'Herlihy, Walter Matthau.

Fire. USA. 1977. p.c. Irwin Allen/Warner Brothers TV. d. Earl Bellamy. l.p. Ernest Borgnine, Neville Brand, Gene Evans.

Five. USA, 1951. p.c. Colombia. d. Arch Oboler. l.p. William Phipps, Susan Douglas, James Anderson.

Flight to the Holocaust. USA, 1977. p.c. Aycee Productions (for NBC). d. Bernard Kowalski. l.p. Patrick Wayne, Chris Mitchum, Desi Arnaz Jr.

Flood. USA, 1976. p.c. Warner Brothers. d. Earl Bellamy. l.p. Robert Culp, Martin Milner, Richard Basehart, Carol Lynley.

The Giant Spider Invasion. USA, 1975. p.c. Cinema Group 75 (for Transcentury Pictures). d. Bill Rebane. l.p. Steve Brodie, Barbara Hale, Alan Hale Jr.

The H-Man. Japan (original title: *Bijo to Ekitai-Ningen*), 1958. p.c. Toho. d. Inoshiro Honda. l.p. Kenji Sahara, Yumi Shirakawa, Akihito Hirata.

The High and the Mighty. USA, 1954. p.c. Warners. d. William Wellman. l.p. John Wayne, Claire Trevor, Robert Stack.

The Hindenburg. USA, 1975. p.c. Universal/Filmakers Group. d. Robert Wise. l.p. George C. Scott, Anne Bancroft, William Atherton, Gig Young.

The Hurricane. USA, 1937. p.c. United Artists. d. John Ford. l.p. Dorothy Lamour, Jon Hall, Mary Astor, Raymond Massey, C. Aubrey Smith.

The Incredible Shrinking Man. USA, 1956. p.c. Universal International. d. Jack Arnold. l.p. Grant Williams, Randy Stuart, April Kent.

In Old Chicago. USA, 1937. p.c. 20th Century-Fox. d. Henry King. l.p. Tyrone Power, Alice Faye, Don Ameche.

Invasion USA. USA, 1952. p.c. Columbia. d. Alfred E. Green. l.p. Gerald Mohr, Peggie Castle, Dan O'Herlihy.

It Came from Beneath the Sea. USA, 1955. p.c. Columbia. d. Robert Gordon. l.p. Faith Domergue, Kenneth Tobey, Donald Curtis.

La Jetée. France, 1962. p.c. Argos-Films/RTF. d. Chris Marker. l.p. Hélène Chatelain, Davos Henich, William Klein, Lygia Borowczyk.

Juggernaut. Britain, 1974. p.c. United Artists. d. Richard Lester. l.p. Omar Sharif, Richard Harris, David Hemmings, Roy Kinnear.

Krakatoa – East of Java. USA, 1968. p.c. Cinerama-Krakatoa. d. Bernard Kowalski. l.p. Maximillian Schell, Diane Baker, Brian Keith.

The Last Days of Pompeii. Italy (original title: *Gli ultimi giorni di Pompeii*), 1908. p.c. Ambrosio. d. Luigi Maggi. – Britain, 1909. p.c. Warwick Trading Company (probably a pirated version of the 1908 Italian film). – Italy

(original title: *Gli ultimi giorni di Pompeii*), 1913. p.c. Gloria Film. — Italy
(original title: *Gli ultimi giorni di Pompeii*), 1913. p.c. Ambrosio. d. Mario
Caserini. l.p. Fernando Negri Pouget, Eugenia Tettoni. — Italy (original title:
Gli ultimi giorni di Pompeii), 1913. p.c. Ambrosio. d. Mario Caserini. l.p.
Pasquali, Enrico Vidali, Suzanne de Labroy, Ines Melidoni. — USA, 1913. —
Italy (Original title: *Gli ultimi giorni di Pompeii*), 1926. p.c. SASP/Grande
Films. d. Carmine Gallone. l.p. Amletto Palermi, Maria Cordi, Victor Varconi,
Hernard Goetzke. — USA, 1935. p.c. RKO. d. Ernest B. Schoedsack. l.p.
Preston Foster, Basil Rathbone, David Holt. — France/Italy (original title:
Les Derniers Jours de Pompeii), 1949. p.c. Salvo D'Angelo/Films Universali.
d. Marcel l'Herbier. l.p. Micheline Presle, Georges Marshall, Marcel Herrand. —
Italy/Spain/Monaco (original title: *Gli ultimi giorni di Pompeii*), 1959.
p.c. Filmar (Rome)/Procusa (Madrid)/Transocean. d. Mario Bonnard. l.p.
Steve Reeves, Fernando Rey, Christina Kaufmann.
The Last Voyage. USA, 1959. p.c. Andrew and Virginia Stone Productions.
d. Andrew L. Stone. l.p. Robert Stack, Dorothy Malone, George
Sanders.
The Last War. Japan, 1961. p.c. Toho. d. Shue Matsubayashi. l.p. Yuriko
Hoshi, Frankie Sakai.
The Last Woman on Earth. USA, 1960. p.c. The Filmgroup. d. Roger Corman.
l.p. Anthony Carbone, Betsy Jones-Moreland.
Lifeboat. USA, 1943. p.c. 20th Century-Fox. d. Alfred Hitchcock. l.p. Walter
Slezak, Tallulah Bankhead, John Hodiak.
Logan's Run. USA, 1976. p.c. MGM. d. Michael Anderson. l.p. Michael York,
Richard Jordan, Jenny Agutter, Farrah Fawcett-Majors, Peter Ustinov.
Madam Satan. USA, 1930. p.c. MGM. d. Cecil B. DeMille. l.p. Kay Johnson,
Reginald Denny, Lillian Roth.
Metropolis. Germany 1926. p.c. UFA. d. Fritz Lang. l.p. Brigitte Helm, Gustav
Frohlich, Rudolf Klein-Rogge.
The Monster that Challenged the World. USA, 1957. p.c. Jules V. Levy and Arthur
Gardner Productions. d. Arnold Laven. l.p. Tim Holt, Audrey Dalton, Hans
Conreid.
The Most Dangerous Man Alive. USA, 1961. p.c. Bogeanus. d. Allen Dwan.
l.p. Ron Randell, Debra Paget, Elaine Stewart.
The Naked Jungle. USA, 1953. p.c. Paramount. d. Byron Haskin. l.p. Charlton
Heston, Eleanor Parker.
The Night of the Lepus. USA, 1972. p.c. MGM. d. William F. Claxton. l.p. Stuart
Whitman, Janet Leigh, Rory Calhoun.
The Night of the Living Dead. USA, 1968. p.c. Image Ten. d. George A. Romero.
l.p. Judith O'Dea, Russell Steiner, Duane Jones.
A Night to Remember. Britain, 1957. p.c. Rank. d. Roy Ward Baker. l.p. Kenneth
More, Jill Adams, Michael Goodliffe.
The Night the World Exploded. USA, 1957. p.c. Clover Productions. d. Fred
F. Sears. l.p. William Leslie, Kathryn Grant.
1984. Britain, 1955. p.c. Holiday Productions. d. Michael Anderson. l.p. Edmond
O'Brien, Jan Sterling, Michael Redgrave.
The Omega Man. USA, 1971. p.c. Walter Seltzer (for Warners). d. Boris Sagal.
l.p. Charlton Heston, Anthony Zerbe, Rosalind Cash.

On the Beach. USA, 1959. p.c. Lomitas Productions. d. Stanley Kramer. l.p.
Gregory Peck, Ava Gardner, Fred Astaire, Anthony Perkins.

Panic in the Year Zero. USA, 1962. p.c. American International. d. Ray Milland.
l.p. Ray Milland, Jean Hagen, Frankie Avalon.

Phase IV. Britain, 1973. p.c. Alced Productions. d. Saul Bass. l.p. Nigel Davenport,
Michael Murphy, Lynne Frederick.

Planet of the Apes. Britain, 1967. p.c. Apjac Productions. d. Franklin D. Schaffner.
l.p. Charlton Heston, Maurice Evans, Kim Hunter, Roddy McDowell. —
Beneath the Planet of the Apes. USA, 1969. p.c. Apjac Productions. d. Ted
Post. l.p. Charlton Heston, Maurice Evans, Kim Hunter, James Franciscus. —
Escape from the Planet of the Apes. USA, 1971. p.c. Apjac. d. Don Taylor.
l.p. Roddy McDowell, Kim Hunter, Brad Dillman. — *Conquest of the Planet
of the Apes*. USA, 1972. p.c. Apjac/20th Century-Fox. d. J. Lee Thompson.
l.p. Roddy McDowell, Don Murray, Natalie Trundy. — *Battle for the Planet
of the Apes*. USA, 1973. p.c. Apjac. d. J. Lee Thompson. l.p. Roddy McDowell,
Claude Akins, Natalie Trundy.

The Poseidon Adventure. USA, 1972. p.c. Kent Productions (for 20th Century-
Fox). d. Ronald Neame. l.p. Gene Hackman, Ernest Borgnine, Red Buttons,
Shelley Winters, Stella Stevens, Carole Lynley.

The Rains Came. USA, 1939. p.c. 20th Century-Fox. d. Clarence Brown. l.p.
Myrna Loy, Tyrone Power, George Brent. — *The Rains of Ranchipur*. USA,
1955. p.c. 20th Century-Fox. d. Jean Negulesco. l.p. Lana Turner, Richard
Burton, Fred MacMurray, Michael Rennie.

The Runaway Train. USA, 1973. p.c. Universal. d. David Lowell-Rich. l.p.
Ben Johnson, Martin Milner, Vera Miles.

San Francisco. USA, 1936. p.c. MGM. d. Woody S. Van Dyke. l.p. Clark Gable,
Spencer Tracy, Jeanette MacDonald.

Silver Streak. USA, 1976. p.c. Miller Milkis-Colin Higgins (for 20th Century-
Fox). d. Arthur Hiller. l.p. Gene Wilder, Jill Clayburgh, Richard Pryor, Patrick
McGoohan.

Smash-up on Interstate Five. USA, 1976. p.c. Filmways Productions. d. John
Llewellyn-Moxley. l.p. David Groh, Vera Miles, Harriet Nelson.

Soylent Green. USA, 1973. p.c. MGM. d. Richard Fleischer. l.p. Charlton Heston,
Edward G. Robinson, Leigh Taylor-Young.

Spider Man. USA, 1977. p.c. Danchuck Productions. d. E. W. Swackhamer.
l.p. Nicholas Hammond, Lisa Eilbacher.

Squirm. USA, 1976. p.c. Edgar Lansbury/Joseph Beruh. d. Jeff Lieberman.
l.p. John Scardino, Patricia Pearcy, R. A. Dow.

The Submersion of Japan. Japan (original title: *Nippon Chinbotsu*), 1973.
p.c. Toho. d. Shiro Moritani. l.p. Keiju Kobayashi, Tetsuro Tamba. (There
is also an American release version of the film, starring Lorne Green, and re-
titled *Tidal Wave*).

Suez. USA, 1938. p.c. 20th Century-Fox. d. Allan Dwan. l.p. Tyrone Power,
Loretta Young, Annabella.

Survive! Mexico (original title: *Supervivientes de Los Andes*), 1976. p.c. Conacine/
Productora Filmica Re-Al. d. Rene Cardona Sr. l.p. Hugo Stiglitz, Pedro
Requeiro, Pablo Gorge.

The Taking of Pelham 123. USA, 1974. p.c. Palomar/Palladium. d. Joseph Sargent.
l.p. Walter Matthau, Martin Balsam, Robert Shaw.

Tarantula! USA, 1955. p.c. Universal International. d. Jack Arnold. l.p. John
Agar, Mara Corday.

Tentacles. Italy/USA (original title: *Tentacoli*), 1976. p.c. A-Esse Cinematografica. d. Oliver Hellman (= Sonia Assonitis). l.p. John Huston, Henry Fonda,
Shelley Winters.

Them! USA, 1954. p.c. Warners. d. Gordon Douglas. l.p. James Whitmore,
Edmund Gwenn, Joan Weldon.

Things to Come. Britain, 1936. p.c. London Films. d. William Cameron Menzies.
l.p. Raymond Massey, Edward Chapman, Ralph Richardson.

THX 1138. USA, 1970. p.c. Zoetrope Productions. d. George Lucas. l.p. Robert
Duvall, Donald Pleasence, Don Pedro Colley.

The Time Machine. USA, 1960. p.c. George Pal Productions/ Galaxy Films.
d. George Pal. l.p. Rod Taylor, Alan Young, Yvette Mimieux.

Titanic. Germany, 1943. p.c. Tobis. d. Herpert Selpin & Werner Klinger. l.p.
Sybille Schmitz, Kirsten Heiberg, Hans Nielsen. — USA, 1953. p.c. 20th
Century Fox. d. Jean Negulesco. l.p. Clifton Webb, Barbara Stanwyck,
Thelma Ritter.

The Towering Inferno. USA, 1974. p.c. Fox/Warner. d. John Guillermin. l.p.
Steve MacQueen, Paul Newman, Faye Dunaway, William Holden, Fred Astaire.

Transatlantic Tunnel. Britain, 1935. p.c. Gaumont British. d. Maurice Elvey.
l.p. Richard Dix, Leslie Banks, Madge Evans.

Der Tunnel. Germany 1953. p.c. Vandor. d. Curtis Bernhardt. l.p. Paul Hart-
mann, Olly Van Flint, Gustaf Gründgens.

Volcano. USA, 1926. p.c. Paramount. d. William K. Howard. l.p. Bebe Daniels,
Ricardo Cortez. — Italy, 1950 (original title: *Vulcano*). p.c. Artisti Associati/
Panaria. d. William Dieterle. l.p. Anna Magnani, Rossano Brazzi, Geraldine
Brooks.

War of the Colossal Beast (Alternative title: *Revenge of the Colossal Man*. British
release title: *The Terror Strikes*). USA, 1958. p.c. American International.
d. Bert I. Gordon. l.p. Sally Fraser, Roger Pace.

The War Game. Britain, 1965. p.c. BBC TV. d. Peter Watkins.

When Worlds Collide. USA, 1951. p.c. Paramount. d. Rudolf Maté. l.p.
Richard Derr, Barbara Rush, Larry Keating.

Willard. USA, 1971. p.c. Bing Crosby Productions. d. Daniel Mann. l.p. Bruce
Davison, Ernest Borgnine, Sondra Locke.

The World, the Flesh and the Devil. USA, 1958. p.c. Sol. C. Siegel Productions/
Harbel Productions. d. Ranald McDougall. l.p. Harry Belafonte, Mel Ferrer,
Inger Stevens.

X, the Unknown. Britain, 1956. p.c. Hammer. d. Leslie Norman. l.p. Dean Jagger,
Leo McKern, Edward Chapman.

Zardoz. Britain, 1973. p.c. John Boorman Productions (for 20th Century Fox).
d. John Boorman. l.p. Sean Connery, Charlotte Rampling, Sara Kestleman,
John Alderton.

Zeppelin. Britain, 1971. p.c. Getty-McDonald-Fromkess (for Warners). d. Etienne
Perier. l.p. Elke Somer, Michael York, Rupert Davies.

PART THREE

PROBLEMS AND PROSPECTS

Introduction

Bernard Sharratt

This final section of the book comprises two contributions to the
Kent conference of a rather different kind from the other papers:
an edited transcript of part of the discussion, and my own paper,
which was an attempt to survey the broad field covered by the conference as a whole and to offer an overview by suggesting some
hypotheses about the continuing functions of 'popular' forms of
art and entertainment in the nineteenth century and the present.
The paper was designed, deliberately, as an attempt by a non-specialist
to look afresh at a region of academic research and debate in which
familiar lines of inquiry have long been established; its argument has
been left in a relatively tentative and incomplete form because something of the pressure of thinking, of reflecting upon a wide range of
disparate contributions, is worth retaining, and even insisting on,
in a debate that is bound to remain problematic. The conjunction of
this mainly theoretical paper with a discussion among theatre practitioners is indicative of some of the aims of the conference: to widen
the debate about 'popular theatre' and to bring together academics
and practitioners. Discussion between those participants who worked
mainly in education and those who worked professionally in theatre
was one central element in the experience of the conference, but
writing papers for publication in books of this kind tends to be the
preserve of the former. We have therefore included an extract from
one of those discussions as a way of reminding readers of the otherwise absent participants. Both the context and the content of the
extract are worth commenting on here because they serve to focus
some more general considerations.

The discussion took place after a public rehearsal by the Joint
Stock Theatre Company of some scenes from *Fanshen*, a play by
David Hare written for that company. The rehearsal was a genuine
working rehearsal; the play was being revived for a tour and had gone
into rehearsal only a week or so before the conference; we asked the

271

company simply to transfer their regular rehearsal session from London to Canterbury and to allow us all to watch. This they, courageously, did. After a few preliminary remarks — including the the comment by Max Stafford-Clark, the director, that they really *needed* the rehearsal time, so had definitely *not* prepared anything 'special' for us — the company worked solidly for about two hours, before an absorbed audience of 150 assorted academics and specialists.

That open rehearsal was one of a number of sessions in which the conference tried to break away from the familiar format of papers followed by discussion. Another company, the Strathclyde Theatre Group, put on a production of a new play, *Melmoth: the Wanderer's Dream*, in the university's Gulbenkian theatre and then, equally courageously, submitted to a morning's critical discussion; some students from the university's melodrama course acted scenes from Victorian melodramas as the 'quotations' in a conference paper; a session on the ritual element in folk-culture included a memorable ritual dance; Steve Gooch led a discussion of a videotape of Belt and Braces' production of *The Mother*, which he had translated; a Victorian 'free and easy' occupied one evening, incorporating the more or less spontaneous contributions of more or less talented participants; and, of course, films and television programmes were screened and discussions arranged around them.

The point of such sessions was not simply to enliven the conference, to mingle entertainment or light relief with serious debate. A crucial component of theatre, as of all art, is its immediacy, its *nowness*, its status as *event*. For a conference concerned mainly with forms of drama to distance itself from the experience of drama would have been to risk distorting and muting the very object of our inquiry. And when the object of attention is *political* drama that element of *nowness*, in all its urgent senses, is peculiarly important.

Raymond Williams once remarked that 'The history of ideas is a kind of middle age'; by that cryptic comment I think he meant that in writing, say, a historical work on 'Romanticism' it is possible to capture something of the excitement, the energy, the freshness and attractiveness of feelings and ideas which were new in the late eighteenth and early nineteenth centuries — but only as it were through a curiously taming, deadening or even patronising nostalgia, akin to the feeling that someone now aged fifty may have for the passions and enthusiasms of their own early twenties; the tingle has gone, and only the memory remains, recollected but not revived in tranquillity. When we research into the past of politics, and especially into the

agitational art of previous periods and generations, that sense of
energies once alive yet now dulled beyond even recall can be over-
whelming: the faded photograph of the magnificently innovative
production, the then-startling gesture or design, can seem simply
inert before us. Fellini's *The Clowns* includes that sad, predictable,
anti-climax of actually finding the one genuine clip of film of — does
it matter who they were, those dismally flickering puppets with their
grey antics?

To be in the middle of a process is not to be clear about it. The
kind of clarity academics strive for seems always to come, if at all,
only afterwards. The problems of political drama today are as acute
and difficult, as urgent and present, as they ever were, at the time. In
the discussion after *Fanshen* a lot of those difficulties are legible —
the problems of audience, of style, of venue, of standpoint, of objectives; and in the form of the discussion itself something of the
strangely muffled quality of any actual present struggle is apparent:
those taking part in the discussion, trying to articulate their sense of
their own current work in theatre and drama, are thinking through
their difficulties and concerns as they speak: questions are left
hanging, or circled around, or answered only obliquely, answers
suggest other problems or tangentially relevant facets. Throughout,
there is — it seems to me — a continuing difficulty of language, despite
the articulateness: a difficulty in pinning down the problems, a difficulty in expressing the partial solutions people have found in the
daily work of practice. Even with the hindsight of a mere few months,
or with that colder kind of immediate hindsight that comes from
reading what was originally spoken, it's possible to see more clearly
the uncertainties, simplifications, naiveties; each reader will register
different marginal irritations; but, of course, such clarity is only
achieved with distancing, and it too is fragile and provisional when
the problems remain, insistently, present.

The transcript of the discussion has, inescapably, been edited,
tidied up somewhat, and a selection has been imposed. Some sections
of the debate were too closely tied to the experience of watching
the rehearsal, others were a bit too chaotic to shape into readable
form; the whole was too long to give in full. Names have been used
only for those whose role in relation to the issues raised makes a
difference to the significance of their comments. It should be noted
that the session began with nine actors present but that they left
(for a performance that evening) about half-way through. It would
obviously be useful to have read *Fanshen*; the scenes rehearsed were

Act I, Section 7 and Section 8. i: 'The Gate', and some references are only intelligible if these scenes are already known.

Of course, in using the discussion in this way, we too are trying to recapture a moment, a live performance, that is past: the impressive openness, the sense of shared experience, and particularly the humour of that occasion, as of the conference as a whole, cannot be revived purely on the page. That is one of the reasons why the whole art of drama sometimes imposes itself upon us as necessary and irreplaceable. At one point in the discussion David Hare quotes Len Deighton to the effect that a debate is only dramatic when the loser is to be shot at the end; the debate about political drama does have a certain edge when we remember that, not infrequently, the losers in a political debate have been shot, and that a dramatist or theatre group involved in 'political drama' is committed to that wider conflict in which the bullets are real. It's also worth remembering that — as the comments of one of the actors suggests — the peculiarly English confidence in nuances, subtleties and gradations may sometimes be misplaced; in certain situations, there can be a sharp and unpredictable leap into violence, 'revolutionary' or otherwise. But then David Hare, as a dramatist, dissociates himself from Deighton: it is the debate itself which is dramatic, not the resolution. It seems politically appropriate to end this book with a 'live' debate that could perhaps even be dramatised in some form, but which certainly cannot be resolved simply by the various arts of the dramatist.

The politics of the popular? – from melodrama to television

Bernard Sharratt

This paper attempts two things: to seek connections between some
of the topics covered by the Kent conference, and to explore some
problems concerning the possibility of popular political drama today.
It is not offered as either a report on research or as a fully elaborated
thesis; given the complexity of the issues tackled and limitations on
space, I can present only compressed points and some methodologically
eclectic and schematic hypotheses. A brief comment on some problems
of 'Marxist criticism' can serve as introduction.

There are various difficulties involved in trying to relate the history
of an art-form to the history of class struggle; most attempts to do
so begin from the art-object, the artefact, and seek to connect its
'content' and/or 'form' to the conditions of its production; a work of
art can then be seen as expressing, embodying, working through, or
otherwise 'containing' the ideology of a social class. In Goldmann's
criticism, for example, the work is grasped as the summation or
intensification, the most coherent articulation, of a world-view;
whereas for Macherey the work betrays, in its very silences, incon-
sistencies and contortions, the fissures and gaps which always fracture
and undermine the dominant ideology of a period.[1] Such approaches
have difficulties with the notion of authorship; Lukácsian theories
rely upon a dubious attribution of 'representativeness' to an author,
while for Althusserians the 'author' tends to evaporate into a complex
instance of relatively autonomous signifying practices – six textual
codes in search of a typewriter. An alternative line, which has some
affinities with these Marxist approaches, has developed in recent
work in 'reception theory', which has emphasised the act of reading,
the point of consumption rather than of production, but here too
it has proved difficult to accommodate the individual, the actual
readers; it is the 'implied reader', the response posited and pre-
structured by the operations of the 'text', that is analysed, and critical

theory thereby remains focused on the intestines of the artefact, unable to move onto the terrain of directly political concerns.[2] The intricate methodological issues raised by these various approaches make *any* critical argument today peculiarly tentative, but thinking about the problems of 'popular art' may suggest a further facet, another angle of approach. It's certainly possible to see some forms of 'popular' art as expressing the collective aspirations of a 'people', but that notion of 'the people' has to be recognised, often, as standing in for the self-definition of a dominated class struggling to identify itself against an imposed and degrading definition by a ruling class.[3] It may also be possible to offer a reading *à la* Macherey of the lack of 'fit' between the different textual and dramaturgical codes at work in, for example, 'melodrama', thereby coming to terms with the sense of oscillating between the aesthetic conventions and strengths of dramatic realism and the sentimental emotionalism and moral polarisation of the strip-cartoon which emerges from reading Pixérécourt, Bouchardy and their English successors.[4] But if we try to combine the Althusserian emphasis on *conditions* of production with the Constance school's emphasis on *reception* and seek to analyse the *conditions of reception* of 'popular' art, we may be in a position to understand more clearly some of the peculiar difficulties of creating a 'popular' *political* art today. I want to try, in what follows, to suggest, in a drastically simplified way, some of the conditions of reception which seem to underpin the response of working-class audiences to a variety of forms of art and entertainment which it would be difficult not to label, in some sense, 'popular'. Part of my concern is to understand the experiences and aspirations not of the 'class' as a whole but rather of the individuals and families who comprise the 'audience' for art; it is not 'the working class' which attends a theatre performance; though an audience always constitutes a 'collective', whereby any individual response is shaped, an audience is not the same kind of collectivity as a 'class';[5] as we enter a theatre or switch on the television we enter into relationships with others and with ourselves that cannot easily be mapped onto the relations of production and consumption that constitute the specifically economic and political identity of a class.[6] In the disharmony between the collective strengths of a class and the individual position of the members of a class, one of the functions of 'popular' art may perhaps be located. Some facets of that disharmony can be traced in this paper.

Insecurity and impotence

Insofar as the designation 'popular' indicates that the audience for a particular form of drama or entertainment includes, to some considerable extent, members of the working class, one can say that the life experience of much of that audience is characterised by economic insecurity and political impotence, and that the popularity of a particular form of cultural activity may therefore be related to those components of their experience.[7] By this I mean that in the nineteenth century and in modified ways in the twentieth century one central element in the situation of a working-class family has been acute vulnerability to economic uncertainty and a lack of control over the forces governing their overall condition. In general, it has been characteristic of individual and domestic working-class life that an apparently minor event can have immediately drastic consequences: a rise in food prices may finally erase a narrow gap between income and necessary expenditure; a slight fluctuation in national or sectoral trade conditions may result in lay-off or redundancy; a brief illness, minor accident or momentary 'indiscipline' (drunkenness, 'insubordination') may result in loss of job; a wage-claim may end in a long-drawn-out and difficult strike. This is the experiential obverse of the structural control exercised by a ruling minority over the conditions and prospects of employment. A long history of efforts by working-class organisations, by the class as collective agency, to ensure increased security and achieve some counterbalance of control can, of course, be charted; but it remains true that always at the personal level a degree of insecurity and impotence remains. In contemporary terms, this can be seen not only in the persistence of large numbers on the poverty-line or on the dole but also in a wide-spread sense of unknown or ill-understood forces affecting and governing social and economic conditions. The psychological result of this situation can be a constant, if latent, sense of fear and of living in a state of permanent risk.[8]

Escapism, dream and nightmare

One familiar way in which a link has been suggested, or presumed, between working-class experience and popular art-forms is the notion of 'escapism': that in enjoying certain forms of entertainment, sport or other activities, an economically deprived audience seeks 'escape' from mundane pressures and anxieties into a world of fantasy, daydream, wish-fulfilment, or simply an obliteratingly colourful and spectacular excitement; a variant of this interpretation emphasises the 'release' of pent up emotions in an exaggerated or vivid form.[9]

But if we consider a range of cultural activities normally labelled 'popular', some doubt about this familiar line arises. For in a large number of cases, though in various ways, what seems an essential element in many popular cultural activities is precisely an experience by the audience of an actual or vicarious *fear*. The essential attraction of a circus, for example, surely lies in the acts which involve physical danger: the trapeze artist, lion tamer, high-wire acrobat, knife thrower, fire-eater, high diver and human cannon-ball are all experts in personal risk. It is not so much the spectacle or skill (the glittering girls on white stallions, the trick cyclist or juggler) that makes a circus memorable, as the tension in the pit of the stomach at the possibility of terrible failure or mistake; it is the high stakes that grip us, the lonely vulnerability of the performer in which, open-mouthed and edgily silent, we tinglingly participate. The same element seems present in that other great place of popular entertainment, the fairground; but there it is we ourselves who take the risks or simulate them: it is the Big Dipper and the giddy Big Wheel, the gyrating aerial torpedoes and the sickening slide of the helter-skelter that are the tempting high points — the other booths, those of skill or luck, seem a tame second-best, literally side-shows. In the fairground ghost train, as in its cinematic cousin the horror movie, we expose ourselves to the psychological frights without the physical risks; disaster movies, war movies and supernatural terror movies (*The Exorcist* and all its breed) exemplify the same pattern. In some sports, part of the thrill lies in the possibility of disaster: it is the flashing blue light of the ambulance in the centre of the speedway circuit that underpins the tension in the stadium. In its muted form, even gambling offers its own risks, of loss, failure, even disaster.

Much popular drama can also be viewed from this angle. The spectacular sensation scenes of Victorian melodrama (crashing trains, burning houses, sinking ships, avalanches and explosions) are the precursors of today's disaster movies; the melodramas of incantation anticipate *The Exorcist*; gothic melodramas revive in the Hammer horror. And in domestic melodrama it is the persecuting pursuit of the helpless heroine by the malignant villain, the succession of 'hair's-breadth perils' engineered by the machinations of evil antagonists, that constitute the main content of the plot; the old serials of the

278

children's matinee gave a cinematic half-life to these patterns of
endlessly suspended peril.

In the standard accounts of melodrama this overwhelmingly obvious
feature is, of course, acknowledged and dwelt upon; but it is then
often subsumed under an account which puts emphasis rather upon
the moral dichotomies that control the plot and characterisation: the
stereotyping of Good and Evil characters, the 'poetic justice' of the
(last-minute) triumph of the Sunday School virtues, the final evap-
oration of evil. Michael Booth's formulation can stand for many:

> Essentially, melodrama is a dream world inhabited by dream people and dream
> justice, offering audiences the fulfilment and satisfaction found only in dreams.
> An idealisation and simplification of the world of reality, it is in fact the world
> its audiences want but cannot get. Melodrama is therefore a dramatisation of
> this second world, an allegory of human experience dramatically ordered, as it
> should be rather than as it is. In this world life is uncomplicated, easy to under-
> stand, and immeasurably exciting. People are true to their surface appearances
> and always think and behave in a way these appearances dictate. One of the
> great appeals of this world is clarity: character, conduct, ethics, and situations
> are perfectly simple, and one always knows what the end will be, although
> the means may be temporarily obscure. The world of melodrama is thus a
> world of certainties where confusion, doubt, and perplexity are absent; a world
> of absolutes where virtue and vice coexist in pure whiteness and pure blackness;
> and a world of justice where after immense struggle and torment good triumphs
> over and punishes evil, and virtue receives tangible material rewards. The
> superiority of such a world over the entirely unsatisfactory everyday world hardly
> needs demonstration, and it is this romantic and escapist appeal that goes a
> long way to explain the enduring popularity of melodrama.

The last sentence particularly puzzles. A world of fear, terror, horror,
violence, disaster, agony, of (in Booth's own phrasing) 'shootings,
stranglings, hangings, poisonings, drownings, stabbings, suicides,
explosions, conflagrations, avalanches, earthquakes, eruptions, ship-
wrecks, trainwrecks, apparitions, tortured heroines, persecuted heroes
and fearsome villains' seems a distinctly odd one to choose to *escape
into* — even if it does constitute 'only a lengthy prelude to inevitable
happiness'. James Smith somewhat similarly claims: 'poetic justice
permits the free indulgence of our fears'.[10] But neither critic seems
to me very convincing about *why* a (working-class) audience should
want this 'free indulgence' of its 'fears' in the first place. However,
if we remember, and relate melodrama to, those other forms of popular
entertainment in which considerations of 'poetic justice' or the 'triumph
of good' seem irrelevant but where the element of fear also seems

crucial, it may be suggested that it is the experience of fear itself which
is enjoyed rather than the long-suspended and last-minute 'catharsis'.

Various explanations of why a 'free indulgence in fears' might be
welcome are, of course, possible: both Aristotle and Freud come
to mind.[11] But if we place the experience of watching a melodrama
within the surrounding experience of its audience, if we consider
not just the internal trajectory of the plot itself (from initial, brief
security through long and elaborate perils to re-established security)
but also the over-arching 'before-and-after' of the whole performance
for its audience (their life before they come to the theatre and
after), it may be that a formulation from Strindberg (that sophisticated melodramatist) offers us a more interesting perspective. For
if melodrama presents a dream-world, for much of its time that
dream is a nightmare, and it is precisely as a nightmare that Strindberg describes his own *Dreamplay*: 'Sleep, the liberator, often appears
as a torturer, but when the pain is at its worst, the sufferer wakes —
and is thus reconciled with reality. For however agonising real life
may be, at this moment, compared with the tormenting dream, it
is a joy.' The escape, and fantasy, provided by melodrama may
essentially have been not so much an escape *into* its world as an
escape back from its world into the familiar world which, however
insecure, irrational and hostile it might actually be, was then experienced by comparison as not as horrific and risk-laden as it might
be.[12] Melodrama may have primarily presented for many of its
audience not a (morally) 'superior' world but a decidedly worse and
more physically frightening one in which to live. As the father,
returning from a debtors' prison in *Luke the Labourer* (1826), put
it: 'no man truly knows the blessings of his home but he who has been
shut out from it'. There is, indeed, a parallel here to the actual
experience of Samuel Bamford, almost the same year, who, having
led a contingent at Peterloo, been tried for treason and imprisoned,
finally returned home not to continued political agitation but to a
settled domesticity, to a withdrawal into a privatised 'security'.[13]
The attractions of the 'normal', the familiar, may well be enhanced
by a thrilling venture into adventure and that enhancement can have
a deeply disabling effect politically. One might claim that, after
coming out of a melodrama, it is the *normal* world which is made to
seem more attractive — and, indeed, the internal structure of some
melodramas rests not upon a final betterment of the initial situation
but simply on the peculiar satisfaction of a return, more or less, to

the *status quo ante*: it is the normal which becomes the normative ideal; that endorsement of 'normality' is at the root of conformism, of acquiescence, of ideology.

Expertise and intimacy

Winton Tolles has suggested a general formula for melodrama:[14]

Two human forces, A and B, are opposed to each other in a struggle to be decided by brains and chance . . . The action then leads the opposing forces through a series of artfully contrived crises, each more exciting and piquant than the last. Suspense is constantly present, and surprise occurs repeatedly as first A and then B gains the supremacy through the amazing influence of some apparently trivial factor. The most common device to throw the weight first on one side and then on the other is the shifting possession of some material object, preferably a letter. As the play develops the pace with which the commanding position changes accelerates, until in a whirlwind climax one force attains final victory.

This description could serve also as a formula for an exciting football match, and further elaborations of the parallel might be pursued: the black/white dichotomisation that governs the committed supporter's viewpoint, the low 'thrill-threshold' of the massed audience, the applicability of social-psychological interpretations in terms of escapism and release of emotions, etc.[15] But I want here to emphasise two other aspects of spectator enjoyment of football which seem to be present in other forms of popular culture. The first is that each man on the terraces is his own expert: he claims to *know* what the players, and referee, should do. Secondly, he often claims a curious kind of knowledge of the players as persons, almost an acquaintanceship or friendship: characteristically, players in your own team are referred to by their first names and treated with the affectionately insulting disrespect reserved for close friends (consider for example the advice freely given by the crowd just behind a throw-in). The same two features can be observed at a local boxing or wrestling stadium and increasingly, perhaps, at county cricket grounds. It was the 'expertise' of the spectators which attracted Brecht to the model of the boxing match. But both the expertise and the intimacy seem to be, to a large extent, forms of self-pretence or semi-fantasy. Yet they both seem, in various ways, constitutive of the pleasure of much popular entertainment. The stand-up comedian in a working men's club, for example, is treated by the audience precisely as a kind of old acquaintance and the success of his act often depends upon his establishing a knowing intimacy with that audience (thereby enabling him, often, to get laughs from the fears and insecurities he knows they know he knows about).[16] The same is true of the pantomime dame and perhaps was true of the melodrama villain. What is involved in all these cases is a complex interplay between the player and the role: the panto dame, or villain, makes no sense unless we simultaneously see through the character to the actor, and react 'exaggeratedly' to the personality of both character and performer — we are allowed to subvert the role *and* asked to make it live, in quite explicit ways (boos, hisses, 'Watch out behind you', etc.).[17] The mark of the professionally assured club comic is that he *might* be a mate cracking jokes at the bar — but, subtly, isn't. The attraction of a Tommy Lawton or (though less so?) a Kevin Keegan is that you might have been playing instead of him (or so you half-think) — after all, you know as much about football as the experts, don't you. I suspect, though it would be difficult to show, that these elements are far less present in (what I think of as) characteristically 'middle-class' sport and entertainment: the crowd at Wimbledon may cheer Virginia Wade but they don't swear affectionately at her like an old friend, and though we may marvel at or envy Olivier's skill few of us really think of him as Larry.

This peculiar blend of real and pretended knowledge, real and fantasised acquaintanceship, can, obviously, be seen in other areas. For example, the fascination with the life style of 'stars' and royalty feeds upon a desire for anecdote, and 'inside knowledge' about the people behind the image, coupled with some sense that their extraordinariness is only a variation of ordinariness (so that I could, given the luck, turn out to be Tom Jones, Prince Charles or Georgie Best).[18] And obviously in the case, of, say, a star of melodrama this 'knowledge' deeply shapes the response to the 'terror' of the villain, since the audience both 'knows' the actor behind the role and claims an expertise in the techniques of his art: the sense of 'fear' is accompanied by, though not fully replaced by, an awareness of the illusory nature of its source.[19] A perhaps related aspect of this complex of attitudes is the urge to pass comments on a performance while it is in progress: the 'aside' and the 'ad-lib' are as much a feature of the audience's contribution as of the performer's in a club or even music hall act, while the louder and more physical expressions of opinion (catcalls, whistles and flying fruit) may be merely an appropriate and natural extension, to a larger setting, of the *sotto voce* critical remark! Even *if* the audience kept silent during a favourite pantomime, as Thomas

Dibdin's Colombine claimed in 1814, I presume they didn't sit mute during the five-minute scene changes.[20]

What is perhaps being *displaced*, or compensated for, here is a relative lack of kinds of knowledge elsewhere. Since the people who actually control our society are not known personally to many of us, and since the systematic nature of that control is itself difficult to grasp,[21] it may become important to assert an expertise and quasi-acquaintanceship in areas which at least masquerade as important. If all we 'know' is what we actually know then most of us would have to acknowledge our almost complete ignorance and impotence as individuals in those areas of economic and political decision making that we uneasily know are 'beyond our ken' (to use that symptomatic phrase from a once popular radio programme), but which crucially affect us. Of course, the insecurity and impotence, the displacement of knowledge, that I've sketched have to be grasped as the *effects* of a whole system of control: ignorance of economics and politics, for example, is one *product* of an educational system which is institutionally *geared* to the 'failure' of most of its pupils (think, as a minor pointer, of the consternation of management if *every* shop steward had a degree in economics and business studies!). Royalty-adulation and strong personal feelings expressed about individual political leaders (Tony Benn or Maggie Thatcher) may be one way in which the economic and political system is rendered ideologically, i.e. 'safely', 'knowable' — as a music hall turn, derby match or melodrama.

Television

If we now ask what today is the most 'popular' form of cultural activity (in at least a crudely head-counting sense of 'popular'), the obvious answer has to be 'watching TV'. Television, as a medium, has of course incorporated and modified various older forms of popular entertainment: we can see the adaptations in *The Good Old Days*, *Match of the Day*, *The Comedians*, the Christmas fare of pantomime and Billy Smart's Circus, and we can add the TV screening of horror movies, Westerns, Ealing comedies, cartoons, Chaplin and Whitehall farces.[22] The significance of television can be explored in various ways — as, for example, the continual 'dramatisation' of society to itself or as the quintessential expression of the Society of the Spectacle.[23] What interests me here is how the experience of watching TV — with the family, in the normal domestic sitting-room — seems to combine and blend the elements of intimacy and expertise with something akin to escapism back into the *status quo*, an enhancement and endorsement of the 'normal'.

Variants on the elements of intimacy and expertise can be easily listed: the use of close-ups, the familiar faces of newscasters and actors, the sense of acquaintance with characters derived from regularly watching a long-running series, the personal interviews, the chat-shows, indeed the whole notion of a 'television personality' — all these tend to induce a reaction similar to that in the relation between the football supporter and a local player: the same kind of advisory or derisory comments, friendly insults, back-chat, directed at the screen personality but also aired to the rest of the watching family, a shared acquaintanceship. And this goes with a kind of confirmation of 'knowledge' in other, and overlapping, areas: the critical or scoffing remarks about the 'experts' on *Match of the Day*, the family's interpolated anecdotes about the chat-show guests, the anticipatory answers during *University Challenge*; much current affairs presentation depends upon an implicit insinuation that the viewer really knows a great deal more than he or she is likely to; some informative programmes seem to want to convey the impression to the viewer that their explanations of complex material are really directed at someone else, necessary only for some other viewer; some quiz shows seem designed to test the contestant while implying that the audience already know the answers (on radio particularly, the appeal to the studio audience not to help the contestants highlights this); the slow-motion replay of a catch or the use of telescopic lens during a Test Match cater to exactly this impression of viewer-expertise.[24] And of course the conversations about and derived from TV which occur between members of a watching family — and which seem an almost essential part of watching many kinds of programme — continue elsewhere, in the factory, at the shops, in the pub; television provides us all with both a common knowledge and an instant expertise. If once it might be claimed that there was no 'popular' museum or art gallery, philosophy or science, one might now suggest that television provides all these as well as a 'popular' (armchair) theatre.[25]

But the kind of 'knowledge' that television offers is often moulded in precisely the form of 'knowing' *personalities*: a programme about Schoenberg, Einstein or John Ford presents a pictorial biography and anecdotes from old acquaintances but scarcely discusses the structure of a twelve-tone composition, the mathematics of relativity

theory or the semiotics of film; a current affairs programme stages
a polemical contest between 'well-known' economists rather than
examining their economic theories; perhaps most obviously, political
issues are transformed into clashes between individual politicians.
What is offered in these forms of presentation is a peculiar form
of mystified demystification: history is seen as made by actual men
(and even, occasionally, women) but history (and art and science)
is thereby reduced to biography and anecdote. *I, Claudius* and
Panorama link hands.[26]

Perhaps the most consistently popular TV programme is the
News, where personalisation and anecdote dominate most clearly.
But the *News* also provides one of our contemporary equivalents of
the melodrama sensation-scene: clips of earthquakes, train disasters,
sinking ships, fires, explosions and shootings. And such 'actual'
scenes are in continuity with the flow of other forms of natural and
man-made violence presented to us fictionally. 'Violence on TV' has
been endlessly examined,[27] but one facet not much discussed is that
part of the acceptability or even attraction of 'violence' on TV may
lie in the way its reality evaporates at the flick of a switch: the streets
of Kojak's New York or the Sweeney's London, the creepy terrors
of Transylvanian castles, the napalmed villagers of Viet-Nam, all
enhance the reassuring, solid presence of the surrounding sitting-room
once the programme moves on or clicks off; our own reality is
intruded upon by another, frightening reality but one that *we* can
render invisible, absent, by switching over or off and making a cup
of tea; it's a very peculiar, and historically unprecedented, power to
enjoy. And while actually watching TV, the real home in which we
watch operates as a norm which is curiously suspended but still
present while another reality takes its place and takes place in it;
the living-room becomes a palpable 'off-screen space' which continually
reassures us against the lurking threats in the imaginary off-screen
space of the horror movie. As we watch the violence and horrors of
the world 'outside', brought 'inside' the home by the screen, the quiet
and safety of that home becomes simultaneously an almost impossible
ideal and an actual reality.[28] Television may provide an escapist
avenue into a beautiful and impossible fantasy-world at times, but
perhaps the main form of 'escapism' it offers is that repeated escape
back into our own, safely familiar and familial living-room: whatever
insecurities, fears or problems hover over our actual situation we
are less at risk than in the world that glows through the darkness
from the set in the corner.

It's possible to see why this structure of experience should be a
particularly seductive one for an audience largely composed of
people whose normal existence is constantly, if latently, under
threat: in that situation the 'normal' *is* an almost impossible ideal,
rather precariously maintained, while the dangers threatening it
(illness, unemployment, inexorable price rises) are both frighteningly
real and yet invisible, lurking in an apparently different world that
yet can intersect unexpectedly, inexplicably and disastrously with
the familiar domestic world of everyday experience. To survive without neurotic anxiety one has then either to believe that the reality
of those threats is an illusion which in the clear light of the next
tomorrow will somehow evaporate or is a nightmare we can switch
off when we wish — or one has to analyse, understand and defeat
the sources of those threats. But to remove working-class insecurity
in practice would mean collectively challenging and changing a
whole society, an entire version of 'normality'.

Problems of popular political drama

With some exceptions, and for some obvious reasons, television itself
has not been used to any great extent as a medium for (left-wing)
'political' drama. A great deal of politically motivated theatre this
century has sought rather to use other forms of popular entertainment or to reproduce a popular format and setting. Thus we have
seen agitational groups using melodramatic stereotyping for characters
or adapting a ceilidh evening; others have staged rituals, festivals and
pageants before 'mass' assemblies in sports stadiums; others have
taken the circus or music hall as their model. There are problems with
these tactics, however, since what is taken over and adapted may
be only the *surface* appeal of the models imitated. For example,
the circus model may be seen in terms of spectacle and skills (lots
of movement and colour, clowns and jugglers, Fellini-fashion), but
what possible political use could be made of the crucial high-risk
acts in terms of the vicarious fear involved? Or how could the actors
in a play performed before 50,000 people achieve an intimacy with
each spectator and how can the play itself become the affectionate
target of self-confident and participatory 'expertise' from the audience?
More basically, if at the heart of much popular entertainment is a
displacement of the experience of vulnerability and ignorance, and
if political art seeks to present and analyse the determinants of that
experience, how can this be achieved without destroying the very

286

displacement which underpins the popular form being imitated? There are, of course, various partial solutions to these difficulties, but they often raise other problems. An agit-prop drama may be used to precede political discussion or be designed as an intervention in a specific situation the audience is already involved in and knowledgeable about (a strike, an occupation, a campaign); or a political theatre group may be attached to and performing for a party whose members regard the group as, in some sense, their 'team'. But in these situations the effectiveness of the performance rests very much on a prior political rapport between performers and audience and thereby the dramatic activity itself can easily become a variant on the limited exercise of preaching to the already devout.

These are familiar points and have often been debated.[29] But given the massive popularity of television perhaps one crucial problem affecting all such tactics is the sense of cultural nostalgia that seems to permeate them: the utilisation of a largely *superseded* sub-text, model or medium. It is relatively easy to sketch a history of the communications media in terms of a repeated pattern of 'control lag': with each new technical development the previously crucial medium becomes increasingly accessible to dominated groups, while the dominant group retains control over the new medium; when writing itself was the technically most advanced medium, only the ruling elite was literate; with the development of print a monopoly over the printing process was maintained while basic literacy became common; only when radio and television became the dominant media could oppositional groups operate with a fair degree of freedom in print — there are political as well as economic reasons for the relative ease with which an 'underground' press can flourish in the electronic era.[30] There is perhaps a corresponding control lag in the cultural media; the battle for 'artistic freedom' — i.e. the struggle against censorship — seems to be regularly won only for modes of literary and artistic production which are already losing their social influence. It's not surprising that the major area of 'political aesthetics' is now film — a generation after the cinema ceased to be the dominant entertainment medium. The emergence of a breed of 'radical' dramatists may be precisely the sign that theatre is, in Truffaut's phrase, 'a fabulous anachronism'. The point can be made, very crudely, in terms of audience figures: after twelve years' work, one French 'popular theatre' group had been seen by about five million people; in the week I wrote this paper, 7.35 million watched the Monday

287

Coronation Street episode and none of the 'top twenty' ratings was below 5 million — and that was a summer week.[31]

   This sense of 'lag' can extend to debates about political art even when the medium in question is television itself. Most considerations of such obviously political TV dramatists as Trevor Griffiths, Jim Allen, Loach and Garnett, have tended to focus on the one rather faded issue of 'naturalism'; criticism has concentrated on the limits of naturalism as a relapse into a pre-Brechtian mode or, more sophisticatedly, as a confirmation of the ideological positioning of the viewing subject.[32] But the comparison is thereby drawn mainly with other forms of theatre-drama rather than with other aspects of television itself, and it is then sometimes too easily presumed that 'naturalism' is the distinguishing mode of television, rather than recognising that many popular programmes on TV have little to do with naturalism and yet constitute a kind of, or utilise elements of, 'drama': situation comedies, quiz shows, Morecambe and Wise send-ups of naturalist theatre, even *News at Ten* itself. And, as Walter Benjamin recognised forty years ago, the nature of a technical medium may enforce a different awareness of what counts as 'art' — of what counts on television, for example, as 'drama'. I suspect that the search for 'popular political drama' on television may itself be mainly a form of political as well as cultural nostalgia, and that political intervention in television has to operate not so much in terms of the 'drama' slots as in the field of 'Light Entertainment'; it could, after all, be argued that the radio programme which most memorably subverted the ideological complex of its period was *The Goon Show*, while, more recently, the Anti-Nazi League has had more success with 'Rock Against Racism' than with street-theatre. But if we are to try to think beyond the familiar debate about 'naturalism', to try, for example, to carry over into television some of the political insights developed in the theatre by Brecht, then we seem to need a model of 'drama' which offers something different from a story, an anecdote, a reduction of issues to personalities or stereotypes, or merely a clash of perspectives. I can only, very tentatively, instance one TV programme which perhaps met some of these difficulties in a new way. Since I know of few references to it, it is worth outlining and commenting on as an example of an alternative model.[33]

Your Move

In 1967 Granada Television presented a programme called *Your Move*.

It was basically a cross between a war game and an improvised play. A dozen members of a studio audience who had no professional connection with the educational system were assigned roles associated with the running of a school: Headmaster, Deputy Head, local NUT official, a teacher in Rank and File, PTA Chairman, Local Education Officer, School Governor, Conservative Councillor, etc. A situation was sketched by the programme's presenter: the Head is known to be against corporal punishment, but while he is away at a conference the Deputy Head severely canes some boys for trampling on flower beds; the Head returns and the boys' parents complain to him. The players then sat at a table and put earphones on. From then on there was no script and any player could make any 'move' they wished, subject to two limitations. First, the presenter controlled access to the microphones and earphones through which the moves were made, so a player had to request 'air-time', but it was up to the player making the move to decide who, among the other players, heard his move, though the studio audience and the viewers heard every move. Thus we could see what tactics and alliances were developing, how 'characters' were being elaborated or revealing themselves, what moves were backfiring or cutting across others, etc., though the players remained in various states of ignorance about the overall state of play. The game quickly became complex and exciting while remaining intelligible and open-ended. After about twenty minutes it was simply stopped and the studio audience was invited to comment on the various moves and the overall situation that had been reached — which by that stage included a parents' demonstration, a teachers' strike, an abortive arson attempt by some pupils, a deal concerning the promotion of the Deputy to be Head of a new comprehensive, engineered by the Tory councillor, etc. The second limitation on moves is worth noting at this point: throughout, an 'expert' from the educational world advised the presenter if any move contravened definite regulations and laws or went against 'normal practice'; at the end of the game this expert's interventions were also subjected to scrutiny and critique by the audience and players.

This forgotten programme seems to me to have combined many of the elements that have preoccupied practitioners of political drama since Brecht.[34] It made explicit the notion of role-playing within an institution but subverted those roles, estranged them by assigning them to 'amateurs'. The educational apparatus itself was represented not as a fixed abstraction but as interacting agencies,

289

shaped by particular individuals' decisions within the constraints of others' decisions. The agents in the process were revealed as both subjects and objects of that process. The audience found itself thinking both within and above the flow of the game. The issue involved was an ordinary 'minor' crisis but we could see how major issues and powerful interests intersected with and converged upon it, how almost every move was overdetermined. No pre-given solution to the problems was imposed externally, by either an author or a political leadership who 'already knew' the 'answers'. At the same time, the programme employed some of the features of 'popular' television: it allowed us access to a 'privileged' area of knowledge; it treated the ordinary person as competent and responsible in an unfamiliar field while allowing the rulings of the acknowledged expert to be queried; we could see 'ourselves' in the roles depicted and in the ordinary people playing them; it encouraged viewers at home to comment on both specific moves and general issues; we could participate vicariously in the risks of each move, with no script as safety-net or guarantee; it touched directly on something familiar but opened wider perspectives, clarified relations of power and control beyond our own experience of the educational system, as pupils or as parents of pupils; it brought us closer to the 'figures' who control events in an important sector without either offering stereo-typed caricatures or actual officials anxious to whitewash them-selves; while departing from 'naturalism' it remained representational, but what was represented was not a story or anecdote so much as a *structure* of *relations*. The programme thereby offered an exercise in *understanding* rather than simply involvement in a plot or per-sonalities; the 'real world' was suspended for a time but what re-placed it was a dramatic reality structurally homologous to a sector of that real world.

In various ways the format of *Your Move* could be used in con-nection with such *issues* as racism, discrimination against women, redundancy, abortion, unfair dismissal, a campaign for an adventure playground, a strike, eviction, an attempt to unseat an MP, a rent tribunal action, etc. etc. Viewed another way, the format lends itself to a specific dramatisation of crucial *sectors* of control and decision making; one could easily envisage an instructive version of *Your Move* for each of what Althusser terms the 'Ideological State Ap-paratuses'.[35] The basic format could also be adapted for use outside the television medium, as a form of 'live' drama, for example as prologue to a public meeting on some issue or as a form of rehearsal

290

for, say, a factory occupation. The effect of such a game/drama should be to show both participants and spectators how a political situation can develop and how it can be controlled, what tactics and alliances are perhaps viable, what the possible consequences of certain moves might be. One of the various major reasons for insecurity is ignorance and a sense of impotence, a timidity about trying to change a situation because one isn't, one thinks, equipped with the 'right' skills or knowledge to devise appropriate strategies and tactics against powerful forces felt to be waiting with preplanned counter-moves ready. By taking part in as well as watching 'dramatic games' we might learn not only to feel more confident of our capacities in an insecure world but also begin to acquire some of the capacities necessary to change that world: a real knowledge of the structures of control and exploitation within which we live and practice in working effectively both within and against those structures.

A television programme like *Your Move* might be regarded as having little to do with 'theatre', but if we are searching for a 'popular theatre' we might take one more cue from Brecht. In the epilogue to *The Good Person of Setzuan* he invited the audience: '*You* write the happy ending to the play!' Perhaps it's time the 'audience' wrote the rest of the play as well, time the 'readers' became 'authors' themselves, time the process of 'reception' controlled and modified the conditions of 'production'.

NOTES

1 Cf. Lucien Goldmann, *Le Dieu caché* (Paris, 1955), and Pierre Macherey, *Pour une théorie de la production littéraire* (Paris, 1966). Goldmann's work is influenced by that of Georgy Lukács, Macherey's is indebted to that of Louis Althusser. For a useful introductory survey of Marxist literary criticism, see Terry Eagleton, *Marxism and Literary Criticism* (London, 1976).

2 For a representative example of this approach, see Wolfgang Iser, *The Implied Reader* (London, 1976). Iser is the main figure in the 'Constance school' of 'reception theory'.

3 Work along these lines might be developed by elaborating the notion of 'popular-democratic interpellations' advanced by Ernesto Laclau in his *Politics and Ideology in Marxist Theory* (London, 1977), esp. pp. 100—11 and 196—8. A paper given at the Kent conference, 'Punch and Judy to Andy Pandy' by Malcolm Knight, offered a similar analysis with reference to the theories of the Marxist aesthetician Sanchez Vazquez and the theatre of Dario Fo. I am grateful to Malcolm Knight for his critical comments on an earlier version of my paper.

4 Cf. the papers by James, Howarth and McCormick in Part One of this volume.

5 Sartre's analyses of different kinds of collectivities, groups and series in his *Critique de la raison dialectique* (Paris, 1960) might provide a useful starting-point for understanding the nature of an 'audience'.

6 See the points raised concerning the internal relations of production in theatre-work itself, in 'After *Fanshen*: a discussion', this volume.

7 Obviously, 'insecurity' can be a feature of anyone's experience, but my argument presumes that vulnerability to economic vagaries is more character-istic of some social groups than of others and that it is the more insecure groups who make up the characteristic audience for 'popular' art. Cf., however, Douglas Reid's analysis of audiences in his paper in this volume.

8 For aspects of the argument in this paragraph, see, for example, *Power in Britain*, ed. J. Urry and J. Wakeford (London, 1973); *Elites and Power in British Society*, ed. P. Stanworth and A. Giddens (London, 1974); M. Benyon, *Working for Ford* (London, 1973), especially ch. 7; K. Coates and R. Silburn, *Poverty: the Forgotten Englishman* (London, 1970); F. Wilson, *Dockers* (London, 1972); T. Lane and K. Roberts, *Strike at Pilkington's* (London, 1971). One aspect of working-class insecurity in nineteenth-century London has been explored in the analysis of 'casual labour' in G. Stedman Jones, *Outcast London* (London, 1971). For an exceptional example of local control *by* nineteenth-century working-class radicals, see the analysis of the Oldham situation in J. Foster, *Class Struggle and the Industrial Revolution* (London, 1974). One might also bear in mind some lines from two plays: 'A man stands up to his neck in water, so that even a ripple is enough to drown him' (David Hare, *Fanshen*), and 'At one point it looked as if they were going to go back to work and suffer defeat at the hands of the American imperialists, so their Sandra could have a white wedding' (John McGrath, *Fish in the Sea*).

9 Cf. e.g. R. Dyer, *Light Entertainment*, BFI Television Monograph 2 (London, 1973), especially quotations on pp. 10–11, and ch. 3, 'The Aesthetics of Escape'. It is possible, incidentally, that certain forms of emotional reaction only seem 'exaggerated' to those whose very survival is *not* threatened by 'minor' events; consider, for example, the eruptions of violence in *Luke the Labourer*, Act I, Scene 2, in James Joyce's 'Counterparts' in *Dubliners*, and in Walter Brierley's *The Means Test Man*. Melodramatic styles of acting may even have been as close in some respects to working-class quotidian experience as, say, German expressionist film-acting was to the panic reactions visible in clips of the 1920s Stock Exchange crash: post-war hyperinflation had deeply affected the security of the German middle classes and one rather wonders just how 'exaggerated' those staring eyes seemed to someone actually facing imminent bankruptcy.

10 Quotations are taken from M. R. Booth, *English Melodrama* (London, 1965), p. 14 and J. L. Smith, *Melodrama* (London, 1973), p. 35. Cf. also F. Rahill, *The World of Melodrama* (Pennsylvania, 1967). One might query other aspects of Booth's claims: I'm not sure that 'life', plots and situations in many melodramas are best described as 'uncomplicated, easy to understand' and 'perfectly simple', and it's worth noting that Smith devotes a chapter to the 'melodrama of *defeat*'.

11 Particularly Freud, though De Sade or Sacher-Masoch might be felt to be

more appropriate. Freud's grandson playing his game of *Fort/Da* can serve as one analogue: the eighteenth-month-old boy negotiated the intermittent absences of his mother by displacing her disappearance onto those of his toy, throwing it away in order to have it returned; he thus played with his fear, turned his real insecurity into a reassuring game, a simulation and experiment. It may be that one function, and satisfaction, of much popular entertainment is to provide not so much an outlet for 'primitive' or 'exaggerated' emotions but rather a displacement, a way of coming to terms with actual fears by deliberately experiencing the emotions appropriate to vulnerability but in a controlled situation where a reassuring outcome is guaranteed. Obviously, the question of the relation between 'popular' and 'children's' forms of entertainment could be explored along these lines. Cf. S. Freud, *Beyond the Pleasure Principle*, Standard Edition, vol. 18, pp. 14f; cf. also the discussion of 'the drama of reassurance' in J. S. R. Goodlad, *A Sociology of Popular Drama* (London, 1971).

12 The same pattern is, interestingly, discernible in that other Victorian dream/ nightmare, *Alice in Wonderland*; cf. e.g. Terry Eagleton, 'Alice and Anarchy', *New Blackfriars* (Oct. 1972).

13 See my analysis of Bamford's *Passages in the Life of a Radical* in 'Autobiography and Class Consciousness', unpublished PhD thesis, Cambridge 1974. Cf. too the middle-class response to the problem of casual labour, in terms of an emphasis on the 'housing question', in Jones, *Outcast London*, pt 2.

14 Quoted in J. O. Bailey, *British Plays of the Nineteenth Century* (London, 1966), p. 33.

15 For some interesting comments on football, cf. C. Critcher, 'Football and Cultural Value', *Working Papers in Cultural Studies*, 1 (Spring 1971). My term 'thrill-threshold' is adapted from Basil Bernstein's notion of differential 'guilt-thresholds' as between working and middle classes, cf. B. Bernstein, *Class, Codes and Control*, vol. 1 (London, 1971). Bernstein's work suggests an interesting approach to differences between 'popular' and 'middle-class' drama, in terms of both plot construction and character depiction, which cannot be elaborated here.

16 See the problems explored in John Osborne's *The Entertainer* and in Trevor Griffiths's *Comedians*. Cf. also the instructions to the actors in McGrath's *Fish in the Sea* and the note 'On the Play' in 7:84's *The Cheviot, the Stag and the Black Black Oil*. Brecht's 'alienation' acting devices are to some extent in continuity with this strand in popular styles.

17 Cf. e.g. M. Booth (ed.), *English Plays of the Nineteenth Century*, vol. 5 (London, 1976), p. 14.

18 Cf. e.g. R. Dyer, 'The Meaning of Tom Jones', *Working Papers in Cultural Studies*, 1 (Spring 1971).

19 Cf. e.g. Dickens on 'the theatrical young gentleman's' expertise concerning melodramatic acting conventions, quoted in Booth, *English Melodrama*, p. 198.

20 Cf. Booth, *English Plays*, vol. 5, p. 1, and *English Melodrama*, pp. 170–1.

21 Cf. e.g. the analysis of 'The Controllers of British Industry' by M. Barratt-Brown in *Can the Workers Run Industry?*, ed. K. Coates (London 1968),

and the list of Scottish landowners given by J. McEwen, 'Highland Land-lordism', in *The Red Paper on Scotland*, ed. Gordon Brown (Edinburgh, 1975).

22 Cf. e.g. *Football on Television*, ed. E. Buscombe, BFI Television Monograph 4 (London, 1975), and L. Masterman, 'Football on Television: Studying the Cup Final', *Screen Education*, 19 (Summer 1976). Dyer, in *Light Enter-tainment*, pp. 15—16, notes how different TV producers highlight or efface the element of dangerous risk in their handling of circus acts. On Ealing comedies cf. C. Barr, 'Projecting Britain and the British Character', *Screen* 15:1 (Spring 1974) and 15:2 (Summer 1974), and J. Ellis, 'Made in Ealing', *Screen* 16:1 (Spring 1975).

23 Cf. e.g. Raymond Williams, *Television: Technology and Cultural Form* (London, 1974) and *Drama in a Dramatised Society* (Cambridge, 1975); Guy Debord, *La Société du spectacle* (Paris, 1967).

24 One of the few useful analyses in this area is J. Tulloch, 'Gradgrind's Heirs: The Quiz and the Presentation of "Knowledge" by British Television', *Screen Education*, 19 (Summer 1976).

25 Cf. Jean Vilar, 'Memorandum' (1960), translated in *Theatre Quarterly*, 23 (Autumn 1976), esp. p. 54.

26 Cf. e.g. Stuart Hall, I. Connell and L. Curti, 'The "Unity" of Current Affairs Television', *Working Papers in Cultural Studies*, 9 (Spring 1976). This analysis has been criticised for, in effect, endorsing personalisation; cf. R. Coward, 'Class, "Culture" and Social Formation', *Screen*, 18:1 (Spring 1977); but when the controlling agents in an economic—political conflict are *not* generally known to the public a 'personalised' account can sometimes be revealing; cf. e.g. the analysis of GEC—AEI—EE in R. Jones and O. Marriott, *Anatomy of a Merger* (London, 1970).

27 A. Glucksmann, *Violence on the Screen*, BFI Education Department (London, 1971), summarises much of the debate. For a number of different perspectives, see the special issue of *Screen Education*, 20 (Autumn 1976), devoted to *The Sweeney*.

28 To some extent, these two planes of reality can be seen operating *within*, say, a horror movie, where the hero and heroine are nice and ordinary (i.e. acted more or less naturalistically) whereas the villains are melodramatic caricatures. The 1966 Hammer horror movie *Plague of the Zombies* includes an interesting use of a nightmare which arouses and then defeats expectations of a sequence being only a bad dream.

29 *Theatre Quarterly*, 24 (Winter 1976), includes a useful discussion among various practitioners of many of these issues. One might extend the discussion of the use of nostalgic and media-based sub-texts by considering, say, *Sgt Pepper's Lonely Hearts' Club Band*, the albums of Pete Atkins and Clive James, or the work of the Liverpool Poets. For somewhat related problems in another medium, cf. E. and J. Cockcroft and J. Weber, *Towards a People's Art: the Contemporary Mural Movement* (New York, 1977). It would be interesting to know if the National Front have any budding 'popular' dramatists.

30 Cf. Robin Murray and Tom Wengraf, 'The Political Economy of Communi-cations', *The Spokesman*, 5 (Summer 1970), and G. Murdock and P. Golding,

'For a Political Economy of Mass Communications', in *The Socialist Register 1973* (London, 1974), pp. 205–35.

31 Cf. the chronology in *Theatre Quarterly* 23 (Autumn 1976), p. 60, concerning Vilar's Théâtre National Populaire from 1951 to 1963, and *Financial Times*, 9 July 1977, p. 2. For various attempts at 'popular theatre' in France, see E. Copferman, *Le Théâtre populaire pourquoi?* (Paris, 1968), and P. Madral, *Le Théâtre hors les murs* (Paris, 1969).

32 Cf. the debate in *Screen*: C. MacCabe, 'Realism and the Cinema', 15:2 (Summer 1974), C. McArthur, 'Days of Hope', 16:4 (Winter 1975/6), C. MacCabe, 'Days of Hope: a Response', 17:1 (Spring 1976), C. MacCabe, 'Principles of Realism and Pleasure', 17:3 (Autumn 1976), R. Williams, 'A Lecture on Realism', 18:1 (Spring 1977). For other approaches, cf. Janet Wolff *et al.*, 'Problems of Radical Drama: the Plays and Productions of Trevor Griffiths', in *Literature, Society and the Sociology of Literature*, proceedings of a conference held at the University of Essex, July 1976 (University of Essex, 1977).

33 I once sketched an analysis of this programme in *Radical Arts*, ed. Bruce Birchall (London, 1968) — a publication which also includes some guerilla theatre scripts of that vintage.

34 Cf. especially 'The Literalization of the Theatre', Brecht's notes to *The Threepenny Opera*, included in *Brecht on Theatre*, ed. J. Willett (London, 1973).

35 Cf. 'Ideology and the Ideological State Apparatuses', in L. Althusser, *Lenin and Philosophy* (London, 1971).

After *Fanshen*: a discussion

David Hare, playwright: I'll try to fill you in as briefly as I can on
the history of the play, how it came to be written and what's happened
to it since it was written. *Fanshen* is a book of about five or six
hundred pages by William Hinton, who was himself in China at the
time of the story he describes. He spent some six or eight years
writing what he wanted to be the definitive record of one village's
life during those years of change. In summer 1974 Bill Gaskill and
Max Stafford-Clark asked me to read it and to dramatise it for Joint
Stock. Joint Stock had been started by them, from a much more
aesthetic point of view than has since developed. That is to say,
their original interests were in using theatrical spaces differently and
in developing the work of certain actors in workshop. The first
show that they did was *The Speakers*, which was a recreation of
Speakers' Corner. But the material of the book *Fanshen* pushed us
all off in a direction which we didn't really know we were heading
in. It's very important to stress this because, particularly in the
hindsight of success, which always makes things seem very clear-
cut, it's always assumed that you know exactly what you were doing
in creating a play. But like most plays *Fanshen* was created out of
chaos and out of a very unclear sense of what our objectives were;
and all the things that now seem apparent and definitive to us in
Fanshen were achieved through struggle and through deep confusion and disagreement. If the play had been a failure at its first
appearance that would be much more apparent, but success con-
cretes things over in a way that makes it almost impossible to retrieve
them.

We originally did five weeks' workshop on the six hundred pages,
trying all sorts of different approaches to this apparently intractable
material. Just in sheer stage-time the book was enormous, but also
the problems of presentation seemed to us insuperable. So we tried
various kinds of slogan theatre, various ways of telescoping the

297

material, various arts of story-telling, various exercises to do with
how to tell the essence of a story in the shortest possible time. And
the actors also addressed themselves to the problem of how to play
Chinese peasants; that's a whole sub-heading which I'm not really
qualified to speak on — but which the actors have a lot to say about.
But in the course of those five weeks we didn't settle on a way in
which we were going to reduce the material. The way the play emerged
was finally fixed first of all by the two directors and me deciding a
scenario and then by me deciding which of the many plays inside
Hinton's book I was going to write. And the play *Fanshen* is very
different from the book *Fanshen*; both its aims and the play's
selection from the book, its route through the book, make it a very
different kind of project. It was a personal response to certain themes
inside the book, notably the questions how does any democracy
know it's a good democracy, how do the led look after the leadership,
how do the ruled rule the rulers? It was out of a personal interest
in these questions that the play was written.

The material in the book that is apparently dramatic I found to
be the least dramatic of all; that's to say, all the stuff to do with the
violence of the early years of the revolution — the first 150 pages
of the book, the hangings, shootings, scalps coming away from
skulls, trials, uprisings — are, oddly, the undramatic material. There's
a comment of Len Deighton's which interests me very much; he says
'I have no interest in going to a debate — unless I know that the loser
of that debate is going to get shot at the end. *That* is dramatic.' I
feel the exact opposite. I have no interest in who's going to be shot at
the end. I feel that the debate itself is what is interesting. For me,
therefore, there is a lucky coincidence between the nature of the
Chinese Revolution and the nature of what works in the theatre.
Just as some revolutionaries are photogenic, so some revolutions
adapt themselves to theatre better than others, and this one adapts
itself well to theatre because of the struggle between theory and
practice which you can exactly parallel in a play. Because people
sit down in small rooms to discuss the course that the revolution
should take, it is possible to represent it in the theatre. An example
of the opposite which springs to mind is Robert Bolt's play *State of
Revolution*, where, faced with very similar problems to those we
faced in *Fanshen*, he comes up with an exactly opposite and, to my
mind, disastrous series of options. He cannot find a theatrical equivalent
to represent external reality; that's to say, a lot of guys sit around,
called Lenin and Trotsky etc., and their scenes together have a

theatrical life, but they refer all the time to something called historical reality which can only be represented by six National Theatre extras running fast across the stage! So the game is rigged against Bolt before he has begun; he can't win because he can't find a theatrical equivalent for the forces of that history, he can't find metaphors, impressive ways of staging that — because, finally, extras are extras and nothing you can do will make them seem as impressive as four men sitting together. So he presented an inevitably bourgeois view of history; it must be bourgeois because the impersonation of Lenin is bound to be more interesting than the mass movements of extras. Whereas what is fortunate about the Chinese Revolution is that you can take a microcosm: the problems that each village faced were typical, and although the objection that the Chinese leadership had to Hinton's book and which the Chinese Embassy had to our play was that Long Bow was a particularly unhappy village, yet the problems it met were the typical problems of a village during that revolution. And so, because the whole essence and spirit of the Chinese Revolution can be represented by no more than nine actors, you start with a chance of succeeding; you start with chamber politics, and that is really the form that the play takes, the form we chose to tell the story.

Once the text was written it stood more or less. We changed a few sections — those that always gave difficulty were the scenes of village life where it was necessary to return to some kind of reality in the lives of the peasants, which we found much more difficult than the scenes of argument and debate, which fell out almost at once, almost played themselves. The scenes where we Westerners represent the daily life of the village we found much more difficult. Once the play opened and William Hinton — who assumed that the play would fail, as previous attempts to dramatise the book had — heard that it was doing well, he arrived on a plane from America with a whole series of emendations. The play was therefore rethought over and over again between him and the Company and between him and me. The finally agreed text is a compromise between him and us simply because the view he takes of the Chinese Revolution and of events in that village is inevitably a slightly rosier one than that which I and the Company took. That's to say, we tried to present the problems of the village as typical; we tried to represent tendencies within the revolution and said that these classical tendencies of populism or commandism, of the people being allowed to indulge their worst feelings too much and its opposite — too tight a party structure commanding the people to behave as the party wishes — are classical

Members of the Joint Stock Theatre Company in a scene from *Fanshen*, by David Hare.

poles that you would find within any revolution, and we did not really judge the question in the village of Long Bow; were *these* people duped by the Party or was the Party genuinely responsive to their needs? We tried to present that question dispassionately and we did not come down on one side or another. We simply said that there will inevitably be this tension all the time, that if people take control over their own lives they will nevertheless always feel that those people who are giving them control are in some way conning them. But that will always be a shifting feeling *within* the revolution and that is what we tried to represent through the ebb and flow of the play. Whereas Hinton was always extremely uneasy about that, because he is a Marxist and we were not and because his own personal experience of these people inevitably pushed him towards a more committed view.

The last thing I would like to say is that what united us on the material, what kept us going through what, as I say, was an extremely confused period, was the feeling that we were at least showing a group of people whose lives had been incontrovertibly improved in every way: we never for a moment considered anything but the possibility that physically, materially, politically, spiritually, these

300

people's lives got better and better and better through that period.
To those of us who had worked in the West, as we had, as actors and
writers and directors, it was therefore an extremely refreshing
project to be able to work on.

Audience: Would any member of the company like to talk about your
own work as actors on the project — for example, learning how to
play a Chinese peasant?

Paul Freeman, actor: Well, we took it as axiomatic from the start
that we wouldn't employ make-up or screw our eyes up, because
that would be just absurd and patronising. It then became apparent
that what we had to do was somehow relate our lives to the lives
of the Chinese peasants. For me the breakthrough came when we
recognised that the way these people are reacting, to a large extent,
in the early section of the book is to seem to be very passive peasants,
yet they showed that they were able to become extremely violent
and emotional in a way that's quite alien to us. So we felt that we
had got to be able to be quite passive one moment and explode the
next moment; we had to feel that the emotion, the suppression that's
been bottled up for years, has now got the potential of being released
— and that's something we don't experience in our lives very much.
That seemed to be a sort of key; that you didn't have to go through
grades of emotion, didn't have to pass through subtleties in order to
arrive at violence, you could reach it in one step. We had to tap *that*,
but it's not something English actors are attuned to and we worked
on that for some time. We worked also on just being violent, on just
hitting each other, pretending we were hitting each other, which
was a sort of release and aided that. The other thing we worked on
was somehow maintaining all those positive qualities of the peasant
that we wanted to show. OK, there are great descriptions in the book
about how the Chinese peasants continually smoke, much more than
we do in the West, and spit all the time and clear their noses with
their hands and that sort of thing; and there was a section in the
rehearsals when we went through this, and the floor was filthy!
That too, it became apparent, was an irrelevancy, as the squint eyes
indeed were. What was important was just these people's attitudes to
their work, to their daily life, and somehow you had to tune into
that. So that was what we concentrated on, how do they sit, how
do they hoe? That's all.

Audience: David Hare talked about Joint Stock's original orientation
being an aesthetic one and a change in the company as a result of
Fanshen. Can you tell us more about that change?

301

Will Knightley, actor: As a result of *Fanshen* we turned into a collective. The company had previously been run by a board, made up
of David, Max, Bill, with various others and a couple of actors'
representatives. We then decided to turn it into a collective, and that
side of things actually worked and does work very well — we have
endless meetings! Just being an actor living and working with Joint
Stock is one of the best preparations you could have for a kind of
chamber political theatre like this. Politically, the group tends towards
the left, but we have no united political opinion or standpoint, which
may or may not be a weakness.
Audience: As the writer of the book, William Hinton, is a Marxist
and David Hare isn't and most members of the company aren't, how
did this work out? Did you find, throughout the course of the production, that your political consciousness was changing by being
involved in trying to reproduce something that had been written from
a different political point of view, or did the process work somewhat
the other way? Were you really able to get into the mentality of
people who were seen in the original book through a Marxist perspective, or were you imposing your own non-Marxist interpretation
on what was happening? Was it a two-way process or what?
David Hare, playwright: The Marxists leave. It may be in the nature
of Marxists that they leave, but they do leave the production, or they
leave the play. There are always ructions, and there is always a
faction that leaves. That's what I was trying to say about struggle.
It's all very well for us to look fresh-faced and beaming about it now,
but it really was miserable; the arguments really were often attritional.
That's why I now said, retrospectively, that all we're trying to do
is present certain classical problems, dispassionately. But in the case
of the text itself, it was argued and argued with Hinton, point by
point: he would ask for an upward inflection at the end of many
lines, for the tail of a lot of scenes to be flicked up. And there are
various classical objections to the play which you can't argue line
by line; for instance, the Chinese Embassy objected that whereas
the violence of the revolution is shown, the violence of the landlords
isn't, and all you can say is that it's referred to, that from the passion
of the peasants you can tell that they've suffered a great deal even
though there are no actual incidents of landlord violence. The other
bone of contention was the role of Little Li; in my play he's the
man who objects, who says 'this is not just', and he keeps getting
told that justice in a Marxist state is very different from his old-
fashioned ideas of justice. His part got consistently down-rated

302

through the period of attrition to the point where he was pushed to
the side of the play.
Audience: What then would you consider to be the ideological
position from which you approach these classical problems?
David Rintoul, actor: There isn't one. That's the continuing problem
of the company; that's why the ructions continue to take place.
Because there isn't an ideological base-line, you really have to fight
through each point as it comes. *Fanshen* can't be overestimated as
the watershed it was for the company; an enormous amount has
been drawn from it, but at the same time the situation the play is
dealing with is the overthrow of feudalism, and we're dealing with
very different problems in Britain today. Joint Stock is one of the
companies that tries to represent those problems, but that struggle
is a very hard one.
Max Stafford-Clark, director: That's what I would say too. We are
constantly struggling among ourselves as to what it is we want to
say and what standpoint we start from. For me at any rate the work
we've done over the last few years has been very educative — I knew
nothing about China at all before we started work on *Fanshen!*
In that sense you learn and acquire a viewpoint through working. But
we are unlike 7:84 or other companies whose aim is to propagate a
particular point of view and who come together in order to say something specific, and the play is written and the actors chosen presumably with that point of view in mind — that's not how we've
worked, at any rate in the past.
David Hare, playwright: The real nightmare of writing a play is when
you are getting towards the end of the second act and you will be
expected to say something definitive in the last twenty minutes. It's
a killer and it is the death of more playwrights than you can name.
When we came to this material, there was no way you could give
a definitive answer to that classical question of whether in fact
those peasants had been the victims of a series of directives of the
most cynical kind of *realpolitik* or whether they had themselves had
a great deal of influence over those changes of policy. That was
unknowable; there is no possibility, ten thousand miles away, of my
answering that question. I can't answer it. Hinton can't answer it.
He went back ten or fifteen years later and found the situation was
completely different from what he had understood it to be. For
instance, one part of the play is concerned with the problem of Chang
Ch'uer being attacked by a man with a white scarf; he later found
out that that Chang Ch'uer 'attacked' himself in order to get off sick.

That's the truth of that particular incident. So there's no way that
this material is ever going to be resolved in the sense that conventional
dramatic material can be resolved. You can resolve plays about 'will
he marry her, won't he', or plays about invented things, but you can't
resolve plays about this kind of subject: you can only offer them as
a slab and say to the audience 'is your tendency to believe this or
to believe that?' That's why that play is rigged on a kind of carrot
system; I've deliberately slipped in clues so that if the audience is
reacting genuinely to a scene, like today's scene maybe, when that
scene is finished then you should think 'these people are being a bit
hard on that comrade' — so that later when they're corrected by the
regional sub-leader who says that they did go too far, the audience
should think 'yes, I thought that at the time'. What I'm trying to get
all the time is the audience's own personal response to witnessing
this particular event.

Audience: Can I go back to something David Hare said about *State
of Revolution*? I agree with you about the weaknesses of that play,
but why would it be impossible to write a study of the Russian
revolution from the point of view of a Russian village? — except that
we haven't got the information. Do you think there was something
inherently different in the two situations?

David Hare, playwright: I don't know the answer to that. But why is
it that China is so attractive to intellectuals, why are there crazed
Sinologists all over this country? It appeals to them because it's a
country in which theory is taken seriously, theory is written down on
paper and related to practice; they believe in the ideal of what you
write down, a system of thought and theory you put down on paper,
take to the people, see if it works in practice, return to rewrite it,
take it back modified, and so on — that's what's so attractive to them
and also what holds things in a microcosm that a writer, in the
theatre, can easily deal with. As to how to write about the Russian
revolution, I don't know; but there aren't many successful examples.

Audience: Can I try to pull together a couple of threads? You've
talked about ideological confusion, and David Hare has said that you
can't resolve the issues in the play. But you could resolve them in a
naturalistic-realistic form. You've chosen a non-naturalistic form, a
style of theatre without consistency of character, with switches of
role and switches in style; you're choosing a type of theatre which
leads you to a position where you have to consider the overview —
which you can ignore if you're only concerned with characters in

a situation. In other words, you've chosen a style of theatre which is leading you to make a comment on society, which must in the end lead you to work out your ideological confusion.

Max Stafford-Clark, director: I think that on the whole we're a rather colourless company, in the sense that we take on the colour of the material and of the writer we're working with. It's not difficult, for example, to direct by a dialectical method if you're directing *Fanshen*; it's much more difficult to use the same method if you're directing *Epsom Downs*, Howard Brenton's play about Derby Day, which is our most recent production. In the work we've done over the last four years we've changed enormously, because the subjects we've chosen and the writers we've worked with have been different and varied. A company like Peter Brook's or the Pip Simmons Group take on a very particular identity because of the person who's running it; as an actor, you step into that company, or into 7:84, because you want to do that particular kind of work. But we've set up projects like *Yesterday's News* which started off as a show about racial minorities in Camden Town and ended up as a show about the massacre of Angolan mercenaries; the actors who went into that thought they were doing a show about immigrants — it was only once rehearsal had been started and writers had been brought in that we actually changed direction. What I'm saying is that as a group we try, perhaps perversely, to prevent ourselves from falling into a particular slot.

Audience: But you are still making shows which make comments upon society, or political issues or social issues. That is what, as a member of your audience, attracts me to the company, as well as your expertise. You must in the end accept that there will be a judgement on your ideological position from the audience. I wondered why you picked your particular style of acting, your approach to theatre.

David Hare, playwright: I don't think we have an 'acting style'. Our 'approach' comes from wanting to do shows which involve a great deal of documentary and research material; that's what has held the company together. It's my own opinion that the work has been deteriorating because that principle has been harder to hold on to; or rather because when we worked in *Fanshen* we could use definitive political principles and we can't use them any longer on English material which eludes the simplicity of some of the criteria we evolved for the other project. It's the documentary material,

the size and scale of public subjects that demands that the actors
change roles, because such subjects can't be contained within two
hours' passage in the lives of individuals.

Audience: Does the company have a shared notion of what kind of
audience they want, what type of audience they presuppose for their
work?

Max Stafford-Clark, director: We don't set out to attract a particular
audience; we don't start the work from a particular political viewpoint — so we haven't in the past consciously set out, for example,
to play non-theatrical spaces, to tour working men's clubs, say; so
that the audiences we've got are really determined by the places
we play in. We've toured in university theatres like the Gulbenkian
on this campus, or places like the Traverse in Edinburgh, the Third
Eye Centre in Glasgow, the Sherman in Cardiff — so we've played in
theatres, and in that sense we've chosen to play before pre-existing
theatrical audiences. Maybe that is a weakness; maybe you do need
consciously to set out to attract a particular kind of audience, to
decide that we are going to do a show that will be able to tour pubs,
that will be resilient enough to play there; but we haven't in the past
taken that as a starting point.

Audience: So far in the conference no one has risked a definition of
'popular' except in a quantitative sense; perhaps today we might have
a qualitative expression of what it could be. I wonder if Trevor
Griffiths, particularly, would like to comment on the combination
of quantitative and qualitative elements in popular culture, as regards
television and theatre?

Trevor Griffiths, playwright: I think my own position is that a popular
culture today will clearly have to take account of the quantitative aspect.
If you're working today, there are technologies available to reach
large numbers of people. It's for that reason that I spend two-thirds
or three-quarters of my writing time doing work for TV and/or film.
I can't really think of a reason for writing a play for theatre unless it
is to write for the kind of people sitting at this table, and the kinds
of situation they play in — though I do wish they would play rather
more in non-institutional spaces, or spaces in different kinds of institution. I don't necessarily mean working men's clubs; I'm thinking
of a popular play — and I think *Fanshen* could be that — playing in
secondary schools instead of much of the 'theatre in education' work
that I see all the time, which is honest, earnest and committed, but
not on the whole particularly relevant to the lives of the kids in schools.

I think *Fanshen* could be felt to be relevant by the kids themselves, which is the test of a popular work.

Audience: David Hare was talking earlier about the problems of finding a dramatic metaphor for objective reality, for the historical process. I was wondering if television as a form offered any special advantages for depicting social reality, or does it just have the advantage of sheer numbers?

David Hare, playwright: My position is the direct opposite of Trevor's on this point. I think the qualitative sacrifices involved in the making of a videotape are intolerable for any artist. That's to say, I don't like videotape, I think it's an ugly and very limited medium. I don't like television drama, I don't like the look of it, the way it's produced; I don't like the censorship within the medium; I don't like the absurd circumstances under which the work has to be produced – the eight weeks of production time that we enjoy are unimaginable in television. I like film, but it's a fact that the BBC is running down the amount of film it shows on television, and so the qualitative sacrifice involved in putting things on television is too great in my opinion. In the case of *Fanshen*, a work we had spent months preparing was put on television in ten days: the whole process lasted barely ten days. That's just a joke: you can't do serious work in those conditions. In my view, it's a triumph when you see a television play that is half-way good; it's a triumph of determination and often of egoism.

Trevor Griffiths, playwright: This is the extent to which David Hare has retained his aesthetic impulse! – and I think that's good. I agree with a lot of what he said. I'd just reply with Brecht's dictum: 'if you're going to work in a sewer, you can't refuse to handle shit'. It is grotesquely difficult to do good work on television, because the serial drags down the series and the series drags down the single play – and those categories are so false anyway. I think we did *some* good work in *Bill Brand*, and we did that in an eleven-day turn-around – which means that you read it on a Saturday morning and you go into the studio a week the following Thursday, and in two days somewhere in there you have to go and film your exterior scenes – and of course it's obscene to work that way. There's also a double-bind: if you manage to do it in eleven days, then it's scheduled for nine days the next time, and that's nine days for everybody, even the people who need three or five or eight weeks. I would love to have eight weeks in television, but I don't think we're going to get it by avoiding television, if we make no penetration at all. I do believe,

with Marx, that you've got to attack whatever it is you are attacking —
and in my case it's capitalist society, capitalist formations — at their
strongest point and not at their weakest. The theatre is anybody's;
all you've got to do is write the play, and it will get put on somewhere and it might be very successful — God knows, there's enough
rubbish around in the theatre. But television! Try to work in television and tell them what you really want to say, and you're in
trouble: they'll put you in outer Siberia — BBC2 at 10.30.

Audience: Can I ask Trevor Griffiths to elaborate a bit on one
aspect of that? Am I right in understanding that for a number of the
TV plays you've been able to retain the same more or less collective
group operating between you and the television production company,
the same producer, the same director and to some extent the same
team of actors? How did you achieve this, what were the difficulties,
and how did you manage to 'sell' that as a package to the TV company?

Trevor Griffiths, playwright: Any full answer to that would have to
be very complex and layered. I have been able to develop working
relationships with a number of people who are key to my work and
to the presentation of my work, one or two directors and several
actors. The best provisional strategy I've come up with is finding an
independent producer who will commission the whole lot, and give
me, as it were, executive producer control over casting and directors
and designers, and sell it to a company who will then find it very
difficult to intervene in the 'ongoing artistic process'. That's what
happened with *Bill Brand* and insofar as that's succeeded in achieving
anything, it was because of that.

Audience: Was that ruse successful because you were 'Trevor Griffiths',
or could anyone get away with it — perhaps offering it to the TV
company as a way of saving labour-time for them; a company might
welcome such a development for other reasons.

Trevor Griffiths, playwright: I don't know. Let me draw examples
from my own experience when I wasn't, as you put it, 'Trevor
Griffiths'. One of the very first things I ever did were seventeen half-
hour plays — they called them 'episodes' — in a series that went out
in the 'God-slot', 6—6.30 on Sunday evenings, for Granada. I was
writing under a pseudonym anyway, so I really wasn't 'Trevor
Griffiths'! This was in the early 1970s, not so long ago. I not only
had no control over the direction and who produced and who
designed, I had no control over most of the things those people did,
including the text — which they insisted on calling a script. I had a

308

text in which a new character in the play was discovered by the
camera in a studio sitting-room playing some music; the music that
I'd specified was Bartok's 6th String Quartet. When I saw it in
final rehearsal they were playing a song from *Hair*. I told them that
if they could do that, they had clearly misread my intention, and I
tried to talk it through with them as gracefully as I could; I was then
asked if I would, you know, leave the studio, because they were busy
and had a deadline to meet and so on. I suppose this is a point where
it matters whether the Marxists 'leave' or not. I then write a four-
page memo to the Managing Director of Granada. Subsequently to
that, but in the same series, I had a copy made of a piece that they
had sliced fourteen minutes out of, on purely political grounds,
took it down to the IBA who — I had been told — had banned it;
they'd never seen it; I showed it to them; they rang up the Managing
Director . . . The upshot of all that was that I was actually banned
from entering Granada TV studios in Manchester. Then I got a
reputation for being a very 'awkward' writer and that lasted for a
couple of years and nobody wanted to work with me on that account.
There *is* a lot of struggle inside television; it's not always aesthetic,
but it is purposeful and it does have a point. You just have to win
through on all those levels and you still have to keep some sense of
what it is you want to say. It's very potent medium — why do you
think they're called 'Controllers'!

Audience: Have any of the writers on the platform got a clear idea
of what 'popular theatre' is?

David Hare, playwright: I think that all of us, people who write, we
all want to write a play after which things will be seen differently.
We all want that and I imagine it would be a very popular play. And
most of us are very jealous of Osborne because he pulled it off and
because things are seen differently because of what Osborne wrote.
Whether you think it's a good play or a bad play, it was a rallying
point. I imagine a popular play would do that — but as for 'popular
theatre' as a concept, I see almost no sign of it in this country. It's
what plays are actually saying that is either attractive or unattractive
to huge groups of people, that either strikes a chord in people or
doesn't. I can't imagine something called 'popular theatre' because
I don't think anybody can keep that up for long, actually being close
to the pulse, so that people feel that they need to know what it is
that this particular play is saying.

Steve Gooch, playwright: I think that the question of 'popular theatre'
is very much a question of the social context in which it takes place,

and that presumably it's theatre by and for the people. That's something you have to work on at both ends; you have to work on it at the end of the production system, you have to be working towards occupying the big theatres and the small theatres and the secondary schools and the streets — all those places are places where you can do theatre. None of them is a place in which you could unambiguously say that the work that goes on in them is necessarily popular. You have to be working, hopefully, towards a new kind of audience. And you have to be constantly examining your own work to see whether it is actually going to take your thinking about popular theatre further. But I think it would be naive to say that there is any one place, any one answer, one kind of theatre, even one kind of audience, that can offer us a 'popular theatre' now.

Audience: When you say it's 'by and for the people', who do you mean by 'the people'?

Steve Gooch, playwright: Roughly, I'd say, take the poor peasants as the people on your side, take the middle peasants as your allies, and take the rich peasants as your enemies! The point I'm making is that if the word 'popular' simply means all the people, it's probably the wrong word for what we're actually talking about. I'd use the analogy of the poor, middle and rich peasants, because I think that the forces for change in our society are going to come from first examining our own class structures along similar lines — you can say that the poor peasants are roughly equivalent to the industrial working class, the middle peasants to the white-collar workers, and so on.

Audience: But isn't that very divisive? Don't we want plays that are going to appeal to as many people as possible in the community?

Trevor Griffiths, playwright: I think that recognising the nature of this society as a class-divided society is to take the very first steps in doing something about it, in reconstituting it as a classless society. I've absolutely no difficulty in knowing who 'the people' are; they're the people who don't go to the theatre. Which is why I'd rather talk about popular *drama*, not 'popular theatre'.

Audience: But if you talk about people who don't go to the theatre, doesn't that bring the argument back to the theatre that goes to the people? No one's really talked about touring theatre or groups like 7:84 which try to 'go to the people'.

Steve Gooch, playwright: I've done some work with 7:84 and with other companies which take work to working-class audiences, working-class venues. I think you can do different kinds of work in different circumstances. Touring theatre has to be small-scale, light, and punchy.

310

In other words, what you can actually get on the road, out to working-class audiences, is limited in form and so sometimes in content as well: the complexity of argument you can deal with, unless you present it simply as argument and don't dramatise it very much, isn't all that great. So the task tends to produce a particular form of theatre, and while that area of work is very important and we need to support it, to help its growth, as individual artists we're almost bound to move in and out of it, because for a writer it's not the most exciting form of theatre.

Audience: What would you say about your work with the Half Moon Theatre, which is more a theatre in a local community situation?

Steve Gooch, playwright: One of the important things about working in places like the Half Moon is that you are actually very close, physically, to your audience when you're performing, and that can make a very big difference. This relates too to the special power of theatre as against TV, which is the potential to communicate much more vividly and directly to your audience. It also demonstrates its essentially more dramatic nature in that actors behind stage will say 'We've got a group in tonight from such-and-such a trade union', for example, and that affects the work on the spot, at each performance. But I think the more important thing is that it affects the work before it's done. If you know that you're playing in certain venues, doing a tour of the clubs for example or playing for a lot of tenants' association meetings, it actually does condition quite strongly the way you approach a show, and the same goes for the Half Moon, in the sense of attempting to do shows that will have something to say to a working-class East End audience.

Audience: Can you use television to 'go to the people' but in order to bring them eventually to the theatre? I'm thinking of how Pinter's *Birthday Party*, for example, was shown on television before it became a great success in the theatre. I realise, of course, that you can't simply transfer a work of art, a creative organism, from one medium to another — as David Hare pointed out in the case of *Fanshen* itself.

Trevor Griffiths, playwright: I think you can, and I think you must. Sometimes we fail and sometimes we succeed, but we've got to try. I've talked to people who didn't see *Fanshen* live, but who did see it on TV, and said what a magnificent creation it was; large numbers of people may well have been mobilised to think, and maybe even act, politically, on the basis of seeing an inferior version of *Fanshen*. It may hurt this theatre group's pride that the very best that they

311

did wasn't achieved, or even one-hundredth of it, but one-hundredth of something very remarkable may still be very remarkable. I think that somehow we ought to get rid of this notion of the sacredness of the work, the notion of the work of art as an organism. You don't plant a play; it's *made*, like anything else, like chairs, tables, houses; they're made, plays are *made*. We make them, we unmake them, we can test them, find out whether they work or not, and if they don't work we can make them work. It's like that description David gave of the Chinese leadership going to the people to test a theory that's on a piece of paper, taking it back, modifying it, rewriting it. I'm still rewriting *Comedians* — I'll never get the damn thing right!

Audience: Can I develop that a bit, using two of the things we saw in the rehearsal this morning. We saw there the process of work itself, the forming, the making of that production; we also saw, in the content of one scene, Section 7, the process of classing, of one group of people putting other people into classes, classifying them. But if, as Trevor Griffiths implied earlier, a political drama has to recognise, and explore, the class nature of our society, how can you represent the nature of class division in a play? The way it has normally been done has been to take class 'representatives', and that can be done by naturalist means or by agit-prop stereotypes or cartoons or whatever; but underlying that tactic is a notion of 'class' as a 'group' — the 'industrial working class', 'the poor peasants' etc. If, however, you take 'class' as referring rather to the *relations* of production, to the process whereby people are classed in a system of production relations, how can you dramatise that? This morning we saw a rehearsal; but we didn't, and couldn't, *see* the overall system of relations shaping that rehearsal: the relations between not just the director and the actors, but also the relations with Equity, or the relations with the source of finance — in this case the Arts Council and the conference itself. That scene from *Fanshen* is almost unique because it shows class relations being re-drawn very explicitly, it catches a social process at the point where the operation of classing is made visible — and it's no wonder that producing the play stimulated a change in the internal relations of production of the company towards a more collective relation. The paradox that seems to hover over political drama is that the more you recognise the need to analyse class relations the more difficult it becomes to represent those class relations precisely as relations of production, to dramatise not groups in society but the very nature of classing.

Steve Gooch, playwright: It's very difficult to do that as a totality,

in the overall sense you've been describing; especially when you consider that theatre, as a form, tends to want to stay in one place at
one time. What tends to happen, therefore, is that class relations
are represented tangentially, or through a fragment, a section of
relations.

Audience: But then can't that section or fragment be rejected by
an audience as an 'unrepresentative' example of class relations, as
'not typical'? As happened with *Fanshen*: the Chinese leadership
objecting to Hinton that Long Bow wasn't representative.

David Hare, playwright: It was actually Chou En-lai who said that
Hinton's book was 'bad news' for China. He didn't say that the
problems weren't typical; he said that the problems were worse
there than elsewhere — that the typical problems were particularly
grave there.

Audience: There was one aspect of that contribution I'd like to take
up — the point about Joint Stock changing their own internal relations.
If you ask how work in theatre can contribute to the revolution, to
changing class relations, one of the things you have to work through
is how the theatre can change its own 'internal' class relations.
Theatre, like education, like this conference itself, has its own relations of production, and we can modify those relations, in detailed,
sometimes even tiny, ways. At most conferences I go to, there's a
chairman and a speaker up there, and the rest of us listen to a paper
for an hour or so and then there's maybe half-an-hour of questions;
to change from that to watching the rehearsal this morning and then
having this discussion has already been one tiny but important change
in the relations of academic production! And, as Brecht recognised,
if we can learn to change the relations of production in one sector —
the theatre — that learning process can be extended and applied in
other sectors.

Steve Gooch, playwright: That's a very immediate way of looking at
the problem. But there are two sides to this problem. On the one hand
there is, of course, the extent to which every individual working in
whatever system of production they're in can be politicising that
situation, drawing attention to class relations. On the other hand the
most common contradiction we face is that we are also engaged in
making a product which has to be sold on the market, which has a
certain value and is looking for buyers. If, for example, actors during
a production, during a play, try to modify their relation with the
director, perhaps to assert some collective control over the process
of production, they are changing their work situation; but in doing

313

so, they may conflict with the producer or the director or the writer, who have mounted the project as a whole from scratch and who may also have *their* political intentions in the work. In that sense the director's or writer's interest will be in the product, in getting it into the can or getting the first night on. That's where the contradictions begin, because a piece of political theatre as product can make one kind of intervention in society, and the internal processes which make the product are the field for another kind of political intervention. It's unfortunate that our work can't all be seen as process. As it is, we're making products for audience consumption on a semi-commercial market. And one thing that is quite evident in theatre production at the moment, particularly in alternative theatre, is the conflict between those two things: getting shows out to a working-class audience, for example, on the one hand, and the problem of how you govern the internal process on the other. I remember the same kind of contradiction being present in the production of socialist plays when I first started work in 'conventional' theatre eight years ago. The sad thing is that these contradictions often put theatre workers off, make them cynical about socialist theatre. One of our most important tasks now is not to let that disillusionment recur.

Audience: I was just recalling one rather disillusioning incident about class relations within the theatre: that when the Berliner Ensemble came here in 1956, we organised a trip on the Thames for them — and the actors were simply horrified when they discovered that the stage hands were coming!

Audience: I'm not sure whether it's depressing to be reminded of the way such blockages can continue, even among radical theatre groups — or to be optimistic because we can all now realise how absurd that reaction was!

Appendix

TEMPO, TEMPO (1930)

An agit-prop play by the Prolet Buehne, New York, translated from the German by B. Stern, WLT, NY. This originally appeared in the *Worker's Theatre Magazine.*

(Characters: Capitalist and seven or ten workers.)

CAPITALIST:

    Tempo, tempo, watch your step
    Hold on tight and show some pep.
    Move your hands and bend your body
    With out end and not so shoddy.
    Faster, faster shake it up.
    No one idles in this shop.
    Time is money, money's power.
    Profits come in every hour.
    Can't stop profits for your sake.
    Tempo, tempo, keep awake.

WORKER:

    We are humans, not machines.

CAPITALIST:

    You don't like our fast routine?
    Get your pay and get out quick.
    You speak like a Bolshevik.
    Tempo, tempo, watch your step.
    Hold on tight and show some pep.

WOMAN WORKER:

    My head, My head, O help [me], help me.

CAPITALIST:

    You want attention, that's your game.
    Get your pay and get out quick.
    There's no place here for the sick.
    Tempo, tempo watch your step.
    Hold on tight and show some pep.
    Number fifteen, number ten,
    I must fire two more men.
    There's a youngster strong and willing
    Will not find the pace so killing.

To do the work for much less pay,
That's the problem of the day.
Tempo, tempo, work with me.
Help bring back prosperity.
Speed them up and cut their pay,
Tempo, tempo, that's the way.
CAPITALIST AND WORKERS:
Tempo, tempo, tempo, tempo,
Tempo, tempo, no delay.
Tempo, tempo, tempo, tempo,
Tempo is the cry today.
POLICEMAN:
Tempo, tempo, move along,
Do not idle here too long.
Streets are free for all to tread
Except for unemployed and red.
Tempo, tempo, one, two, three,
You cannot get away from me.
To distribute leaflets free
That tell of workers' misery
Is a crime and not permitted
It's high treason to commit it.
Tempo, tempo, one, two, three,
In the name of law and order
I'll deport you across the border.
Tempo, tempo, one more victim
First we club him then convict him.
You're not allowed to strike for bread,
Devil take you, goddamn red.
Unemployed are demonstrating,
There they march unhesitating.
Watch them shout and storm and rage as
They demand their work or wages.
Tempo, tempo, one, two, three,
You cannot get away from me.
In the name of law and order
We'll deport you across the border.
Tempo, tempo, no delay,
Tempo is the cry today.
WORKERS AND POLICEMAN:
Tempo, tempo, tempo, tempo,
Tempo, tempo, no delay.
Tempo, tempo, tempo, tempo,
Tempo is the cry today.
WORKER:
Soviet tempo — worker's might
Onward without parasite.

Appendix

WORKER:
  Soviet tempo — worker's power
  Moving, growing, every hour.
WORKER:
  Soviet tempo — every man
  Helps complete the five year plan.
CAPITALIST:
  Insane tempo, absurdity,
  Respect for private property.
WORKER:
  Fight the thief and profiteer
  Onward, onward, without fear.
CAPITALIST:
  Have respect for your tradition
  Honor god and your religion.
WORKER:
  Fight the hypocrite and priest
  Who do not work and always feast.
CAPITALIST:
  Stop this aimless merriment
  Adopt me for your government.
WORKER:
  Down with all the wealthy classes
  All power to the toiling masses.
CAPITALIST:
  Such words, such tones, I'm in confusion
  The mob is ruling, it's revolution.
WORKER:
  Soviet tempo — every man
  Helps complete the five year plan.
WORKER:
  Industries are socialized.
  Farms are being collectivized.
WORKER:
  Production reaches higher stages,
  Shorter hours, higher wages.
CAPITALIST:
  Take your time and do not worry,
  Slowly, slowly, what's the hurry[?] .
WORKER:
  Faster, faster, drive ahead.
  Tempo makes for triumph red.
WORKER:
  Soviet tempo sets the pace
  Soviet tempo wins the race.
ALL WORKERS:
  Tempo, tempo, tempo, tempo,

Appendix

Tempo, tempo, no delay,
Tempo, tempo, tempo, tempo,
Tempo is the cry today.

Soviet tempo! Workers' tempo!
Lenin tempo! Stalin tempo!
Masses' tempo! Builders' tempo!
Fighters' tempo! Victors' tempo!

Tempo, tempo, tempo, tempo,
Tempo, tempo, no delay,
Tempo, tempo, tempo, tempo,
Tempo is the cry today.

Select bibliography

Ansorge, Peter. *Disrupting the Spectacle*, London, 1975
Artaud, Antonin. *Le Théâtre et son double*, Paris, 1938
Bailey, P. *Leisure and Class in Victorian England. Rationed Recreation and the Contest for Control, 1830–1885*, London, 1978
Baldick, Robert. *The Life and Times of Frédérick Lemaître*, London, 1959
Barker, Clive. 'The Audience of the Britannia Theatre, Hoxton', *Theatre Quarterly*, 34 (1979)
Barna, Yon. *Eisenstein*, Bloomington, 1973
Baskerville, C. R. 'Mummers' Wooing Plays in England', *Modern Philology*, 21: 3 (February 1924), pp. 225–72
Benjamin, Walter. *Illuminations*, London, 1970
    Understanding Brecht, London, 1973
Bergman, Andrew. *We're in the Money: Depression America and its Films*, New York, 1971
Bigsby, C. W. E. *Approaches to Popular Culture*, London, 1976
Booth, Michael. *English Melodrama*, London, 1965
Bradby, David and McCormick, John. *People's Theatre*, London, 1978
Bratton, J. S. *The Victorian Popular Ballad*, London, 1975
Braun, Edward. *The Theatre of Meyerhold*, London, 1979
Brecht, Bertolt. *Brecht on Theatre*, New York, 1964
Brockett, Oscar G. and Findlay, Robert R. *Century of Innovation: a History of European and American Theatre and Drama since 1870*, Englewood Cliffs, New Jersey, 1973
Brooks, Peter. *The Melodramatic Imagination: Balzac, Henry James, Melodrama and the Mode of Excess*, New Haven, 1976
Carter, Huntley. *The New Spirit in the European Theatre 1914–1924*, London, 1925
    The New Spirit in the Russian Theatre, 1917–1928, New York, 1970
    The New Theatre and Cinema of Soviet Russia 1917–1924, New York, 1970
Caughie, John (ed.). *Television: Ideology and Exchange*, BFI Television Monograph 9, London, 1978
Cawte, E. C., Helm, A. and Peacock, N. *English Ritual Drama*, London, 1967
Chambers, Edmund. *The English Folk Play*, London, 1969
Cheshire, David. *Music Hall in Britain*, Newton Abbot, 1974
Clinton-Baddeley, V. C. *The Burlesque Tradition in the English Theatre After 1660*, London, 1952

Copeau, Jacques. *Le Théâtre populaire*, Paris, 1941
Culture and Agitation, London, 1972
Davis, R. G. *The San Francisco Mime Troupe: the First Ten Years*, Palo Alto, California, 1975
Davison, P. (ed.). *The Songs of the British Music Hall*, London, 1971
Descotes, Maurice. *Le Public de théâtre et son histoire*, Paris, 1964
Dort, Bernard. *Théâtre public*, Paris, 1967
  Théâtre réel, Paris, 1971
Dyer, R. *Light Entertainment*, BFI Television Monograph 2, London, 1973
Ellis, J. 'Made in Ealing', *Screen*, 16: 1 (Spring 1975)
  (ed.). *Screen Reader I: Cinema/Ideology/Politics*, London, 1977
Enzensberger, Hans Magnus. *Raids and Reconstructions: Essays in Politics, Crime and Culture*, London, 1976
Fisher, John. *Funny Way to be a Hero*, London, 1973
Flanagan, Hallie. *Arena: The History of the Federal Theatre*, New York, 1965
Furhammar, Lief and Isaksson, Folke. *Politics and Film*, London, 1971
Gailey, Alan. 'Chapbook influence on Irish Mummers' Plays', *Folklore*, 85 (1974), pp. 1–22
Garnham, Nicholas. *Structures of Television*, BFI Television Monograph 1, 2nd edn, London, 1978
Garrett, Dan. 'Documentary Drama: its Roots and Development in Great Britain', PhD thesis, University of Hull, 1977 (with list of plays)
Ginisty, Paul. *Le Mélodrame*, Paris, 1910
Glassie, Henry. *All Silver and no Brass: an Irish Christmas Mumming*, Dublin, 1976
Goldstein, Malcolm. *The Political Stage*, New York, 1974
Gontard, Denis. *La Décentralisation théâtrale en France 1895–1952*, Paris, 1973
Gorelick, Mordecai. 'Legacy of the New Deal Drama', *Drama Survey*, 4: 1 (Spring 1965)
Halinaux, Rene and Bonnat, Yves. *Stage Design Throughout the World Since 1960*, London, 1973
Hippisley Coxe, Antony D. *A Seat at the Circus*, London, 1951; rev. edn Connecticut, 1979
Hood, Stuart. *The Mass Media*, London, 1972
Hoover, Marjorie L. *Meyerhold: The Art of Conscious Theater*, Amherst, 1974
Hunt, Albert. *Hopes for Great Happenings*, London, 1976
Innes, C. D. *Erwin Piscator's Political Theatre*, Cambridge, 1972
Lesnick, Henry (ed.). *Guerilla Street Theatre*, New York, 1973
Macbean, James Roy. *Film and Revolution*, Bloomington, 1975
Macherey, P. *Pour une théorie de la production littéraire*, Paris, 1966
MacCabe, C. 'Principles of Realism and Pleasure', *Screen* 17: 3 (Autumn 1973)
McCarthy, Todd and Flynn, Charles (eds.). *Kings of the Bs: Working Within the Hollywood System*, New York, 1975
McNamara, Brooks. 'Spartakiade', *The Drama Review*, 17: 4 (December, 1973)
Madral, Philippe. *Le Théâtre hors les murs*, Paris, 1969
Mayer, David. *Harlequin in his Element: English Pantomime 1806–1836*, Cambridge, Mass., 1969

Select bibliography

Mayer, David and Richards, Kenneth (eds.). *Western Popular Theatre*, London, 1977

Meyerhold, Vsevolod. *Meyerhold on Theatre*, ed. and trans. E. Braun, New York, 1969

Piscator, Erwin. *Das Politische Theater*, Berlin, 1929

Rahill, Frank. *The World of Melodrama*, Pennsylvania, 1967

Renevey, Monica (ed.). *La Grande Livre du cirque*, Geneva, 1977

Richards, Kenneth and Thomson Peter (eds.). *Essays on Nineteenth Century British Theatre*, Manchester, 1971

Rolland, Romain. *Le Théâtre du peuple*, Paris, 1913

Russell, Ian. 'The Derby Tup', *Folk Music Journal*, 4 : 1 (1979)

Saxon, A. H. *Enter Foot and Horse*, New Haven, 1968
    The Life and Art of Andrew Ducrow, Connecticut, 1978

Schevill, James. *Break Out! In Search of New Theatrical Environments*, Chicago, 1973

Schnitzer, Luda and Jean and Martin, Marcel. *Cinema in Revolution: the Heroic Era of the Soviet Film*, London, 1973

Smith, J. L. *Melodrama*, London, 1973

Stedman Jones, G. 'Working-Class Culture and Working-Class Politics in London 1870—1900; notes on the remaking of a working class', *Journal of Social History*, 7: 4 (1974)

Taylor, Karen M. *People's Theatre in Amerika*, New York, 1972

Thethard, Henri. *Merveilleuse Histoire du cirque*, Paris, 1947; revised L. R. Dauven, 1978

Toll, Robert C. *Blacking up; the Minstrel Show in Nineteenth Century America*, Oxford 1974

Toller, Ernst. *Gesammelte Werke*, 5 vols., ed. Wolfgang Frühwald and John M. Spalek, Munich, 1978

'Trim' (ed.). *Old Wild's*, London n.d. [1888]

Vilar, Jean. *Le Théâtre, service public*, Paris, 1975

Welsford, Enid. *The Fool: His Social and Literary History*, London, 1968

Whitman, Willson. *Bread and Circuses*, New York, 1972

Willett, John. *The Theatre of Bertolt Brecht*, London, 1967
    The Theatre of Erwin Piscator, London, 1978

Williams, R. *Drama in a Dramatised Society*, Cambridge, 1975
    Television: Technology and Cultural Form, London, 1974

Reviews

Drama Review. Especially 17: 1 (March 1973), Russian Theatre
    18: 1 (March 1974), Popular Entertainments
    19: 2 (June 1975), Political Theatre
Arts Council Pamphlets. 'Art in Revolution', 1971
    'Erwin Piscator', 1971
Revue des Sciences Humaines, 162 (1976), Le Mélodrame
Theatre Quarterly. Especially 1: 4 (Oct.–Dec. 1971). People's Theatre
    2: 5 (Jan.–Mar. 1972), People's Theatre
    2: 8 (Oct.–Dec. 1972), Theatre for Social Change

Select bibliography

3: 9 (Jan.–Mar. 1973), Theatre Workshop
5: 18 (Jun.–Aug. 1975), Interviews with Mnouchkine, Davis *et al*.
6: 23 (Autumn 1976), People's Theatre in France
6: 24 (Winter 1976), Political Playwriting in Britain

General index

See also index of titles of plays, films, sketches, and index of theatres, theatre companies and groups.

Ackerman, *Microcosm of London*, 95, 96 (illustration)
Aeschylus, 2
Agit-prop, 1, 168, 170, 173, 178, 201–12, 216, 222, 224, 233, 235, 236, 237, 241, 287, 312
Aldebert, Pierre, 234
Allen, Jim, 288
Althusser, Louis, 275, 276, 290
Amherst, J. H., 113, 130; *Battle of Waterloo*, 1, 113, 117, 126, 130, 132
Andrews, R. C., 100
Aragon, Louis, 231–5; *Front Rouge*, 231
Aristotle, 3, 109, 280
Artaud, Antonin, 27
Astley, Philip, 9, 110, 112, 115

Balzac, Honoré de, 3, 28
Bamford, Samuel, 280
Barker, Kathleen, 104
Bazin, André, 240
Benjamin, Walter, 237, 240, 288
Birmingham Journal, 73
Blitzstein, Marc, *The Cradle Will Rock*, 211
Bloch, Jean-Richard, 234, 235, 241; *Birth of a City*, 169, 234, 235, 241
Blondin, 115
Blum, Léon, 169, 231
Bolt, Robert, *State of Revolution*, 298, 304
Bond, Edward, 169
Bonn, John (Hans Bohn), 201, 202, 205, 209, 212; *Red Revue*, 209; *Was Uns Fehlt*, 202
Booth, Michael, 7, 78, 79, 85, 279
Bost, Pierre, 109
Bouchardy, Joseph, 33–48, 276; *for complete list of plays, see* 48
Boucicault, Dion, 12, 14; *The Corsican Brothers*, 14

Brecht, Bertolt, 2, 141, 169, 170, 171, 177, 217, 240, 241, 281, 288, 289, 291, 307, 313; *Good Person of Setzuan*, 291; *The Mother*, 272; *Mother Courage*, 2
Brenton, Howard, *Epsom Downs*, 305
British Drama League, 226
Brook, Peter, 305
Brooks, Peter, 3, 27
Buckstone, J. B., *Luke the Labourer: or the Lost Son*, 13, 280

Čapek, brothers, 216; *R.U.R.*, 218
Chaplin, Charles, 198, 283; *The Gold Rush*, 198
Chevalier, L., 34
Clarion League, 214, 215, 216, 221
Clurman, Harold, 210
Cochran, C. B., 117
Coleridge, Samuel Taylor, *Rime of the Ancient Mariner*, 10
Colman, George, 92
Commedia dell' Arte, 174, 175, 176, 181
Commune, 232
Communist Party (Britain), 219, 220, 224; Young Communist League, 219
Communist Party (France), 169, 231, 232, 233, 238
Communist Party (Germany – KPD), 168, 192, 194, 198, 202, 231
Connolly, Michael, 53
Cooke, T. P. (actor), 11, 112, 128, 129
Co-operative Guilds, 214; *Co-operative News*, 218
Corrie, Joe, 218
Creswick, William (actor), 83, 84
Crommelynck, Ferdinand de, *The Magnificent Cuckold*, 173, 180
Cruikshank, George, 7

323

General Index

Dada, 168
Daily Mirror, 29
Daily Worker, 209, 220, 224, 225
Darwin, Charles, *Expression of Emotions*, 6
Deighton, Len, 274, 298
Democratic Party (USA), 204
Dibdin, Charles, the younger, 92—103
Diderot, Denis, 18, 19, 26, 27
Dort, Bernard, 170
Drame bourgeois, 18, 27
Dryden, John, *The Indian Emperor*, 91
Ducrow, Andrew, 9, 110, 111 (illustration)
Dullin, Charles, 241

Edwards, Ness, 218; *Workers' Theatre*, 217, 218
Egerton, 98, 102
Eisenstein, Sergei, 3, 12, 167, 173—81, 184, 187, 201; *Battleship Potemkin*, 178, 180, 237; *Ivan the Terrible*, 174, 178; 'Montage of Attractions', 175; *October*, 178, 180; *Old and New*, 180; *Strike*, 178
Elliston, R. W., 73, 103
Engel, J. J., 7, 11, 12; *Ideen zu einer Mimic* (translated as *Practical Illustrations of Rhetorical Gestures*), 7
Engels, Friedrich, 5, 179

Fanshen (book by William Hinton), 297, 298
Federal Theatre (USA), 170, 206 (illustration), 211 (illustration); Living Newspaper *Injunction Granted*, 212
Field, Dick, 80, 85
Fitzgerald, Percy, 50, 51, 52, 54
Folk drama, 1, 139, 141
Freeman, Paul, 301
Freud, Sigmund, 7, 280

Garnett, 288
Garrick, David, 7, 66
Gaskill, Bill, 302
Geoffroy, 18
Glover, Jimmy, 51
Gogol, Nikolai, 179; *The Government Inspector*, 179
Goldmann, Lucien, 275
Gooch, Steve, 272, 309, 310, 312, 313
Gorky, Maxim, *The Lower Depths*, 222
Granach, Alexander, 191
Granville-Barker, Harley, 49
Greuze, 26, 27
Griboyedov, Alexander, *Woe from Wit*, 179

Griffiths, Trevor, 288, 306, 307, 308, 310, 311, 312; *Bill Brand*, 307, 308; *Comedians*, 312
Grimaldi, 101
Grosz, George, 192
Gyseghem, André van, 225

Hagenbeck, 115
Hare, David, 271, 274, 297, 301—13; *Fanshen*, 271, 273, 297—314
Hauptmann, Gerhardt, *The Weavers*, 218
Hinton, William, 297, 299, 300, 302, 303, 313
History Workshop, 213
Hogarth, William, 7, 176
Holcroft, Thomas, 10, 11; *A Tale of Mystery*, 9, 10, 14
Hughes (actor), 110, 112
Hughes, Langston, *Scottsboro Ltd*, 204

IBA (Independent Broadcasting Authority), 309
Ibsen, Henrik, 49, 217; *A Doll's House* (version entitled *Nora*), 173
Illustrated London News, 126
Isherwood, Wilfred, 153, 154

James, William, 7, 8
Jerome, Jerome K., 55, 62
Jerrold, Douglas William, 3—16; *Black Ey'd Susan*, 3—16
Jones, Henry Arthur, 49, 53

Kabuki, 175, 179
Kaiser, Georg, *Gas*, 218
Kean, Charles, 14
Kean, Edmund, 11
Keegan, Kevin, 282
King, T. C. (actor), 85
Knightley, Will, 302
Knowles, Sheridan, *Virginius*, 82, 85
Kölnische Zeitung, 194
Kosma, Joseph, 240

Labour Party (including Labour Publishing Co., Labour Choral Union, Dramatic Societies, Choirs, Orchestras), 214, 216, 218, 219, 226, 227; Independent Labour Party, 214, 216, 219, 221; *Labour Leader*, 216, 217
Lavater, Johann Caspar, 9; *Essays on Physiognomy*, 6
Lawton, Tommy, 282

General Index

General Index

Index of titles of plays, films, sketches

For titles of plays by Bouchardy see complete list on p. 48; for titles of plays by Shakespeare, see under 'Shakespeare' in the general index; for titles of films mentioned in Nick Roddick's article see 'A Skeleton Filmography' pp. 264–9.

Index of titles of plays, films, sketches

Index of titles of plays, films, sketches

Index of theatres, theatre companies and groups

Index of theatres, theatre companies and groups